THE RENAISSANCE AND THE OTTOMAN WORLD

The Renaissance and the Ottoman World

Edited by

ANNA CONTADINI
SOAS, University of London, UK

CLAIRE NORTON
St Mary's University College, UK

LONDON AND NEW YORK

First published 2013 by Ashgate Publishing

2 Park Square, Milton Park, Abingdon, Oxfordshire OX14 4RN
52 Vanderbilt Avenue, New York, NY 10017

Routledge is an imprint of the Taylor & Francis Group, an informa business

First issued in hardback 2019

Copyright © Anna Contadini and Claire Norton 2013

Anna Contadini and Claire Norton have asserted their right under the Copyright, Designs and Patents Act, 1988, to be identified as the editors of this work.

All rights reserved. No part of this book may be reprinted or reproduced or utilised in any form or by any electronic, mechanical, or other means, now known or hereafter invented, including photocopying and recording, or in any information storage or retrieval system, without permission in writing from the publishers.

Notice:
Product or corporate names may be trademarks or registered trademarks, and are used only for identification and explanation without intent to infringe.

British Library Cataloguing in Publication Data
A catalogue record for this book is available from the British Library

The Library of Congress has cataloged the printed edition as follows:
The Renaissance and the Ottoman world / [edited] by Anna Contadini and Claire Norton.
    p. cm.
  Includes bibliographical references and index.
  ISBN 978-1-4724-0991-1 (hardcover) 1. Renaissance--Turkey. 2. Turkey--Civilization--1288-1918. 3. Turkey--Relations--Europe. 4. Europe--Relations--Turkey.
I. Contadini, Anna, author, editor of compilation. II. Norton, Claire, Dr., author, editor of compilation.
  DR486.R46 2013
  956'.015--dc23

2013006869

ISBN 978-1-4724-0991-1 (hbk)

Cover image: Ottoman silk (*kemkha*), second half of sixteenth century. Prato, Museo del Tessuto, inv. no. 75.01.316. Courtesy of Museo del Tessuto.

Contents

List of Figures vii
List of Plates ix
Notes on Contributors xi
Foreword and Acknowledgements xv

SECTION I   COMMERCIAL, ARTISTIC AND CULTURAL CONTEXTS

1   Blurring the Boundaries: Intellectual and Cultural Interactions between the Eastern and Western; Christian and Muslim Worlds   3
    Claire Norton

2   Sharing a Taste? Material Culture and Intellectual Curiosity around the Mediterranean, from the Eleventh to the Sixteenth Century   23
    Anna Contadini

3   The Lepanto Paradigm Revisited: Knowing the Ottomans in the Sixteenth Century   63
    Palmira Brummett

SECTION II   TEXTS, ART AND MUSIC AS MEDIA FOR THE TRANSMISSION OF INTERCULTURAL INFLUENCES

4   The Role of the Book in the Transfer of Culture between Venice and the Eastern Mediterranean   97
    Deborah Howard

5   The 'Reception of the Venetian Ambassadors in Damascus': Dating, Meaning and Attribution   109
    Caroline Campbell

6   Giacomo Gastaldi's Maps of Anatolia: The Evolution of a Shared Venetian-Ottoman Cultural Space?   123
    Sonja Brentjes

7   Turning a Deaf Ear   143
    Owen Wright

SECTION III   RENAISSANCE THOUGHT

8   Old and New Demarcation Lines between Christian Europe and
    the Islamic Ottoman Empire: From Pope Pius II (1458–1464) to
    Pope Benedict XVI (2005–2013)   169
    Zweder von Martels

9   *Turco-Graecia*: German Humanists and the End of Greek
    Antiquity – Cultural Exchange and Misunderstanding   181
    Asaph Ben-Tov

10 Positive Views of Islam and of Ottoman Rule in the Sixteenth
    Century: The Case of Jean Bodin   197
    Noel Malcolm

SECTION IV   THE RENAISSANCE AND THE OTTOMAN EMPIRE

11 Binding Relationships: Mamluk, Ottoman and Renaissance
    Book-Bindings   221
    Alison Ohta

12 Ottoman Textiles in European Markets   231
    Suraiya Faroqhi

13 Mehmed II as a Patron of Greek Philosophy:
    Latin and Byzantine Perspectives   245
    Anna Akasoy

Bibliography   *257*
Index   *299*

List of Figures

2.1 Qur'an printed by Paganino and Alessandro Paganini, 1537–38, Venice — 27
2.2 Vase of the Queen of Aquitaine. Sasanian or early Islamic rock crystal, Iran or Mesopotamia, fifth to ninth century. Silver gilt mount with precious stones, Paris, twelfth century. — 33
2.3 Marble capital, carved in relief. Spain, Madinat al-Zahra, tenth century. — 34
2.4 Bronze griffin, Spain (?), eleventh to mid-twelfth century — 35
2.5 Woollen table carpet, Cairo, mid-sixteenth century — 38
2.6 Girolamo da Carpi, *Portrait of a Gentleman with a Cat*, ca. 1526 — 39
2.7 Cimabue, *Crucifix*, 1265–8, tempera on panel — 41
2.8 Drawing of the Madonna and the *mandīl* from Cimabue's *Crucifix* — 43
2.9 Detail from Gentile da Fabriano, *Adoration of the Magi*, 1423, tempera on panel — 44
2.10 Parrasio Michiel or Micheli, *Portrait of a Lady*, ca. 1565 — 49
2.11 Woven silk brocade, Bursa, second half of sixteenth century — 51
2.12 *Çatma* (brocaded velvet), Bursa, sixteenth century — 52
2.13 Molino ewer and detail of the coat of arms, brass, Germany, Netherlandish with Middle Eastern decoration, second half of fifteenth century — 54
2.14 One of a pair of candlesticks, brass, engraved and inlaid with silver, Italian, probably Venice, mid-sixteenth century — 57
2.15 Pattern in Islamic style, from Francesco Pellegrino, *La Fleur de la science de pourtraicture: façon arabicque et ytalique*, Paris, 1530 — 59

3.1 Giovanni Francesco Camocio, The 'true order of the two potent armadas', at Lepanto, Venice, 1571 — 65
3.2 Giovanni Francesco Camocio, 'The success of the miraculous victory of the armada of the Christian Holy League against the most powerful and vainglorious … Sultan Selim', Venice, 1572 — 66
3.3 Matthias Gerung [The Turks persecuting the Christians], ca. 1548 — 75
3.4 Giacomo Gastaldi [Anatolia], Venice, 1566 — 76
3.5 Antonio Lafreri, 'The Order with which the Turkish army presents itself in the field against the Christians or the Persians', Rome, 1566 — 78
3.6 Antonio Lafreri, 'The true portrait of Sighetvar', Rome, 1566 — 79
3.7 'Brazo de Maina' [1560] — 81
3.8 Nicolo Nelli, 'Tripoli City of Barbary', Rome [1570] — 82

3.9	J.S., 'Scheme of Hatvan fortress, besieged and captured by the Christians on September 3, 1596' [1596?]	84
3.10	Giovanni Francesco Camocio, 'Soppoto fortress ... taken by Sebastian Venier ... 10 June 1570', Venice [1570]	85
3.11	Antonio Lafreri, 'Image of the Island of Cyprus ...', Rome, 1570	87
3.12	Jodocus Hondius, 'Turcici Imperii Imago', cartouche [Amsterdam, ca. 1606]	89
5.1	Follower of Gentile Bellini, ca. 1511, *Study of a Young Man*. Pen, ink and body colour on paper.	113
5.2	Workshop of Titian, *Portrait of Pietro Zen*, around 1520, oil on canvas	117
6.1	Map of Anatolia by Giacomo Gastaldi, produced in 1564, copy from 1570	125
7.1	Piero della Francesca, *Natività*, 1470–1475, oil on poplar	146
7.2	Turkish musicians – the ensemble of the governor of Belgrade	150
7.3	Notation of a Turkish song	153
7.4	Notation of a Mevlevi melody, with bass line added by Chabert	154
7.5	Notation of a song from an untitled collection made by Ali Ufki	163
7.6	Burlesque Turks dancing	164
11.1	Upper cover, Petrarch, *Canzoniere and Trionfi*, Florence, 1460–1470. Oxford, Bodleian, Ms.Canon.Ital.78, 21.8 × 13.8 cm	224
11.2	Upper cover, al-Dimyati, *Mashāriʿ al-ashwāq ilā maṣāriʿ al-ʿushshāq*, Cairo, 1490. Topkapı Palace Library, A.649/1, 36.5 × 26 cm	225
11.3	Upper cover, Fra Giocondo, *Sylloge*, Venice, ca. 1520–1530, Chatsworth, 25.1 × 15.9 cm	229

List of Plates

1. Astrolabe with Arabic and Latin inscriptions, Fez, dated 699/1299–1300
2. Arabic-Latin dictionary, Spain, end of thirteenth – early fourteenth century
3. Title page. Giovan Battista Raimondi, *Alphabetum Arabicum*, Rome, 1592.
4. Cup with one handle – from the ambo of Henry II, Iraq or western Iran, tenth century (?)
5. Dish, from the ambo of Henry II, Fatimid Egypt (?), late tenth – early eleventh century (?)
6. Lothar cross, c. 1000
7. *Grotta della Vergine* (The Virgin's Grotto), rock crystal, Fatimid Egypt (?), eleventh century (?); crown: silver-gilt, enamels and precious stones, Constantinople, ninth–tenth century; statuette of the Virgin: silver-gilt, Venice, thirteenth century
8. Rock crystal ewer, Fatimid Egypt, late tenth – early eleventh century; European silver gilt and enamelled mount, early seventeenth century
9. Small-pattern Holbein carpet, West Anatolia, third quarter of the fifteenth century
10. Gentile da Fabriano, *Madonna of Humility*, c. 1420
11. Dish, sheet brass incised and inlaid with silver and gold, Egypt or Syria, 1300–1350
12. Ottoman silk (*kemkha*), second half of sixteenth century
13. *Çatma* (brocaded velvet), Ottoman, late sixteenth – early seventeenth century
14. Short-sleeved kaftan, probably belonging to Osman II (1618–22), European, probably Italian
15. Velvet, Florence, sixteenth century
16. Agnolo Bronzino, *Eleonora of Toledo with her son Giovanni de' Medici*, c. 1545
17. Velvet, probably Venice, sixteenth century
18. Mahmud al-Kurdi, bowl-shaped box with cover of engraved brass inlaid with silver, disputed provenance, fifteenth century
19. Bookbinding, *dogal commission* to Michele Foscarini, 1587
20. Gilded and varnished hanging leather with a horizontal band in Ottoman style, Venice (?), sixteenth century
21. Gilded leather shield and detail of the arms of the Foscarini family, Venice, 1550–1600
22. Hans Memling, *The Virgin and Child with Saints and Angels*, Donne triptych, centre panel, 1478
23. Cornelius de Iudaeis [Cornelis de Jode], 'Newly delineated, Croatia and the surrounding region against the Turk', undated

24 Cornelius de Iudaeis [Cornelis de Jode], inset, 'Croatia against the Turk', undated
25 Ioani Bussemechers [Johan Bussemacher], 'Thrace and Bulgaria and Surrounding Territory' [Cologne], 1596
26 *Pyramids at Giza*, 1560, from the travel diary of Alessandro Magno
27 *View of Alexandria*, from Archivio di Stato di Venezia, Cinque Savii alla Mercanzia, 'Capitolare cottimo Alessandria'
28 Follower of Gentile Bellini (Girolamo da Santacroce?), *The Reception of the Venetian Ambasssadors in Damascus*, after 1511
29 Giovanni Mansueti, *Symbolic Representation of the Crucifixion*, probably around 1492
30 Workshop of Giovanni Bellini, *The Adoration of the Magi*, 1475–80
31 Vincenzo Catena, *Holy Family with a warrior adoring the Infant Christ*, after 1520
32 Girolamo da Santacroce, *Martyrdom of Saint Lawrence*, c. 1550
33 *Tabula Asiae Prima*, from the first Italian translation of Ptolemy's *Geography* prepared by Pietro Andrea Mattiolo, Venice, 1548
34 *Natolia, Nova tabula*, added to the first Italian translation of Ptolemy's *Geography* by the cosmographer Jacopo or Giacomo Gastaldi
35 Muslim and Christian musicians playing the same instrument. *Cantigas de Santa Maria* for Alfonso X, Spain, thirteenth century.
36 *Intemperance*, Anon. *Tractatus de septem vitiis*, Genoa, late fourteenth century.
37 Fra Angelico (Guido di Pietro), detail of 'Angel beating a drum', from the Linaiuoli Tabernacle, 1433
38 Fra Angelico (Guido di Pietro), detail from *Christ Glorified in the Court of Heaven*, 1423–4
39 Depiction of the ending of the dance during a Mevlevi *mukabele* (*Les Dervichs dans leur Temple de Péra, achevant de tourner*), de Ferriol, 1715
40 Detail of musicians from the painting of the circumcision festival of Bayezid and Cihangir, Arifi, *Süleymanname*, Ottoman, 965 AH / 1558 AD
41 Upper cover, *Commission*, Venice, 1500
42 Doublure, L. Bruni, *Commentarius rerum in Italia suo tempore gestarum*, Bologna?, 1464–5
43 Upper cover, *Commission*, Venice, 1571

Notes on Contributors

The Editors

Anna Contadini is Professor of the History of Islamic Art, Department of the History of Art and Archaeology, SOAS, University of London. She is also Director of the 'Treasures of SOAS', and of the 'Griffin and Lion' projects. She has been a Curator at the V&A and the Chester Beatty Library and Lecturer in Islamic Art at Trinity College, Dublin. Her doctoral thesis examined early Arab and Persian miniature painting, a research topic still central to her work, and has just published *A World of Beasts: A Thirteenth-Century Illustrated Arabic Book on Animals (the Kitāb Naʿt al-Ḥayawān) in the Ibn Bakhtīshūʿ Tradition*, Leiden-Boston: Brill, 2012. Her interests extend to the material culture of the Islamic Middle East, including rock crystal, ivories and metalwork (on which she has extensively published), and the artistic contacts between the Islamic World and Europe. Other publications include: *Fatimid Art at the Victoria and Albert Museum*, V&A, 1998, and – with regard to the subject of this volume – 'Translocation and transformation: some Middle Eastern objects in Europe', in L.E. Saurma-Jeltsch and A. Eisenbeiss, eds, *The Power of Things and the Flow of Cultural Transformation. Art and Culture between Europe and Asia*, Berlin-Munich: Deutscher Kunstverlag, 2010, 42–65, plus col. pls.; 'Middle Eastern Objects', in *At Home in Renaissance Italy*, ed. M. Ajmar-Wollheim and F. Dennis, London: V&A Publications, 2006, chapter 21, 308–21; 'Le stoffe islamiche nel Rinascimento italiano tra il XV e il XVI secolo', in *Intrecci Mediterranei. Il tessuto come dizionario di rapporti economici, culturali e sociali*, ed. by D. Degl'Innocenti, Prato: Museo del Tessuto, 2006, chapter 3, 28–35; 'Beasts that Roared: The Pisa Griffin and The New York Lion', in *Cairo to Kabul – Afghan and Islamic Studies* (presented to Ralph Pinder-Wilson), ed. by W. Ball and L. Harrow, London: Melisende, 2002, chapter 6, 65–83 (with contributions by R. Camber and P. Northover); and *Islam and the Italian Renaissance*, London: The Warburg Institute, 1999 (edited with Charles Burnett).

Claire Norton is Senior Lecturer in History at St Mary's University College, Twickenham. She has authored a book (with Mark Donnelly) on historiography, *Doing History* (Routledge, 2011) and has also edited a volume on nationalism and historiography, *Nationalism, Historiography and the (Re)Construction of the Past* (Washington: New Academia Press, 2007). Her other research interests concern the cultural identities of communities living in politically and culturally liminal areas, conversion, Western European and Ottoman conceptions of the 'other', and Muslim-Christian interactions throughout the Mediterranean and Indian

Ocean areas. She has published a number of articles on identity formation among early modern communities living along the Habsburg-Ottoman border as well as articles on English and Ottoman imaginations of the 'other' including: 'Lust, Greed, Torture and Identity: Narrations of Conversion and the Creation of the Early Modern "Renegade"', *Comparative Studies of South Asia, Africa and the Middle East*, 29/2 (2009). She is currently finishing a book on Ottoman and modern Turkish narrative representations of the 1600 and 1601 sieges of Nagyakanizsa castle.

The Contributors

Anna Akasoy studied Oriental Studies, History and Philosophy at the University of Frankfurt, where she obtained her doctoral degree in 2005. Her main fields of expertise are Islamic intellectual history, in particular philosophy and Sufism, the history of the Muslim West as well as contacts between the Islamic world and other cultures.

Asaph Ben-Tov, PhD (2007) in history, Hebrew University Jerusalem. Author of *Lutheran Humanists and Greek Antiquity* (Brill, 2009) and several articles on Late Humanist and Baroque scholarship. Currently working on the evolving nature and role of Oriental studies at German universities in the seventeenth and early eighteenth centuries.

Sonja Brentjes is a historian of science who works on Islamicate societies between the ninth and the seventeenth centuries (mathematical sciences, maps, institutions, narratives, cultural processes) and on cross-cultural exchange of knowledge in the medieval and early modern period (Mediterranean, western and southern Asia). She has published extensively on Euclid's Elements in Islamicate societies, the teaching of mathematical knowledge, the creation of cross-cultural knowledge spaces and travellers from Catholic and Protestant countries in Europe to the Ottoman and Safavid empires. Her latest publication is 'Medieval Portolan Charts as Documents of Shared Cultural Spaces', in R. Abdellatif, Y. Benhima, D. König, E. Ruchaud, eds, *Acteur des transferts culturels en Méditerranée médiévale*, München: Oldenbourg Verlag, 2012, 134–46.

Palmira Brummett is Visiting Professor of History at Brown University and Professor Emerita of History at the University of Tennessee. Her work addresses the rhetorics of cross-cultural encounter in the Ottoman and Mediterranean worlds. She is the author of *Ottoman Seapower and Levantine Diplomacy in the Age of Discovery* (1994), and *Image and Imperialism in the Ottoman Revolutionary Press, 1908-1911*, as well as multiple articles in the fields of Ottoman, Mediterranean and World history. She is editor and contributor for *The 'Book' of Travels: Genre,*

Ethnology and Pilgrimage, 1250-1700 (2009). Her current work analyses the mapping of Ottoman territory, sovereignty and identity in the early modern period.

Caroline Campbell is Curator of Italian Paintings before 1500 at The National Gallery, London. Prior to this she was Schroder Foundation Curator of Paintings at The Courtauld Gallery, London, and held junior curatorial positions at The National Gallery and the Ashmolean Museum, Oxford. Following a degree in Modern History at University College, Oxford, she took an MA and PhD in Renaissance Italian art at the Courtauld Institute of Art, writing her dissertation on Florentine wedding chests. She has published extensively on *cassoni*, the Bellini family, Titian, and the reception of Italian Renaissance art, and has curated many exhibitions, including *Bellini and the East* (London, National Gallery and Boston, Isabella Stewart Gardner Museum, 2005–2006).

Suraiya Faroqhi taught history at Middle East Technical University, Ankara (1972–87) and served as a professor of Ottoman Studies at the Ludwig Maximilians Universität in Munich, Federal Republic of Germany (1988–2007). After retirement from LMU she now works as a professor at the Department of History, Istanbul Bilgi University in Istanbul. In 2001–2002, she was a Fellow at the Wissenschaftskolleg Berlin and in the spring of 2007, a Visiting Professor at Dartmouth College, New Hampshire. She is an honorary member of the Middle East Studies Association. She is the author of numerous books and articles on Ottoman history. With Kate Fleet and Reşat Kasaba, she is a co-editor of the *Cambridge History of Turkey*.

Deborah Howard is Professor of Architectural History in the University of Cambridge, where she is also a Fellow of St John's College. A graduate of Cambridge and of the Courtauld Institute of Art. Her books include *Venice & the East* (2000), *The Architectural History of Venice* (rev. edn., 2002), *Sound & Space in Renaissance Venice* (with Laura Moretti, 2009) and *Venice Disputed* (2011).

Noel Malcolm is a Senior Research Fellow at All Souls College, Oxford, and a Fellow of the British Academy. He has published widely on early modern intellectual history and the history of the Balkans: his books include *Bosnia: A Short History* (London, 1994), *Kosovo: A Short History* (London, 1998) and *Aspects of Hobbes* (Oxford, 2002), as well as editions of Hobbes's *Correspondence* (2 vols, Oxford, 1994) and *Leviathan* (3 vols, Oxford, 2012). In 2010 he gave the Trevelyan Lectures at Cambridge University on 'Early Modern Europe's Encounters with Islam'.

Zweder von Martels is lecturer in Classics at the University of Groningen. He has published on Augerius Busbequius, Aeneas Sylvius Piccolomini, Travel Literature and Humanist Scholarship.

Alison Ohta is Director of the Royal Asiatic Society of Great Britain and Ireland. She studied Arabic and Politics at the University of Durham and Japanese at the University of Western Australia as an undergraduate and completed her MA and PhD in the Department of the History of Art and Archaeology at SOAS. Her PhD thesis traced the developments in technique and ornament in Mamluk bookbinding reflecting her interest in the Islamic Arts of the Book. She has lectured and published on the subject and is currently working on the bindings of the Mamluk Qur'an Collection in the National Library of Egypt.

Owen Wright is Research Professor of Musicology of the Middle East at the School of Oriental and African Studies, University of London. He has a particular interest in historical musicology, and works on Arabic ('Die melodischen Modi bei Ibn Sīnā und die Entwicklung der Modalpraxis von Ibn al-Munağğim bis zu Ṣafī al-Dīn al-Urmawī', *Zeitschrift für Geschichte der Arabisch-Islamischen Wissenschaften*, 16, 2004/2005, 224–308), Persian (*Touraj Kiaras and Persian Classical Music: An Analytical Perspective*, Aldershot: Ashgate, 2009) and Ottoman material ('Mais qui était 'Le compositeur du Péchrev dans le makam Nihavend'?', *Studii și Cercetări de Istoria Artei: Teatru, Muzică, Cinematografie* (Academia Română, Institutul de Istoria Artei 'George Oprescu'), serie nouă, vol. 1 (45), 2007 [2008], 3–45).

Foreword and Acknowledgements

The thirteen cross-cultural and inter-disciplinary articles that make up this volume bring together some of the latest research on the cultural, intellectual, and commercial interactions between Western Europe and the Middle East, in particular the Ottoman Empire, during the Renaissance.[1] Recent scholarship has brought to the fore the economic, political, cultural, and personal interactions between Christian Western Europe and the Islamic Eastern Mediterranean, and has thereby highlighted the incongruity of conceiving of a political and ideological iron curtain-separating communities located in the same Mediterranean space. Instead, the emphasis here is on interpreting the Mediterranean world as one knit together not just by the trade routes along which goods regularly travelled but also by associated cultural and intellectual networks.

Accordingly, the various articles provide a stimulating scholarly dialogue that explores elements of contact and exchange between the two areas, and perceives the Ottoman Empire as an integral element of the geo-political and cultural continuum within which the Renaissance evolved.

These contributions from major scholars in the field include discussions of commercial contacts; the acquisition and reception of objects and their impact on the evolution of design in both Western Europe and the Middle East; the exchange of technological, cartographical, philosophical, and scientific knowledge; the role of Venice in transmitting the culture of the Islamic East Mediterranean to Western Europe; shared sources of inspiration in Italian and Ottoman architecture; the musical imaginary; and the use of Eastern Mediterranean sources in Western scholarship and European sources in Ottoman scholarship. Their aim is to refine current understandings of the diverse artistic, intellectual and political interactions in the pre- and early modern Mediterranean world and, in so doing, to advance the discussion of the scope and nature of the Renaissance.

---

[1] The book emerged out of a conference *The Renaissance and the Ottoman World* organised by Charles Burnett, Anna Contadini and Claire Norton and held at the Warburg Institute and the School of Oriental and African Studies (SOAS, both part of the University of London) in 2006.

Acknowledgements

We are pleased to be able to thank those individuals and institutions who have helped this project come to life: Charles Burnett and staff of the Warburg Institute; SOAS faculty of Arts and Humanities and the Department of the History of Art and Archaeology, especially Farouk Yahya; and St Mary's University College. In particular we would like to thank John Law who first suggested that we organise a conference on this topic and the Society for Renaissance Studies for providing ongoing support and encouragement.

Various foundations provided generous financial support for the conference for which we are very grateful. These include: The Society for Renaissance Studies; The British Academy, The British Institute of Archaeology at Ankara, St Mary's University College, the Gladys Kriebel Delmas Foundation.

Lastly, we would like to thank the two anonymous readers whose comments were thoughtful and instructive, and John Smedley and his team at Ashgate for making the editing and production process go smoothly.

The Editors

SECTION I
Commercial, Artistic and Cultural Contexts

Chapter 1
Blurring the Boundaries: Intellectual and Cultural Interactions between the Eastern and Western; Christian and Muslim Worlds

Claire Norton

Introduction

Although a number of Ottomanists have, in recent years, integrated the Ottoman Empire successfully into discussions of European history, studies of intellectual, artistic and socio-political developments in the Renaissance, with some notable exceptions, have tended to ignore the Ottoman Empire. Alternatively, they have employed it as a counterpoint designed to foreground Christian European cultural development; approached it as a source for Western artistic development; explored it as a repository for transmitted Christian European Renaissance developments; or examined it as the subject of Western Christian humanist inquiry.[1] It has therefore been conceived of as being conceptually and qualitatively different to other European states and as existing in a separate world, isolated or immune from the cultural innovations and developments occurring throughout the rest of Europe: a bystander viewing events from the periphery. As such the Ottoman Empire is figured as a quintessential Islamic, oriental, or Asian, empire, where such terms carry the frequently pejorative connotations common in orientalist discourse. Very little attention has therefore been given to the extent to which the Ottoman Empire benefited from, participated in and contributed to, what, has been categorised and defined as the Renaissance.

---

[1] Such Ottomanists include Goffman 2002; Aksan 2004, especially Aksan 1999; Finkel 2008; many of the articles in Aksan and Goffman 2007 especially those by Brummett 2007, Goffman 2007b and Ágoston 2007; Greene 2000; and Necipoğlu 2005. Renaissance scholars who constitute notable exceptions include many of those cited below as well as the authors of some of the chapters in MacLean 2005 including Finkel 2005, Matar 2005, and MacLean 2005b; and some of the papers in Maclean 2011, especially Landry 2011 and MacLean's introduction. Matar in his many articles and trilogy of books examining Anglo-Maghrebi interactions has also done much to reconceptualise the traditional division between states and communities in the wider early modern Mediterranean World: see Matar 1998; *Matar, 1999; Matar 2005b; and MacLean and Matar 2011.*

The more that becomes known about the economic, political, cultural and personal interactions between Western European Christian states and the Eastern Mediterranean Islamic states, the more incongruous it is to continue to conceive of an iron curtain bisecting the mentalities of the various socio-political and religious communities located in the same Mediterranean, and in the case of the Ottoman Empire, European geo-political space. To this extent, the Ottoman Empire, extending around the Mediterranean, straddling Europe, Africa and Asia, proves an illustrative example that foregrounds the constructed, rhetorical nature of the conceptual dichotomy between Christian and Islamic, Western and Eastern worlds. The Ottomans did not occupy a different intellectual, commercial, or political world to the Christian Europeans. The Mediterranean was a world traversed by commercial, cultural and intellectual networks through which ideas, people and goods regularly travelled. What sense does it make to discuss the Renaissance solely as an Italian, or Western-European phenomenon when we know that Ottoman and Italian architects were influenced by each other's designs and techniques; artists crossed borders and worked for different patrons; rulers in the East and West employed the same vocabulary and iconography of sovereignty and political legitimisation, engaged in the same practices and ceremonies designed to promote their own power, read the same books, commissioned the same maps, and exchanged military, scientific and philosophical knowledge? The degree and extent of trans-culturation and exchange that occurred in intellectual, commercial, political and personal contexts necessitates, I argue, the abandonment of the prevailing dominant discourse of difference between East and West, and the adoption, in its place, of a more heuristically beneficial and cogent framework of analysis within which to reconceptualise not only the Renaissance, but all interactions within and beyond the early modern Mediterranean world. In this chapter I intend to articulate, in general and introductory terms, not only why such a reconceptualisation is necessary, but what form this new meta-framework might take.[2] I will argue that examples of artistic practices translating between communities, the existence of shared cultural texts, and correlative uses of political rhetoric were not simply random instances of cultural and intellectual exchange occurring between qualitatively different western European, Christian states and their Eastern Mediterranean, Muslim counterparts, but that on a deeper, more significant, level these states and communities inhabited a co-extensive geo-political space where they competed over access to trade routes and raw materials, were motivated largely by the same concerns and where a shared intellectual, cultural and political heritage not only provided common vocabularies with which to

---

[2] As such I am not claiming originality on this point, rather I would hope that this chapter be understood as a continuation of the work of the scholars cited above, and perhaps more specifically as a contribution to the reformulation discussion as articulated by MacLean 2007 in his introduction and the introduction by Birchwood and Dimmock 2005.

express legitimacy and authority, but also engendered the development of mutually comprehensible art motifs and practices.

The Context of Acculturation and Cross-Cultural Convergence

The Mediterranean world (particularly the Eastern Mediterranean world) at the beginning of the early modern period was a patchwork of different political and commercial powers including city states, larger, older empires and colonial outposts. While Islamic powers predominated in the Levant region with the Mamluks in Egypt and a profusion of Turkic *beyliks* (small proto-states) in Anatolia, the islands of the Aegean were under Latin or Byzantine control, as were parts of the Anatolian coast. This patchwork was further complicated by the establishment of independent commercial colonies by Italian city states such as Venice and Genoa throughout the Eastern Mediterranean world, and the presence of ex-patriot communities of foreign merchants living and working in various states and empires. While the development of the Ottoman state into an empire that stretched across three continents in the fifteenth and sixteenth centuries may have provided a degree of political homogeneity in the Eastern Mediterranean, religious, cultural and linguistic heterogeneity was maintained. Moreover, this expansion brought Islam back into immediate contact with the Western Christian European world.

Fleet has argued that from a commercial perspective, the Ottoman Empire in the early modern period (fourteenth and fifteenth centuries) cannot coherently be viewed within a conceptual framework of an East-West dichotomy, nor in terms of conflict between Christian Western Europe and the Muslim Eastern Mediterranean.[3] Instead she has demonstrated that commercial pragmatism was the overriding criteria in determining relations between the various states with an interest in the Eastern Mediterranean, be they Christian or Muslim: the Genoese, Venetians, Ottomans, Mamluks, and other Turkic *beyliks* were all competing to control key commercial networks and territories, and to acquire access to goods and raw materials in the East Mediterranean, often at the expense of the faltering Byzantine Empire. Such was the drive of commercial and political pragmatism in determining relationships between states that even during the siege of Constantinople in 1453, the Genoese in Pera maintained close relations with, and offered help to, both the besieged Byzantines and the besieging Ottomans.[4] Moreover, as scholars have demonstrated, the siege and change of ruler did not damage relations between the Ottomans and the Christian West.[5] Commercial and diplomatic treaties were renewed: an alliance

---

[3] Fleet 1999, 141.
[4] Ibid., 12.
[5] Ibid., 123.

was even agreed with the Venetians a year after the capture of Constantinople, despite their previously professed support for the Byzantine Emperor.[6]

The decades of friendly and hostile interaction that this competition engendered ultimately facilitated closer diplomatic and cultural links between Venice and Genoa and the Ottoman Empire. In particular, the ex-patriot communities of Italian merchant-bankers resident in Ottoman lands helped integrate the Ottoman state into a wider network of Western European humanist scholarship, artistic patronage and princely gift-exchange through their close affiliation with, and acculturation into, the Ottoman military-administrative structure: for example, Genoese merchants were not only present at Mehmed I's court, but they, and their Venetian counterparts, were often absorbed into the Ottoman administrative-military structure through their employment as tax farmers for the Ottoman state.[7]

Such commercial pragmatism continued through the sixteenth and seventeenth centuries with Western European Atlantic states vying to agree favourable commercial treaties with the now powerful and very wealthy Ottoman Empire. Communities of English and Frenchmen resided in Ottoman lands in the East and West Mediterranean, and Ottoman merchants, both Muslim and Christian, travelled as far as England, although were mainly resident in the rather more receptive Venice.[8] The example cited by Faroqhi in this volume further illustrates the commercial and thus the social and cultural interconnectivity of the Mediterranean world: the caravan of merchants travelling from Istanbul to Venice that she describes was composed of Muslim Ottomans, Christian Venetians and Jewish merchants.[9]

Connections across the Mediterranean world, the development of a co-extensive cultural and intellectual context, and the diffusion of common ceremonial practices and legitimising strategies, were all further facilitated by the absorption of foreign, non-Muslim skilled labour into the Ottoman

---

[6] Such inter-faith alliances were fairly common: for example, Venice allied with the Muslim Aq-qoyunlu against the Ottomans, Necipoğlu 2012, 4; and there is a description of the Byzantine Emperor allying with the Muslim Karamanids, in *The Holy Wars of Sultan Murad Son of Sultan Mehmed Khan* in Imber 2006, 44–5, see also Imber's introduction, 13.

[7] Fleet 1999, 128 and 136. This was not particularly innovative practice as Latins had previously acted as tax farmers in Islamic North Africa in the thirteenth century, ibid., 137. The Mamluks, other Turkic *beyliks* and also the North African city-states also had close relationships with Latin states (particularly the Genoese and the Venetians), ibid., 11.

[8] Ibid., 141 notes that clauses introduced into various peace and trade treaties stipulated the necessity for bilateral rights for merchants which suggests that Ottoman merchants may well have traded in areas ruled by Franks or Latins. See also Kafadar 1986; Matar 1999 *especially* ch. 1 for the presence of North African Ottoman Muslims in England. See Goffman 1998 for English merchants in the Ottoman Empire.

[9] Faroqhi 2013, 231–44.

Empire at all levels, and the incorporation of ex-members of the households and administrative elites of conquered states and dynasties, particularly the Byzantine Palaeologan house.[10] The tendency of elite families to intermarry and establish connections across states and empires meant that with the absorption of ex-Byzantine officials into the Ottoman Empire there then existed high-ranking Ottomans with close family connections across Eastern Europe and further afield. For example, Mehmed II's grand vizier was Mahmud Pasha Angelovic, a convert to Islam whose brother was Grand Voivode of Serbia and whose cousin was George Amirutzes, previous treasurer of the Comnene kingdom of Trebizond who subsequently became philosopher royal to Mehmed II.[11]

Moreover, the Ottomans throughout the early modern era competed with other European states for the loyalty and service of the most talented scientists, artists, administrators, engineers and mercenaries, and many chose to forge a future in the service of this dynamic, vibrant and wealthy empire.[12] While those with military, or administrative skills could always find lucrative employment in the Ottoman Empire, there is evidence that Christian Habsburg peasants also moved across the Habsburg-Ottoman border zone to settle in Ottoman lands, ostensibly encouraged by lower tax rates.[13] Such liminal, border spaces constituted a 'middle ground,' a place where people, commodities, ideas and cultures met in a rather more accepting and heterodox atmosphere and which therefore contributed significantly to wider cultural exchanges.[14] The transmission of ideas did not solely happen in an *ad hoc* fashion through the mediation of migrants, or the communities of Florentine and Genoese merchants resident in Pera, there was also an institutional framework for such exchange: the *ta'ife-i efrenciyan*, a group of paid retainers in the sultan's service who, through contact with Western Europe, ensured that the Ottoman Empire was cognisant of the latest scientific and technological advances in the Christian world.[15]

---

[10] Finkel 2005b, 57, 60–63.

[11] Raby 1982, 3–8; Finkel 2005b, 62–3.

[12] Isom-Verhaaren 2004, 109–34, has described the careers of a few high-level migrants to the Ottoman Empire. Matar 1999, ch. 2 has described the *ad hoc* temporary, or more permanent, migration of soldiers, craftsmen, gunners and sailors to the Ottoman Maghreb and Morocco.

[13] Wessely 1973–74, 55–110 and 91. Finkel 1992, 451–71 and 452 also mentioned that the Ottomans tried to encourage the migrations of Christian peasants into the Ottoman-controlled border lands with tax incentives. Stein 2007, 93–7 comments that young men from both sides of the borders, both Christian and Muslim, were encouraged to seek their fortune in the Habsburg-Ottoman border zone either through military service, working as skilled labour, or by acquiring a plot of arable land.

[14] For more on the Habsburg-Ottoman border zone functioning as a middle ground see Norton 2008, 79–101 and 85–8.

[15] Murphey 1983, 287–98.

Commercial and other economic or political interactions also engendered personal interactions with the 'other' and instances of acculturation and conversion. Conversion to Islam by non-Muslim migrants resident in the Ottoman Empire in the early modern period largely arose from the development of close personal and communal partnerships: intermarriage or a close working relationship, be it in a military, administrative, urban or naval context, often engendered a desire to share a common identity, and thus encouraged conversion.[16] Such interactions were not restricted to the Ottoman and Islamic lands; Andrews and Kalpakli have argued that the Venetian attempt, through the proclamation of various laws and decrees, to limit or restrict sexual relations between the Turks in the *fondaco die Turcei* and Christians of both genders was probably a response to the prevalence of existing relations.[17]

Such relationships and the offspring they produced can stand as a metaphor for the complex, tangled web of inter-relations between political, economic and cultural communities inhabiting the wider Mediterranean space. Andrea Gritti, a Venetian merchant and nobleman, moved between the worlds of Venice and Istanbul, spending twenty years living in the latter, yet finally becoming Doge of Venice. He had sons by both his Venetian wife and his Ottoman consort and his offspring were therefore assimilated into the Venetian and Ottoman sociopolitical worlds respectively. Most famously, one of his sons by his Ottoman consort, Alvise Gritti was born in Istanbul, educated in Padua and Venice and then returned to Istanbul where he became jeweller to Sultan Süleyman and a close intimate in the household of the Ottoman grand vizier, Ibrahim Pasha.[18] Alvise occupied a liminal position: having access to both Venetian and Ottoman networks of patronage, commercial connections and intellectual and cultural contexts, and yet completely belonging to neither. He was thus in a position to be instrumental in not only establishing close political, diplomatic and commercial ties between the two states, but also in translating and appropriating artistic and political rhetorical vocabularies. In particular he, and Ibrahim Pasha, were responsible for commissioning and designing the Venetian-made crown that Süleyman wore in his 1532 campaign against the Habsburgs and which clearly articulated, in a vocabulary familiar to Western European, Christian audiences, Ottoman claims to universal sovereignty through the presentation of the Ottoman sultan as the new Caesar, heir of the Roman Empire.[19]

---

[16] For more on conversion in the Ottoman Empire see Norton 2007; Greene 2000, 94 explores court records for evidence of conversion in order to marry.

[17] Andrews and Kalpakli 2005, 115. As the title of their work suggests, Andrews and Kalpakli read Ottoman love poetry as being part of a Mediterranean-wide Renaissance 'age of beloveds'.

[18] Raby 1989, 41–6, 43; Klinger and Raby 1989, 50.

[19] Necipoğlu 1989. For other references to this crown see Pulido-Rull 2012. For information on Alvise Gritti see Howard 2006, 24, and Valensi 1993, 17–19. See also Raby 1989.

Artistic Interactions

Over the past few years, a number of scholars have cogently illustrated how Venice's economic and political interactions with Eastern Mediterranean civilisations had an impact on the artistic output and culture of the city state.[20] To argue that such an interaction would not also have had an effect upon the Ottoman and Mamluk states is redolent of orientalist accusations concerning the closed, introspective-nature of Islamic societies, and more pertinently ignores the available evidence. Political and commercial interaction between communities in the Mediterranean led to an exchange of art objects particularly textiles, carpets, ceramics, metal and glassware, both as diplomatic gifts, booty and as curios brought home by merchants. For example, rock crystals from the Fatimid treasury were kept in the San Marco Treasury in Venice, while Burgundian late-Gothic rock crystals were also valued and collected in the Topkapı Palace treasury.[21] Objects from the Islamic world achieved an elite and desirable status in the Italian states and later throughout Europe because of their quality and rarity, and the fact that they connoted the wealth and power of the powerful Islamic Empires of the time.[22] Similarly, for the Ottoman sultan and elite, luxury European goods signified the allure of the foreign other. This mutual fascination and curiosity extended to depictions of the prosperous and exotic cities of the 'other'. Just as the Marquis of Mantua requested that Bellini paint views of Venice, Genoa, Cairo and Istanbul in his villa, so too did Mehmed II ask the same artist to paint him a view of Venice in his palace.[23] It was not simply the 'otherness' of these art objects that made them attractive for various Mediterranean communities though, the calligraphic and geometric designs, knotwork and plant, animal and hunting motifs commonly found embellishing them, transcended cultural borders and were therefore equally desirable to a Christian Western European audience. The existence of pseudo-Kufic bands on Western European Christian textiles attests to not only the translatable nature of Arabic calligraphy, but also to the value that Islamic textiles had within Western European Christian society.[24] This cultural mimesis was intensified by a shared interest in harmony of design and the balance of parts by Christian and Muslim Renaissance states across the Mediterranean world and by a shared

---

[20] Howard 2000; Carboni 2007; Raby 1982b; Mack 2002; Grube et al. 1989; Contadini 2006.

[21] Contadini 1999, 8.

[22] MacLean 2007, ch. 1 discusses the English elite's fascination with not only acquiring carpets from the Ottoman Empire and other Islamic states, but also having their portraits painted standing on them. Faroqhi 2013, 235–6, comments that Ottoman silks and other textiles were so valued that they were often used in a religious context i.e. were transformed into synagogue curtains and church vestments.

[23] Howard 2006, 14.

[24] Contadini 2013, 41–4 for details and examples of pseudo-Kufic bands.

conceptual system of symbolism.²⁵ For example knotwork in both a Christian and Islamic context was understood to have associations with and thus refer to the intellectual pursuits of astronomy and astrology.²⁶

The exchange of diplomatic gifts often created a wider demand for the art objects of the 'other' and thus led to increased commercial interaction. Mack has argued that the Venetian Senate's generous gifts of luxurious robes to Ottoman ambassadorial delegations ultimately led to the purchase of huge quantities of Venetian silks and velvets by the Ottoman court.²⁷ Likewise, gifts of Chinese porcelain by the Mamluks to various 'Italian tastemakers' was probably done in order to promote the re-export of quality merchandise which had recently begun to be imported into the Mamluk realm in some quantity.²⁸ Furthermore, the development of a repertoire of shared decorative motifs in turn enabled goods to appeal to potential customers from both Western and Eastern markets and therefore not only created an import market, but also encouraged the development of native industries producing imitations of the art objects: Italian imitations of Ottoman textiles and ceramics for the home and foreign markets were common as were in the sixteenth century Venetian manufactured varnished leather shields based upon original Ottoman models.²⁹ The Ottomans similarly produced gauche costume books for sale to European merchants and travellers as a response to their initial production by Western Europeans but also were interested in acquiring Venetian style gilded leatherwork.³⁰

It was not only objects that were exchanged as diplomatic gifts: Mehmed II also requested that master-builders, bronze workers, *christallini* craftsmen, intarsia artists, makers of clocks, sculptors, artists, scabbard makers and other craftsmen be sent to the empire. Although Bellini is the most famous of these artists and craftsmen, Raby has argued that so many came during Mehmed II's reign that there was a sizeable European atelier based in Istanbul.³¹ This exchange of objects and men also facilitated a diffusion of techniques: the Ottomans learnt and developed sculptural, architectural, painting and medal casting practices from the Venetians and others, while artists from the Italian city states adopted Ottoman book-binding and lacquerwork, and Mamluk metalwork practices

---

25   Mack 2002, 4.
26   Auld 1989, 190.
27   Mack 2002, 24.
28   Ibid., 23; and Spallanzani 1997.
29   Howard 2006, 27–8; Faroqhi 2013, 232 and 235; Mack 2002 provides numerous examples of the transfer and adoption of Islamic motifs and designs. The reverse also happened: Faroqhi 2013, 237 notes that the Ottomans copied European motifs such as the crown.
30   Raby 1989, 44; and Contadini 1989.
31   Raby 1982, 5. Rogers 1990, also suggests that as a result of the similarities between Ottoman and Venetian book-bindings and leather work it is reasonable to conclude that there were either Venetian workshops in Istanbul copying and adapting Ottoman court style leatherwork, or that Italian craftsmen had access to Ottoman palace workshops.

and motifs.³² Out of such collaborations also arose new artistic syntheses. For example, there is evidence that a Ragusan, Maestro Pavli (Paolo da Ragusa), trained the Ottoman court artist Sinan Bey in portraiture and, in turn, Sinan Bey passed on a synthesis of Italian and Ottoman artistic practices and techniques to his pupils.³³ Moreover, Sinan Bey's ability to translate Western and Eastern artistic vocabularies and traditions, together with his ability to speak Italian, meant that he was sent as a cultural ambassador to Venice at the same time that Bellini was performing a similar role in Istanbul.³⁴

Artistic and intellectual exchanges were not limited to art objects and techniques. Architectural reciprocity and synthesis also developed against a background of Ottoman-Western European shared intellectual contexts and a common rhetorical heritage which both Western European states and the Ottoman Empire used to fashion an imperial identity: namely their common preoccupation with idealised architectural forms and spaces, and a shared Byzantine heritage. This co-extensive ideological context and vocabulary will be explored in more detail below, so here I will simply offer a few examples of how both Renaissance Italians and the Ottomans translated Byzantine architectural traditions in order to authorise their own claims to imperial dominion and express current developments in architectural form.

Early Ottoman mosques through the establishment of intertextual references to previous architectural traditions appropriated the imperial iconography of powerful neighbouring states and empires including those of the Ilkhanid Mongols, the Timurids and the Mamluks.³⁵ With the conquest of Constantinople in 1453, a new imperial heritage and rhetorical vocabulary was made available to the Ottomans: that of the Romano-Byzantine Empire. As such, post-conquest imperial Ottoman mosque building began to incorporate, and dialogue with, architectural features of the archetypal Byzantine Church of Hagia Sophia. In particular, the imperial mosque built by Mehmed II, Fatih Cami, epitomises these interconnections between the Christian and Muslim Mediterranean world in that it exemplifies and exploits not only the Romano-Byzantine heritage, but also contemporary Italian Renaissance ideas concerning ideal planning. Mehmed II did not, however, slavishly imitate, instead he, or rather his architects, appropriated and re-interpreted facets of this heritage as well as contemporary Renaissance architectural concepts and combined them with existing features of the Ottoman architectural tradition. For example, the half dome and tympanum arches perforated by windows acknowledged the mosque's, and by implication also the empire's, shared genealogy with the Byzantine church of Hagia Sophia,

---

³² On book-binding see the article in this volume by Ohta 2013; on gilded and varnished leather work see Grube 1989b, and Contadini 1989. On metalwork see Mack 2002, ch. 8; and Auld 2004.

³³ Raby 1982, 5; Necipoğlu 2012, 4, see also 55, n. 18.

³⁴ Ibid., 4.

³⁵ Necipoğlu 2005, 77–8.

whereas its bilateral, symmetrical axial layout is very reminiscent of the Ospedale Maggiore designed by the leading Italian Renaissance architect Filarete.[36]

However, the influence of Italian Renaissance architectural ideas was not limited to the design of Ottoman mosques: Necipoğlu has noted intriguing parallels in attitudes towards architecture and urban planning in Rome and Istanbul in the fifteenth and sixteenth centuries. In both cities one can observe a concern to renew ancient water systems; the select preservation of ancient monuments, but the destruction of others; the creation of new urban axes to link together important and iconographic landmarks; and the patronage of monumental buildings that not only exalted the greatness of God, but also made direct allusions to past imperial grandeur.[37] Both the Ottomans and the Italians appear to have virtually simultaneously embarked upon a revival of the architectural traditions of late antiquity in order to articulate and legitimise their current dynastic claims. Just as Mehmed II's architects dialectically engaged with Byzantine structures in their re-fashioning of Istanbul, Bramante's design for St Peter's cathedral also bore a significant resemblance to Hagia Sophia.[38] Pope Julius II, through his building of the monumental St Peter's, hoped to re-establish the ancient imperial power of Rome, and by visually articulating the humanist argument concerning the shared cultural heritage and desired unity of both the old and new Rome (Rome and Constantinople) challenge the Ottoman's rhetorical claim to legitimate rule in Constantinople.[39] Moreover, both the sixteenth-century chief Ottoman architect Sinan Pasha and contemporary Italian architects did not simply employ earlier iconic architectural works as a point of reference, but crucially re-interpreted and modernised their inherited models, thus creating their own distinctive styles. As Necipoğlu has demonstrated, the debate as to the ideal balance to be attained between imitation and creativity occurred throughout the Mediterranean world and not simply in the Christian West.[40]

The connections between monumental architecture in Rome and Istanbul were not restricted to the exploitation of a common Byzantine heritage for politico-rhetorical purposes; there is evidence that the ongoing political, diplomatic and personal contact and interaction between different communities also facilitated a degree of cultural mimesis that evidenced itself in shared architectural practices, idioms and techniques. Along with artists and craftsmen,

---

[36] Ibid., 84 and 86. Allusions to the Hagia Sophia became more pronounced in later Ottoman imperial mosques such as those built by Beyazid II and Süleyman I.

[37] Ibid., 83.

[38] Necipoğlu 2012, 22–30 discusses in more detail the Ottoman renovation and re-use of Byzantine relics as well as the manner in which Ottoman architecture in Istanbul was in dialogue with extant Roman and Byzantine antiquities.

[39] Necipoğlu 2005, 91. This desire to re-unite the old and new Rome in one world empire also encouraged the Ottomans to look West and dream of capturing Rome.

[40] Necipoğlu 1993, 176.

architects were frequent travellers between the Italian states and the Ottoman Empire: the Bolognese architectural engineer Aristotile Fieravante and possibly his associate Filarete came to Istanbul; and later the services of Michelangelo and Leonardo da Vinci were requested to design a bridge to cross the Bosphorus: there is a sketch for the bridge in the latter's notebook as well as a Turkish translation of a letter from him to the Ottoman sultan in which he describes his design.[41] Michelangelo may also have acquired information about contemporary technologies of dome construction in the Ottoman Empire through diplomatic and architectural contacts because the double-shell dome that he uses for St Peter's is very reminiscent of that employed not only in the Hagia Sophia, but also in mosques designed by the Ottoman architect Sinan.[42] Ottoman architects and travellers also visited Western European cities: the diplomatic position of çavuş (messenger, but more akin to an *ad hoc* ambassador) was frequently occupied by the corps of architects; and an Ottoman delegation also apparently visited the construction site of St Peter's while they were in Rome.[43] In addition, çavuşes acted as escorts for European architects and artists in Istanbul: Melichor Lorichs who accompanied Busbecq's embassy to Istanbul in the 1570s depicts himself with his çavuş. A picture album from a Habsburg embassy to Istanbul attests to this means of diffusing architectural knowledge as it includes two bath plans by an Ottoman architect, one of which includes German translations of the Ottoman terms.[44] One could therefore conjecture that the similarities between Palladio's Redentore in Venice and minarets designed by Sinan might be the result of diplomatic connections. One possible source for the connection is the Venetian *bailo* and amateur architect Marcantonio Barbaro who not only mentions Sinan's mosques in his official correspondence with Venice, but whose brother had also written a commentary on the architectural treatise by Vitruvius which was illustrated by Palladio. As Barbaro was friendly with the Ottoman grand vizier Sokullu Mehmed Pasha, it is reasonable to hypothesise that he may have given him a copy of this commentary as a gift. Nonetheless, even if Palladio and Sinan were not directly aware of one another's work, the affinity of their designs and their design practice suggest that the intellectual context, or cultural milieu, in which both worked was remarkably similar.[45]

Intellectual Connections

The Ottomans and their Western European counterparts not only inhabited a shared cultural or artistic world; there is substantial evidence that the

---

[41] Necipoğlu 2005, 88.
[42] Ibid., 89–90 and 92.
[43] Necipoğlu 1993, 174–5.
[44] Necipoğlu 2005, 98.
[45] Ibid., 100–101.

intellectual developments and interests associated with the Renaissance also traversed religious and geographical boundaries. In particular, libraries, patronage networks and comments by travellers and scholars attest to an interest by the Ottoman elite in the philosophy, literature and cartography of the ancient Greeks and Romans, as well as in other typical Renaissance subjects such as jurisprudence, military science, fireworks, history, medicine and narratives of origin.[46] The non-Islamic manuscripts in Topkapı Palace Library, while previously assumed to have been rescued from the library of the last Byzantine Emperor, are now understood to have been actively commissioned by Mehmed II.[47] These manuscripts include works on classical literature, geography, cosmography, history and natural history which, as Raby has noted, essentially constituted the core subjects of an early-modern Byzantine school curriculum.[48] Indeed, Raby has argued that these manuscripts may have been commissioned for use in training Ottoman chancellery scribes thereby providing them with what was, effectively, a quintessential humanist education.

This interest in Graeco-Roman civilisation was also expressed through a preoccupation with the fashioning of a Greek lineage. Both Western humanists and the Ottomans participated in the humanist politics of ethnology and articulated their own and their enemies' origins with reference to the same myths and peoples: the idea circulated in both the Ottoman Empire and Western European states that various peoples including the Italians, French and the Ottomans were the descendants of the Trojans, the *Teucri*, who were the descendants of the Greek God Apollo and Cassandra, the daughter of the King of Troy.[49] Although such a ethnographical explanation was common in Renaissance poetic and literary works it was far less common in more historical texts which posited instead the supposedly barbaric Scythians as ancestors of the Ottoman Turks less out of a concern for historical accuracy and more from a desire to denigrate the Turks and demonstrate their political illegitimacy.[50] However, as

---

[46] For a common interest in fireworks see, Faroqhi, 'Fireworks in Seventeenth-century Istanbul' (unpublished manuscript) I thank the author for allowing me to read this draft; and Raby 1987, 300; See Necipoğlu 2012, for multiple references to Ottoman interest in Greek philosophy, narratives of origins, and histories. See n. 47 below for an interest in the military text *De re militari*.

[47] Raby 1982, 6.

[48] Rogers 2005–2006, 82.

[49] Raby 1982, 6.

[50] Meserve 2008, 63–4, chapter one of this work is a detailed description of Renaissance claims that the Ottomans were descended from the Trojans or *Teucri* whereas chapter two explores authors who argued that they were descended from the Scythians. Depicting the Ottomans as descended from the Scythians also conveniently allowed Renaissance scholars to differentiate between different Islamic states and consequently to legitimise those Islamic states that might be potential allies in future conflicts between Western Christian European states and the Ottoman Empire, Meserve 2008, 3 and 17.

Necipoğlu has pointed out, the Ottomans also employed the polemical trope of the barbaric Sythians to describe their enemies: in this case they asserted that the Timurids were descended from the Sythians.[51] Such discussions are not really about genealogy, but are instead arguments over political legitimacy. What is pertinent in this context is that the argument and the references were engaged in by both Christians and Muslims, Westerners and Easterners, suggesting that the different Mediterranean states and communities, despite the often hostile and violent realities of their relations were united, at some level, in a rhetorical, or discursive, commonality. This common rhetorical heritage is explored by Akasoy in her discussion of Pope Pius II, Amirutzes and George of Trebizond's intellectual interactions with Mehmed II and the common ground they established through a shared interest in Aristotelian philosophy and the importance of reason.[52]

Likewise, just as humanist writers were keen to acquire manuscripts of works by the ancients and Arabic commentaries on such works from Constantinople/Istanbul, so too were the Ottomans, particularly Mehmed II, desirous to acquire copies of key humanist texts that they felt were missing from Ottoman collections, and they often requested them as gifts from foreign elites. Most commonly cited is the attempted journey of Matteo de'Pasti, sent by Sigismondo Malatesta, the ruler of Rimini, to the Ottoman Empire with a copy of *De re militari*. Although he and the work were seized on route by the Venetians, a copy printed in Verona in 1472 did eventually find its way into the Topkapı Palace Library.[53] Moreover, Mehmed II also made a request of the Rectors of Ragusa to help him acquire two works on Avicenna's *Canones*, the Latin translation of Ibn Sina's *Qānūn fi'l-tibb*.[54] All of this suggests that the Ottomans, as well as Western Europeans, were keen to (re)discover and (re)create a Graeco-Roman intellectual heritage, and that they all shared a reverence for the same ancient sources be they in Arabic, Latin or Greek.

Further testimony to Mehmed II's interest in typical Renaissance subjects is attested to by his patronage of George Amirutzes. Mehmed II commissioned Amirutzes to both up-date Ptolemy's *Geography* and to produce a composite world map from the discrete maps.[55] Cartographic knowledge, like artistic motifs and architectural influences, moved back and forth between the Eastern and Western Mediterranean: for example, Francesco di Lapaccino used a copy of Ptolemy's *Cosmographia* that had been brought to Italy from Constantinople as his source for his transcription of the work, and subsequently copies of his

---

[51] Kritolovulos describes Timur as Scythian in his Greek language *Historia* dedicated to Mehmed II and designed to immortalise his deeds and exploits. Necipoğlu 2012, 11.

[52] Akasoy 2013, 245–56.

[53] Raby 1987, 300–301. Sigismondo Malatesta had previously sent copies of the same work to other European princes, Rogers 2006, 82.

[54] Raby 1987, 303.

[55] Rogers 2006, 80.

transcription were sent back to the Ottoman Empire.[56] Brentjes in this volume has demonstrated the shared cartographic world that existed in the Mediterranean with maps traversing a broad Mediterranean intellectual space, and place names as well as geographical features being transmitted, appropriated and amended.[57] Similarly, Brummett argues that gradually through the early modern period European cartography began to acknowledge, albeit in a partial manner, the place of the Ottoman Empire in Eurasian geopolitical space, not only in the body of their maps and in the captions, but also though the figural depictions of the Ottoman sultan on maps: the sultans were no longer exclusively portrayed as incorrigible, malevolent infidels, but were instead presented as one of the many rulers of Eurasia.[58]

That the early-modern Ottomans were perceived by their Western European Christian contemporaries as inhabiting a shared political and intellectual world, as well as a geographical space, is evidenced by the interconnected and trans-Mediterranean networks of patronage and clientship that existed. A number of European Christian cartographers dedicated work to the Ottoman sultan, or worked for him: Berlinghieri chose to dedicate his revised version of Ptolemy's maps not to an Italian Renaissance prince, but to the Ottoman sultan; George of Trebizond journeyed from Italy to Constantinople to meet Mehmed II, and while there, he, together with Amirutzes, composed an introduction in Greek to Ptolemy's *Almagest* which was then dedicated to Mehmed; and the Italian Conte Ottomano Freducci, father of one of the leading map-makers of the Benincasa school, regarded himself as a client of the Ottoman imperial family.[59] At least in the early centuries of Ottoman rule, Ottoman sultans also utilised similar strategies of incorporation to create ties of loyalty between patron and client: Mehmed II appropriated and re-interpreted the titles of the European equestrian orders as Ottoman honours thereby emulating the European practice of conferring honours on artists and diplomats, and more effectively demonstrating his participation in European networks of diplomacy and patronage. He thus knighted the Italian artists Bellini and Costanzo di Moysis, and the Venetian diplomat, Giovanni Dario. In particular, Bellini was appointed *miles auratus ac comes palatinus* (golden knight and palace companion); the *comes palatinus* in this instance signifying that Bellini was a palace companion, and possibly one of a number of foreigners who were enrolled in the *müteferrika* corps of intellectuals, artists and craftsmen who were directly employed by Mehmed II.[60] That these Ottoman honours were understood and recognised by Christian European contemporaries is demonstrated by Bellini's explicit visual

---

[56] Raby 1987, 302–3; Brotton 1997, 100.
[57] Brentjes 2013, 123–41.
[58] Brummett 2013, 63–93.
[59] Raby 1987, 301–2; Brotton 1997, ch. 3.
[60] Raby 1982, 7; Rogers 2006, 95; Chong 2006, 114–15.

reference to them in his paintings and Francesco Sansovino's mention of them in his survey of knighthoods.[61]

Renaissance rulers from across the Mediterranean world not only employed shared ceremonies and clientship networks, but they also, through references to the same iconographic historical personages, established parallel methods of articulating their claims to universal sovereignty. For example, both Western European and Ottoman rulers projected themselves as world rulers through allusions to Alexander the Great and the Roman caesars. Mehmed II, commissioned copies of various histories of Alexander the Great including Arrian's *Anabasis* and his daily discussions with philosophers caused his contemporaries to draw a direct comparison with Alexander and Aristotle's discussions.[62] Both textually and visually, the correlation between Ottoman sultans and Alexander was established: Ottoman authors frequently used Qur'anic references to Alexander to augment their descriptions of the heroic deeds of Ottoman sultans and Ottoman pictorial representations of Alexander often depicted him in Ottoman costume.[63] A motif of a nude male reclining on a rocky landscape holding a victory torch on the reverse side of a medal made for Mehmed II in the 1460s or 1470s, probably by a follower of Pisanello, indirectly references Alexander. Moreover, Pisanello had earlier used a similar motif on the reverse of a medal designed for the Duke of Ferrara.[64] This cross-Mediterranean appeal of Alexander as an emblem of imperial power is further evidenced by the Burgundian Philip the Bold's gift of Arras-made tapestries depicting the deeds of Alexander as the ransom price paid to the Ottoman sultan for the release of Philip's son. It demonstrates that Philip was aware that the figure of Alexander played a similar rhetorical role in the Ottoman Empire as in Western Europe.[65]

As was suggested above in the discussion of architectural intertextuality and mimesis, Byzantium as a paragon of imperial might and majesty played an important rhetorical role in both Western European Christian states and the Ottoman Empire: by establishing parallels with this great civilisation, rulers sought to appropriate the lineage of the Romano-Byzantine Empire and thus present themselves as the rightful heirs of the Roman empire, the new Caesar of their time. As a result of close commercial ties, but also arising from periods of conflict and occupation, the Byzantine Empire had a pivotal

---

[61] Ibid., 116.
[62] Raby 1987, 305, 309; Raby 1982, 4; and Necipoğlu 2012, 8. It was reported that Mehmed II not only had daily discussions with an Arabic-speaking philosopher, but also with two physicians who spoke Greek and Latin respectively, 7.
[63] Ibid., 8.
[64] Campbell 2006, 70.
[65] Jardine and Brotton 2000, 76, also 88, 118 for references and allusions to Alexander the Great in a series of canvases and tapestries made for the Holy Roman Emperor Charles V, and the King of Portugal respectively.

influence on Venetian culture, art, architecture and ceremonial practices.⁶⁶ In a similar manner, the empire had comparable effects on the nascent Ottoman state through commercial ties, intermarriage, diplomatic contacts and conflict. More specifically, the Ottomans' territorial, commercial and imperial ambitions, especially post-1453, encouraged them to engage in a conscious self-fashioning that strove to present the Ottoman dynasty and state as the heirs and successors of the Byzantine Empire. This induced them, not only to emulate Byzantine politico-diplomatic and administrative practices, but also to appropriate and adapt their artistic, iconographic and rhetorical heritage as well. Thus, Byzantine books of ceremonies and the practice of royal seclusion influenced Ottoman protocols and performances of sovereignty, and the monumental domed architecture of early Byzantine churches was revived by Ottoman architects in post-conquest imperial mosque complexes.⁶⁷ Furthermore, Mehmed II was known by titles similar to those of the Byzantine emperors: Kritovoulos in the dedication of his history of Mehmed II addressed him as 'the Supreme Autocrat and Emperor of Emperors', while Amirutzes eulogised him as the legitimate ruler of the Romans or Byzantines.⁶⁸ The significance that the Ottomans placed on their claim to being the heirs of the Byzantine emperors was also known in Western Europe, hence Pope Pius's recommendation to Mehmed II that he follow in the footsteps of Emperor Constantine and embrace Christianity, in order that the imperial power and legitimacy associated with the Byzantine crown be fully transferred to him.⁶⁹

This use of a shared imperial iconography and vocabularies of sovereignty is perhaps most potently exemplified in the Renaissance practice of casting and exchanging medals: a custom that transcended religious and geographical divides. Italian Renaissance rulers, other European sovereigns and the Ottomans engaged in this practice by which claims to legitimate rule and authority were articulated and promulgated. Moreover, the motifs and visual idioms were also remarkably similar and show that all parties had recourse to shared myths and means of representing authority. Medals commissioned by Mehmed II and also those designed to be presented to him utilised the same combination of a profile of the ruler on one side, equestrian images on the reverse, imperial titles and often Latin legends. These medals alluded to a Roman heritage by depicting the sultan as a Roman Emperor and thus can be interpreted as part of the Ottoman attempt to present themselves as the true heirs to the Holy Roman Empire.⁷⁰ The

---

⁶⁶ For the Byzantine influence on Venetian architecture see Howard 2004; for its influence on Venetian painting see Bacci 2008; see also Campbell 2006b.

⁶⁷ Necipoğlu 1991, 16–17; Necipoğlu 2005, 77.

⁶⁸ Necipoğlu 2012, 7.

⁶⁹ See von Martels 2013, 169 and for more on Pius's letter to Mehmed II.

⁷⁰ Campbell 2005–2006c, 76. For example, the medal by Bertoldo di Giovanni depicts a turbaned, bearded figure holding a victory figure aloft and standing on a triumphal cart pulled by two horses guided by Mars the Roman god of war.

desire of many northern Mediterranean rulers to depict themselves as the new Caesar was something that continued into the sixteenth century: Francis I of France, Charles V and Süleyman I all projected themselves in texts, ceremonies and art objects as the rightful heir to the Holy Roman Empire: a comparison is made between Francis I and Caesar in François Demoulins' *Commentaires de la guerre gallique*, while Charles V's elaborately staged coronation as Holy Roman Emperor in 1530 in Bologna, and subsequent triumphal entry into Rome, involved visual motifs such as ceremonial arches and columns, sculptures of Roman caesars, and pages carrying pseudo-Roman ceremonial helmets, that all evoked a Roman imperial past.[71] As Necipoğlu has demonstrated, Süleyman responded to his rival's coronation by staging his own theatrical appropriation of this Roman legacy, commissioning an elaborate crown and other European objects of sovereignty including a sceptre and throne, and staging similar processions in Hungarian towns while on his way to besiege Vienna in 1532.[72]

Beyond East-West Dichotomies: New Frameworks for Analysis

The Romano-Byzantine and Graeco-Roman heritage does not belong exclusively to, nor was it only exploited and re-invented by, Western European Christian states. As demonstrated above, it instead belongs to the whole Mediterranean world and transcends simplistic religious differences. Both Ottoman and Western European interest in reviving or renewing the ancient Roman Empire in the fifteenth and sixteenth centuries suggests that there existed not only similar geo-political and material conditions permitting the rise of empires that could make such assertions, but also a shared intellectual tradition which contextualised and articulated such claims.

This use of shared conventions of representation, and a common vocabulary for voicing claims to power and authority, highlights further commonalities between states in the wider Mediterranean world and militates against a narration of the early modern period predicated upon a religious dichotomy dividing East and West. While the discourse of humanism in early-modern Western Europe emphasised, or accentuated the divide between West and East, Christendom and the *dār al-Islām*, we should not uncritically accept such

---

[71] François Demoulins, *Commentaires de la guerre gallique*, BL: Harley ms.6205, fol. 3, vol. 1, cited in Knecht 1994, 78; For ceremonial arches and columns and sculptures of Roman figures see the engraving of Charles V's triumphal entry into Bologna by Robert Péril in the catalogue of the exhibition by Soly and van de Wiele 2000, 261 and Dunbar 1992; for Charles use of pseudo-Roman ceremonial helmets and people shouting 'Caesar' as Charles passed see references in Necipoğlu 1989, 204.

[72] Necipoğlu 1989; Pulido-Rull 2012, analyses the visual and verbal means by which an Italian-produced panegyric legitimises Ottoman rule and promotes Ottoman power though the depiction of various Ottoman sultans wearing the aforementioned crown.

assertions as necessarily completely accurate. As Faroqhi points out in her article in this volume, there is a tension between the rhetoric of humanist scholars who are 'otherising' the Muslim Eastern Mediterranean communities as barbaric and culturally and racially inferior, and the rather more fluid, multicultural reality of the Mediterranean world: a world in which diplomats, intellectuals, merchants, artists, architects and skilled migrants and elites, through their traversing of geo-political, ideological and cultural boundaries were, in a sense, reifying and asserting the opposite.[73] We must learn to distinguish the rhetorics of difference that served 'official representational needs', that were employed for political ends such as mobilising support for anti-Ottoman alliances, or were a constitutive part of the process of identity formation, from the pragmatic realities of interaction, exchange and cooperation.[74]

These interconnections can no longer be ignored or dismissed. We need a framework that acknowledges and encompasses the heterogeneity of the Mediterranean commercial, cultural and intellectual worlds and that engages with the dynamics of interaction. No longer can Western, European, Christian, re-naissance be unproblematically posited as a counterpoint to Eastern, Asian, Islamic, Ottoman re-entrenchment. We need to redefine the interpretative frameworks that we employ in order to situate and acknowledge the role that the Ottoman Empire played in the Renaissance. It was subject to the same influences, responded to the same environment and political problems, shared a world influenced by the same philosophies, artistic motifs and trends; utilised the same vocabularies of power and legitimacy and revered the same texts. A new model of the Mediterranean world, to be useful, must abandon the discourse of irreconcilable difference and the heuristically simplistic dichotomy of East-West, Christian-Muslim, and instead acknowledge the complexities and contradictions inherent in a world which was politically, culturally, militarily and economically as united as it was divided, integrated as it was segregated. While at certain times, in particular places, the divisions may well have been along religious or geographical fault lines, at as many other times they were not.

However, we must be wary of exchanging one homogenising historiographical frame for another. Simply replacing the paradigm of hostility and isolation with one of interaction and cooperation will neither adequately explain the available evidence nor reflect the complexity of relations between the Christian, Western European states and the Islamic Eastern Mediterranean. As Brummett argues, we need to synthesise the distinct historiographical approaches implicit in the histories of trade with the histories of intellectual or literary culture, and create a balance in our perception of the Mediterranean as a zone of diffusion *and* difference.[75] Such a framework will enable us to more coherently explore how different states and communities responded to similar cultural, economic,

---

[73] Faroqhi 2013, 233.
[74] Wilson 2005, 163 quoted in Brummett 2013, 73.
[75] Ibid., 92.

political and military developments. It is, for example, far more heuristically beneficial and intellectually coherent to investigate and interpret the 'exchange' of medals, the interest in Graeco-Roman scholarship, and developments in dome building/architecture shared by the Ottoman Empire and Western European states as a Renaissance Mediterranean phenomenon arising from a shared Graeco-Byzantine heritage rather than bisect the Mediterranean and assume that the impact was only felt by, or interested, the Christian West.

Perhaps more importantly, a new, more coherent, less problematic, interpretative framework is required because of the adverse assumptions with which the old model requires us to acquiesce. The notion of the Renaissance as a Western European, Christian phenomenon uncritically situates it in a wider European intellectual tradition linking in a linear manner the medieval and early modern period to the present day. Therefore implicitly assuming a historicist vision of global historical time in which events occur first in Europe and then diffuse to the rest of the world: the rise of the West meta-narrative. Renaissance Europe becomes *the* site of modernity and thus any, or all, intellectual or cultural movements are perceived, and narrated, as leading up to this teleological conclusion. Historicism provides a secure homogeneous narrative of previous times and knowledge, which places the narrative emphasis on explaining the path of the apparent winners.[76] The existence of counter-narratives that displace this teleological unfolding are airbrushed from the story, and thus the cross-cultural convergences that constitute the Renaissance are subordinated to a dominant teleological insistence on depicting the artistic, intellectual and technological progress of a retrospectively defined Christian Western Europe. Such a framework not only does not cohere with the evidence but, paraphrasing the term used by Fabian, denies coevalness to other societies and thus elides their contribution, and effectively disregards them as stagnant, backward or uncivilised: assumptions that can have a profound and deleterious effect, not only on our construction of the past, but also on how some contemporary states and communities are perceived.[77]

---

[76] For an argument that historicism is the narration of the victory of the winners see Chambers 2000, 7–19.

[77] Chakrabarty 2000, develops the issues surrounding the politics of historicism and cites the phrase by Johannes Fabian.

Chapter 2

Sharing a Taste? Material Culture and Intellectual Curiosity around the Mediterranean, from the Eleventh to the Sixteenth Century

Anna Contadini

Within the context of a research project that seeks to explore new concepts and, possibly, arrive at more productive paradigms, it is interesting to observe the degree to which the study of the transfer of artefacts between the Islamic Middle East and Europe has already evolved away from early art-historical modes of enquiry. It has become increasingly attuned to the need to take account not only of political and economic factors but also of ideological issues, and has begun to address what may be couched in contemporary terms as hybridity and transformations of meaning and identity. Above all, alongside the perennial concern with periodic conflict set against a background of wary coexistence, recent approaches have shown a greater awareness of transcultural impingement, so that however fundamentally a European phenomenon the Renaissance may be, it can be seen as one within which contacts with the Islamic world were embedded.

It is also worth stressing that the trade in artefacts and the artistic exchanges across the Mediterranean that took place during the Renaissance period were a continuation and development of already established patterns of contact and acquisition. Alongside what survived from Classical antiquity,[1] Eastern artefacts had long been appreciated and collected in Europe, as is demonstrated by the presence of medieval Middle Eastern rock crystals, ivory, glass, textiles and metalwork in many church treasuries and aristocratic collections, and although some were pillaged, others were gifts and yet others traded.[2] The Geniza documents, which record the activities of Jewish merchants in Fatimid Egypt, give evidence of healthy trans-Mediterranean trade connections as far back as

---

[1] See, for example, Knapp and Dommelen 2010; Carrié 1999.
[2] Howard 2000, 59–62; see various articles in Schmidt Arcangeli and Wolf 2010. For a discussion of these objects between the church and princely treasuries and those of the 'cabinet of curiosities' see Raby 1985.

the eleventh century,[3] and the account of the dispersal of the Fatimid treasury (in 1067) specifically talks about precious objects, including rock crystals, being sold in the markets.[4]

Given such information, it is hardly surprising that the old emphasis on empires, which even when used as seemingly neutral taxonomic tools still carried the implication that they were the major actors in the generation and transfer of artefacts, has gradually receded.[5] The role of Byzantium, for example, had traditionally dominated the landscape of eastern Mediterranean scholarship, and more recently it has still been viewed as a bridge between East and West, especially in the transmission of ornament or technique (with reference, for example, to the use of pseudo-Kufic inscriptions, or to the origins of enamelling on glass in the Western world).[6] But such generalised appeal to the mediation of Byzantium merely prolongs the traditional scheme. It is problematic not merely because the evidence for it may be inconclusive, but also, and especially, because it perpetuates the appeal to monolithic states and hence shores up a too schematic set of temporal and geographical demarcations. What is needed, rather, is a number of detailed case studies that might allow us to arrive at a better understanding of the complexities and nuances of developments within Byzantine territories, for given the permeability of borders and the frequent absence of centralised state patronage, it is rather the case that we need to heed the complexities of trading patterns and look at the Mediterranean less in terms of large-scale power blocs and more in terms of a patchwork of cultural centres participating in a set of loosely structured transactions. Accordingly, it might be more profitable to plot patterns of acquisition, and trace the responses to the different categories of artefacts as they variously maintain their original function, inspire emulation, are transformed, or are represented in other media.

Such retentions or adaptations point to conceptual flexibility, reflecting varied modalities of reception. Nor is the world of material culture the only forum of contact and reception, for in Renaissance Europe an interest in the Islamic world extended to certain areas of intellectual enquiry: to languages and to disciplines such as medicine and philosophy; and there was, further, an

---

[3] Indeed, Goitein named the collection of volumes of his major publication on the documents (the first of which dates from 1967) 'A Mediterranean Society': Goitein 1967–93.

[4] This is the eye-witness description by the *qāḍī* (judge) Ibn al-Zubayr of the dispersal of the palace treasures of the Caliph al-Mustansir (427–87/1036–94), as reported by the fourteenth-century historian al-Maqrizi (Al-Maqrīzī 1853); Contadini 1998, 20 and 27.

[5] For views on the Mediterranean as a pool of exchanges and transactions see the fundamental work by Braudel 1949; and more recently, Abulafia 2003 and 2011; also Horden and Purcell 2000, esp. 342–400; Cameron 2012, esp. 101–2; and Hoffman 2007 for the arts.

[6] Fontana 1999; Tait 1999.

openness to its technology, as witness the widespread adoption of the astrolabe, an appropriate example being the one dated 699/1299–1300 from Fez with Arabic and Latin inscriptions[7] (Plate 1). As is well known, Middle Eastern scholarship, including classical scholarship mediated through Arabic, had provided an important part of Europe's intellectual landscape since the twelfth century, when Latin translations were made of important texts by such major figures as al-Farabi (Alpharabius), Ibn Sina (Avicenna), and Ibn Rushd (Averroes).[8] In Italy the teaching of Arabic started as early as 1310, with the Dominicans in Piacenza, while a contemporary or slightly earlier Arabic-Latin dictionary was produced in Spain[9] (Plate 2). This precious document, a witness to the Arabic spoken and written in Spain, was probably commissioned by the religious authorities in order to teach Arabic to friars seeking to convert Muslims. Within the general context of growing concern with the historical development of languages and the relationships between them,[10] the study of Arabic was to develop further during the Renaissance, and in the late fourteenth century this manuscript was acquired by Niccolò de' Niccoli (ca. 1364–1437), a Florentine humanist scholar whose library contained Arabic and other oriental codices.[11] But the interests of such scholars were not restricted to the languages themselves: they had, rather, a broader humanistic concern with their related cultures. Accordingly, fresh manuscripts were sought, new editions and translations were produced, and the study of Arabic was recognised as a desideratum alongside that of Greek and Hebrew.[12] The major areas of concern remained medicine and philosophy,[13] and the treatise on medicine (*Qānūn fi'l-ṭibb*) by Avicenna (the tenth to eleventh century Iranian polymath) was to remain on the syllabus of many European universities until well after 1600, with more than one translation being printed in Venice during the sixteenth century.[14]

---

[7] Florence, Museo di Storia della Scienza, inv. no. 1109. See Marra 1993.

[8] A brief summary of the transmission of medical knowledge from the Islamic world to the West can be found in Siraisi 1990, 12–16. Lists of publications relating to the influence of Ibn Sina on the West can be found in Janssens 1991, 237–58 and Janssens 1999, 137–61.

[9] Now in Florence, Biblioteca Riccardiana, no. 217. The dating is based on codicological and script features of both Arabic and Latin.

[10] 'la storia e la ragione delle lingue', as Michele Amari put it: Schiaparelli 1871, viii.

[11] Niccoli's library went to enrich the library of St Mark's in Florence, in 1441. For Niccoli's library see Ullman and Stadter 1972. Also, Schiaparelli 1871, xii and xx–xxi.

[12] Burnett 1979–80; Burnett and Dalen 2011.

[13] Also history, and for a recent study of humanist historical thinking regarding the empires of Islam see Meserve 2008.

[14] For one such example, published by Giovanni Costeo and Giovanni Mongio in Venice in 1564, see Hamilton 1994, 34–5. Incidentally, the First Book of the *Canon of Medicine* has been translated into English by O. Cameron Gruner and published in 1930, based on 'the Latin versions published in Venice in 1608 and 1595, supported by a study

The audience for works in the original would still have been tiny, so that unless commissioned by a wealthy patron they must have been uneconomical to print. Yet there is one recently rediscovered copy of a Qur'an printed in 1537–38 in Venice by Paganino and Alessandro Paganini that provides one of the earliest instances of movable type being created for Arabic script[15] (Figure 2.1). This copy was in the possession of Teseo Ambrogio degli Albonesi (ca. 1469–1540), Lateran canon and renowned scholar of Near Eastern languages, who lived in Pavia, and we can see his annotations and also, in some places, his interlinear translation into Latin.

It was not until 1584 that printing in Arabic resumed, but it was then undertaken on a larger scale at the Stamperia Orientale Medicea (Medici Oriental Press) in Rome directed by Giovan Battista Raimondi.[16] Two of the aims, to produce propaganda to attract Eastern Christians to Roman Catholicism and, given that printing was unknown in the Arab world, to make a profit by creating a new market, lie beyond our present concerns, but the third is directly relevant. This was to provide good editions of the Arabic originals of certain standard non-religious texts such as Avicenna's *Qānūn*; and, as is shown by an Arabic alphabet printed in 1592, to aid European students wishing to read a text[17] (Plate 3). It thereby extended and deepened lines of enquiry and speculation central to Renaissance thinking, and provided on the intellectual level a parallel to the commercial strands that joined Renaissance Italy to the world of Islam.

But no evidence has come to light that might indicate that the aesthetic appreciation of Middle Eastern artefacts was conceptualised in ways connected with the world of ideas and scholarship, or that the Renaissance scholar perceived the desk rug and the astrolabe that adorned his studio as products of

---

of the Arabic edition printed at Rome in 1593 and the Bulaq edition' (quote taken from Gruner 1930, 18). Hamilton 1994 and 2011 are useful learned overviews on European interest of the Arab and Islamic world through the collection of the Arcadian Library.

[15] Venice, Biblioteca dei Frati Minori di San Michele ad Isola, coll. A.V. 22. Nuovo 1987, and English translation Nuovo 1990; Fontana 1993b; Pelusi 2000; also see Dijk 2005, 140. The earliest known printed Arabic text is found in *Poliphili Hypnerotomachia*, published by Aldo Manuzio in 1499. According to Angelo Michele Piemontese, this is the first Arabic printed text in the world. However, here the Arabic texts are brief phrases, containing one bilingual Greek-Arabic epigraphy, and one quadrilingual Arabic-Hebrew-Greek-Latin: Piemontese 1999, 199–220 and 218, figs 1 and 2. The earliest Arabic complete book in movable type seems to be the *Book of Hours*, printed in 1514, see Hitti 1942; Krek 1979. A chronological list of Arabic books printed in movable type between 1514 to 1585 is given in Jones 1994, 104, footnote 13. A history of printing in Arabic can be found in Lunde 1981.

[16] For a background on the Medici Oriental Press, see Jones 1994, 88–108. Also see Lunde 1981, 21–2, who places the Press within the context of the history of printing of Arabic texts. For Arabic printing in Venice see Vercellin 2000.

[17] Giovan Battista Raimondi's *Alphabetum Arabicum*, Rome 1592, see Hamilton 1994, 60–61, cat. 15.

Figure 2.1   Qur'an printed by Paganino and Alessandro Paganini, 1537–38, Venice

Source: Venice, Biblioteca dei Frati Minori di San Michele ad Isola, coll. A.V. 22. After Curatola 1993, 481.

a culture the alterity of which demanded intellectual attention. Rather, as Sabba da Castiglione demonstrates,[18] artefacts from the Levant could be inserted within a list of objects listed to adorn the home, amongst others from various parts of Europe, thereby underlining the fact that both the scholarly and the mercantile spheres of activity need to be seen as part of the same, complex cultural milieu. It is as such that they were treated in the 1999 Warburg publication on *Islam and the Italian Renaissance* which, with its emphasis on cultural history, covered both areas and, whether dealing with the visual and decorative arts or with aspects of language, philosophy and medicine, was expressly intended to promote a multidisciplinary approach.[19]

The following attempt to characterise the flow of material culture across the Mediterranean during the Middle Ages and the Renaissance from this wider perspective, and to address its aesthetic impact as registered by differences in response, is deliberately selective. Rather than striving, unrealistically, for

[18]   Castiglione 1554, chapter CIX (109), on 'Cerca gli Ornamenti della Casa', 53.
[19]   Burnett and Contadini 1999. See also Kraemer 1992.

comprehensive coverage, preference has been given to consideration of a small number of representative case studies. The material is introduced in a broadly chronological sequence, and thus can be plotted against changes in the political, economic and social spheres, even if the emphasis is on the evolution of differing uses and related perceptions, thereby taking account of shifts in attitude towards the 'other'.

Discussing Pirenne's theory, Francesco Gabrieli judiciously commented that '... [he] considered the state of war (endemic and recrudescent at stated periods) in the society of the early Middle Ages as automatically paralysing international social and economic relations ...; [but] on the evidence of medieval texts such a comparison seems false'.[20] By interpreting the reaction of the West towards the Middle East as fundamentally antagonistic, traditional scholarship did not give due weight to the positive aspects of contact between the two cultures: without wishing to deny times of tension and the realities of military engagement, for present purposes we may remark upon the simple fact that trade continued even during periods of war.

The first examples relate especially to the earliest stage of contact with the Middle East, beginning in the medieval period, and are associated with the acquisition, use and display of a whole host of artefacts. That these were collected and admired for their beauty and their technical qualities is demonstrated by the fact that their value as luxury or display pieces was deliberately enhanced by the addition of often sumptuous mounts.

Some of the most striking objects are rock crystal vessels carved in relief, which were to be used in both secular and sacred contexts. Among the first extant, arriving in the tenth or early eleventh century, are the two found on the ambo presented to the palace chapel at Aachen between 1002 and 1014 by the Ottonian emperor Henry II[21] (plates 4 and 5). They consist of a cup

---

[20] Gabrieli 1974, 68–9. Henri Pirenne's theory was that the end of Roman civilisation, and the beginning of the European Middle Ages, could be placed during the seventh century, as a result of Arab expansion into the Mediterranean that blocked Europe from trade with the East, see a summary in his posthumous book *Mohammed and Charlemagne* (Pirenne 1939, 284–5). This idea has been challenged on the basis of archaeological evidence: Hodges and Whitehouse 1983, 169–76. For a study of Western European views of Islam during the Middle Ages, see Southern 1962; Gabrieli 1974; Lewis 1993; Agius and Hitchcock 1994.

[21] Which I had the privilege of studying recently in my trip to Aachen in November 2009. Thanks are due to the Chapel's authorities for allowing me to study the ambo closely and for photographic permission. I am also grateful to Jens Kröger with whom I discussed the two rock crystal pieces at length and who allowed me to study the calco of these two objects deposited in the Museum of Islamic Art in Berlin at an early stage of my research, prior to my direct examination of the objects in Aachen.

with one handle and a dish with raised foot, both carved in relief with vegetal motifs of palmettes, and they are often referred to as 'cup and saucer', a rather cosy interpretation that is interesting as well as amusing, as it may readily be understood as an example of the 'domestication' of a foreign object. It is, however, inappropriate, as they do not seem to constitute a related pair.[22] They are differently decorated in carved relief and the typology of the cup points to it being probably earlier and from a different artistic sphere: its shape is related to Eastern Mesopotamian works of the ninth–early tenth century, while the dish could be assigned, on stylistic grounds and the type of cut, to the early Fatimid period, late tenth–early eleventh century.[23] Other objects have been assembled on the ambo, making it an extraordinary and unique object: we have sixth-century carved ivories at either side; a central, large, green glass Roman vessel cut in relief; and two agate vessels, around which are placed coloured stones and chalcedon and agate chess pieces of the typically non-figural Islamic type.[24]

---

[22] The 'cup and saucer' terms is used by Lamm 1929–30, vol. 1, 199, vol. 2, Tafel 68, 2 and 3, who put forward the hypothesis (on p. 199) that the cup could have been placed on the outer foot of the dish placed upside down; Wentzel 1972, 70, Abb. 72a following Lamm published the two vessels with the cup on top of the upside down dish, indeed as if they were cup-and-saucer. However, it is unlikely that this would have been their original function, it rather seems a modern, Western interpretation. Further, no other examples are known, though this in itself is not a reason for discounting the possibility, and the decoration in carved relief is different in the two pieces. For the objects and their interpretation of them see Lamm 1929–30, vol. 1, 199, vol. 2, Tafel 68, 2 and 3; Schnitzler 1957, 30, no. 36, Tafeln 110 and 111; Mathews 1999, 177–8, and figs 6 and 7 on 163. Works on the ambo in general include Doberer 1957, which still remains the most comprehensive study to date; Appuhn 1966; Mathews 1999, in footnote 1 lists a bibliography of works concerning the ambo written in the twentieth century. To this we may now add a forthcoming article by Gabriella Miyamoto, whom I thank for having sent me a copy of her lecture given in 2008 (see Miyamoto 2008). A colour picture of the ambo is found in Kramp 2000, 340. A recent study of the ivories on the ambo is Lepie and Münchow 2006, 26–57.

[23] Erdmann 1940, 144–5 and Erdmann 1951, 146 include them with a group of objects that belong to the high production of Fatimid rock crystal, late tenth – early eleventh century. However, the shape and decoration of the cup points to a Mesopotamian, western Iranian area, possibly ninth century. The typology of both cup and plate will be discussed in detail in my forthcoming publication on the two objects.

[24] For a discussion of the 'style sets' of abstract chess pieces in the Islamic world see Contadini 1995.

As the assemblage includes *spolia*²⁵ from ancient Rome and contemporary Byzantium it has been interpreted as symbolizing *translatio imperii*,²⁶ with the inclusion of Middle Eastern objects indicating parity with contemporary Islamic cultures. An allusion to the Islamic world, however, is by no means certain, and if, as has been suggested, the pieces came via Byzantium as part of the treasure that Theophanou,²⁷ wife of Otto II, brought with her,²⁸ they would most probably have been considered Byzantine pieces. However, it has not been possible to associate any particular object with Theophanou,²⁹ so that certainty eludes us.

Rather, it is worth noting that they retained their original form, with no attempt having been made to rework them in order to disguise or neutralise their original shape. Nor is it clear what symbolic value the chess pieces might have had. That they have been organised so as to represent armies on a field seems unlikely; rather, together with the other stones on the ambo, they should be considered primarily as part of an aesthetic programme, assembling pieces that were not manipulated but were included exactly as they were because of their colour and beauty. The use of coloured stones is significant, as it is also possible that it was associated with the characteristically medieval rhetorical concept of *varietas*, since there is evidence that this was extended to the sphere of material culture.³⁰ Accordingly, the ambo could be aligned aesthetically with the deliberately contrastive assemblages of differently coloured gems and rock crystal found on contemporary *Cruces Gemmatae*, such as the Lothar cross, also in Aachen, to be dated ca. 1000³¹ (Plate 6).

Abbasid or Fatimid glass and rock crystal objects are similarly found alongside late-classical pieces in several church treasuries. Many are now reliquaries, and those that arrived in Venice via Acre or Jerusalem might have

---

²⁵ I use the term *spolia* as in German and Italian scholarship and in Byzantine studies generally, i.e. for objects taken from one context and reused in another, no matter how they were acquired. For *spolia* see, for example, the seminal essay by Esch 1969. A distinction between 'reuse' and 'recycling' of objects has been made in more recent times, and the keynote address I gave at the Society of the Medieval Mediterranean in 2011 ('Cultures, Communities and Conflicts in the Medieval Mediterranean', University of Southampton, 4–6 July 2011) was entitled 'Sacred Recycling: the Appropriation of Middle Eastern Artefacts in Europe'. But we do not have evidence that all the objects considered here were ideologically/symbolically restaged, so that for many of them 'reuse' would be a more appropriate term. For such a discussion see, for example, Dale Kinney in Brilliant and Kinney 2011, 4 and chapter 5.

²⁶ For the concept of *translatio imperii* see Pocock 2005, especially chapter 7.

²⁷ For Theophanou, see among others Euw and Schreiner 1991; Euw and Schreiner 1993.

²⁸ Wentzel 1971, 1972 and 1973. But see articles in Davids 1995 that challenge Wentzel's suggestion that the treasury came with Theophanou from Byzantium.

²⁹ See Westermann-Angerhausen 1995, 245, 252.

³⁰ Carruthers 2009.

³¹ See Barasch 1997, 30–32.

already served in that function before 1204 and the sack of Constantinople, their probable source.³² It is certainly the case that some of the mounts pre-date 1200, and these are most probably Byzantine, as in the case of the *Grotta della Vergine* in St Mark's treasury³³ (Plate 7), a substantial fragment of a rock crystal vessel that has been turned upside down, and its neck mounted with a ninth–tenth century enamelled diadem of Leo VI. Placed in the centre is a later insertion, a silver-gilt statuette of the Madonna. This is Venetian and was evidently added after it arrived in Venice in the thirteenth century. In addition to its intrinsic significance as a composite object that has been refashioned in different times and places, this piece is also of interest because of the scholarship related to it. The crystal, already identified early in the twentieth century as Middle Eastern, possibly Egyptian or Iraqi, ninth to eleventh century, has been referred to as such in Islamic art scholarship ever since. In Byzantine scholarship, however, this is overlooked: usually there is no reference to the possibility of it being a Middle Eastern piece and it is referred to variously as a fourth to fifth-century late-antique object or a ninth to eleventh-century Byzantine one.³⁴

As a number of the vessels that are now reliquaries reached Venice well after 1204,³⁵ they may have formed part of that significant portion of the booty that was systematically divided up among the Crusader prelates and went with them to the Holy Land.³⁶ Whether or not they already contained a relic when brought to Europe,³⁷ the connection with the Holy Land raises the possibility of an association with holiness that singled them out as particularly suitable for this purpose, a judgement that might have been reinforced by the beauty and quality of the vessels, and even by a symbolic value inspired by the play of light on the rock crystal itself. Just as it has been suggested that the erection or refurbishment of shrines would help to revive the cult of that particular saint,³⁸

---

32 Riant 1875 and 1885.

33 Inv. Tesoro 116: Hahnloser 1971, 81–2, cat. 92 (entry by André Grabar).

34 A Fatimid attribution is given by Lamm 1929-30, vol. 1, 213–14, vol. 2, Tafel 76, 1; Christie 1942, 167–8; Shalem 1996, 223–4, no. 73 and 1996b, 58–60. A Byzantine attribution is given by Grabar 1971 (tenth-eleventh century) and Galuppo 2001 (ninth century). An attribution to Late Antiquity fourth-fifth century is given by Alcouffe and Frazer 1986 (Alcouffe on the rock crystal, Frazer on the votive crown) and Urbani 2008 where a possible Middle Eastern provenance for the piece is not even considered. Rogers 1998, 135 doubts a Fatimid attribution and speculates that it could be a European piece.

35 As the earliest inventory of 1283 makes clear: Hahnloser 1971, xiii.

36 What Patrick Geary 1986, 184 calls 'the greatest theft'. For an account of relics being used by Ottoman sultans (in particular Bayazid II, r. 1481–1512) for diplomatic relationships with the Papal state see Babinger 1951b.

37 The reliquary of the Holy Blood in St Mark arrived in Venice already with the blood inside the rock crystal bottle. See Hahnloser 1971, 116–18, cat. 128 (entry by Erdmann on the rock crystal and by Hahnloser on the mount).

38 Geary 1986, 179–80.

so a splendid rock crystal reliquary, especially when endowed with an elaborate mount, could have served a similar purpose. Without documentary evidence all this is decidedly speculative, but it is at least certain that such mounts were expressly designed to enhance the beauty of an already beautiful object and, in the case of a royal donation, to express gratitude and recognition by adding to its preciousness: such is clear both from the catalogue entry made by the abbot Suger (ca. 1081–1151) on the rock crystal vase of the queen of Aquitaine and from the extraordinary inscription on the wonderful metal mount that the monks added to it, which records a gift from an Arab king[39] (Figure 2.2).

The best-known rock crystals are the celebrated ewers, two of which, housed in the Treasury of St Mark, may ultimately have come from the Fatimid treasury and reached Venice in the mid or late thirteenth century.[40] Another striking example, now in the Treasury of the cathedral in Fermo[41] (Plate 8), can also, according to style and cut, be dated to the Fatimid period, perhaps to the eleventh century, and what we know of its later history reveals something of the esteem in which such objects were held in Europe. It was given to the Cathedral by Giovan Battista Rinuccini, Archbishop of Fermo from 1625 to 1653, who received it as a present in 1649 from the Grand Duchess of Tuscany, Vittoria della Rovere, daughter of Claudia de' Medici and wife of Ferdinando II de' Medici. That the ewer formed part of the Medici heritage is confirmed by the Medici coat of arms enamelled on the mount at the base. The mounts, in silver gilt and enamels, have recently been tentatively attributed to the early seventeenth century and to the workshop of Hans Karl, a goldsmith first in the service of Wolf Dietrich von Raitenau, Prince-Bishop of Salzburg, and later in the service of the emperor Rudolf II at Prague.[42] (Wolf Dietrich von Raitenau was himself a lover of things exotic, and was responsible for commissioning gilded leather shields in Ottoman style from Venice in the late sixteenth century,[43] some of which will be discussed below.) Like other Fatimid or pre-Fatimid rock crystals, the Fermo ewer acquired value as a sacred object by being transformed into a reliquary: to it was consigned a bone of St Cesonio, the martyr. It is interesting to note that it was manipulated to fit this new function: apart from the beautiful

---

[39] Suger 1996, vol. 1, 151–3, ch. 19; Suger 1946; Gaborit-Chopin 1986, 289–91; Alcouffe and Gaborit-Chopin 1991, 168–72, no. 27 (Alcouffe on the rock crystal, Gaborit-Chopin on the mount); Beech 1992 and 1993, 75 and 3 respectively; Contadini 2010, 48–9.

[40] As documented in the 1283 inventory of St Mark. Hahnloser 1971, 112–15; also Contadini 1998, ch. 1.

[41] The ewer has an Arabic inscription running along the shoulders, *baraka wa surūr bi'l-sayyid al-malik al-manṣūr*, the interpretation of which is, however, unsure, for there has been some disagreement as to whether it is possible to identify here a specific al-Mansur. One may add that it could also be simply read as 'Blessing and joy to the victorious king'. For an up-to-date bibliography on the object see Barucca 2004 and Piazza 2006.

[42] Barucca 2004, IX.9, 369.

[43] See Contadini 1989, 236–7 and notes 36–40.

Figure 2.2 Vase of the Queen of Aquitaine. Sasanian or early Islamic rock crystal, Iran or Mesopotamia, fifth to ninth century. Silver gilt mount with precious stones, Paris, twelfth century.
Source: Paris, Musée du Louvre, MR 340. Courtesy of the Musée du Louvre.

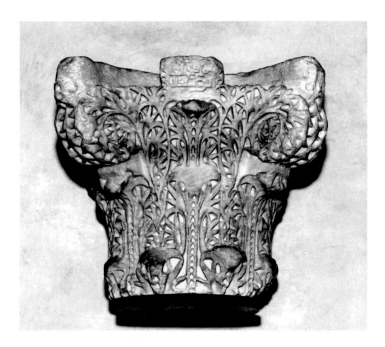

Figure 2.3   Marble capital, carved in relief. Spain, Madinat al-Zahra, tenth century.
Source: Pisa, Museo dell'Opera del Duomo, sala 1, no. 30. Copyright Opera Primaziale Pisana.

silver gilt and enamelled mount and lid attached to it, an attempt was made to enhance its beauty by adding an incised decoration of tendrils with bunches of grapes[44] on the plain area of the body under the missing handle. Together with the smoothing out of the points at which the missing handle had been broken off, this was probably done contemporaneously with the addition of the mount and lid, sometime in the early seventeenth century.

The rock crystals were not, however, the only pieces that could be invested with a particular symbolic importance. In Pisa this was demonstrated by setting two pieces of a quite different order on the roof of the cathedral: on the north transept, placed on a short column, it housed a marble capital from al-Andalus, more precisely from the Umayyad regnal capital, Madinat al-Zahra,[45] and above the apse, facing East, a bronze griffin (figures 2.3 and 2.4). The capital, which is

---

[44] Piazza 2006, 616. Guidi 1899 has drawings of the crystal, one of which shows the added incised decoration of the part under the handle, so this later decor was already there before 1899 when the article was published.

[45] According to Monneret de Villard 1946, 17, the capital was 'discovered' during the restoration works that took place in 1918.

Figure 2.4   Bronze griffin, Spain (?), eleventh to mid-twelfth century
Source: Pisa, Museo dell'Opera del Duomo, sala 3. Copyright Opera Primaziale Pisana.

dateable to the second half of the tenth century and has an Arabic inscription mentioning Fatḥ, the name of the maker,[46] was eventually taken down and

---

[46] This belongs to a well-known group of signed capitals from Madinat al-Zahra. See Contadini 1993, 122–3, cat. 39, Cressier 2004, and fig. 7, and Contadini 2010, all with relevant bibliography.

placed in the Baptistery where, in the centre of the baptismal font, it served as the pedestal for a bronze figure of St John the Baptist. The Pisa Griffin is an extraordinary bronze sculpture with an Arabic inscription of good wishes, eleventh to mid-twelfth century, a dating that recent carbon 14 analyses of organic material found inside one of the wings have confirmed.[47] It remained on top of a short column set on the roof from the Middle Ages until it was taken down in 1828 and put in the Camposanto before entering the Diocesan museum where it is now housed, together with the capital.[48] Monneret de Villard suggested that both were seized from Spain, most probably after either the battle of Almeria of 1089 or the conquest of the Balearic Islands in 1114,[49] although the latter seems more likely.[50] To enhance the visual impact of a cathedral for which the Pisans had already used the most precious materials, the Griffin was positioned where it would be visible to those coming from the city.[51] Apart from its striking visual appearance and its material value as a large piece of bronze, the Griffin had the symbolic property of a terrifying guardian, for when the wind was blowing through its open belly it emitted eerie sounds that were amplified by an internal resonating vessel.[52]

Although in some respects distinct from the rest of the material considered below, this first group of objects initiates the complex process of changing functions and perceptions that will develop further. If its most characteristic features are the acquisition and display of rare and valuable objects, it is also marked by significant transformations of function and symbolism. The European response to the arts of the Middle East was to be marked by further such shifts as it evolved and mutated thereafter – indeed continuing to do so down to the present day – and associated with this evolution was a shift in modes of acquisition. Although valuable objects might continue to appear as items of booty, trade now predominates, with extensive and increasingly dependable networks being developed, both responding to demand and further stimulating it.

---

[47] Contadini 1993, 129–30. The carbon 14 analyses were carried out in February 2013.

[48] Presently the Pisa Griffin, together with the Lion in the Mari-Cha collection and the Lucca Falcon are the subject of a project with Pisa Opera del Duomo, Pisa University, Pisa Consiglio Nazionale delle Ricerche, Lucca Soprintendenza, Oxford University, and the Istituto Superiore del Restauro e Conservazione in Rome. See http://vcg.isti.cnr.it/griffin/. For discussion of provenance, dating and function of the Griffin see Contadini 1993, no. 43, 126–30; Contadini, Camber and Northover 2002 where a comprehensive bibliography is also found; and also Contadini 2010. See also Carletti 2003. The piece presently on the roof is a copy.

[49] Monneret de Villard 1946.

[50] As the sources talks at greater length about the wonderfully rich booty from the Balearic conquest of 1114: see Contadini 1993, 131, note 10.

[51] Baracchini 1986, 67, figs 71, 72.

[52] Contadini in Contadini, Camber and Northover 2002, 68–70.

As far as Italy is concerned, the city states, and especially the maritime republics, were to become increasingly important, so that Middle Eastern artefacts were transmitted not only through Sicily and Southern Italy but also through the commercial activities of Genoa, Pisa, Lucca, Siena, Florence, Amalfi and, of course, Venice, particularly with regard to carpets and textiles. We know from documents in the Venetian archives that one of the biggest yearly expenses of the Republic, starting already in the early thirteenth century, was the import of precious textiles from various parts of the Middle East, and in particular from Fatimid and, later, Mamluk territories in the Eastern Mediterranean.[53] But there were also sources further afield: after the fall of Acre in 1291 and until the early fifteenth century, textiles from Central Asia (Turkestan) and China, especially silk, were imported in great numbers by Florentine and Sienese merchants via Persia and Iraq, which by then formed part of the Ilkhanid Empire.[54] In addition to these long-standing if fluctuating patterns of commercial exchange between East and West, significant developments were to take place during the Renaissance.[55] With the rise of the Ottomans as the new major power of the Islamic world, Turkish centres of production, already of some importance, came even more to the fore, and after 1453 the newly dominant position of Ottoman Constantinople attracted a strong Italian mercantile presence. The Genoese, long resident in considerable numbers in Constantinople, gradually lost ground in this new climate. This was to the advantage of Venice, which, after being granted trading capitulations in 1454, took over certain enterprises previously held by the Genoese and, within a few decades of the conquest, came to enjoy a commercial status that far exceeded its position under the Byzantines. It is interesting to note that the ascendancy of Venice occurred in spite of the considerable tensions – sometimes escalating into actual military conflict – that existed between the Sublime Porte and the Serenissima. Florence, too, came to be an important player in this new commercial arena, with the Ottoman sultan granting the city trading capitulations in 1460. Such trading opportunities encouraged the development of mercantile fleets and contributed to the economic growth of the Italian city-states. The number and activity of Italian merchants and overseas agents engaged in trade with the East increased considerably during the Renaissance, and this, of course, helped promote the importation of artefacts into Europe.

The import of rugs from the Middle East and North Africa to Florence and Venice is already documented from the early fourteenth century,[56] and fifteenth-century documents bear detailed witness to Florentine transactions involving

[53] Jacoby 2000, 271. Also Molà 1994, 23.
[54] Wardwell 1989.
[55] For a useful survey with much detailed information see Rogers 2002. Howard 2007 provides a great synthesis of the cultural and artistic transfer especially between Venice and the Ottoman empire in the fifteenth and sixteenth centuries.
[56] Spallanzani 2007, 11–12.

Figure 2.5   Woollen table carpet, Cairo, mid-sixteenth century
Source: San Gemignano, Museo Civico. After Curatola 1993, 397.

merchants and their agents in complex trading networks. The presence of a Florentine colony in Constantinople soon after the city fell in 1453 reflected the increasingly favourable trading circumstances there, and in the fifteenth century Ottoman Turkish rugs, some from Bursa, became a significant element of Levantine trade. Once in Florence, they were distributed through yet another network, one catering for various categories of customer[57] (Plate 9).

For Venice, too, we know of the presence of merchants and agents overseas, buying or commissioning carpets both for other merchants and for patrician families who may have required the inclusion of the family coat of arms, as is testified by a document relating to a commission for Lorenzo il Magnifico,[58] and

---

[57] Spallanzani 2007, ch. I: 'Importation'.
[58] Spallanzani 1989, 88–9.

Figure 2.6 Girolamo da Carpi, *Portrait of a Gentleman with a Cat*, ca. 1526
Source: Rome, Galleria Nazionale D'Arte Antica a Palazzo Barberini, inv. no. 0912 (F.N. 632). Copyright of Soprintendenza SPSAE and Galleria Nazionale D'Arte Antica a Palazzo Barberini.

as is shown by a table carpet in San Gemignano[59] (Figure 2.5). Instructions for carpets commissioned by Italian families were very precise, with regard not only to type but also to dimensions, as is demonstrated by a 1555 dispute between the

---

[59] See Boralevi 1993, 396–8, cat. 247; Spallanzani 2007, 56.

Venetian Francesco Priuli, an agent living in Alexandria, and the family of the trader Piero da Molin in Venice.[60]

The use of these carpets varied, but usually they were not intended to be walked on, although they could be arranged around a bed (those that are depicted at the feet of the Madonna are a special case, as they demarcate a sacred space). They were used, rather, to cover furniture, in particular beds, benches, tables and chests,[61] and the visual record testifies to the high regard in which they were held. A scholar saint, ancient philosopher, or Renaissance humanist is often represented in his study surrounded not only by books but also by various symbolic objects, including ones of Middle Eastern origin such as astrolabes, various types of metal bowls, pomanders, and, typically, a beautiful carpet that covers the table, as in the case of the fresco by Domenico Ghirlandaio of *St Jerome in His Study*, of 1480, where the splendid border of a colourful carpet with pseudo-Kufic motifs is visible,[62] or the painting attributed to Girolamo da Carpi, *Portrait of a Gentleman with a Cat*, ca. 1526, where a small-pattern Holbein carpet is represented[63] (Figure 2.6).

Given such a variety of functional uses it hardly comes as a surprise to find that rugs were by no means the preserve of patrician families and the church: more modest individuals are also recorded as being able to afford a medium size rug.[64] For fabrics, on the other hand, such evidence is hard to find, and although silks and velvets were traded westwards in significant quantities the visual record points to them more as luxury commodities for the upper strata of society. Reflections of the commerce in fabrics that would contribute to Italy's economic ascendancy appear in art from the thirteenth century onwards: Middle Eastern textiles are reproduced in paintings of the main Italian masters where, in general, they symbolise individual or family wealth,[65] being, quite possibly, a direct representation of the possessions and hence status of the commissioner as well as a vehicle for the painter's expression of rare beauty.

Particularly prominent here are *ṭirāz*, a well-known type with epigraphic bands, the production of which is documented especially during the Umayyad, Abbasid and Fatimid periods,[66] while also well represented are brocaded textiles, including also a particular Spanish type, for Spanish-Islamic textiles begin to arrive in Italy with increasing frequency in the thirteenth and fourteenth

---

[60] Curatola 2004.

[61] Curatola 2004, 130; Spallanzani 2007, 50 and numerous images that testify to the various uses of the carpets throughout the fifteenth and sixteenth centuries.

[62] Florence, Church of Ognissanti. Spallanzani 2007, fig. 46.

[63] Rome, Galleria Nazionale D'Arte Antica a Palazzo Barberini, inv. 0912 (F.N. 632). Thornton 1997, fig. 87. The small-pattern Holbein is a type of Anatolian carpet of the early sixteenth century.

[64] Spallanzani 2007, 35, 44.

[65] Contadini 2006b, 29.

[66] See Contadini 1998, chapter 2 with relevant bibliography. Also Sokoly 1997.

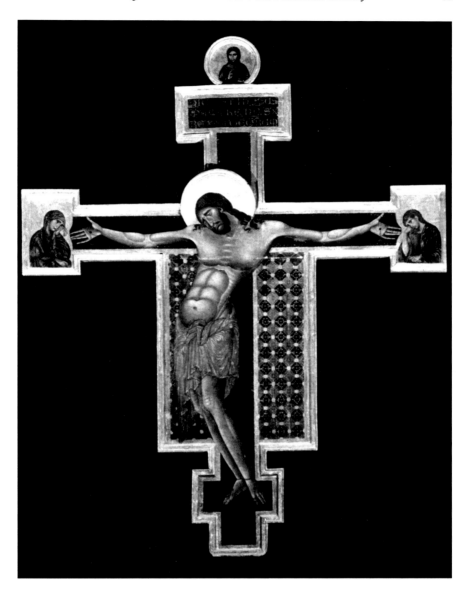

Figure 2.7   Cimabue, *Crucifix*, 1265–8, tempera on panel
Source: Arezzo, Chiesa di San Domenico. After Maetzke 2001, 58.

centuries as trade with Lucca and Pisa grew. The crucifix by Cimabue in San Domenico, Arezzo, 1265–8 (Figure 2.7), contains perhaps the earliest known examples of Middle Eastern textiles to be found in a Western painting. One, at the back of Christ, is possibly Spanish, while the other, held by the Madonna,[67] is a *mandīl* (a fine handkerchief) with epigraphic *ṭirāz* bands in pseudo-Arabic, 'Kufic' script (Figure 2.8). In the fourteenth century such representation of luxury materials continues, as exemplified by Giotto frescoes in the Cappella degli Scrovegni (ca. 1305), which show several textiles with pseudo-Arabic inscriptions in both angular and cursive scripts, as well as scripts of other oriental languages, such as the Tibetan/Mongolian Phagspa.[68] In the early fifteenth century we find Hebrew in Andrea Mantegna,[69] while Gentile da Fabriano makes considerable use of Middle Eastern elements in his paintings. His *Adoration of the Magi*, for example, is full of 'oriental' references: turbaned men and Arabic or pseudo-Arabic inscriptions on the luxurious textiles[70] (Figure 2.9). The inscriptions are not, though, restricted to textiles (and other objects such as leather belts[71]): many are to be found on haloes, for example those of the Madonna and St Joseph. They were previously thought to approximate to the *shahāda* (the Muslim declaration of faith), but it has more recently been persuasively argued that Gentile's source was metalwork, on which inscriptions are, rather, expressions of good wishes.[72] Both these and other haloes bearing pseudo-Arabic inscriptions, such as Gentile's *Madonna of Humility*[73] (Plate 10), resemble Ayyubid and Mamluk metalwork both with regard to the layout of inscription and decor, as a dish in the Aron collection shows[74] (Plate 11), and in the script, which is the typical *thuluth* used on metalwork of the period. As

---

[67] Contadini 1999, 4–5 and figs 3a, 3b (the textile held by the Madonna was first noticed by Bagnera 1988).

[68] Basile 1992, colour plates on 192, 268–9; Tanaka 1989 is on other alphabets represented in the Scrovegni paintings (such as the Phagspa script); and Tanaka 1994 for East Asian connections.

[69] See Busi 2007, pp. 99–105. For Hebrew inscriptions in general see Barasch 1989.

[70] Florence, Galleria degli Uffizi, inv. no. 8364. The bibliography on this painting is vast. For a work that deals with the pseudo-Arabic inscriptions see Auld 1989 and for a recent discussion of the textiles in this painting see Monnas 2008, 102–105. For an overview of pseudo-script in Italian art see Nagel 2011.

[71] Another example of pseudo-Arabic inscription on the representation of a leather belt is found in Verrocchio's David (1473–75) in the Museo Nazionale del Bargello in Florence, for which see Fontana 1993, 457.

[72] Leemhuis 2000. Also Auld 1986, 256–9; and Mack 2002, 65, fig. 57, who draws attention to the divisions of these inscriptions on the haloes into four sections divided by rosettes like those found in Mamluk metalwork (a type of division, however, that is also found on haloes with traditional Latin texts). Even in the case of Ayyubid metalwork with Christian imagery, the inscriptions are not religious but of the general, good wishes type (Baer 1989, 10–11). For the reading of the inscriptions as the *shahāda* see Sellheim 1968 and Forstner 1972.

[73] Pisa, Museo di San Matteo. See Contadini 1999, figs 22a and b where a detail of the halo is reproduced.

[74] Allan 1986, 92–3, cat. 12.

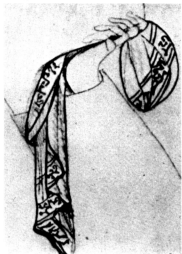

Figure 2.8 Drawing of the Madonna and the *mandīl* from Cimabue's *Crucifix*
Source: After Bagnera 1988.

far as can be ascertained, the content of the halo inscriptions is derivative of the typical Mamluk formula '*izz li-mawlāna al-sulṭān al-mālik al-'ādil*, etc. It may therefore be concluded that, whether on clothing or halos, the inscriptions reference prized luxury artefacts, metalwork as well as textiles.[75]

Textile designs with Islamic elements, including inscriptions with the same *thuluth* script, also appear in the sketchbooks of Jacopo Bellini (ca. 1424–ca. 1470), in particular that on parchment now in the Louvre.[76] Both the elements of the design and the inscriptions recall textiles from Lucca, as demonstrated by a late fourteenth or early fifteenth-century silk in the V&A, or perhaps from Venice,

---

[75] An Arabic inscription in *thuluth* is found on a fourteenth-century stained glass window in the Church of SS Annunziata in Florence (see Bernardini 1999), again most probably taken from a Mamluk metalwork.

[76] For instance on fol. 88v of the sketch book, Paris, Musée du Louvre, Départment des Arts Graphiques, inv. no. RF. 1556: see Degenhart and Schmitt 1984.

Figure 2.9　Detail from Gentile da Fabriano, *Adoration of the Magi*, 1423, tempera on panel
Source: After Monnas 2008, fig. 105, detail.

as demonstrated by a fourteenth-century silk formerly in Berlin that might even have been a textile from the Lucchese colony in Venice.[77] The style of some of the drawings already suggests that Bellini was using an older sketchbook, and it is indeed clear that his own drawings are added on top. The earlier date of the designs is of interest because it points to the existence of 'pattern books' with orientalising motifs, usually associated with a later period (see below), already in the fourteenth century.

The textiles themselves present us with problems regarding provenance, as they are often difficult to track. At the same time, this very difficulty is of theoretical interest, pointing as it does to a variety of economically driven adaptations that result in the production of similar materials in several locations, and in a circulation of style features that ought to result in homogeneity, but is counterbalanced by further local specialisation. During the fifteenth and sixteenth centuries the most notable Muslim land in terms of international trade was the Ottoman Empire, and this certainly holds true as far as textiles are concerned. The great quantity of silk fabrics produced there are called in the documents by a bewildering number of terms whose meanings in many cases remain unclear, but the most important types were *kemkha* (brocaded silk, Plate 12) and *çatma* (velvets brocaded with silver or gold thread, Plate 13).[78] Production of these textiles was concentrated in the West Anatolian town of Bursa, which rose to prominence as a weaving centre from the later fourteenth century onwards. Bursa was, moreover, an entrepôt in the international trade in raw silk, which, until the development of local sericulture in the late-sixteenth century, was brought to it mainly from Iran.[79] Italian merchants settled and traded in Bursa throughout the fifteenth and sixteenth centuries, but they concentrated on purchasing raw silk to be taken back to Italy,[80] either for the thriving and long-established local weaving industries, particularly in Venice, Florence and Genoa, or to be traded on, via Venice, to France or the Netherlands. Because of the existence of these domestic manufactories the demand in Italy for worked – as opposed to raw – silk from the East became with time rather

[77] V&A, inv. no. 8286-1863. See Auld 1986, 256-8 and fig. 9 for the Lucchese silk now in the V&A that has motifs and pseudo inscriptions in *thuluth* relatable to drawings in Bellini's sketch book. See also Monnas 2008, 49-51, fig. 40 which reproduces a page, fol. 88v, of Bellini's sketch book (mentioned in footnote 75) with orientalising motifs and pseudo inscriptions; and fig. 41 which illustrates a reconstruction drawing of the Venetian silk formerly in the Kunstgewerbemuseum in Berlin (lost in the war) relatable to Bellini's drawing; and notes 50-57 on page 345 for details of both sketchbooks and textile, and for the scholarly debate on both.

[78] Baker 1995, 92-3. For the terms and their meanings, see Denny 1982, 122; Rogers 1986, 15-17; Gürsu 1988, 27-30; Atasoy, Denny, Mackie and Tezcan 2001b, 16, 217-25.

[79] Denny 1982, 122; Rogers 1986, 15; Gürsu 1988, 19, 22, 39-40; Baker 1995, 86; Atasoy, Denny, Mackie and Tezcan 2001b, 155, 157-60.

[80] Gürsu 1988, 22; Molà 2000, 60.

low,[81] so that while Ottoman fabrics were exported in large numbers to Eastern Europe and to Russia[82] comparatively few ended up in Italy: earlier reliance on imported luxury textiles such as Fatimid *ṭirāz* and Spanish-Islamic brocade was thus replaced not so much by Ottoman as by local production.

It is thus hardly surprisingly to find that very few Italian Renaissance paintings depict Ottoman fabrics,[83] in contrast to their abundant portrayals of Ottoman carpets. In fact, far from being reliant on Ottoman textile manufacture, Italy was itself a major source of silk fabrics for the Ottoman court and upper strata.[84] Until the 1480s, all the velvets listed in Ottoman court documents were imported from Europe and, to a lesser extent, Iran.[85] During the reign of Mehmed II, much was spent by the court on purchasing Italian fabrics:[86] in 1505 alone the sum of 60,000 ducats – over 7 per cent of the Porte's total annual expenditure – was used for this purpose.[87] These textiles were bought to be tailored into imperial caftans and robes of honour.[88] Indeed, only a few of the surviving velvet caftans in the Topkapı Palace collection are made of Ottoman velvet; the majority are tailored from Italian material,[89] and it is notable that even robes of honour made for foreign visitors to the Ottoman court might be made of imported Italian fabric.[90] One imperial caftan, possibly for Osman II (r. 1618–1622) (Plate 14), the design of which closely resembles a velvet in the Museo di Palazzo Mocenigo in Venice (inv. no. 491/191) (Plate 15) seems to be of sixteenth-century Italian, probably Florentine, manufacture, and is, indeed, extraordinarily similar to the one worn by Eleonora de' Medici (married to Cosimo I de' Medici) in the

---

[81] Atasoy, Denny, Mackie and Tezcan 2001b, 182.

[82] Rogers 1986, pp. 33–4; Baker, Tezcan and Wearden 1996, 28–9; Atasoy, Denny, Mackie and Tezcan 2001b, 176–81, 186.

[83] Andrews Reath 1927, 304; Denny 1982, 122. For those paintings that do depict fabrics that may be of Turkish manufacture, see V&A 1923, 13–14; V&A 1931, 10–11; V&A 1950, 6–7.

[84] Goldthwaite 1993, 20; Molà 2000, 93.

[85] One must keep in mind, however, that for Iran the documentation is inadequate. Wearden 1985, 26; Gürsu 1988, 28; Atasoy, Denny, Mackie and Tezcan 2001b, 182–90.

[86] 110,000 ducats: Baker 1995, 92, although many of these would have been woollens. For internal production of textiles and woollens in the Ottoman Empire, see Faroqhi 1980; Faroqhi 1982–83.

[87] Baker, Wearden and French 1990, 133. This will change in the mid-sixteenth century during the vizierate of Rüstem Pasha, when an embargo on the large-scale importation of luxury textiles from Italy was imposed: see Necipoğlu 1990, 155.

[88] For royal Ottoman caftans made of imported Italian fabric, see Rogers 1986, cat. nos and col. pls 14, 27–8, 31, 42–3, 46, 49; Baker, Wearden and French 1990, 133, 137 and figs 4, 15; Baker, Tezcan and Wearden 1996, 178–99; Atasoy, Denny, Mackie and Tezcan 2001b, figs 36, 38, 40, 46, 54; Denny 2007, cat. 80.

[89] Atasoy, Denny, Mackie and Tezcan 2001b, 182, 223.

[90] Wearden 1985.

portrait of her by Bronzino of ca. 1545[91] (Plate 16). Both contain, further, design elements that could be read as either Spanish-Islamic or Italian.[92] The suggestion, therefore, is of a constantly shifting pattern of exchanges, both at the level of trade, with enterprising manufacturers and merchants feeding and creating new markets, and at the level of design, with pattern elements from one part of the Mediterranean being incorporated in a fabric designed in another that might then be exported to an appreciative buyer in a third. But designs could also be created with a particular market in mind. Thus while the Ottomans did import fabrics with a distinctly Western appearance, Italian textiles produced in imitation of Ottoman models, especially silks, were sold there too, and it is generally agreed that they were produced for the export market.[93] A particularly fine example of a textile in Ottoman style but probably of Italian (and possibly Venetian) manufacture is a sixteenth-century velvet in the Bargello Museum[94] (Plate 17).

The market for such fabrics was by no means limited to the courtly sphere:[95] one Italian manufacturer of silk textiles whose dealings with the Ottomans are particularly well recorded is Andrea Banchi, a Florentine who owned a large and important workshop during the second and third quarters of the fifteenth century, and his account books, which survive in the Spedale degli Innocenti, Florence, document in some detail the substantial sales he made to various Ottoman buyers through agents resident in Pera.[96]

While Italians copied Ottoman designs, the Ottomans returned the compliment. In Bursa about the middle of the fifteenth century (and in Istanbul a century later)[97] we find, in reaction to the market success of fashionable Italian designs, velvet-weaving looms producing fabrics virtually indistinguishable from them,[98] and although technical features can sometimes help clarify

[91] The caftan is in Istanbul, TKS, inv. 13/360. See Rogers 1986, cat no. and col pl. 42. For the velvet in Venice see Degl'Innocenti 2006 (other pieces from the same velvet are kept in different collections). The Bronzino painting is in the Galleria degli Uffizi in Florence, inv. no. 748. See also colour reproductions in Orsi Landini and Niccoli 2005, fig. 1 on 14; Monnas 2008, figs 199 and 216 on 180 and 195 respectively. For a discussion of the textile in this painting see Orsi Landini 2005, 25; Monnas 2008, 191–2.

[92] See discussion in Thomas 1994.

[93] Denny 1982, 125; Baker, Wearden and French 1990, 137; Atasoy, Denny, Mackie and Tezcan 2001b, 182–3, 186–90.

[94] Museo Nazionale del Bargello, Florence, inv. Franchetti 639. Suriano and Carboni 1999, no. 25.

[95] Öz 1950, 73.

[96] Edler de Roover 1966, 270–75.

[97] On the establishment of these industries, see Gürsu 1988, 45–6; Atasoy, Denny, Mackie and Tezcan 2001b, 155, 171–2; V&A 2004, 125.

[98] V&A 1923, 7–9; V&A 1931, 12–14; V&A 1950, 7–9; Mackie 1973–74, 13; Gürsu 1988, 41, 72, 89, 165, 167, 182–3; Atasoy, Denny, Mackie and Tezcan 2001b, 187, 190; V&A 2004, 125.

provenance, the degree of mutual imitation in this period is such that certain pieces cannot be assigned with any certainty to either an Ottoman or an Italian place of manufacture.[99]

Although never achieving the technical standard of their Italian equivalents, the Bursa and Istanbul silk fabrics were of fine quality and much admired both within and beyond the Ottoman Empire; moreover, they were only half as expensive on the Ottoman market as those from Italy.[100] The industry quickly developed its own characteristic style and excelled in the production of brocaded velvets, in particular *çatma*,[101] that were also competitive in Italy. It is known that Ottoman traders were allowed to settle in Venice and sell fabrics amongst other wares,[102] and that Italian merchants were engaged in importing Turkish silks into Italy.[103] Such fabrics were versatile, being put to different uses:[104] for upholstery, for the tailoring of costumes, and as floor coverings, and their popularity was such that at times the influx of Levantine brocades was substantial enough to cause the Venetian *Signoria* to place an embargo on their importation.[105]

Evidence for the import of such fabrics, and for their use for clothing, survives in a repeated order mentioned in a letter, dated 1501, by Giovanni Maringhi, a Pera-based Florentine agent, informing his patron in Florence that he had sent to Bursa for four dress lengths of a type he had dispatched before.[106] Another insight is provided by a portrait of a Venetian noblewoman in the Palazzo Rosso in Genoa, which, although traditionally misattributed to Paris Bordone, was probably executed around 1565 by Parrasio Micheli (Figure 2.10). The lady is depicted lavishly attired in a gold-brocaded robe whose floral design is distinctly Ottoman in inspiration, and a brocade of Ottoman manufacture with

---

[99] Gürsu 1988, 43, 72. 167. 182; Atasoy, Denny, Mackie and Tezcan 2001b, 300, 333–5 and col. pls 67–8, 70–72. For discussions of the technical differences between Ottoman and Italian velvets, see Andrews Reath 1927; V&A 1923, 15; V&A 1931, 21–2; V&A 1950, 15–16; Atasoy, Denny, Mackie and Tezcan 2001b, 183, 187, 224.

[100] V&A 1923, 15; V&A 1931, 21–2; V&A 1950, 15; Wearden 1985, 27. For the prices of these velvets see Atasoy, Denny, Mackie and Tezcan 2001b, 183.

[101] For this type of velvet, see Rogers 1986, 16; Gürsu 1988, 28; Atasoy, Denny, Mackie and Tezcan 2001b, 222–4.

[102] Gürsu 1988, 167; Atasoy, Denny, Mackie and Tezcan 2001b, 186; Pedani 2008, 9 for Ottomans, 7 for Persians.

[103] Mackie 1973–74, 14; Gürsu 1988, 165.

[104] For the uses to which Ottoman textiles were put, see Mackie 1973–74, 14; Denny 1982, 137; Gürsu 1988, 28. An inventory of the Topkapı Palace, Istanbul, dated 1504 lists various types of objects made from velvet, including cushion covers, cloths for mules, and night-caps. Öz 1950, 38.

[105] Rogers 1986, 28.

[106] Richards 1932, 137; Atasoy, Denny, Mackie and Tezcan 2001b, 186.

Figure 2.10   Parrasio Michiel or Micheli, *Portrait of a Lady*, ca. 1565
Source: Genoa, Palazzo Rosso. Copyright of the Palazzo Rosso.

a pomegranate pattern similar to that of the fabric in the painting may be found in the Victoria and Albert Museum (Figure 2.11).[107]

---

[107]   The brocade in the V&A (inv. no. 1356&A-1877) was first compared to the fabric shown in the portrait in V&A 1923, 13–14 and pl. IV.

Illustrated in Figure 2.12 is a *çatma* velvet, probably sixteenth century, that is typically of the output of Bursa:[108] the cut silk pile of the velvet is dyed a deep crimson (the favourite colour in Ottoman textiles) that is probably derived from lac,[109] and its design is rendered in gold thread. The pattern, one of the most frequently encountered in Ottoman textiles, consists of an ogival lattice that provides a framework for rows of staggered floral motifs, in this case carnations,[110] and it presents us with another instance of the diffusion of a particular design feature along an irregular path. The origins of the lattice layout are ultimately to be found in East Asia, whence the design travelled westwards via the Mongol Ilkhanids who ruled Iran. From the Mamluks of Egypt and Syria it then passed to Renaissance Italy, and it is likely that Ottoman adaptation of it in the fifteenth century was indebted to Italian rather than Eastern models.[111] A similar complexity concerns the transfer of flower motifs, but there is here an additional fluidity that can render hazardous any attempt at hard-and-fast categorisation. The carnation – which, along with the tulip, hyacinth and rose, was central to the new floral repertoire created by court artist Kara Memi known as *quatre fleurs*[112] – may also have been of Western derivation. Although flowers had long featured in Islamic art, this new style, which is best known through the ceramics of Iznik, was distinguished by its relative naturalism: the flora rendered in this manner were recognisable species rather than unreal hybrid creations, and the impetus for this move to naturalism may well have come from illustrated European herbals and books of floriculture.[113] However, such motifs acquired distinctive forms under the Ottomans, and the carnation in particular, or possibly the Sweet Sultan (*Centaurea Moschata*), took on a rather abstracted, fanlike shape that is instantly discernible as Ottoman and was especially favoured for use in the decoration of textiles.[114] Crimson velvets brocaded

---

[108] London, V&A, inv. no. 100–1878. Although it is currently not possible to distinguish between the products of different centres (Rogers 1986, 15), the *çatma* weaving was particularly associated with Bursa, whereas the Istanbul ateliers appear to have specialised more in brocaded silks and cloths of gold and silver. Denny 1982, 124; Gürsu 1988, 19; Atasoy, Denny, Mackie and Tezcan 2001b, 156.

[109] Denny 1982, 124; Rogers 1986, 19; Gürsu 1988, 26.

[110] For discussion of this layout, see Atasoy, Denny, Mackie and Tezcan 2001b, 208, 229–30, 233.

[111] Mackie 1973–74, 14; Denny, 128; Gürsu 1988, 43, 67–8; Atasoy, Denny, Mackie and Tezcan 2001b, 208, 227.

[112] Atasoy and Raby 1989, 222. For an example of the *quatre fleurs*, see Atıl 1987, 59; for Kara Memi, see Rogers 1992.

[113] See Rogers and Ward 1988, 60; Atasoy and Raby 1989, 222–3.

[114] As on the example here illustrated, the carnations are usually arranged in staggered rows, often within an ogival lattice. See Denny 1982, 129; Gürsu 1988, 182; Atasoy, Denny, Mackie and Tezcan 2001b, 317. For similar velvets, see Atasoy, Denny, Mackie and Tezcan 2001b, 305 and figs 309, 310.

Figure 2.11   Woven silk brocade, Bursa, second half of sixteenth century
Source: London, V&A, inv. no. 1356&A-1877. Courtesy of the Victoria and Albert Museum.

Figure 2.12 *Çatma* (brocaded velvet), Bursa, sixteenth century
Source: London, V&A, inv. no. 100-1878. Courtesy of the Victoria and Albert Museum.

with gold lattices and flowers were as commonly woven in Italy as they were in Anatolia,[115] and so that they come to represent a type of textile that was of especially broad international appeal. At the same time, the distinctly Ottoman carnations (or Sweet Sultan), lends the fabric a recognisably Turkish flavour that would have served to differentiate it from similar Italian stuffs. By introducing an Eastern note into a rather Italianate format, velvets such as this would

---

[115] Atasoy, Denny, Mackie and Tezcan 2001b, 182.

have held considerable appeal as variations on the kinds of textile commonly produced in Italy itself, and would thus have featured alongside locally produced weavings in the furnishing of Renaissance interiors or in the attire of the upper classes. There was thus a considerable measure of stylistic overlap and a mutual awareness of needs and tastes in Italy and the Ottoman Empire that encouraged the production of goods for export.

Another striking example of transcultural production is provided by a group of multifarious inlaid metalwork objects, many of which are found in European collections.[116] As with velvets, assessment is complicated by the fact that they present us with sometimes intractable problems with regard to provenance, but it is likely that some were made for a local market and later acquired by Europeans, some may have been intended for a European market or even commissioned by Europeans, while others, finally, are European imitations, identified as such by stylistic and technical features. Those that cannot be so identified may be assigned broadly to two types.[117] One consists of pieces where the decorative design can be identified as late Mamluk, typical examples being globular perfume burners, bowls and candlesticks. The other is stylistically akin to late fifteenth and sixteenth-century Iranian metalwork,[118] but yet distinct, and is further distinguished from the first type by the use of silver wire inlay. Among the pieces of the first type some have a European morphology, which suggests that craftsmen were sometimes consciously creating shapes that would appeal to a European market, and a corresponding piece of the second type, now in the Courtauld, includes on one rim an Arabic formula identifying the maker, the 'Master Mahmud' (usually identified with Mahmud al-Kurdi, whose name appears on other pieces of metalwork[119]), while on the rim opposite there is a partial translation in Roman characters,[120] thus clearly indicating that it was intended for Europe (Plate 18). There are also pieces belonging to both types that contain the further and quite explicit feature of a European coat of arms, such as that of the prominent Venetian Contarini family, which appears on a pair of candlesticks now in the Museo Correr.[121] However, in some instances, as with the

---

[116] Previously dubbed 'Veneto-Saracenic'. For a review of the scholarship on them see Auld 2004, 7–8, 36–43.

[117] Auld 2004, 8.

[118] Ward 1993, 102–3.

[119] Other names appear in other objects, such as that of Zayn al-Din.

[120] London, Courtauld Institute, O.1966.GP.204. See also Auld 1989, figs 1 and 2. The Roman transliteration is not, as often reported in the literature, a Persian version, being 'AMALEI MALEM MAMUD' (Robinson 1967, 170–73; Auld 2004 and 2007, cat. 103; and Mack 2002, 214, note 17, for example), but an abbreviated 'AMAL ELMALEM MAMUD', from the Arabic one on the other side of the rim: 'amal al-muʻallim maḥmūd yarjū al-maghfira min mawlāh (the work of the master Maḥmūd who hopes for forgiveness from his lord).

[121] Venice, Museo Correr, inv. no. CIXII nn. 22, 23. See Contadini 2006, 311, col. fig. 21.3.

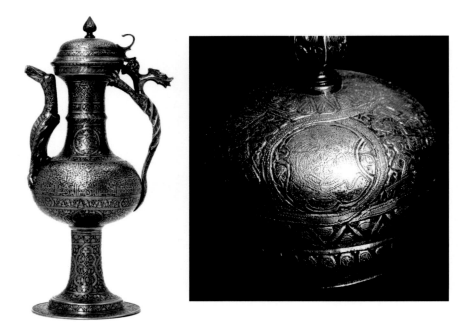

Figure 2.13   Molino ewer and detail of the coat of arms, brass, Germany, Netherlandish with Middle Eastern decoration, second half of fifteenth century

Source: London, V&A, inv. no. M.32-1946. Courtesy of the Victoria and Albert Museum; coat of arms photo by Rowan Bain.

famous Molino ewer[122] (Figure 2.13), although the decoration is characteristically Middle Eastern in style, the object has a European shape[123] as well as a coat of arms, and here the presumption is that the vessel is of European manufacture, but with the surface worked by a Muslim craftsman.

This suggests either a back-and-forth trading process, or the presence of Middle Eastern craftsmen in Europe, and in fact it was long thought, as proposed in the middle of the nineteenth century by Vincenzo Lazari, that all the pieces discussed so far were produced in Venice by Muslim craftsmen settled there. This hypothesis remained unchallenged until 1970, when Huth argued that it was not supported by evidence and that the Venetian guild system would have not have permitted foreign craftsmen to work there.[124] Further, James Allan has provided comparisons (from Qur'anic illumination and architectural

---

[122]   Contadini 2006, 310–11, 356, cat. 62.
[123]   See European ewers in the same shape in V&A 2004, 126–7 (entry by Tim Stanley).
[124]   Lazari 1859; Huth 1970.

decoration) with the decoration on the Mahmud al-Kurdi group that point to a Mamluk (Cairo) provenance for this group and a dating to the third quarter of the fifteenth century;[125] Rachel Ward has proposed, on the basis of metallurgical analyses and details of design, for a Western Iranian provenance; and Sylvia Auld, subsequently, has argued, referring to inlay technique as well as design, for an Aq-qoyunlu provenance.[126] Yet evidence that such pieces were imported is hard to come by. There are Florentine documents of the fourteenth century that refer to metal cargoes coming from ports such as Beirut and *Tana* (Azov), with Famagusta (Cyprus) and Modon (Peloponnese) as intermediate stops. As Marco Spallanzani points out,[127] however, even though they cast light on prices and usage and, albeit rarely, refer to ornamental motifs, they make no mention of places of origin.

The presumption of Middle Eastern manufacture may, though, need to be revised in the light of the recent discovery of an extraordinary document in the National Archive in Florence that mentions a certain 'Antonio Surian' from Damascus who, in 1563, was said to be making inlaid metalwork in Venice better than any Italian.[128] It thereby reopens the debate about Middle Eastern craftsmen working in Venice, leading to a reappraisal of earlier scholars who had argued for their presence.[129] But whatever the place of production, we are dealing with objects, many found in European collections, that often bear European coats of arms, and in some cases have a morphology that is less mainstream Middle Eastern than European. Future progress in our understanding of them may need, as Auld (2004) has indicated, further engagement with the intricate problems of the design of the inlay decoration, and to this may be added the need for further technical analyses, to supplement what Ward and La Niece (1995, and La Niece 2007) have done for some of the material in the British Museum, and which would characterize items of European manufacture versus those of Middle Eastern provenance.

---

[125] Allan 1986, 55–7 and 1989, 168–70. More recently Behrens-Abouseif 2005 has taken up James Allan's attribution including a discussion of the inscriptions on some of these objects.

[126] Ward 1993, 102–3. Auld puts forward the hypothesis that masters like Mahmud al-Kurdi and Zayn al-Din might have been itinerant artists working for the Aq-qoyunlu Turkmen in and around north-west Iran or Anatolia: Auld 2004, 8–9, and ch. 7. There are two types of silver inlay – linear and spatial – and the method of attaching them varies: Allan 1979, 64–5.

[127] Spallanzani 2010, 7–10.

[128] This extraordinary document is mentioned in Spallanzani 2010, 11–12, and footnote 22. Similarly, the Egyptian 'Sabadino', working as a tapestry maker in Ferrara at the court of Ercole I, was judged to make 'panni figuradi' better than anybody else: see Forti Grazzini 1982, 55. Thanks to Isabel Miller for the reference.

[129] See review of literature in Allan 1989, 167–8.

As a further complication, there are metalwork pieces of similar style which this time are European, mainly Italian, imitations of imported Middle Eastern artefacts, as in the case of two candlesticks in the V&A[130] (Figure 2.14). The stylistic similarity is sufficiently close for this group to have been identified only relatively recently on the basis of differences in design, the European imitations having a more clearly compartmentalised organisation of the decoration, and in material, as they contain no trace of the black organic compound that provides the background for the silver inlay of those produced with Middle Eastern techniques.[131] They properly represent, then, the phenomenon of a fascination with Islamic art that led to the incorporation of its design in various media.

Numerous further instances of this phenomenon are supplied by leatherwork. There are several book-bindings, including varnished ones, made for doges and prominent Venetian families, such as the commission of the doge Michele Foscarini dated 1587 (Plate 19), where the binding is similar to a known Middle Eastern type, but with the addition of the Lion of St Mark on one side and the Foscarini coat of arms on the other.[132] Similarly, shields and bucklers were produced in Venice, probably during the late sixteenth century, with decoration in Ottoman style, the shields with an oval and convex shape, the bucklers with a round and conical shape. Twenty-three such gilded and varnished leather shields and bucklers, and a number of quivers are preserved in the Armoury of the Doge's Palace (although unfortunately all the bucklers have the metal boss missing, so that the skin in the middle is laid bare), and similar pieces are scattered in various museums and private collections.[133] A particularly important collection is to be found in Salzburg, consisting of a group of twenty shields that Wolf Dietrich von Raitenau, the prince-bishop of Salzburg already mentioned above in relation to the possible maker of the enamelled mounts of the Fermo rock crystal ewer, ordered from Venice for his horsemen. Since von Raitenau was prince-bishop from 1587 to 1611 we actually know the period during which these shields were produced. This allows us to suggest a date for the other shields too, for the Salzburg ones are practically identical in decoration and technique not only to the items in Venice, but also to those in Florence, Rome, Milan, London, New York, Offenbach am Main and Munich.

The Venetian group is the one I was able to study and research in detail while the pieces were being restored.[134] The restoration process made it possible to

---

[130] Inv. no. 553–1865 and 554–1865, see Contadini 2006, 313–14, 360, cat. 135.

[131] Ward, La Niece, Hook, and White, 1995, 235–58; La Niece 2007; also Auld 2007.

[132] Venice, Biblioteca Nazionale Marciana, Cod. It. VII, 1724 (=8126), published in Zorzi 1988, tav. CXLIV. For varnished book-bindings in the Islamic style, see among others Zorzi 2003, 75–8.

[133] Contadini 1989, 236–7.

[134] Contadini 1989. This publication includes an analysis of their history within the 'cuoridoro' industry, drawn from archival documents, and of their decoration. 'Cuoridoro' is a dialectal version of 'cuoi d'oro', which literally means gilded leathers. The word 'cuoridoro'

Figure 2.14 One of a pair of candlesticks, brass, engraved and inlaid with silver, Italian, probably Venice, mid-sixteenth century
Source: London, V&A, inv. no. 553-1865. Courtesy of the Victoria and Albert Museum.

establish the exact technique used, that of *cuoridoro*, and to conclude that the shields probably functioned primarily as display objects, paraded on special occasions and prominently exhibited on the wall of the entrance hall of Venetian patrician houses as a symbol of power, with spears behind it in a fan-like arrangement.[135] Alternatively, the weapons might be put in the study of the master of the house, where at times shields and other arms with the family coat of arms were displayed and proudly shown to important visitors and friends.[136]

Examination of the bucklers and shields in the Doge's Palace revealed that they were produced by the technique used on gilded and varnished leather wall hangings, a kind of wall tapestry very much in fashion all over Europe during the sixteenth to eighteenth centuries. A wonderful Italian example is the one in the

---

was used indiscriminately for the art, the craftsmen, or the product. My finds have been used recently by Rizzo 2007 who adds further technical analyses recently conducted on various varnished and gilded objects. In this publication, instead of 'varnished' the objects are still unfortunately called 'lacquered', a misleading term as the process involved is totally different.

[135] Thornton 1991, 269; Brown 2004, 19–20, 73, 224; Brown 2006, 57. Such an arrangement can be seen in a print of 'Palazzo Cappello on the Grand Canal', from the 1843 book *Interiors and Exteriors in Venice* by Lake Price (published in Brown 2004, fig. 22).

[136] Thornton 1997, 80–83, especially the reference to Bartolo's study on 83.

Museo Civico at Bologna, which can be dated to the late sixteenth or the early seventeenth century, and is additionally of interest because it includes a form of decoration in the horizontal band that is quite clearly derived from a type of pattern found in Ottoman sixteenth-century silks[137] (Plate 20).

Plate 21 shows one of the shields with the Foscarini coat of arms, and bearing the initials A F, for Antonio Foscarini, an admiral of the second half of the sixteenth century. The overall style and appearance of the objects is so pronouncedly Ottoman that one could be forgiven for mistaking them at first glance as genuinely Turkish, although close inspection of their design patterns reveals striking similarities with some of the metalwork pieces discussed above, thus further illustrating the complexities of style transfer between media.

Beyond such processes of absorption we arrive, finally, at a stage where forms and concepts taken from the exotic are creatively recombined and/or recontextualised, often in a different medium. This process had already been exemplified in the way, say, that the halo of the Madonna in a painting might incorporate a pseudo-Kufic inscription, but we now enter the more dynamic realm of ornament, explicitly identified as a transferable element.[138] Admittedly, the transmission of ornamental features is common within a given culture (motifs pass happily from book illumination to architectural decoration or to metalwork design, for example, in Mamluk Egypt just as well as in Yuan China), but what is important to emphasise in the present context is the transcultural dimension, and what the international transfer of motifs may tell us about cultural fluidity.

In Europe, an interest in Middle Eastern ornament starts to be felt particularly keenly during the Renaissance, with Middle Eastern motifs of knots and stars being used, for example, by Leonardo and Dürer.[139] In the first half of the sixteenth century, pattern books such as those of Peter Flötner and Francesco Pellegrino include large sections of 'oriental' motifs (termed *moresque* by Flötner and *façon arabicque* by Pellegrino)[140] (Figure 2.15). However, Pellegrino's patterns are closer to what is found on early sixteenth-century Venetian book-bindings and brassware than on Middle Eastern objects, and as in other European pattern books of the period such terms are used generically to encompass a variety of styles within the global vocabulary of ornament that could be used in different media: there is no attempt to identify specific origins.

---

[137] Contadini 1988.
[138] Rogers 1999; Rawson 1984, 145–98; Grabar 1992; Necipoğlu 1995, 91–126.
[139] Sannazzaro 1982, fig. on 151; Albrecht Dürer 1971, nos 110–111.
[140] Pellegrino 1908 (facsimile of the original edition, Paris 1530); Flötner 1882 (facsimile of the original edition, Zurich 1546). Examples from these can be found in Contadini 1999, figs 23–4 on pp. 47–8. Little is known about Francesco Pellegrino (d. 1552?), the artist whose sixty woodcuts of Islamic-style ornament were published as a pattern book in Paris in 1530. Only one copy of his pattern book survives (Paris, Bibliothèque de l'Arsenal, Sciences et Arts no. 11952).

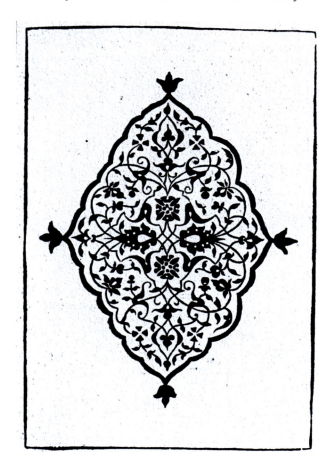

Figure 2.15   Pattern in Islamic style, from Francesco Pellegrino, *La Fleur de la science de pourtraicture: façon arabicque et ytalique*, Paris, 1530
Source: After Pellegrino 1908.

Equally important, elements were creatively combined: as Rogers points out,[141] it is the very eclecticism of Venetian Islamicising bookbinding designs that serves as a diagnostic tool to distinguish them from their Ottoman counterparts, which have an austere unity of design. Such recombination of motifs also appears in paintings, where textiles and carpets in some cases have complex designs that cannot be simple reproductions. Thus, in addition to some striking representations of real objects (as for example in the Holbein

---

141   Rogers 1999, 139.

and Lotto carpets),[142] we also encounter displacement and creative reworking: Jan van Eyck, Quinten Massys and Hans Memling all juxtapose separate motifs to create pseudo-Islamic carpet and textile designs, which they would probably have claimed to be 'Ottoman'[143] (Plate 22).

The above discussion, which touches on acquisitions and exchanges, on transcultural cross-fertilization and competition, essays a move away from traditional art-historical scholarship towards, it is hoped, a more productive engagement with the contexts within which artefacts were produced and consumed, and also, however faint the traces, with the ways in which they were perceived. In doing so, it raises further questions and compels the recognition that the current state of our knowledge is not always sufficient for confident conclusions to be reached. With regard to early acquisitions, we may reasonably suppose that the use of rock crystal vessels, particularly as reliquaries with lavishly decorated mounts, indicates on the one hand an appreciation of their aesthetic grace and symbolic potential, and on the other ignorance of, or disregard for, any Islamic associations they may originally have had. Yet when we move to the much better documented Renaissance, we find, paradoxically, that the ascription of meaning becomes more elusive. The record suggests a high degree of commercial competitiveness, with a range of differently priced goods being made for both local consumption and export, some evidently luxury objects. But if the importation of these can obviously be understood as a recognition of value, their reception otherwise is obscure, and is certainly not verbalised in ways that might allow interpretation in the light of the re-emerging engagement with the world of Islam in intellectual circles.

Indeed, it may be argued that the very notion of a meaning associated with alterity is suspect, and that the pooling of design features meant that the fact of a Middle Eastern place of production for a given artefact might be incidental, even insignificant: the intensification of trading networks clearly demonstrates the increasing international appeal of certain types of artefact, leading to an eclectic sharing of features and the creation within them of significant local variations (resulting in an extraordinary complex scenario with related problems of identification and provenance).

With this process can be associated the enrichment of the language of ornament. Here we reach a stage where motifs are detached from their original contexts to be integrated creatively within others. At the same time, paradoxically, notions of origin are not wholly erased. Labels such as *arabesche* preserve an identification of certain style features that will eventually be brought into play as part of a growing characterisation of the Islamic Middle East, especially in its Ottoman manifestation, first as a threatening other and then later, especially as we move into the rococo domain of *turquerie*, as a world

---

[142] Spallanzani 2007, 202–5, 210–13 for Holbein carpets, 233–7 for Lotto carpets.

[143] Ydema 1991, but more recently Monnas 2008, ch. 5: 'The transmission of textile designs in fifteenth and early sixteenth century Netherlandish Paintings'.

onto which can be projected, with increasing extravagance, the various fantasies that will prove to be such an enduring element in Western visual art.

Chapter 3

The Lepanto Paradigm Revisited: Knowing the Ottomans in the Sixteenth Century

Palmira Brummett

Lepanto: a narrow channel connecting the Gulf of Patras and the Gulf of Corinth, dividing the Peloponnesus from the Greek mainland. Lepanto: a famous sea battle on October 7, 1571, in which the combined fleets of Venice, the Holy League and Don Juan of Austria defeated the Ottoman fleet under Grand Admiral Müezzinzade Ali Pasha.[1] We have all seen the paintings (perhaps in the Doge's Palace in Venice, perhaps in our Western civilisation texts) of two large fleets representing two monotheistic religions arrayed against each other in permanent enmity. For an anxiously observing, early modern, European audience, Lepanto was mapped not simply as a 'famous' sea battle, but as a triumph for Christendom against an apparently unstoppable foe.

Here, for example, we see Lepanto as the map-maker Giovanni Camocio conjured it for a Venetian audience: 'The true order of the two potent armadas, Christian and Turkish, as they approached to engage in battle' (Figure 3.1).[2] This map was distributed in single sheet and also bound into a celebratory atlas, an *isolario* which placed Lepanto in an array of islands and port bases linking the Venetian and Ottoman polities across the Adriatic and Aegean seas. The very next image in Camocio's atlas provides an alternative view (which seems logically to follow the arraying of 'Christian' and 'Turk' fleets in crescent formation), a view of the naval battle, the engagement itself (Figure 3.2). This map is entitled, 'the success of the miraculous victory of the armada of the Christian Holy League against that of the most powerful and vainglorious prince of the Ottomans, Sultan Selim II' (r. 1566–1574).[3] This characterisation of the Ottomans provided

---

[1] This essay is dedicated to Dr Tom Goodrich, pioneer of mapping the Ottomans. It was delivered, originally, at the conference, 'The Renaissance and the Ottoman World', Warburg Institute and School of African and Oriental Studies, London, April 26–27, 2006.

[2] Giovanni Francesco Camocio, '*Il vero ordine delle due potente armate...*', Venice, 1571, map 38, in *Isole famose, porti, fortezze, e terre maritime, sotto poste alla Sigma Sig.ria di Venetia, ad altri Principi Christiani, et al Sig.or Turco, novamente poste in luce*, In Venetia, alla libraria del segno di S. Marco. Folger Shakespeare Library, G1015 C3, 1574.

[3] Camocio, 'Il successo della mirabile vittoria della armata di la Santa Lega Christiana, contra la potentissima, et orgogliosa [di] Sultan Selim principe Ottomano...', Venice, 1572, map 39, in *Isole famose*. Folger Shakespeare Library, G1015 C3, 1574.

in Camocio's caption was an elemental part of the late sixteenth-century image of 'the Turk' which was circulated in Christian Europe. The Ottomans were characterised as enormously powerful, a trait which engendered fear, but also as arrogant, a trait which opened up the possibility for their defeat. Taking both map images together, the message is simple. There are two sides, one victory, and battle is the natural mode of encounter. That message, along with Camocio's maps, was disseminated widely and endured long after the battle and the subsequent peace treaty.[4] Lepanto, a struggle between *'Turchi e Christiani'* would seem to have captured the imagination of the late sixteenth-century Mediterranean world.

In more recent times, Lepanto serves as a place, a space, a time and a marker for the historiography of what is still too often called 'Islam and the West', or the Ottomans and Europe. In more traditional historiography it is battle space, the point at which a Christian coalition demonstrated that the mighty 'Turk' could be beaten, the end of an era. Or, as Fernand Braudel put it, 'The spell of Turkish supremacy had been broken'.[5]

In other historiographic constructions, the destruction of the Ottoman fleet is simply (as the Ottoman grand vizier is said to have noted) the shaving of the Ottoman 'beard', a dramatic transformation, but a transient one.[6] The contemporary Ottoman chronicler, Mustafa Ali, called it 'the campaign of the broken fleet', a condemnation of a military misstep but hardly the death knell of an era.[7] For

---

[4]   The new treaty was confirmed in March 1573; see de Groot 2003, esp. 593.

[5]   Braudel 1995, 1088.

[6]   This phrase is repeated in various sources. It is attributed to the grand vizier Sökülü Mehmed Pasha, who compared Ottoman victories to the taking off of Venice's arm and Lepanto to the Christian fleet merely shaving the Ottoman beard, thus making it grow back (rebuilding the fleet) even thicker. Capponi 2006, 320-21, in his recent, thoughtful treatment of Lepanto, has concluded that 'The Ottoman beard had indeed grown again at lightning speed, but was no stronger'. He sees the battle as confirming 'the viability of Western military strategy and tactics ... Military victory was now in European hands, although ultimate success was not assured. Western military superiority would not be a confirmed fact until the end of the eighteenth century, and until then the Ottomans remained a formidable foe.'

[7]   Mustafa Ali 1975, 59. In describing the 'second category' of begs, the 'walls' of the structure of the Ottoman state, who had served in the imperial divan for many years and reached that status through service to high-ranking statesmen, Mustafa Ali mentions Mehmed Bey, 'the Admiral of Egypt with the sanjak of Alexandria, the son of the admiral [Müezzinzade] Ali Pasha who perished in the 'campaign of the broken fleet' [Lepanto] and disappeared on the bottom of the sea like a singular pearl. [He] was thus one of those begs who rule over the land as well as over the sea. He was basically a commander of sincere and serene character, a lover of fair lads and of wine'.

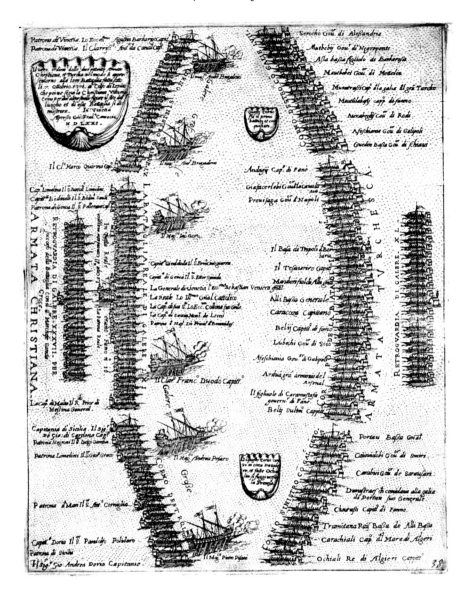

Figure 3.1 Giovanni Francesco Camocio, The 'true order of the two potent armadas', at Lepanto, Venice, 1571
Source: By Permission of the Folger Shakespeare Library.

Figure 3.2 Giovanni Francesco Camocio, 'The success of the miraculous victory of the armada of the Christian Holy League against the most powerful and vainglorious ... Sultan Selim', Venice, 1572

Source: By Permission of the Folger Shakespeare Library.

Ottomanist historians, Lepanto does not loom very large, it plays a small role in our mental landscapes, or seascapes.[8]

Historiographically, however, Lepanto is more than either a moment of victory, or the beginning of a major shift in Mediterranean power relations. Lepanto is supposed to signal an attitudinal shift as well as a shift in power. It

---

[8] İnalcık 1973, 44, does posit the Ottoman navy at this point as 'ineffective', noting also: 'The extraordinary taxes levied to finance the fleet caused widespread discontent and unrest, and after Lepanto the provincial military forces did everything in their power to avoid participating in naval campaigns. The empire had, in fact, exceeded its material capabilities.' More recently, Imber 2002, 63, while noting the destruction of the Ottoman fleet, calls Lepanto (also called the battle of Navpaktos) 'a battle without strategic consequences', noting the construction of a new fleet and that the war ended with the ceding of Cyprus to the Ottomans. In Finkel 2005b, 160, she notes that 'Lepanto is an event graven on the Western consciousness as having only narrowly saved Christendom from being overrun by the "infidel Turk". It was much described by eye-witnesses and later historians alike, but no Ottoman contemporary thought to preserve his recollections for posterity – indeed there were few survivors among the Ottoman seamen.' Yildirim 2007, demonstrates that Ottoman chroniclers did pay attention to the defeat at Lepanto.

is a paradigm for the ways in which early modern Europeans 'knew' the 'Turk', and for the ways in which contemporary historians have crafted the Afro-Eurasian world. According to this paradigm, it is in the years after Lepanto that the 'West' becomes scientific in its measuring of space; European mentalites shift to incorporate a more complex understanding of the Turk; and the English enter the Mediterranean, rewriting the Ottomans in narrative and theatrical literature, supplanting Venice as chief mediator or interpreter of the Ottomans to Europe. Lepanto is thus considered emblematic of a significantly different mode of knowing.

The periodisation of knowing the Turk seems to begin and then reach a midpoint of sorts with two military 'shocks', the conquest of Constantinople in 1453 and Lepanto in 1571. The first is followed by an apparently enlightened Ottoman era (in which Mehmed II collected world maps and commissioned Gentile Bellini to paint his portrait); the second is followed by the long reign of Murad III (r. 1574–1595), a reconfiguration of Ottoman-European relations, and the so-called 'sultanate of the women'.[9] The *Christian Science Monitor*, for example, reporting on an exhibition of Bellini paintings, 'Bellini in the World', at the National Gallery in London in 2006, described the first period as one imbued with a 'spirit of curiosity' that 'ran both ways'.[10] Characterisations of the Lepanto era (both before and after) are somewhat different. Cultural reaction is presumed to have set in after Süleyman the Magnificent executed his companion and grand vizier Ibrahim Pasha (d. 1536).[11] The Ottomans soon became embroiled in a long European war that spanned the reigns of Murad III, Mehmed III (r. 1595–1603), and Ahmed I (r. 1603–1617). And the latter sultan, far from being celebrated for his cultural vision, is known for destroying Dallam's marvelous organ, a gift to his predecessor from the English queen.[12]

Thus Lepanto, beyond the direct implications of naval triumph, in contemporary historiography has been made to stand for an era in which the Ottomans (and the Venetians for that matter) are no longer 'magnificent', in various senses of that term, and in which the states of Western Europe, with their advancements in science, technology and the will to trade across vast spaces, stand poised to carve out new political and commercial realities in the 'East'.[13] That historiographic juxtaposition of ambition and stagnation,

---

[9] On Bellini and his sojourn in the Ottoman court, see, for example, Pedani Fabris 1996–97; and Schmidt Arcangeli 2007. On the role of women in the Ottoman palace, see Peirce 1993, esp. 267–85.

[10] Austin 2006, 19.

[11] On Süleiman, see İnalcık and Kafadar 1993; Kunt and Woodhead 1995; and Turan 2006 (not yet seen by this author).

[12] MacLean 2004, 3–47. See also, Dimmock 2005, 43–63.

[13] Matar 1998, 4–5, notes that 'major hostilities were suspended in the Mediterranean between Christians and Muslims', although the war of piratic raiding continued. Vitkus 2003, 16, highlights the later decades of the sixteenth century as the era in which this

cultural exploration and cultural isolation, has coloured the appreciation of later sixteenth century realities in the trans-imperial space between Ottomans, Venetians and Habsburgs in rather anachronistic ways. Neither the rhetorics of celebration that sped across Europe in the aftermath of Lepanto, nor the swagger of Ottoman viziers as the Porte's navy was rebuilt signal the decisive advent of a new era or the inevitable continuity of an old.[14] Instead the types of rhetoric by which the Ottomans were consumed and understood in the later sixteenth century remained variable and complex. Lepanto was neither the beginning nor the end of the story; it was one episode, albeit a comforting one, in a saga, both epic and dreary, of the European endeavour to comprehend (in narrative, image, imagination and memory) the Ottoman Empire.

In this chapter, I propose to examine elements of the Lepanto paradigm, as it shifts from a military emphasis to an emphasis on knowledge, reflecting on the ways by which Europeans knew the Ottomans in the long sixteenth century. The Ottoman Empire was, of course, a European empire. That said, maps, images and narratives produced in the European territories ruled by Christian lords crafted the Ottomans as occupying a separate though familiar space, one characterised by an intrusive Islamic faith, stunning military prowess, a matrix of trading networks, and the shades of Western classical and Biblical history. European knowledge of that space and its occupants came in different forms, through maps, histories, itineraries, trade goods, art objects, ceremonies of magnanimity and intimidation, and interactions with envoys, artisans, captives and converts (among other sources). I will focus on some of the historiographic possibilities, and particularly on maps.

Historiography

First let's examine some aspects of the historiography. Lepanto serves as a dividing line or a set of dividing lines for the historiography of the sixteenth century. Andrew Hess, in an article on Lepanto published in *Past and Present* in 1972, pointed out the different realms of Ottoman action. He argued that assessments of the post-Lepanto Ottoman Empire had been skewed by a focus

---

transformation took place for the English: '... by the end of the sixteenth century the continuous, expanding trade in the region made the Mediterranean world more familiar to English culture'. Dimmock 2005b, 84–7, seconds the notion that 'events following the battle of Lepanto in 1571 marked a fundamental shift away from the Mediterranean as an area of conflict ...' (87); but he also emphasises the idea of 'Turkishness' and the internal European and English implications for England and its monarchy of the Ottoman defeat at Lepanto (84). In both cases 1571 serves as a pivotal date.

[14] See Peirce 2004. In terms of periodisation, Peirce would choose, not Lepanto, but the reorganisation 'of the Eastern Mediterranean by the Ottomans between 1453 and 1555 (23)', as the crucial period.

on the Balkans at the expense of North Africa (where Ottoman expansionism was in full swing after 1571).[15] I would add to that argument by suggesting that we look at the sixteenth-century Ottoman world in terms of regional zones and points of diffusion (in the Adriatic/Balkan region, in North Africa, and in the East along a line stretching roughly from Georgia to the Indian Ocean). That diffusion would include information, personnel, material culture and ideas (in much the same way that Marshall Hodgson considered the diffusion of culture in the Afro-Eurasian Oikumene).[16] Thus, for example, Mehmed the Conqueror's patronage of Bellini does not seem quite so unusual when one considers the long sixteenth century as an era of opportunistic Ottoman patronage which supported (and imported) artists from both East and West in the context of Ottoman claims to hegemony in both realms.[17] Historiographical preoccupation with relations between 'Christians' and 'Turks' has tended to preclude the consideration of the Eastern zone as comparable to the Western zone; but assessments based on the entire circuit of Ottoman frontiers, taken as a whole, could prove quite revealing, and put Lepanto in its place. The latter part of the sixteenth century is, after all, a time during which the empire was reaching into Georgia and Iraq as well as into the Western Mediterranean. The comparison to Rome is not an illogical one.

Like Hess, Nabil Matar has also looked at the Ottoman impact on the Western Mediterranean region. His focus, however, is on the impact of Lepanto on Spain, the Iberian reach across the Atlantic, and its contingent representational options:

> By 1492 the Spaniards had succeeded in defeating the last Moors of Granada and by 1571 they had defeated, with support from the Papacy, the Turkish fleet at Lepanto. As they began their conquest of the Americas they transported their anti-Muslim ideology of religious war across the Atlantic and applied it to the American Indians ... The Spaniards had treated the Muslim infidel as an object of polarization and holy destruction, and they began viewing the American Indian in the same light.[18]

Matar poses the question: What is the content of information about the Ottomans that flows across the ocean along with the Spanish fleets? We can turn that question back onto Europe and ask what information, visions, and rhetorics of the Ottomans were available. How were they selectively received?

---

[15] Hess 1972. See also, İnalcık 1974; and Guilmartin 1980, 221–52. Guilmartin argues that the loss of a generation of bowman was a much more crucial factor than the loss of ships (251).

[16] Hodgson 1974. See Murphey 1983; and Ágoston 2007, on the diffusion of technology and information. See also, Günergun 2007.

[17] Beyazid II (r. 1481–1512), for example actively sought out Persian and Turkish works and gave elaborate gifts in his efforts to entice Persian poets to the Ottoman court.

[18] Matar 1999, 130. Both Muslims and Indians were 'worshippers of the devil'.

Did Lepanto really loom as large as reports of celebrations across Europe would seem to suggest?

Nancy Bisaha, in a recent book, entitled *Creating East and West: Renaissance Humanists and the Ottoman Turks*, has argued that the legacy of late medieval humanists to the Renaissance both 'promoted a greater openness and understanding of Muslim cultures and religion' and 'served to nurture incipient ideas of Western superiority to Eastern rivals', especially the Ottomans.[19] Nonetheless, it was the negative impulse, she proposes, that was dominant. Bisaha (in order to challenge the notion of scholars like Jerry Brotton, that Renaissance Europeans, or at least some of them, were more 'multicultural', as Bisaha terms it, than previously thought) points to the vast body of hostile writings produced by European humanists.[20] She goes on to note, rightly, that while travel writers may have presented a more balanced vision of 'the Turk' [as the Ottomans were called]..., 'many writers returned home with blinders intact and prejudices confirmed'; they even created new stereotypes of the Ottomans.[21] While that is certainly the case, other scholars, like Kenneth Parker and Gerald MacLean, have suggested that the incidence of permanent blinders was not perhaps as high as Bisaha would seem to suggest. Their work, unlike Bisaha's, focuses on the post-Lepanto era and the English discovery of the Mediterranean.[22] But if we take the Lepanto paradigm at face value, as one embodying the rhetoric of hostility, then the post-Lepanto era should resemble the earlier period. I would suggest, instead, that neither the earlier nor the later sixteenth century can be read unilaterally in terms of anti-Ottoman hostility. Bisaha, despite focusing on the earlier period, raises a point that is crucial for both periods: What were the influential writings of the sixteenth century and how were they read? That is, what was the available universe of representations from which visions of the Ottomans derived? Juxtaposing hostile evaluations of the 'Turks' to complimentary ones (and finding the hostile side more weighty) may not

---

[19] Bisaha 2004, 174–5, 270, n. 62. For further assessment of classical, Renaissance and early modern paradigms of Eastern princes and their rule, see Springborg 1992, which ends with the Ottomans; and Valensi 1993, which focuses on sixteenth and seventeenth century constructions of Ottoman rule.

[20] See Brotton 1997, 87–118, which includes a pioneering treatment of mapping and European constructions of the Ottomans.

[21] Bisaha 2004, 180–81. Bisaha also takes on the Turk v. Native American issue, noting that, 'In many ways the Turkish advance provided compelling conditions under which humanists constructed a coherent vision of Western culture and its inherent superiority to other societies' (183).

[22] MacLean 2004, xiii, and throughout, esp. Dallam (1599) and Blount (1634–36); Parker 1999. Archer 2001, 3 (Shakespeare, Milton, Dryden) has argued that England, like the Ottomans, was still turned towards the East. This is an era that Vitkus 2003, 21, has called 'a period of intensive intelligence-gathering' by the English on the Mediterranean and the Ottomans.

give us a clear understanding of the possibilities.[23] That approach simplifies the complexity of the available representations and rules out the selectivity that was applied to those representations. Hostility, with its inevitable conflict, and alternating 'victories', then remains the default lens through which we view the sixteenth century.

It is clearly the case that the rhetorics (and realities) of religious difference and cultural or political hostility were a primary frame for Renaissance visions of 'the Christians' and 'the Turks'. It is also clearly the case that there were complex networks of interrelations between Ottoman lands and the rest of the Mediterranean world, networks that predated the Ottoman Empire and submerged religious, cultural and political differences. Among other factors, proximity to the Ottomans meant a different set of objectives and a different set of understandings for some of the peoples of Christian Europe from the understandings of those located at a distance. Some saw the Ottomans as potential political allies or as regular trading partners. Others saw opportunities to benefit from the prosperity of the Ottoman court in the sixteenth century. Our options for the ways that 'Europe' (or 'Asia' for that matter) related to the Ottomans thus comprise both fear and conversation. We have rationalised these two historiographic frameworks by separating them, focusing on individual instances of contact, pointing to exceptional individuals, or arguing, as I myself have done, that economic imperative tends to trump religious zeal.[24] But fear and conversation were often tightly intertwined in European dealings with or narratives of the 'Turk'.

One of the forms of conversation that linked Ottomans and their Christian counterparts in Europe was translation, a mode by which various authors made sense of the Ottomans in visual works and narratives crafted for Christian audiences. Translation could take multiple forms, whether the narration of friendships forged by Venetian diplomatic personnel in Istanbul with Ottoman citizens, the rendering of Ottoman texts into European languages, or the production of nuanced portraits and other images inscribed in maps, travel accounts and letters which equated the Ottomans with Christian Europeans

---

[23] Or even finding the complimentary ones more weighty; see Valensi 1993, and Springborg 1992.

[24] Brummett 1994. Schmidt 2001, 103-5, has noted that both 'radically inclined Calvinist elements' and William I of Orange were quite open to the possibilities of negotiation with the Porte: '… it is speculated that Orange's diplomacy may have prompted the Sultan to send his navy in full force to Tunis in September 1574, a moment that found Spanish resources particularly overextended' (103). Also, 'Those *Geuzen* who liberated Leiden from a Spanish siege in 1574 made this point ["Calvinoturcism"] more stylishly when they fastened onto their caps crescent-shaped badges bearing the slogan, "Better a Turk than a Papist"' (104).

rather than drawing them as irreparably enemies and 'foreign' creatures.[25] Matthew Dimmock, for example, has demonstrated the ways in which the Ottoman royals were equated with other European monarchic houses in terms of their competitive ceremonial dramas.[26] The universe of available images of the Ottomans went well beyond constructions of the sultan as the Anti-Christ and of the Ottomans in general as Muslim heretics and ferocious holy warriors.

Contemporary historiography is now fruitfully addressing such questions of representation and reception through examining the sixteenth century in terms of a diverse set of alternatives of knowledge, representation and reception.[27] Bronwen Wilson, for example, in a study entitled *The World of Venice: Print, the City, and Early Modern Identity*, notes the multiple filters through which Ottoman culture was presented in the sixteenth century (via interpreters, diplomatic reports, histories, costume books and travel narratives). She indicates that there was little interest among Venetian humanists in learning Turkish, but that there were numerous interactions and many people moving from Venetian to Ottoman employ.[28] She points out, for example, that it was not only artists seeking patronage who 'went over' to the Ottoman side. It was also interpreters, as well as skilled seamen who, according to the Venetian bailo's secretary in 1562, could earn 'in four months on the galleys of the Grand Turc, what they earn in an entire year on the galleys of your Lordship'.[29] Thus, while Francesco Sansovino, whose *Annali Turcheschi* was published in Venice in 1571, was slandering Sultan Selim II (in a tract addressed to Christian soldiers) as voluptuous, illegitimate, and Hebrew to boot, some of those 'Christian soldiers' may have been serving in the sultan's fleets, the same fleets that seized Cyprus in 1570 and then moved on to defeat at Lepanto. While political conflict and religious hostility are critical frameworks for crafting 'European' knowledge of the 'Turks', so too are

---

[25] See Çagman 2000. See also, Dursteler 2006; and Soykut 2001. McJannet 2006, 91–121, discusses the 'Eastern' sources available in translation which were employed in England in the early modern era, particularly Johannes Leunclavius' (d. 1593) translation, *Annales sultanorum Othmanidarum*, Frankfort, 1588, of the Ottoman chronicler Sadeddin (1536–1599) which was used by Richard Knolles and others. For an analysis of the question of translation more broadly and European translation of the Ottomans in particular, see Burke 2007, esp. 75–80; and for one treatment of Ottoman translations of European, in particular cartographic, texts, see Günergun 2007.

[26] Dimmock 2005b, 66–7, uses an English account (dating to 1565) of the coronation of Prince Maximillian, attended by an Ottoman ambassador, to show how the Ottoman sultan's household was equated with that of other European royal houses: 'It was to this kind of text (along with the examples of Venice and France) that the English would turn in the late 1570s and 1580s to defend their increasingly close links with the Ottoman Empire.'

[27] See, for example, MacLean and Dalrymple 2005.

[28] Wilson 2005, 147–63, analyses the dissemination of images and print culture on Lepanto.

[29] Ibid., 142.

opportunism and the exigencies of regular or irregular contact by those coming from, journeying to, or processing news about Ottoman lands. Wilson calls the Turks, 'too familiar to be made exotic'.[30] And that very paradigm of familiarity, dependent in part on proximity, needs far greater elaboration than we yet have available. Venetian images of Lepanto expressed that familiarity at the same time that they conformed to what Wilson calls: the republic's 'official representational needs'.[31] That notion of 'official representational needs', regardless of what level of official exigency is addressed, serves us well as an analytical paradigm.

Maps

The tension between familiarity and 'official representational needs' can be illustrated using maps as a marker of European knowledge of the Ottomans. The map is one type of rhetoric that breaches the historiographic boundaries between the histories of war and the histories of knowledge. Maps are records of battle, conceptualisations of imperial space, indicators of networks of travel and of trade, and records of conventions of representation. Even when they are depicting battle, they are also the canvas upon which knowledge, conventional or not, and geographic space are inscribed. Returning to the broad frontier zones of Eurasia that connected the Ottoman Empire to its Western rivals, one might view Lepanto not so much as a victory that signaled the long, gradual overtaking of the Ottomans, or provided a sense of the limits of their apocalyptic power, but as a primary case study, a spatial and temporal hot spot, for the transmission and visualisation (consumption and reading) of the Ottomans in the sixteenth century.

Especially for territories in south-eastern Europe, the Ottomans were a topic of much interest and speculation. And Venice, for early modern Europe, was the centre for the production, processing and dissemination of news about the Ottomans. One important form in which that news travelled was the map. Maps, of course, are not necessarily good indicators of contemporary knowledge. They make use of outdated engraving plates; and they cleave to old conceptualisations of geography, cartographic conventions and historical tropes of representation, long after new visions of cultural and political space have emerged. But maps also serve as bulletin boards of contemporary events – they are evolving visuals of so-called 'eye-witness' accounts, especially accounts of battle. Thus, maps provide one avenue for assessing the merits of the Lepanto paradigm.

In the mid-sixteenth century, visions of Ottoman space were likely to come in certain stock forms. In the woodcut shown here, the German artist, Matthias Gerung (1500–1570), has mapped the Ottomans onto undesignated European

---

[30] Ibid., 147.
[31] Ibid., 163.

space (Figure 3.3).[32] There, turbaned Turks (as the Ottomans were called) and their demon allies are slaughtering defenseless Christians (men, women and children) and destroying their churches. In the same space, just over the next hill, the Pope and his own demonic minions are tormenting Christ's flock. This is a common image of Reformation, Turks and Papists grouped in the same frame – both as menacing threats and enemies of Christendom. The audience does not see a kingdom which the Ottomans rule, rather it sees only the effects of their onslaught in a territory suspended between the forces of heaven and the forces of hell. This image is a 'map' of sorts, of the forces of evil; it depicts the Ottomans but it does not directly address sovereign territorial space.

The Ottoman Empire ruled from a double territorial core that included Rumelia (the first conquered territories of the southern Balkan peninsula) and Anatolia, the land in which the Ottoman principality originated and grew strong. The Ottoman polity cannot be comprehended without recognition of this territorial identity as both European and Asian. Yet it was not until the later sixteenth and early seventeenth centuries that European maps of the empire began directly to acknowledge Ottoman sovereignty through labelling European territory as part of the Ottoman realm. And even when that recognition was granted, however grudgingly, it was done through a system of dual naming, Turkey in Asia and Turkey in Europe, as if to preserve the sense that the empire was not really a single entity with an imperial capital that bridged the continents just as did the rule of the sultan.

In a typical sixteenth-century map, by the Venetian map-maker Giacomo Gastaldi, the core of Ottoman territory, Anatolia, is depicted as what J.B. Harley has called socially empty space (Figure 3.4).[33] Here Anatolia is apparently part of the unchanging, Ptolemaic 'first part of Asia'. On the body of the map, there is no indication of Ottoman presence or sovereignty. That recognition comes only in the caption. The legend of the first edition of the map, published two years earlier in 1564 begins: 'The design of the modern geography of the province of Anatolia, and Caramania, "patria" of the "Signori Turchi" of the House of Osman, its eastern boundaries at the Euphrates river and its western at the strait of Constantinople ...'. This caption acknowledges the Ottoman Empire, at least in its Asian territories, 'fatherland' of the 'Turks'. In the 1566 edition, shown here, however, the caption begins: 'This image [*disegno*] represents the nature of the province of Anatolia and Caramania and part of Syria, with the Archipelago, and part of Romania, where stands the notable city of Constantinople ...'. Reference to the Ottomans and their state has been omitted.

---

[32] Matthias Gerung (1500–1570), 'Die Türken verfolgen die Christen', woodcut, ca. 1548. Kunstsammlungen der Veste Coburg, no. I.349.13.

[33] Giacomo Gastaldi, [Anatolia], Venice, 1566. Newberry Library, Novacco 4F 377. See Harley 2001, 99–105. Gastaldi was Piemontese by origin but established his print and map shop in Venice around 1539.

Figure 3.3   Matthias Gerung [The Turks persecuting the Christians], ca. 1548
Source: Courtesy of Kunstsammlungen der Veste Coburg.

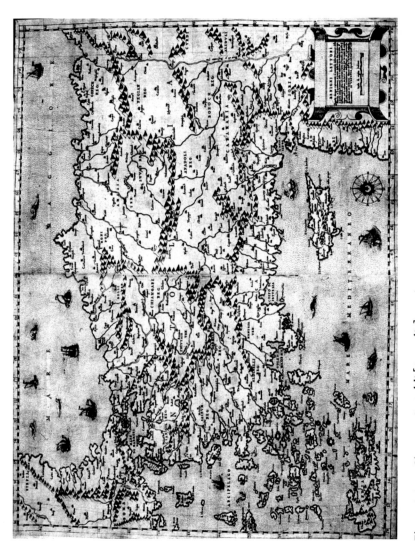

Figure 3.4   Giacomo Gastaldi [Anatolia], Venice, 1566
Source: *Courtesy of the Newberry Library, Chicago.*

In Gerung's woodcut and Gastaldi's map, then, we have either an Ottoman threat in undesignated space, or a designated space with an undesignated Ottoman Empire. Contrast those images to the ubiquitous news-map, which purported to provide its audience with timely, 'true' images of the conflicts between 'Christians' and 'Turks'. In news maps, as in Gerung's woodcut, the 'Turk' often appeared formidable and intimidating. He was a besieger of the cities or ports of the frontier zone, attempting to replace the generic, cross bedecked flag of Christendom with the generic crescent flag which was employed by European map-makers and engravers to represent Ottoman and Muslim possessions.[34]

Another mode of displaying 'the Turk' in European maps was to depict the Ottoman army as a large, and expertly ordered military on its way to do battle with an often undesignated foe, presumably Christian. The image shown here, by the map-maker Antonio Lafreri, represents a common vision of the marching order of the Ottoman army, banners flying and cannons blazing as a fortress falls before its irresistible force (Figure 3.5).[35] The caption reads:

> Order with which the Turkish army presents itself in the field against the Christians or the Persians. So splendid and industrious is it, that it can quickly mobilize, if need be, three or four hundred thousand persons, mostly cavalry ... [and so on].

In this frame the Ottomans are clearly identified, with tags and banners, and praised for their efficiency. The exact place is not mentioned, but this image appeared at the time that the Ottoman army was marching into Hungary in 1566, the same year that Gastaldi's map of Anatolia was published.

The vision of the Turk could thus either respond directly to news of conflict or function as a 'timeless' characterisation of divided space, and military prowess, without reference to specific events.

Interestingly the legend in Lafreri's map places 'Christians' and 'Persians' together as people who fall before the compelling power of Ottoman arms. Thus it is not Eastern or Western space that is at issue, but the apparently unstoppable quality of Ottoman forces. Such an army could wreak havoc on both the empire's western and eastern frontiers, on Christian and Muslim polities alike. Thus the map created a cross-communal, and trans-regional affinity between Ottoman neighbours who were the object of the sultan's expansionist ambitions.

On this particular campaign in 1566, the Ottomans took Sighetvar in northern Romania. The long-reigning sultan Süleyman the Magnificent (r. 1520–1566) died in the midst of this campaign, providing some relief to the beleaguered Christian

---

[34] See Brummett 2008.

[35] Antonio Lafreri (d. 1577), 'Ordine con il quale l'esercito Turchesco suole presentarsi in Campagna contro de Christiani, o Persiani ...', Rome, 1566. Newberry Library, Novacco 2F 48. Lafreri immigrated to Rome from France and set up as an engraver and print seller in 1544. See Tooley 1939, esp. 12; and Karrow 1993, 230n.

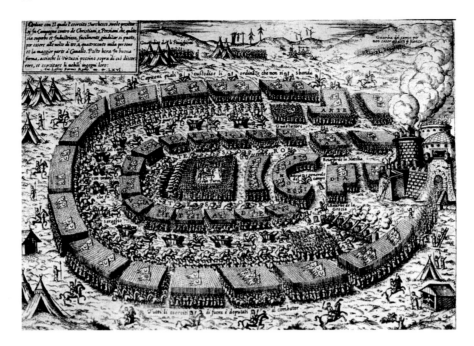

Figure 3.5　Antonio Lafreri, 'The Order with which the Turkish army presents itself in the field against the Christians or the Persians', Rome, 1566

Source: Courtesy of the Newberry Library, Chicago.

forces in the Balkans. Nonetheless, the victory over well-defended Sighetvar was considered an ill omen and was immortalised in many map images and engravings produced in Europe such as the one shown here by Lafreri (Figure 3.6). In this mapping of territory and battle, the target of the Ottoman army is a clearly designated and unique space. The map's caption reads: 'The true portrait of Zighet, with its castle, new fortress, marshes, lake, river, and bridge and other notable things indicated [*per lettere annotate*], showing the "*monte*" [hill shaped earthworks] built by the Turks, and their assault upon the defenders.'[36]

Unlike Gerung's woodcut, this map is linked very specifically to an event. It claims to portray things just 'as they happened', in timely visuals that were counterparts to the ubiquitous 'News' pamphlets and broadsheets that circulated throughout Europe. Publishers in Venice and Rome employed agents whose task was to transmit reports of Balkan battles with all due speed, so that maps and broadsheets could provide 'up to the minute' images of Christian engagements

---

[36] Antonio Lafreri, 'Il vero ritratto de Zighet ...', Rome, 1566. Newberry Library, Novacco 4F 101.

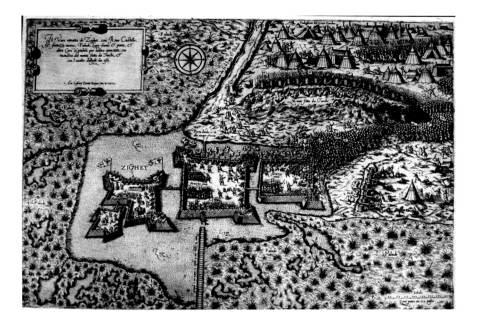

Figure 3.6   Antonio Lafreri, 'The true portrait of Sighetvar', Rome, 1566
Source: Courtesy of the Newberry Library, Chicago.

and victories. These images were posted, as Brendan Dooley has shown us, and became the subject of discussion, in the streets and public squares.[37] In the sixteenth century, the Ottomans and their successes were an important subject of such dramatic portrayals, the details of which were picked up and reproduced in sermon literature. In the context of the Reformation, those successes were often construed as signs of God's punishment of a sinful and unrepentant Christendom.

Nor were all the victories Ottoman. The Venetians and map-makers elsewhere in Europe published news and commemorative maps of victories by the forces of

---

[37]   Dooley 2001; Infelice 2001. Wilson 2005, 149, citing Paolo Preto, notes that dozens of printed pamphlets were circulated when Venice joined the Holy League and used 'as an "antidote" to a demoralised public, a kind of collective illusion that united the classes and was driven by "an aggressive proselytism" fired with the "spirit of the crusades".' Pamphlets published in Paris between 1565 and 1606 carried news reports, often translated from Italian, of Ottoman and 'Christian' victories, including the battle of Lepanto. Venice, Istanbul, Messina, Malta and Ragusa were all cited in such pamphlets as points for the transmission of such news which was consumed by the literate but also presumably read aloud (or cited) to audiences of the illiterate. Transmission time could sometimes be counted in weeks rather than months.

both 'Turk' and 'Christian' rulers. Venice was particularly adept at celebrating the victories of its own commanders.[38] One such map, ca. 1560, depicts the capture of the Ottoman fortress at Brazo de Maina, by the Venetian Marco Querini and the armada from Candia on Crete (Figure 3.7).[39] On this particular map, the insignia of troops and ships are unreadable but the caption tells us who is taking what from whom. While this map does not share the pretensions to accuracy that the map of Sighetvar proclaims, like that map it is an image of a frontier, a point of contact, and a victory in the making.

Victories, of course, might occur on land and sea, or only in the imagination. In another map, ca. 1570, of a port besieged, the identity of besieger and besieged is clear from the flags of the fortress and of the attacking ships and military units, even though the map is missing the key text which provides the identifications to match the coded letters on the map itself (Figure 3.8).[40] The fortress shown bears the crescent flags used to mark Ottoman and Muslim territory on European maps. The forces of the attackers bear the symbols of Christian princes, most notably a cross. This particular plan, produced by the map-maker Nicolo Nelli and published by Claudio Duchetti in Rome, envisions an attack on Tripoli (one of the important North African points of diffusion of information and images of Ottoman expansion) which had been taken by the Ottoman captain Turgut Reis in 1551. The cannons of a Christian fleet blast smoke into the port's harbor while the ships of the Muslim fortress lay vulnerable, unmanned with sails stowed. This vision of victory remained unfulfilled and Tripoli remained in the hands of the Ottomans and their subordinates. Once inscribed on the map, however, it was not necessarily apparent to the audience whether the battle was imagined or real.

The circulation of such images was not limited to the territories most threatened by the Ottoman occupation of Europe (Italy, Croatia or Hungary). Indeed, an indication of the way in which news and its attendant images circulated can be found in the map production of Cornelis de Jode, map-maker of Antwerp. In 1593 de Jode published his *Speculum Orbis Terrae*, a second edition of his father's earlier, 1578 atlas. It contained a map (and accompanying text) bearing the title 'Newly delineated, Croatia and the surrounding region against the Turk' (*Croatia & circumiacentium Regionum versus Turciam nova delineatio*). This map shows the armies of the Ottomans marching in ordered units across Bosnia and

---

[38] Wilson 2005, 14, calls the celebratory procession, such as that in Venice for the Lepanto victory, a 'refracted image of reality'; the same could be said for news maps. See also, Mantran 1985, 260, for an image of a celebratory procession through St Mark's square

[39] 'Brazo de Maina' [1560]. Newberry Library, Novacco, 2F 32. The legend notes that this victory was secured by Marco Querini and the Armada of Candia in 1560.

[40] Nicolo Nelli, published by Claudio Duchetti, 'Tripoli Citta di Barbaria', Rome, [1570]. Newberry Library, Novacco 4F 404. Duchetti was the nephew of Antonio Lafreri.

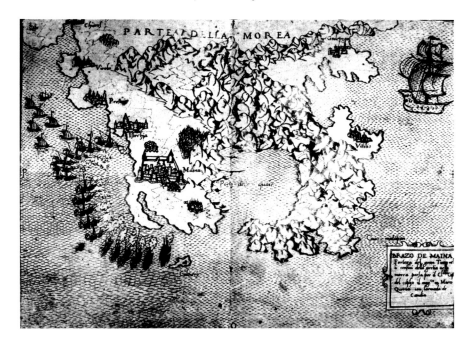

Figure 3.7 'Brazo de Maina' [1560]
Source: Courtesy of the Newberry Library, Chicago.

Croatia (Plate 23).[41] Sometime after it was published, de Jode produced a variant, entitled: '*Croatia versus Turcam*', which was quite similar in its representation of contested space except for the addition of two large vignettes (Plate 24). In the lower corners of this revised map, de Jode has posed two images of submission.[42] In the lower right is a female figure (labelled *T.K. Swester*), the Turkish ruler's

---

[41] Cornelius de Iudaeis,[Cornelis de Jode] (1568-1600), 'Croatiae & circumiacentiu[m] Regionu[m] versus Turcam nova delineatio', undated map, in Cornelis de Jode, *Speculum Orbis Terrae*, Antwerp, 1593. British Library, Maps. C.7.c.13. This is a later edition of the atlas by Cornelis's father, Gerard de Jode (ca. 1509-1591), entitled *Speculum Orbis Terrarum*, published in 1578. The De Jodes, father and son, are treated in Koeman 1967, 205-12; the map of Croatia is listed as no. 52, fol 18.Tt for the second edition. I have not had the opportunity to consult the update of Koeman's work, van der Krogt 2003.

[42] Cornelius de Iudaeis [Cornelis de Jode] (1568-1600), 'Croatiae & circumiacentiu[m] Regionu[m] versus Turcam nova delineatio', undated map. Leiden University Library, COLLBN Port 123 N 138 and Port 168 N 65, published in Teunissen and Steegh 2003, plate 14. The authors identify this image as dating from approximately 1598, but I suspect it was produced earlier to capitalise on the good feelings produced by a Christian victory in the Croatian frontier territory.

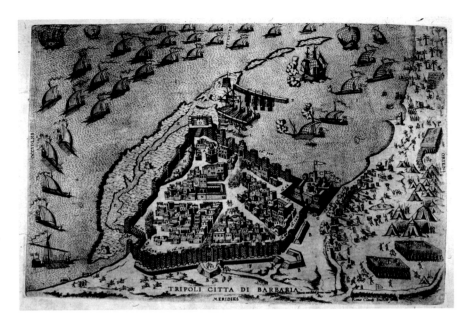

Figure 3.8 Nicolo Nelli, 'Tripoli City of Barbary', Rome [1570]
Source: Courtesy of the Newberry Library, Chicago.

'sister', representing the Ottoman harem, and a male figure representing the Ottoman sultan, Sultan Murad III (r. 1574–1595) (labeled *T.K. Contrafatiur*). In the left-side vignette the Ban of Croatia kneels, gazing up at Kaiser Rudolph (d. 1612), the Habsburg emperor. The Ban holds a tall stake on which is the severed head of Telli Hasan Pasha, beylerbeyi of Bosnia, subordinate of the sultan.[43]

The situation depicted in these vignettes is the struggle for Croatia which took place in the broader context of the long Ottoman-Habsburg war of 1593–1606.[44] On June 22 of 1593, a force led by Telli Hasan Pasha, which was laying siege to the town of Siska, on the Sava River, was attacked and defeated by a

---

[43] The COPAC online map catalogue identification note for the British Library's copy of this map identifies these figures as Ferdinand I, King of the Romans (standing), his general Jean Baptiste Gastaldi (kneeling), and Friar George Martinuzzi (head). This map, however, presumably represents more current events in Croatia. Martinuzzi, treasurer of John Zapolyi, as power behind the throne for Zapolya's son, submitted personally to the Ottomans at Buda in 1541. He died in 1551; and Ferdinand's rule ended in 1564.

[44] See Finkel 1988; and Szakály 1994, esp. 96.

hastily assembled Austrian-Croatian army. Hasan Pasha was killed.[45] I suspect that this amended map was published following the defeat of Hasan, to celebrate one of the few reasons for Christian joy in the region at the time. The vignettes added to de Jode's map are very similar to those found in a German broadsheet dated 1594. De Jode's atelier employed an agent who frequented the German book fairs. Thus, this image is emblematic of the multi-directional transmission of news and images. It derived from accounts of the battle proceeding through Italy or Hungary to Germany where they were immortalised in broadsheets and passed on to Antwerp, there to be inscribed on de Jode's map of Croatia.[46] Unlike Gerung's image of the Ottomans, in these vignettes the sultan appears just as regal and perhaps more benign than the Habsburg emperor. Where Rudolph bears scepter and sword, Murad bears scepter and scroll. The gendered juxtaposition of two figures kneeling before their monarchs serves as a commentary on both the nature of autocratic rule and the equation of conquered territory with the female body. The male 'servant' is a military taker of heads, armed with sword and lance. The female 'servant' may be both petitioner and advisor; but the sultan's scepter is extended over her head, symbol of his enduring control and benevolent protection.

The Ottoman-Habsburg wars at the end of the sixteenth century provided rich material for the production of news maps whether the frontiers in question were land or sea frontiers. In one such German map, the conquest of Hatvan in 1596, north-east of Budapest, is commemorated (Figure 3.9).[47] A key labels the besieging forces and a lone flag bearing the Ottoman crescent leans precariously from the tallest tower of the besieged city. This is not the image of a once imposing foe brought low. It is an image of a hard-won victory by an army familiar with its enemy and aware of the long history of such fortresses changing hands. Like Camocio's depiction of the Battle of Lepanto, such images of conflict have two clear sides, Christian and Muslim (or 'Turk'). They serve simultaneously as news, commemoration, history and communitarian admonition. They map the points and iconographic action of battle. But such maps are also emblematic of the role of such fortresses as points for the diffusion of knowledge and culture. They are

---

[45] This frontier defeat led to the mobilisation of a full-scale Ottoman campaign. See Finkel 1988, 7–20, 36–7. See also, Rothenberg 1960, 52–63; and Heywood 1993.

[46] It is of course possible, but less likely, that the direction of image transmission was West to East. Woodward, 1980, has commented upon the evidence for the consumption and dissemination of Italian maps. Many of the gaps in our knowledge that he pointed out in this 1980 piece still remain.

[47] J.S., 'Abris Der Vöstung Hadtwan, Von Den Christen Belegert Und Eröbert, Den. 3. Septemb: A: 1596'. British Library, Maps, C.7.e.2(.31). Note that I have reproduced the capitalisation as it appears on the map rather than reducing it to a modern capitalisation scheme.

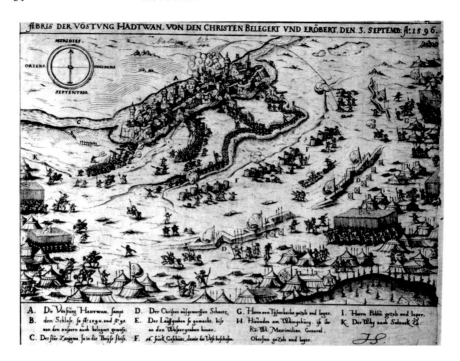

Figure 3.9   J.S., 'Scheme of Hatvan fortress, besieged and captured by the Christians on September 3, 1596' [1596?]
Source: British Library Board. All Rights Reserved, Maps, C.7.e.2(.31).

places where locals fight alternately on one side and then the other; places of trade; places of conversion.[48]

The fortress stands as an emblem of shared and contested space. Another map from the commemorative atlas of Camocio demonstrates the central role of the fortress in Venetian maps. Here the ships of the Venetian fleet lie in the harbor of Sopoto on the (Albanian) Adriatic (Figure 3.10).[49] This is not the generic fleet seen in many maps, identified by its flags, rather each vessel here is labelled with the name of a Venetian officer or patron. The troops and pavilions of the attackers occupy the midground. The fortress, in the background, sports two crescent flags, indicating its status as an Ottoman possession. The legend tells the reader that this is 'a Turkish place, taken by the Illustrious Sebastian Venier,

---

[48] See for a few examples of these interactions, Ágoston 2007; Faroqhi 2000, 80–100; and Bracewell 1992.

[49] Giovanni Francesco Camocio, 'Soppoto fortezza nella provincia della Cimera luoghi del Turcho presa dal Clarissimo M.r. Sebastian Venier ... 10 Giugno 1570', Venice, [1570], map 28, in Isole famose. Folger Shakespeare Library, G1015 C3, 1574.

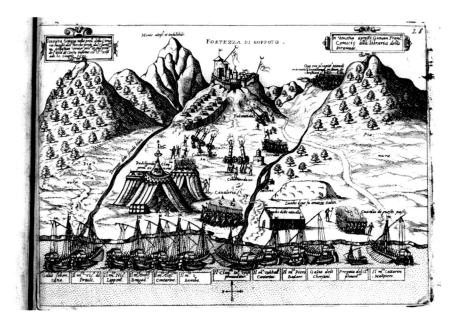

Figure 3.10 Giovanni Francesco Camocio, 'Soppoto fortress … taken by Sebastian Venier … 10 June 1570', Venice [1570]
Source: By Permission of the Folger Shakespeare Library.

provedidor general of the [nearby] island of Corfu, together with the Illustrious Zelfi, on June 10, 1570.' This scene depicts one of the successful Venetian sea actions which took place during the lead-up to both Lepanto and the Ottoman conquest of Cyprus. Soppoto and Lepanto were triumphs, but the loss of Cyprus was considered a disaster for the Venetian Republic's sovereign interests and reputation. While Venice could not, ultimately, protect the big island, it could use small fleets in locales such as that of Soppoto to change the dynamics of the frontier in the Adriatic-Balkan zone of interaction.

Between the news map and the socially empty map, or the small sea-based siege map and the illustrations of the large fleet encounter that was Lepanto, there was another alternative for visualisation of navies and their contexts – the regional map of the Mediterranean. One such pre-Lepanto image of naval force suggests notions of possession and legitimacy through the portrayal of a single contender for power in the Eastern Mediterranean, Venice. Cyprus was a valuable territory of the Venetian Mediterranean empire, but one which in 1570 was surrounded on three sides by Ottoman lands. The map shown here, entitled 'Design of the Island of Cyprus Showing the Borders of Caramania [in Anatolia], Syria, Judea, and Egypt …' from the workshop of Antonio Lafreri, shows a well-ordered and impressive fleet sailing eastwards beneath the Anatolian shore, headed towards Cyprus and the Levant (Figure 3.11).⁵⁰ As in the map of Soppoto, the vessels are labelled; but in this case the labels indicate ship types and their places in the armada. The legend locates Cyprus among the 'maritime places of Caramania, Syria, Judea, and Egypt, such as Tripoli of Syria, Jaffa, and Alexandria', thus including both the armada and the island as part of the regional complex of Eastern Mediterranean travel and trade that formed such a crucial element of Venetian identity.

Lafreri, in this image, depicts Venetian entitlement to Cyprus which was also claimed by the Ottoman Empire.⁵¹ There is here an additional, implied Venetian claim to the 'Holy Land' which the Ottomans had conquered from their Muslim rivals the Mamluks in 1516 and which, the rhetoric of Christian Europe suggested, was in need of redemption. Despite the bravado of this image, the Ottomans would conquer the island (taking Nicosia in 1570 and Famagosta in 1571 after a long siege), cementing their control over the Eastern Mediterranean territories shown on Lafreri's map.⁵² Just as mapping Lepanto was a symbol of Christian victory, mapping Cyprus would become a symbol of the lost Levant and of the continued subordination of Jerusalem and the Eastern Mediterranean matrix of pilgrimage and trade to Muslim lords.⁵³ In maps, then, the Ottoman Empire (its territory and its power) were sometimes clearly designated, sometimes hidden and sometimes assumed. Images of its engagements circulated widely – some fanciful, others claiming to represent the 'truth'. History, news and sovereign claims (realised or unrealised) all contributed to the crafting of Ottoman space and the contested territories of the trans-imperial zone.

At the turn of the seventeenth century, European cartography was increasingly recognising Ottoman sovereignty in the body of the map, as well as in the caption. The figure of the sultan, as in the portraits by Bellini, was also inscribed onto the Afro-Eurasian space, to indicate possession, recognition

---

⁵⁰ Antonio Lafreri, 'Disegno de l'Isola di Cypro con li Confini della Caramania, Soria, Giudea et Egitta', Rome, 1570. British Library, Maps C.7.e.2.(17.). The borders of those regions are, in fact, not drawn in.

⁵¹ See, Wilson 2005, 153–4. One of the earliest printed maps of Lepanto was dated 16 September 1571, by Lafreri in Rome. It was drawn in anticipation of the battle explaining, 'We presume the Turkish fleet will come at us in this way'. The map of Cyprus shown here may also have been anticipatory or perhaps it was designed to bolster the courage of its Christian audience in defense of Cyprus. We do not know how many maps of Lepanto were printed in Venice; but I would speculate that there were hundreds of copies including those published in atlases, single sheet, and book format. The commemoration (in maps, engravings, paintings, sculpture, and other media) was quite active in Venice for a generation.

⁵² On the conquest of Cyprus, see Norwich 1981, 209–22; and Imber 2002, 63, 280–82.

⁵³ Wilson 2005, 133–85, addresses the modes by which Venice mapped the Mediterranean and the Ottomans in map, image and allegory. Her notion of war as landscape is most appropriate for this map of the Venetian fleet which suggests the Ottoman enemy without ever naming him.

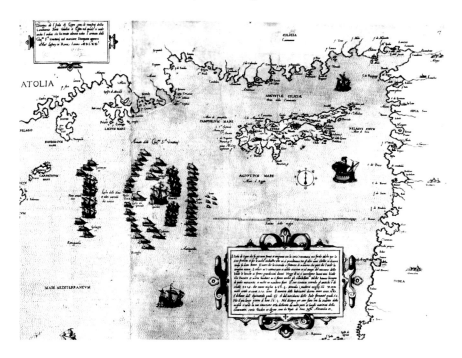

Figure 3.11   Antonio Lafreri, 'Image of the Island of Cyprus ...', Rome, 1570
Source: British Library Board. All Rights Reserved, Maps C.7.e.2.(17.).

and familiarity. Such portraits do not necessarily depict the warrior Turk, or the infidel Turk; sometimes they represent the benign, the sovereign, the imperial Turk. In Johan Bussemacher's 1596 map of Thrace, Bulgaria and surrounding lands, for example, the territory portrayed is all Ottoman space, although the land itself is not marked as the Ottoman Empire. It is, however, stamped with the portrait of Sultan Mehmed III, who ruled 1595 to 1603. He is labeled '*Turcoram Imperator*', the fifteenth Ottoman sultan, and mistakenly designated as Mehmed II, although the year of his accession is indicated correctly (Plate 25).[54] There is no suggestion in this map that the Ottomans have been emasculated in the aftermath of Lepanto. The sultan looks cheerful and kingly; rather more like a potential ally than like a demonic, infidel threat. But his portrait sits astride Europe, his glance aimed back toward Anatolia. Thus the portrait medallion serves to link the Rumelian lands of Europe with the trans-continental imperial Ottoman capital of Constantinople and its Asian hinterlands.

---

[54]   Ioani Bussemechers [Johan Bussemacher], 'Thracia Et Bulgaria Cum Viciniis', [Köln], 1596. British Library, Maps, C.39.c.1(.67).

A similarly noble-looking image of the sultan, labelled '*Sultan Mahumet Turcorum Imperat*', is found in the cartouche of J. Hondius's 1606 map of the Ottoman Empire, '*Turcici Imperii Imago*', from his *Atlas sive Cosmographicae*, published in Amsterdam (Figure 3.12).[55] This is an image of known space, sovereign and imperial. The only hint of enmity or hostility is embodied in the two devils that flank the portrait of the sultan. In this map the scope and nature of the empire of the 'Turks' is identified and inscribed with the image of a monarch who is one among the various emperors of Eurasia. He has a regal look and were it not for his turban he might be mistaken for one of the European Christian kings with whom he was in competition. The decorative aigrette on the turban suggests the artist's familiarity with the trappings of Ottoman sovereignty, while the small crown perched on top of the turban suggests an audience accommodation that dispenses with Ottoman convention and the desire for 'accurate' depiction.[56]

One might argue that such portraits are emblematic of the new knowledge of the Turk that characterised the early seventeenth century – the same familiarity suggested in the frontispiece of Richard Knolles' *Generall Historie of the Turkes*, published in England in 1603.[57] That frontispiece showed a rather bored-looking 'Turk' lounging against a pillar, the counterpart to a Christian knight. Keep in mind, however, that the Turks in Gerung's woodcut were also accompanied by devils. In Hondius's cartouche, the sultan's empire has finally been officially stamped onto Eurasian space. But, while Hondius's devils are more elegant, even more 'civilised', they act as a reminder of the indelible 'difference' of this urbane-looking Ottoman monarch. His is still the empire of the unbelievers: acknowledged and established, but nonetheless an undesirable intruder on European space. If attitudes have changed, in the post-Lepanto world, they have changed in terms of granting partial recognition to the enduring nature of Ottoman conquests and to the familiarity of Ottoman kingship – the sultan as one contending monarch

---

[55] Jocodus Hondius, 'Turcici Imperii Imago' [Amsterdam, ca. 1606]. Library of Congress, Maps, uncatalogued.

[56] European images of Ottoman costume at this time varied enormously, from the carefully ethnographic to the wildly fanciful, to the types of faux classical or 'oriental' dress which were more a function of stock images than of serious attempts to represent Ottoman dress.

[57] The Ottomans had become familiar through translations of Italian works throughout the sixteenth century. Ramberti 1539 was translated under the following title: Ramberti 1542, *The order of the greate Turckes courte, of hys mene of warre, and of all his conquests, with the summe of Mahumetes doctryne*. Giovo, 1531, was translated into multiple languages including English, and printed in twenty one editions within fifteen years of its appearance. See, Raby 2000, esp. 141–4. Cambini 1529 was translated into English in 1562. Marin Barleti's (ca. 1460–1512 or 13) history of the clash with the Ottomans was translated into English (via French) and published in London in 1596 under the following title: *The historie of George Castriot, surnamed Scanderbeg, King of Albania. containing his famous acts, his noble deedes of armes, and memorable victories against the Turkes, for the faith of Christ*.

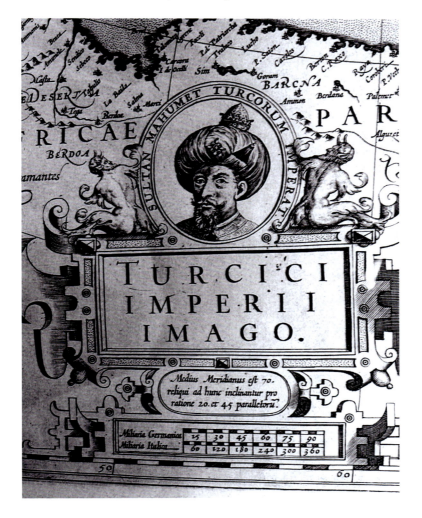

Figure 3.12   Jodocus Hondius, 'Turcici Imperii Imago', cartouche
[Amsterdam, ca. 1606]
Source: Courtesy of Library of Congress.

among others. That recognition followed an evolutionary trajectory which links the reigns of Mehmed II and Mehmed III, a trajectory which was uninterrupted, albeit enhanced, by the event and celebration of Lepanto.

By 1571, Europeans were already well equipped to narrate, embody, historicise and institutionalise the 'Turk'. That familiarity is signified by another image from Camocio's atlas which shows the finial from a battle standard, claimed to be that of the Ottoman admiral himself, captured at Lepanto.[58] The finial bears an inscription which is translated for the viewers of the commemorative atlas. Like other contemporary European images showing representations of Ottoman writing, this image is interesting because it suggests a Venetian audience which already demanded not only a 'true and accurate' depiction of sieges and naval battles, but also a 'true and accurate' reading of Ottoman artifacts and 'Turkish' lettering. This artifact (with its script shown in an approximation of mirror image) is translated for those utilising the atlas to witness the battle, its territorial contexts, and the trophies of war. It is a statement of proclamation, telling who the 'Turks' are, what they revere, and how they script themselves. There is thus a sense that the map-maker felt his audience wanted to know what the characters said, and what divine invocations the Ottoman commander carried with him into battle to inspire himself and his men.[59] Further, the artifact must be apprehended as if the viewer were witnessing the thing itself instead of a two dimensional image stamped onto a page – as if, one might say, he or she could walk around it to see that which in the atlas image was unseen.[60]

Camocio's atlas, in which this image of defeat and of words of triumph appeared, served as news, education and commemoration. It was not simply a canny marketing manoeuver, an assembly of old and new maps celebrating the victory at Lepanto and showing the seascapes in which 'Turks' and 'Christians' had recently engaged in combat. It was a classification of important space – those points (rather than blocks of territory) which were still held or endangered by the Turks, space with which the public did well to concern itself. The atlas included

---

[58] Giovanni Francesco Camocio, 'Il vero ordine delle due potente armate …', Venice, 1571, map 40, in *Isole famose*. Folger Shakespeare Library, G1015 C3, 1574. Legend: '*Forma et vero ritratto del pomo over Cimiero del Standardo principale del Bassa Generale dell'Armata turchesca, il qual era tutto d'Argento dorato et da tutte due le parti vi erano intagliato lettere turchesche, il qual cimiero fu presentato alla ser. [Signor]ia di Venetia; Per Mr. P[au]lo et Mr. Bernardino lancia fratelli orefici, alla insegna della madonna in Rialto; la sua grandezza era tre volte magior di questo disegno.*'

[59] Fenlon 2006, 265, notes that this image of the Ottoman standard was reproduced in Luigi Groto, *Trofeo della Vittoria Sacra*, a 'Lepanto anthology' which was published in Venice in 1572. It is not clear whether the engraving originated in Camocio's print shop or elsewhere, but clearly it was reproduced in at least two contexts, an atlas and a celebratory compilation book.

[60] The caption reads: '*Interpretatione delle lettere Turchesche ché sono nel soprascritto pomo: et prima. dalla parte che si vide IDDIO NON A' ALTRO DIO: MAUMETHO NUNCIO DE DIO. da l'altra parte Alli fideli divino Auspitio et ornamento: nelle degn[e] imprese Dio [sonorisce?] Maumetho.*' (Interpretation of the Turkish letters that are on the above noted finial: On the part which one sees: 'God, Have no Other God: Muhammad [is the] nuncio of God.' On the other part: 'To the faithful, divine, auspicious and ornamented: in worthy [military] endeavors God [*sonorisce?*] Muhammad.') I am not sure what '*sonorisce*' might mean here or if it is a misprinting of some other word (e.g., *favorisce* or favour/support). The attribute 'divine', of course, could only refer to God in Muslim usage.

the presentation of an artifact which symbolised the conflict for territory and honour, and which revealed the nature of the 'Turks' in their own words, as an object of study. Lepanto was thus embedded in a system of portraying and narrating the Ottomans. It could be a specific battle with specific personnel and action, or it could be one in a long chain of events for which Christian audiences were asked to support their rulers and praise their God.[61]

Conclusion

In 1550 Giacomo Gastaldi, the map-maker, and Michele Membré, a Venetian famous for his mission to the Safavid lands of Iran, 'sought permission to publish a map of Asia, beginning 'at the Mediterranean Sea and going to the East where are Anatolia, Syria and Persia, with the lands of the Sufi [the Safavid Shah of Iran], and then towards the north-east where are the lands of Cathay, [and] to the south where India and the spice islands are.'[62] This endeavour illuminates an interesting conjunction between the European experience of the Ottoman Empire and its construction at a distance. Membré combined the roles of government agent, merchant and traveller. His mission to Persia, 1539–1542, involved a journey across Ottoman Anatolia during which he disguised himself, 'in the Turkish fashion', suggesting a certain claim to familiarity with Ottoman costume as well as access to such a 'costume'.[63]

Membré's *relazione*, written when he returned to Venice, illustrates the ways in which a foreign Christian, posing as a merchant, merged readily into Muslim commercial networks of exchange, buying and selling goods as a mode of travel across Ottoman lands. After his return, his knowledge of lands to the east made Membré a valued authority for the creation of maps which in turn helped to fashion or reinforce visions of the Ottomans. In this regard he joined a series of 'official' witnesses who in the sixteenth century publicised their experience of

---

[61] Even today Lepanto still captivates the Venetian imagination, as witnessed by the speeches, celebration and scholarly attention devoted to the subject yearly on 7 October. Thus, for example, on 7 October 2007, L'Associazione I Giovanni Veneziani, 'con lo spirito di conoscere e ricordare il passato per comprendere meglio il presente, promuove e organizza la commemorazione dell vittoria cristiana di Lepanto ...' celebrated the anniversary of the battle at the Church of Santa Maria del Giglio with speeches and a mass. Matar 1999, 146, 153–4, has pointed out some of the ways in which Lepanto was recalled in the seventeenth century, including mock sea battles as parts of various festival occasions and in the dedication to texts like Fairfax's 1624 translation of Tasso's *Jerusalem*. Lepanto was also inscribed in poems, maps and various other narratives.

[62] Karrow 1993, 225. The map was apparently not published.

[63] See Membré 1993, 5, 8. Membré notes that he loaded his merchandise at Candia, 'together with other Turkish merchants'. For a treatment of the nature of travel accounts to these Asian lands spanning the medieval and early modern periods see Brummett 2009.

Muslim kingdoms and parlayed that knowledge into various forms of recognition and status in the courts and capitals of Europe.[64]

Membre's journey, and his collaboration with Gastaldi, illustrate the ways in which imperial aspirations, commercial interest and rhetorics of the 'Turk' intersected in the sixteenth century. These rhetorics employed the language of political and religious divide, but were certainly not limited to them. Ottoman space was, rather, a space to be traversed, explored, exploited, translated and narrated. That intention was present before and after Lepanto, in times of war and in times of peace. Although the universe of those who experienced Ottoman domains changed and expanded in the later sixteenth century, with the English infiltration of the Levant for example, it would be difficult to argue that the level of interest either waxed or waned in the aftermath of 1571.

The dilemma we face in contextualising Lepanto and conceptualising the ways in which the Ottomans were known in the sixteenth century is that our historiographies still tend to run in parallel rather than intersecting tracks. We have imperial history – that which is concerned with battles, treaties and the projection of imperial power. That history, as Andrew Hess put it, designates 'zones of division' between polities, peoples and civilisations.[65] We have the history of trade, which works within imperial frames, but is grounded in economic imperatives and in transnational and transcultural relationships. That history takes for granted zones of diffusion, as opposed to zones of difference; but it is often narrow in scope and disinterested in the attitudes attached to its materials. Then we have the intellectual and literary histories: histories of knowledge, of attitudes, of identity. These histories are interested in translation and the porous boundaries between political entities; but they are also often nationally and linguistically self-absorbed – looking to poets', essayists' and travellers' representations of others as, inherently, representations of self. To understand how Europeans knew the Ottomans in the sixteenth century, these parallel tracks must be joined: retaining the imperial frames and the significance of war, but becoming attuned to the rhetorical and material modes by which imperial zones were used, ignored, breached and traversed. The sophisticated networks of trade that linked the Afro-Eurasian Oikumene constituted networks of news, representation and attitude as well – networks of visualisation along which consumers selected from among a set of diverse representational possibilities, just as they selected from among the available goods. Bellini stands in a long line of those who appreciated and capitalised upon those networks, crafting a set of images that were both for and about the Ottomans and setting

---

[64] These witnesses include the various envoys of Venice to the Porte in Istanbul, whose *relazioni* formed an important source for information about 'the Turk', and a model for representations of the Ottomans, along with the accounts (long and short, fanciful and authoritative) of other travellers, merchants and renegades.

[65] Hess 1972, 73.

the stage for further examples of visual interpretation that 'read' the Ottomans in a complex series of ways not confined to the elements of victory and faith.

SECTION II
Texts, Art and Music as Media for the Transmission of Intercultural Influences

Chapter 4

The Role of the Book in the Transfer of Culture between Venice and the Eastern Mediterranean

Deborah Howard[1]

According to tradition, Gentile Bellini took one of his father's two precious sketchbooks to Constantinople in 1479 as a gift to Sultan Mehmed II. This tradition rests on the fact that the book was in Izmir in Smyrna in 1728, supposedly taken there from the Topkapi Palace. In the catalogue of the exhibition *Bellini and the East* Alan Chong cast some doubt on the story;[2] but whatever the exact circumstances of the Louvre sketchbook's arrival in Constantinople, it was definitely inked in to make the metalpoint drawings more legible, possibly to prepare it as a diplomatic gift. Unless further evidence is discovered in the future, this issue must remain an open question, but it serves to introduce the focus of this essay on the role of the book as a purveyor of cultural and visual information from East to West, both before and after the onset of printing.

The portability of books makes them ideal travel companions. Just as we fly today with checked bags and hand luggage, the possessions of a Venetian traveller called Nicolò de Ruzzino aboard the Beirut galley in 1457 were divided into those in a bag to keep with him on deck and others in a chest in the hold. Sadly, Nicolò died on board ship, but because his possessions were inventoried on arrival in Syria, ready to be sent back to Venice, we know what he read on his journey. To pass the time during the voyage, he had a copy of St Jerome's *Lives of the Saints*, together with Boccaccio's *Elegy of Madonna Fiammetta*.[3] The first of these titles was a standard textbook prescribed in Venetian vernacular schools for the teaching of reading. The version used in school was the Italian translation by the fourteenth-century Dominican friar Domenico Cavalca, who had transformed

---

[1] The first part of this essay draws directly on material contained in my book Howard 2000. The second part is taken from my essay Howard 2005.

[2] Campbell and Chong 2005–2006, 113.

[3] The 'libero di santi pari composto per San Girolamo' (Archivio di Stato di Venezia, Cancelleria Inferiore, Notai, b. 83 (II), Cristoforo del Fiore, reg. III, unnumb. fols). The inventory is published in Bianchi and Howard 2003, 284–6. For the 'libro dito Fiameta', see Boccaccio 1987.

the stories into exciting chivalric romances, ideal for reading on board ship.⁴ Two more books in de Ruzzino's sea-chest offered the same combination of fourteenth-century secular reading and devotional literature, namely 'one book of stories of Griselda and Walter' (the last novella of Boccaccio's *Decameron*), and 'one small prayer-book [*offizieto*] of Our Lady with other things'.⁵

Merchants are often assumed to be pragmatic and lacking in literary imagination, yet the two most important Venetian poets of the fourteenth and fifteenth centuries, Bartolomeo Zorzi and Giovanni Querini, both travelled to the East with books in their luggage.⁶ Francesco Morosini, who died in Damascus in 1346, had in his belongings a songbook of all the sonnets of Petrarch on parchment ('*uno canzonier di tuti soneti del Petrarcha in bergamena*').⁷ Giovanni Querini's brother Guglielmo tried to recover 'many books by fine writers' belonging to his brother who had died in Constantinople in 1453.⁸ Guglielmo Querini was a stay-at-home merchant who traded through agents. In Venice he operated an informal lending library, as well as accepting books as security when others borrowed money from him, creating a direct link between books and commerce.⁹

The intimate relationship between books and travel during the Renaissance was established well before the development of printing. Books were light, compact and personal – they could be read for entertainment or travel advice, or actively used for writing journals and accounts. In the 1470s or 1480s, the Venetian merchant Benedetto Sanudo, son of Matteo, wrote a letter to his brother Andrea, who was about to set off on his first voyage to Alexandria. Anxious to protect the moral virtue of his relatively inexperienced brother, Benedetto recommended the ship's chaplain for companionship:

> You know as well as I do that everyone on board ship gambles, whether playing cards or backgammon – some even travel for this very purpose. But take note: if you care for your honour … while the others gamble, set about reading one of the books that you will take with you. And if sometimes you want to spend time doing something else other than reading or writing, you may play backgammon with the priest.¹⁰

---

⁴ See Grendler 1982, 47–8. For the *Lives of the Desert Fathers*, generally attributed in the past to Jerome but now more correctly to Cavalca, see Delcorno 2000, especially chap. II, 'Diffusione del volgarizzamento'.

⁵ '*1 libro de istorie de Grixeldo e de Gualtier*' and '*1 officieto de Nostra Dona e con altre chosse suxo*'. See Bianchi and Howard 2003, 284–6.

⁶ Folena 1973, 307.

⁷ (Comune di) Venezia 1954, 19.

⁸ Tucci 1981, 25: '*molti libri de bei autori*'.

⁹ On Guglielmo Querini see especially Luzzatto 1954, 167–92.

¹⁰ The letter is contained in Biblioteca Correr, Cod. Cicogna, 3101, no. 4; document published in Howard 2000, 219–21.

Thus Benedetto placed the act of reading firmly on the moral high ground.

Fifteenth-century inventories of the possessions of deceased Venetians even specify the type of paper in the books listed: good-quality paper ('*bona carta*') is distinct from rag paper ('*carta bambaxina*'), though most paper at this date was made from rags. At the time of his death in Damascus in 1455, the merchant Stefano Ravagnino had trade documents in Arabic, a white Turkish book, a bound book of tariffs, a psalter on good paper, and his own big account book. In addition, he owned small books bought in the bazaar ('*libereti de bazaro*'), presumably purchased in the celebrated book market just to the west of the Great Mosque, in the shadow of the imposing ruins of the Roman temple that once stood on the site.[11] Books were crucial transmitters of songs and musical compositions: in 1436 a Venetian merchant who died in Damascus left several musical instruments, including a harpsichord, a *viola da gamba* in a painted case, and a lute, while among his books was a songbook with all the sonnets of Petrarch on parchment.[12]

Well before the invention of printing, owners of books enacted a personal dialogue with their volumes, inscribing their names, adding marginalia, writing on the flyleaves and updating information. Venetian merchants' handbooks were already in circulation in the thirteenth century, as we know from the manual from Crusader Acre analysed by David Jacoby.[13] These guides were normally written in dialect, as if to communicate insider knowledge to compatriots engaged in similarly risky ventures.[14] Benedetto Cotrugli writing in the mid-fifteenth century defended his decision to write his handbook in dialect for its greater usefulness and intelligibility 'even if the work is less dignified than it would have been if I had written it as a Latin sermon'.[15]

Handbooks such as the famous fifteenth-century *Zibaldone da Canal* listed the tariffs, weights and measures current in different ports for a dazzling range of goods.[16] Such books were passed from one user to another – the small manuscript *Tarifa de pexi e spesse* of 1493, now in the Marciana, has notes in four later hands. This manual gives the prices involved in shipping 48 different commodities from

---

[11] Pedersen 1984, 52. For Ravagnino's inventory see Bianchi and Howard 2003, 270–75.

[12] Archivio di Stato di Venezia, Cancelleria Inferiore, busta 122, Atti Tebaldo Manfredi, registro dated 1420–1465, 3 July 1436, fols 16 sin., 24 sin., among goods belonging to Ruberto Morosini in the house of Piero da Molin. Dr Susan Connell Wallington kindly drew these documents to my attention.

[13] Jacoby 1986. The manual is contained in Biblioteca Marciana, Cod. It., Cl. XI, no 87 (=7355), fols 1–7. The Venetian handbook known as the *Zibaldone da Canal* dates from the 1320s or earlier; see Stussi 1967.

[14] Cortelazzo 1976, 674–6.

[15] Cotrugli 1990, 135: '*benche l'opera non sia sì degna come sarebbe stata s'io l'avessi scripta in sermone Latino.*'

[16] Stussi 1967. See also Cortelazzo 1976, 674–7.

Alexandria, listed alphabetically from '*anbra*' to '*zafaran*'.[17] Discouragingly, it also itemises the likely funeral expenses to be incurred by the Western merchant who dies in Alexandria.[18]

Merchant handbooks open a fascinating window into the mentality of the Venetian traveller. As well as the books of tariffs, merchants carried books known as portolans which often contained a bewildering range of contents. Before the sixteenth century, even the navigational information was usually in text form, describing identifiable features on land (such as the Pharos in Alexandria) and the bearings and distances to be sailed in relation to these. In addition the book might contain recipes for medicinal remedies, prayers, information on shipbuilding and rigging, and notes on both astronomy and astrology. The owners inserted wide-ranging titbits of useful information, rather as we might use a Filofax. One of the most famous examples is the commonplace book in the British Library compiled from 1444 onwards by a certain Zorzi Trombetta, a trombone-player from Modon in Greece who sailed on galleys around the Eastern Mediterranean as well as to Santuzzo (Sandwich in Kent).[19] In addition to essential navigation information and other personal annotations in Venetian dialect in his own hand, Zorzi Trombetta's book contains the scores for nine part-songs in the hands of three other scribes.

Another similarly miscellaneous portolan, now in Greenwich, includes a recipe for mixing paints for colouring maps, given to the owner by none other than Gentile Bellini. The entry is dated 1 May 1487, that is, several years after his visit to Constantinople.[20] That Gentile was himself involved in mapping, or at least in decorating maps, is suggested by the Ottoman sultan Mehmed Fatih's request to him for maps of Venice.[21] Probably Mehmed wanted the maps for strategic motives as well as artistic ones. Gentile's evident love of topographical precision would have recommended him as an illuminator of maps, and it should not be forgotten that his less famous cousin Leonardo was a book illuminator.

Pilgrim guides, too, were circulated, copied and revised over the centuries. Volumes listed the indulgences to be earned by visiting the various pilgrim sites in the Holy Land. The late fifteenth-century Milanese pilgrim Santo Brasca makes four prudent recommendations for the pilgrim's spiritual and bodily welfare: first, the pilgrim needs to be clear about his devotional priorities; second, before leaving he should put his affairs in order and make his will; third, he will need two purses, one full of patience (a pun on the phrase *un sacco di*, or a lot of) and the other containing 150 to 200 Venetian ducats; and fourth, he should pack a warm jacket for the homeward voyages as well as clean shirts and linen.[22] Like

---

[17] Biblioteca Marciana di Venezia, Cod. Marc. It, Cl. VII, 545 (=7530), fols 3–30.
[18] Biblioteca Marciana di Venezia, Cod. Marc. It., Cl. VII, 545 (=7530), fol. 49 v.
[19] British Library, Ms Cotton Titus A XXVI, fols 2–60. See Leech-Wilkinson 1981.
[20] Bonfiglio Dosio 1987, 202, 203–4.
[21] Howard 2005–2006, 16–17, 30.
[22] Brasca 1966, 128.

most pilgrims to the Holy Land Brasca sailed on a Venetian ship. Interestingly even religious texts, such as Ravagnino's small *'offizieto'* mentioned earlier, often had bindings described as 'damascene' or 'moorish', in this case *'con coverta damaschina'*.[23]

Some travellers recorded their travel reminiscences in writing on their return, as much for their own pleasure as for posterity, Marco Polo's journey as dictated to Rustichello being the most celebrated example. The self-conscious intention to commit travel reminiscences to paper makes such narratives more effective than merchant letters in the transmission of visual information. The anonymous author of the hand-written *Itinerario da Aleppo in Thauris* in 1496 seems to have intended his narrative to be read by a public audience – even anticipating a readership outside Venice – for he apologises for his incorrect language. Had he been Florentine or Genoese, he suggests, he could have written in verse.[24]

The importance of books for the communication of visual information between East and West goes back at least to the thirteenth century, when the so-called Cotton Genesis was used as the starting point for the mosaics in the north atrium of San Marco.[25] Named after its famous collector Sir Robert Cotton (who also owned Trombetta's portolan), this precious codex was tragically destroyed by fire in the eighteenth century. It is known only from a few charred fragments and the water colours made by George Vertue just after the fire. Probably made in Alexandria, the Cotton Genesis is datable to the later fifth or early sixth century, although we do not know when it reached Venice. I have suggested elsewhere that additional information for the backgrounds and anecdotal detail in the thirteenth-century mosaics in San Marco may have been available to the mosaicists of San Marco in the form of illustrated Arabic manuscripts such as the *Maqāmāt* of al-Hariri.[26]

Visual information could also be communicated more informally within the family through amateur sketches. After a series of voyages between 1557 and 1562, the Venetian merchant Alessandro Magno neatly copied out his journals in a vellum-bound volume, now in the Folger library:

> There being nothing more enjoyable, for those seeking the world, than the memories of past events, I have decided for this reason and as a relaxation to write up the details of my journey.[27]

---

[23] Howard 2003, 147.
[24] Biblioteca Correr, Venice, Cod. Cic. 2727, fasc. 20, fol. 1.
[25] Weitzmann and Kessler 1986, 2-6, 18-20.
[26] Howard 2000, 79-88.
[27] Folger Library, Washington DC, ms. V. A. 259 (De Ricci 1317 / 1), fol. 1: '*Non essendo cosa più dilettevole, che vadi cercando il mondo quanto lo aricordo all'huomo delle cose passate, ho deliberato per questo et per passar l'otio tenir conto particular del presente viaggio ...*', cited in Howard 2000, 44.

The conflation of history and geography in this statement reflects a deeply ingrained habit among Venetians. That Magno surely expected the account of his odysseys to assume the status of a family heirloom is significant when one remembers that, unlike the Florentines, the Venetians were not habitual compilers of family history.[28] Magno himself illustrated his account with his own drawings, which convey a vivid picture of his travel experiences, despite his limited artistic skills (Plate 26). From the Pyramids to the port of London, he sketched whatever intrigued him, just as we commit our own travel experiences to the camera. Evidently informal graphic information was not hard to come by, for it made its impact even in relatively official documents, exemplified by the topographically realistic view of Fort of Qa'it Bey in Alexandria in the statute book of the Cottimo (the system of local taxation of Venetian residents)[29] (Plate 27).

For the merchants of Venice, the limits of known world corresponded closely to the lands of the Bible. But their frontiers were determined not by religious study, but by the frequency of trade. Alexandria, Damascus and Aleppo, with their resident colonies, were regarded as so familiar that few Venetian visitors felt the need to describe them. As Francis Bacon remarked, most people travelling over land write little, whereas on board ship 'where there is nothing to see but sky and sea', many travellers indulge in travel writing.[30] A striking exception was the Venetian ambassador to Persia Ambrogio Contarini, whose highly readable adventures on his overland journey via Russia and Kiev were widely read in the sixteenth century.[31] Interestingly, Giovanni Dario's vivid account of his reception at the 'Persian court' in 1484 is now known to have been wrongly labelled; it refers instead to his visit to the court of Bayazid I while the sultan was hunting at Edirne.

This brings us to a consideration of the role of printing in East-West transmission. No new information system displaces its predecessors at a stroke: even after the invention of printing, numerous manuscripts of travel narratives were still in circulation in the sixteenth century, including the travels of both Marco Polo and the explorer Alvise da Mosto. But printing was to change the public perception of the known world, just at the very time when its frontiers were being extended to hitherto unimaginable limits by the discovery of the Americas and the Cape Route to India.

Printing, most importantly, gave the sense of greater *authority and authenticity.* Traditional merchant handbooks began to appear in printed form, giving their content a definitive aspect that added conviction. The conferring of authenticity was always a preoccupation of travel writers, especially when describing their

---

[28] Grubb 1986.
[29] Archivio di Stato di Venezia, Cinque Savi alla Mercanzia, 'Capitolato cottimo Alessandria', busta 944 bis (neg. no. 306), illustrated in Howard 2000, 98, fig. 108.
[30] Bacon 1985, 113.
[31] Cavazzana Romanelli 1983; Lockhart and Morozzo della Rocca 1973.

more remarkable experiences. A favourite device was to give plausibility to foreign places by comparing them with familiar Venetian monuments. In his description of Pegù in Burma in 1583, Gasparo Balbi compared the width of the main street to that of the Grand Canal at Rialto, and estimated the Pagoda to be the same height as the Campanile of San Marco, and the size of the Doge's Palace, although round rather than square.[32]

Secondly, printed texts reached a *wider audience*. The preface of the 1548 Italian translation of Ptolemy's *Geography* claimed its usefulness not only to philosophers, theologians, astronomers, medical doctors, lawyers, orators, poets and other scholars, but also to princes, colonial administrators, *condottieri*, captains, admirals, private navigators, solders, merchants and gentlemen, as well as '*gentilissime Madonne*', wanderers and pilgrims.[33]

Thirdly, printed texts could be customised by adding illuminations, decorated initials or personalised bindings. Venetian bookbinding in the sixteenth century is profoundly influenced by Ottoman and other Islamic bindings. A copy of Serlio's Book III in the Louvre has an Ottoman-style binding, and another volume from Marcolini's press, a copy of Dante of 1544, still in Venice, is similarly reminiscent of Middle-Eastern models.[34] Because many customers bought books unbound, even before the days of printing, there was no obvious link between authorship and the appearance of the closed book.

Fourthly, the *language* of the discourse of travel was drastically modified by printing. In the thirteenth and fourteenth centuries, under the influence of crusading culture, many texts about the East, including the original version of Marco Polo's travels, were written in French.[35] By the fifteenth century, however, most travel narratives were composed in Venetian dialect, whether in diary form, or under subject headings. Merchant handbooks, too, were written in dialect, using the familiar '*tu*' for the reader.[36] In the sixteenth century, by contrast, a more Tuscan version of Italian became the standard language for the printed texts of travel literature. Dialect disappeared, even when the text was clearly addressed to active Venetian merchants, such as the account of his travels to the East Indies by the jeweller Gasparo Balbi, published in Venice in 1590.[37]

[32] Balbi 1590, fols 96r–96v.
[33] Ptolemy 1548, Proemio ai lettori.
[34] Hobson 1989, 115, fig. 14 on 122; Rogers 1999, 139 and fig. 17.
[35] Howard 2000, 22.
[36] Ibid., 17. The main exception was the odyssey of Niccolò dei Conti, whose travels were written down in Latin by the Florentine humanist Poggio Bracciolini, at the request of Pope Eugenius IV. This unusually humanistic context resulted from the historical circumstances of dei Conti's repatriation. On his return from his voyage to the East Indies in about 1439, he had to go to Florence to seek absolution from the Pope for having renounced the Christian faith while abroad, in order to save his skin. See Ramusio 1967–70, vol. I, 338. For the likely date of this voyage, see de' Conti 1929, 34.
[37] Balbi 1590.

The printing of travel narratives in Venice began in the fifteenth century.[38] The first printed edition of Marco Polo seems to have been that published in Venice in 1496 and reprinted in 1508.[39] Ambrogio Contarini's travels to Persia were printed in 1476–1477 just after his journey, but the extreme rarity of this edition suggests that the print-run was very small.[40] A reprint of 1524 published in Venice was more widely circulated. The title page lists the profusion of topics to be included:

> notable mountains, rivers, plains, deserts, horrid wildernesses, distances, frontiers, difficult passes, the fertility or otherwise of the lands, merchandise, animals and fish of strange kinds, forms of boats and houses, place names, countries, courts of kings, dukes and lords, the nature, customs, religion and stature of the inhabitants (male and female), and endless other things.[41]

The first proper anthology of travel writing, edited by Fracanzio da Montalboddo, was first published in Vicenza in 1507.[42] This selection appeared at the very time when the suspicions of Venetians about the long-term impact of Portuguese competition were beginning to sink in. The emphasis of this book was *exclusively westward*. The only Venetian traveller to be included was Alvise da Mosto, whose West African voyages open the volume. Most of the narratives are concerned with discoveries in the Americas, including those by Columbus and Amerigo Vespucci. The only mention of the East is a little note at the end recording an observation about Christians in the India.[43] The dedicatee of the book, Angiolello, was himself a renowned traveller to the East, best known for his period in the service of Sultan Mehmed II from 1474 – ca. 1483.[44] Fracanzio used Angiolello's previous experience to stress the novelty of the publication: 'Because having travelled in almost all of Europe and a great part of Asia you will recognise in the diversity of the things mentioned how marvellous they are.'[45]

---

[38] As a possible precedent, Francesco Sansovino mentions a certain Vincenzo Querini in the time of Doge Foscari (1524–57) who published '*un libro, De singulis conclusionibus omnium scientiarum. Et alcuni commentarii dell'India, et di Colocuth*', but this may not have been printed (Sansovino 1581, fol. 244 v.). On travel literature in Early Modern Venice, see Lucchetta 1985, 43–68; and Perocco 1997.

[39] Polo 1496 and 1508.

[40] The travels of Ambrogio Contarini are mentioned by Francesco Sansovino in the reign of Doge Andrea Vendramin (1476–1478) (Sansovino 1581, fol. 239 r).

[41] Contarini 1524.

[42] da Montalboddo 1507.

[43] This was a comment made by an Indian called Joseph who had joined a Portuguese caravelle.

[44] See Babinger 1961.

[45] '*Si perche havendo tu quasi tutta la europa & gran parte del asia pagiato, in tanta diversità de cose discerne qual diano piu maraviose*' (cited from da Montalboddo 1517).

The language of publication, Tuscan Italian, was quite deliberately chosen, for Fracanzio declared that in any other form, whether florid Latin, or rough dialect, or Portuguese, the narratives would have been overlooked.[46]

A new edition published in Venice in 1517 by the Milanese publisher Giorgio Rusconi seemed to address a more specifically Venetian readership, for the title page is largely taken up by a woodcut of the centre of Venice, stretching from Piazza San Marco with its quay and warehouses ('*magageni*') to the Rialto market.[47] The importance of this little book lies in the gathering of miscellaneous texts in various languages, including a series of letters collected from Spain and Portugal. The anthology format was to prove highly influential, as we shall see.

Once the *genre* of the anthology of travel writing was established, the idea began to take root. In 1543 Antonio Manutio, heir to the famous publishing house of Aldus Manutius, published a longer anthology of travel writing called *Journeys from Venice to Tana, Persia, India and Constantinople*.[48] Here the emphasis appears to be an attempt to restore the primacy of oriental travel in the Venetian consciousness. In direct contrast to Fracanzio's anthology, the emphasis is *exclusively eastward*. Indeed, it focuses on all the traditional destinations of Venetian merchants.[49]

But Manuzio's introduction stresses that the aim of the book is entertainment rather than practical usefulness.[50] In other words the audience is not the active, enterprising Venetian merchant, but the 'universal' reader. Despite the appeals to the Republic's supremacy in trade and travel, these peregrinations thus entered the realm of literature.

The most celebrated Venetian printing initiative in the realm of travel writing was, of course, that of Gian Battista Ramusio. Ramusio's goal was a

---

[46] Nevertheless, within 10 years of the original publication in 1507, the anthology was also translated into both Latin and French. See Lucchetta 1985, 435.

[47] da Montalboddo 1517.

[48] Manutio 1543,

[49] In his foreword, Manutio stresses their contribution: 'Among all the moderns who have hitherto travelled the world, without any doubt the Venetian nobility [hold the first place]; because of their greatness and power in maritime affairs, both as merchants and as envoys from their most illustrious Republic to various potentates, they have been able to sail to the most remote places, and thus to interact with many barbarous nations ... For the mutual benefit of their descendants they have left faithful accounts.' ['*tra tutti i moderni che prima & con maggior chiarezza hanno in questa parte giovato al mondo, senza alcun dubbio sono stati i Signori Venetiani; i quali per la loro grandezza & potenza cha hanno havuto nelle cose maritime, et come mercanti & spesse fiate come oratori della loro Illustrissima Republica à diversi Potentati, hanno potuto penetrare navigando in luoghi remotissimi; & cosi tenere commentio con molte barbare nationi ... per comune utilità de loro descendenti, hanno lasciato fedel memoria.*'] (ibid., fol. 2r-2v.)

[50] '*per fine principale, piu tosto il giovare universalmente à gli huomini, che al suo privato comodo*' (ibid., fol. 2v.). The book is dedicated to Antonio Barbarigo, the Captain of the Alexandria galley from which the writer of the last narrative was seized.

purely scholarly, scientific one. The sole aim was to update the geographical knowledge of antiquity, on every continent, whether East or West, in order to assist map-makers. Above all, Ptolemy's *Geography* needed supplementary texts, in the light of recent voyages of exploration.[51] For decades Ramusio had been collecting texts, using his network of humanist friends and his connections as secretary in the Doge's Palace.[52] He himself translated all the texts into elegant Italian, including not only those in Latin, Portuguese and Spanish, but also the accounts in Venetian dialect.[53] According to the dedication the intended audience included both scholars and princes.[54]

The publication was a huge enterprise. The three original massive volumes, published by Tommaso Giunti in Venice, appeared in 1550, 1559 and 1556 respectively. They were dedicated to Ramusio's friend Fracastoro, author of a well-known work on cosmology *Homocentricorum* (1538) and of a much-admired Latin poem on syphilis (1530).[55] The second volume was due to appear in 1557, the year of Ramusio's death, but an unfortunate fire in the printer's workshop in that year destroyed the woodblock illustrations, and the book eventually appeared without the intended maps two years later.[56] All three volumes were originally published anonymously, and Ramusio's identity was not revealed until 1563 when Giunti added a tribute to their late editor in the foreword to volume I.

Ramusio's three volumes were organised geographically. The first volume included accounts of Africa, India and the East Indies; the second was concerned with Russia, the Middle East and Central Asia; and the third with the New World. His publisher Giunti mentioned, probably in jest, that Ramusio hoped to publish a fourth volume on the Antarctic, in which case 'there would no longer have been any need to read Ptolemy, Strabo, Pliny or any of the other ancient writers on geography'.[57]

The woodcut maps included in the volumes are anonymous, but may have been made by Ramusio's friend the great cartographer Giacomo Gastaldi, who

---

[51] These editions should be considered in the context of printed editions of Ptolemy's geography: the Latin editions published in Vicenza, (Ptolemy 1475) and in Venice by Bernardo Sylvano 1511, as well as the Italian translation with new maps by Gastaldi published in 1548 (Ptolemy 1548).

[52] Lucchetta 1986, 482–6.

[53] Perocco makes a detailed comparison between the original Venetian dialect of Ambrogio Contarini and Ramusio's Italian 'translation' (Perocco 1997, 9–10).

[54] '*dotti & studiosi*', also '*i Signori & Principi*' (Ramusio 1967–70, vol. I, preface to Fracastoro, unnumbered pp.)

[55] On Fracastoro, see Peruzzi 1997.

[56] Skelton, introduction to Ramusio, 1967–70, vol. I, xii–xiii.

[57] '... *non havesse fatto più di bisogno leggere, ne Tolomeo, ne Strabone, ne Plinio, ne alcun'altro de gli antichi scrittori intorno alle cose di Geografia*' (Preface to vol. I, 1563 edn, by Tommaso Giunti, Ramusio 1967–70, vol. I, unnumbered).

instructed his son in geography.[58] The first volume contained only one woodcut map of the Nile and some plans of Ethiopian churches. Volume III included a number of maps of the New World as well as Africa and the East Indies. All the maps contain anecdotal detail such as exotic animals and fish, natives with weapons, and primitive huts. In addition there are some small woodcuts to give local colour, such as the rather unconvincing rendering of the rhubarb plant and a woodcut of an Indian hammock which appears twice.

The real significance of Ramusio's enterprise in Venice was to broaden the scope of travel-lore to include the New World and Africa south of the Sahara, which lay beyond the frontiers of Venice's communal geographical experience.[59] For the first time, the boundaries of travel lore extended beyond the limits of the traditional sources of knowledge: the Bible, the classics and Marco Polo. As the world became larger, Venice's role in it became smaller, and for many Venetians armchair travel had to satisfy their geographical curiosity.

---

[58] Skelton, introduction to Ramusio 1967–70, I, xii. Two of the maps were very similar to maps by Gastaldi in Ptolemy 1548. Ramusio himself seems to have been the moving spirit behind a nearly contemporary project to decorate the large Sala dello Scudo in the Doge's Palace with up-to-date maps of the world between 1548 and 1553. See Gallo 1943. This was the first room in the private apartments of the Doge, to which the new Scala d'Oro, erected in 1555–1559, would give almost direct access. See Sansovino 1604, fol. 222 v.

[59] A similar story could be told about costume books. See especially Wilson 2005.

Chapter 5

The 'Reception of the Venetian Ambassadors in Damascus': Dating, Meaning and Attribution

Caroline Campbell[*]

The so-called *Reception of the Venetian Ambassadors in Damascus* in the Musée du Louvre (Plate 28) has been the subject of extensive study by generations of Islamicists, and now by students of East-West connections in the Mediterranean world during the Renaissance. Yet it still remains an enigmatic work, because it sits outside the categories we are familiar with for fifteenth and sixteenth-century Venetian representations of the Levant. It neither represents a biblical subject set in the Near East, nor is it a portrait. Furthermore, we do not know its original location, although we can be sure that it was not made as part of a cycle of paintings for one of Venice's *scuole*, or confraternities.

A new interpretation and attribution is presented here for this much-researched canvas, provoked by the campaign of cleaning and restoration which was undertaken in preparation for the painting's inclusion in two recent exhibitions examining connections between Renaissance Venice and the Orient.[1] It has often been said that the Louvre painting was the means by which accurate Mamluk motifs were transmitted to Venice. Yet the date 1511 which was revealed during the conservation treatment makes a reassessment of this statement necessary. The discovery of this date also enables us to make more informed judgements as to what precisely is represented in this most intriguing and perplexing of paintings. It is argued below that it depicts a visual synthesis of events and places of significance for Damascus's Venetian community between 1510 and 1512, particularly those which involved Pietro Zen, the Venetian Republic's consul in this provincial Mamluk city from 1508.

The earliest description of the *Reception of the Venetian Ambassadors* is found in Marco Boschini's *Carta del Navagar Pitoresco* of 1660, which its author describes

---

[*] I would like to thank Alan Chong, Deborah Howard, Jean Habert and Brigitte Arbus for the considerable help they have given me with the research for this chapter. This pa chapter per is based on my article: Campbell 2011, originally delivered at 'The Renaissance and the Ottoman World' conference at SOAS, April 2006, but with the inclusion of new material.

[1] For a summary of the very extensive literature on this painting, see Campbell and Chong 2005–2006, 22–3, cat. 2; Carboni 2007, cat. 29, 305–6.

as a dialogue between a Venetian Senator and a Professor of Painting.[2] Boschini praises the Louvre painting highly, as a master work by Gentile Bellini, calling it an amalgam of: 'such / Variety of curious things, / Of dress, and fantastic people / Among the most beautiful that populate the Levant.'[3] Further details of Boschini's description, and the full information he gives regarding the painting's provenance, makes it clear that his subject is the Louvre painting. He mentions a 'Visir' seated on a sofa, with crossed legs, with two other figures behind him – a 'Mufti' and a 'Cadi', all dressed in white. They are surrounded by councillors, including religious officials. He continues to describe in detail the setting – there is a mosque, which he identifies as the former Church of Hagia Sophia: appropriately, since for Boschini, the painting is a view of Ottoman Constantinople, made for the city's Venetian consul.[4]

For two centuries, the painting retained this identification. But in 1895 Charles Schéfer pointed out that the costumes of the Muslim officials and the setting were Mamluk. Schéfer compared the painting with Zaccaria Pagani's celebrated account of the Venetian Domenico Trevisan's Embassy to the court of the Mamluk sultan Qansuh al-Ghuri at Cairo in 1512, and argued that the painting depicted Trevisan's first audience with the sultan, held on 10 May.[5] Later Pacha's identification of the Mamluk heraldic emblems represented so accurately in the Louvre *Reception* further strengthened Schéfer's argument.[6] Since then there has been no doubt that the picture represents a Mamluk scene.

However, Sauvaget subsequently noticed serious discrepancies between accounts of Domenico Trevisan, his 1512 Embassy, and the Louvre painting, and correctly identified the picture's setting as the Syrian city of Damascus.[7] The dome rising towards the left is that of the city's Great Umayyad Mosque, seen from the south. At the extreme left of the canvas (see Plate 28) is shown the western minaret, decorated with detailing in black and red stone. This minaret was constructed in 1488, and provides the *terminus post quem* for the Louvre painting's execution. Between the mosque's dome and the western minaret rises the bathhouse in the Grain market. In the middle plane, houses are sandwiched between the mosque, the baths and the walls. Elements of their appearance – including the wooden balustrades which surround the roof terraces, their balconies, and the courtyards planted with shrubs and trees – correspond to traditional types specifically associated with Damascus. The accuracy of these

---

[2] Boschini 1966, 49–50.
[3] This translation is by Julian Raby, in the catalogue, Levenson 1991–1992, 210–11, cat. 106.
[4] Boschini 1966, 49–51.
[5] Schéfer 1895, 201–4.
[6] Pacha 1906, 89–90.
[7] Sauvaget 1945–1946, 5–12.

and other architectural details is remarkable: for example the minarets are shown complete with struts from which lamps were hung.[8]

Venetian merchants had long gravitated towards Damascus, a well-watered oasis at the intersection of two important trade routes. As the setting for St Paul's conversion, and the location of important relics, including some of John the Baptist (fifteenth-century travel literature noted that these were set into the fabric of the Great Umayyad Mosque), the city was also host to Western Christian visitors en route for the Holy Land.[9] As Deborah Howard has suggested, Venetians were further attracted by the affinities between this ancient city, served by a network of canals derived from the Barada river, and their home.[10] With Alexandria, Damascus was probably the Republic's most important trading centre in the Near East.[11] It was also a congenial place to live – unlike Alexandria, which Pagani described in his eyewitness account of Trevisan's 1512 embassy as being nine-tenths in ruin.[12] Together with the Catalans the Venetians were the most numerous group of Franks in Damascus, and apparently the most respected and privileged. Venetian merchants resident in Damascus benefitted from special privileges, including the right to wear local costume and – following a treaty of 1442 – to live 'wherever they like in the land' (*habitar in che parte i vuol de la terra*), rather than being confined to the Venetian nation's trading colony, or *fondaco*.[13]

The Louvre painting (Plate 28) is perhaps the most remarkable surviving visual record of the Venetian community in Damascus. The right hand side depicts the reception of a Venetian delegation to a Mamluk official, presumably the viceroy (*nā'ib al-salṭana*) of the province[14] (for this formal occasion, the Venetians wear their customary dress rather than Arab clothing). This reception takes before the Great Gate of the Citadel, as was customary. The viceroy is seated on a dais (*masṭaba*), and wears the great horned turban commonly called *al-nā'ūra* (a nickname which aptly compared it to a waterwheel with projecting spokes), use of which was restricted to the Sultan and his highest officials, while others bear the tall *ṭāqiyya* on their heads.[15] A dragoman, or interpreter, stands between the Viceroy and the leader of the Venetian party: the latter is presumably the consul who was the highest ranking Venetian in Damascus. He wears the crimson toga with open sleeves (*maniche ducali*), a special style of dress to which strictly only the nine Procurators of San Marco, Venetian ambassadors abroad and consuls were entitled. His juniors are clothed in the customary black gowns and caps

---

[8] Ibid. 8; Raby in Levenson 1991–1992, 210.
[9] Casola 1855.
[10] Bianchi and Howard 2003, 240–41; Howard 2006, 20.
[11] Vallet 1999, 106.
[12] Pagani 1875, 17; Howard 2006, 20.
[13] Wansbrough 1965, 495–7; Vallet 1999, 226.
[14] Raby 1982b, 62; Tarawneh 1994, 27.
[15] Raby 1982b, 35.

(*barete*) of Venetian gentlemen and citizens.[16] Interestingly, the cloak worn by the Venetian at the far left resembles Cesare Vecellio's woodcut from the end of the sixteenth century representing the 'ancient costume of Venetian merchants in Syria'.[17] But even closer is a drawing in the Louvre (Figure 5.1), attributed by the museum to Carpaccio's circle, which definitely represents this man: its implications will be discussed further later.

As has been stated above, the architectural details of the Great Mosque, and the Mamluk dress have situated the Louvre painting between 1488 and the Ottoman conquest of Damascus in 1516.[18] Scholarly consensus, following Julian Raby's influential analysis of the 'Mamluk mode' in Venetian painting has further narrowed its chronological range to between 1488 and 1499, the date of Giovanni Mansueti's *The Arrest of Saint Mark* (Vienna, Lichtenstein Collection).[19] Raby argued that the unusual accuracy of the Mamluk motifs in the Louvre *Reception*, notably the heraldic blazons, meant that it must have been the conduit by which accurate visual information concerning Mamluk dress and customs reached Venice. This was used extensively by painters – including Gentile and Giovanni Bellini, Vittore Carpaccio and Cima da Conegliano – to add credulity to their depictions of Middle Eastern saints and the life of Christ.[20] The cleaning of the Louvre painting changes this assessment, for it has revealed the date 1511 in Roman numerals [MDXI] in the middle ground on the wall between the horse's legs (Plate 28).[21]

Any subsequent interpretation of the painting has to take account of this date. This was one of great significance for the Venetian colony in Damascus, during which they were entangled in extraordinary diplomatic intrigues. In July 1510 a Cypriot messenger, Nicolò Soror, and two Venetian merchants based in Aleppo were intercepted at the fortress of Bir on the north-west bank of the Euphrates. They were carrying compromising messages from Isma'il I, Shah of Persia, to the Venetian consuls of Alexandria and Damascus, Tommaso Contarini and Pietro Zen (1458–1539).[22] Both men belonged to families long active in the Levant and further east. Zen's father Caterino had been sent to Persia in the 1470s to negotiate an alliance against the Turks with the Aq-qoyunlu emperor Uzun Hasan. Although the Signoria concluded peace with the Ottoman sultan Mehmed II in December 1478, the possibility of using the Aq-qoyunlu and their

---

[16] Newton 1988, 12 and 15–16.
[17] Vecellio 1590, 71.
[18] Savauget 1945–1946, 9.
[19] Raby 1982b, 62–3; Schmidt Arcangeli 2007, 126; Kennedy, in Stefano 2006–2007, cat. 27, 304–305.
[20] Raby 1982b, 43, 52; Brown 1988, 197–8.
[21] Campbell 2005–2006, cat. 2, 22. I would also like to thank Brigitte Arbus for kindly discussing her conservation treatment and restoration of the *Reception* (in 2006) with me.
[22] Lucchetta 1968, 148.

Figure 5.1 Follower of Gentile Bellini, ca. 1511, *Study of a Young Man*. Pen, ink and body colour on paper.
Source: Musée du Louvre, Paris. © RMN / Thierry Le Mage.

territorial successors, the Persian Shahs, against the Turks was never far from the surface of Venetian diplomacy.[23]

Following his arrival in Damascus in 1508, Pietro Zen actively revived Venetian contacts with the Persian Sofi, as the Venetian documents consistently refer to him. Zen was in a very strong position to do this, since they were blood relations. Shah Isma'il's mother, Marta, was the daughter of Zen's great-aunt (the Despina Katerina, daughter of the last Greek Emperor of Trebizond); and indeed in a further twist, the Despina Katerina's daughters, in exile in Damascus, were alleged to have wished to take Zen's son back to Persia with them in 1512.[24] Acting on the Doge's behalf, Zen corresponded directly with the Sofi, and forwarded his letters to Venice through messengers. On 14 May 1509, as Marin Sanudo recounts, envoys from the Sofi themselves arrived in Venice, and appeared before the College two days later. They had travelled through Damascus, where Pietro Zen had translated their letters into Venetian.[25] Like Mehmed II thirty years earlier, the Sofi wanted Venice to supply him with artillery manufacturers. In return, he proposed that the Venetians join him in sending their combined military and naval forces against the Turkish sultan Beyazid II.[26] This was extremely dangerous ground for a Venetian living in Mamluk territory. During these years, the sultans of Cairo and Istanbul were allies against the Portuguese, who posed a mutual threat to their trading interests (having discovered the sea route to the Far East via the Cape of Good Hope).

Despite Zen's attempts at circumspection and secrecy, the 'Zen affair'[27] quickly gathered pace. The merchants arrested at Bir were soon joined by their patrons in Aleppo. In August 1510 – catastrophically for Venice – the Knights of Rhodes captured the entire Mamluk fleet at Laiazzo. The sultan blamed the Venetians for this, and subsequently ordered the imprisonment of all 'Franks' in his domains.[28] Zen's good relationships with Mamluk officials ensured that the confinement of the Venetian community in Damascus was brief. But their goods were confiscated, and they remained under house arrest. Subsequently, the Venetian consuls of Alexandria and Damascus were summoned to Cairo.[29] Zen arrived in the city in January 1511. His three audiences with the sultan worsened matters further, and the surviving documents suggest that great personal animosity existed between the two men.[30] After the second, the sultan ordered that all Venetian merchants in his lands be placed in chains. Following the third, the diplomat Zen shared the same fate. On the 4 April he wrote to the

---

[23] Ibid., 125, 137–8; Giraldi 1976, 129–31; Rogers 2005–2006, 81.
[24] Lucchetta 1968, 125, n. 60.
[25] Sanudo 1879–1903, vol. 8, col. 232.
[26] Lucchetta 1968, 137–8.
[27] Vallet 1999, 223.
[28] Lucchetta 1968, 159–60.
[29] Sanudo 1879–1903, vol. 9, col. 825; Lucchetta 1968, 161–2.
[30] Sanudo 1879–1903, vol. 11, cols 236–9; Pagani 1875, 31; Thenaud 1884, 196.

Venetian Signoria, requesting that they send either an orator or an ambassador to Cairo.[31] Only after every other possibility had been exhausted was Domenico Trevisan, one of the procurators of San Marco, dispatched to Cairo as ambassador in January 1512.[32]

A lost letter of 13 March, known through Sanudo's mention of it, sent from Damascus by the consul Nicolò Malipiero, records that the sultan eagerly awaited Trevisan's arrival.[33] In May he arrived in Cairo, and relatively quickly arranged for Contarini, Zen and their compatriots to be released from prison.[34] However, the sultan's anger remained directed chiefly at Zen. Narrowly escaping execution, or at least the serious threat of it, he was finally allowed to leave the Mamluk court on 20 May 1512. Ambassador Trevisan promised the sultan that Zen would receive proper punishment in Venice, and personally placed a chain around Zen's neck. Three hours later, Zen was permitted to accompany the Venetian delegation to their lodgings in Cairo – on foot, still in chains, and accompanied by a military guard.[35] But rather than harming Zen, the Mamluk sultan's treatment of him seems to have increased his repute among Venetians. It is notable that he was still called consul of Damascus after leaving the post. Despite his disgrace in Cairo, he returned home in January 1513, and was received on the occasion by the College with public acclaim.[36] Zen subsequently enjoyed a distinguished public career in the service of the Venetian state in the Levant, holding positions as significant as consul of Constantinople and orator to the Ottoman court on several occasions.[37]

I have recounted at some length the history of the Zen affair, because the setting of the Louvre painting, and the date inscribed on it implies its connection to these events. But who is the main Venetian it represents, and which reception might it show? Only four of the Venetians implicated in the 'Zen Affair' were entitled to wear dogal sleeves and crimson as official dress outside Venice: Trevisan, Contarini, Malipiero and Zen, and thus one of these must be the lead 'ambassador' represented in the Louvre painting. The picture's Damascene setting further excludes Contarini and Trevisan from the running (the former was consul of Alexandria, and Trevisan did not visit Damascus on his Embassy). However, both Pietro Zen and Nicolò Malipiero are referred to as the consul of Damascus in the years 1511/12. Which one of them is depicted in the Louvre painting?

Malipiero had arrived in Damascus in 1511, and logically, one might assume that we see him before the viceroy, presenting his credentials to the province's

---

[31] Lucchetta 1968, 169.
[32] Pagani 1875, 1.
[33] Sanudo 1879–1903, vol. 14, cols 246–7.
[34] Pagani 1875, 19–20.
[35] Schéfer 1884, 197.
[36] Sanudo 1879–1903, vol. 15, cols 174–5, 457.
[37] Lucchetta 1968, 109–10; Coco and Manzonetto 1985, 31–3.

authorities as was customary, and is described in numerous surviving accounts of Venetian consular activity.[38] However, while no image of Malipiero survives, there are several still extant of Pietro Zen, and I would like to advance the hypothesis that it is perhaps Zen who is represented in the Louvre *Reception*. In the late 1520s Alessandro Vittoria made a portrait bust of Zen (Venice, Seminario patriarcale). It is hard to connect this terracotta definitively with the lead Venetian in the Louvre *Reception*: however, a little-known portrait now in the Hermitage, probably made in Titian's workshop, makes this suggestion possible (Figure 5.2).[39] At the top of the painting, a strip of canvas added in the eighteenth century identifies the sitter as 'Caterino di Pietro Zen', and gives his age as 63.[40] Stylistically, the painting belongs to around 1520, and it seems far more likely that it represents Pietro di Caterino Zen, who was 63 in 1521. The similarity between the figure in the Louvre Reception and the Hermitage portrait makes this an intriguing possibility. In this context, it is worth returning to Boschini's description of the Louvre Reception in 1660 because – in spite of his mistake about the setting – he clearly knew the painting very well. He says that the painting was commissioned by the consul of Constantinople.[41] Pietro Zen held this post on two occasions in the 1520s, and was one of its two most significant incumbents during the sixteenth century, while Nicolò Malipiero was never consul of Constantinople.[42] This is far from being conclusive evidence, but it is fascinating even to consider that Pietro Zen could be represented in the Louvre painting. Zen's role in the Persian/Mamluk spying scandal gave him a certain celebrity in Venice, and the events provoked by his presence in Syria must have – at the very least – formed the impetus for creating the Louvre Reception. The painting's unique status could thus be explained by the unprecedented significance for Venice of the resolution of their diplomatic impasse with the Mamluks, seen in the context of the latter's precarious position vis à vis the Ottoman Turks (who were to assume control of the Mamluk Empire in 1516). The picture is unlikely to have been made in 1511, as the Venetian crisis in the Mamluk sphere of influence was still unfolding. Instead it seems more probable that the Louvre canvas was intended as a retrospective souvenir or mnemonic of Damascus and perhaps of Pietro Zen's life within it, commissioned following his return to Venice in 1513.[43]

This hypothesis is given credence by the painting's unusual depiction of an actual event – or at the least a highly convincing representation of an event which was known to have taken place – within a carefully constructed, somewhat

---

[38] Sanudo 1879–1903, vol. 12, col. 141. See also Howard 2006–2007, 84 and n. 59-67, who favours the identification of the lead 'ambassador' as Malipiero.
[39] Fomichova 1992, 332–3, cat. 254, where it is optimistically attributed to Titian.
[40] Ibid., 332.
[41] Boschini 1966, 49.
[42] Coco and Manzonetto 1985, 31–8.
[43] Campbell 2005–2006, cat. 2, 22.

Figure 5.2   Workshop of Titian, *Portrait of Pietro Zen*, around 1520, oil on canvas

Source: The State Hermitage Museum, St Petersburg.

imagined but convincingly realistic setting. No official reception of the Venetian community in 1511 is recorded by the numerous accounts of the 'Zen affair', although the meeting depicted accords well with descriptions of Zen's formal audience on his arrival in Damascus in late 1508, or that of Malipiero in 1511. The date on the painting, therefore, should not necessarily be read as the date of the meeting, nor as the date of the work's making, but as a remembrance of the most important of Zen's Mamluk years.

Nor do the buildings represented constitute a strictly accurate topographical view, although the position of the Great Umayyad Mosque suggests that it may have been depicted from the Venetian *fondaco* in Damascus (certainly it was taken from the side of the city where the Venetian trading colony was situated).[44] Rather, the painting is a compendium of several different views, made to assist the viewer to recall the salient features of the city, and also, perhaps, to provoke their memories of their life within it. The structures depicted range from public ones such as the Great Mosque, public baths, and the Great Gate, to private houses and gardens.[45] In the foreground at the left, a generalised street scene conveys the bustle of the busy city, with a man on horseback with two armed attendants in old-fashioned Syrian dress, heavily laden camels, groups of gossiping bystanders, and even a monkey in harness: all watched by women wearing uniquely Damascene head-dresses.[46] Such anecdotal details suggest considerable knowledge of Damascus, but not necessarily by the painter. They could easily have been supplied by a knowledgable patron like Pietro Zen, and depicted by a painter who – like many Venetians – was familiar with aspects of Damascene material culture and customs, despite having never visited Syria.[47]

What role did this painting play in the dissemination of Mamluk motifs in Venice? It is now clear that it was not the first Venetian pictorial evocation of the Mamluk world.[48] That honour must fall to Gentile Bellini's pupil, Giovanni Mansueti (active ca. 1485–1526/7), who made the depiction of aspects of this Muslim civilisation his speciality. As Catarina Schmidt Arcangeli has commented, Mansueti was far more precise than his other Venetian contemporaries, including Cima da Conegliano, in his representation of Syrio-Egyptian costume.[49] The *Symbolic Representation of the Crucifixion* in the National Gallery, London (Plate 29) which seems to belong to the early 1490s,[50] and even more, the *Arrest of St Mark* of 1499 made for the chapel of the Silk Workers Guild in the Crociferi (Vienna, Lichtenstein Collection) show Mamluks in a range of accurately depicted head-dresses and costumes, including the *tāqiyya*.[51] The *Symbolic Representation of the Crucifixion* is a painting of relatively modest scale. It has been called a processional banner, but on no more evidence than it was painted on canvas. It is probably

---

44 Sauvaget 1945–1946, 9.
45 Ibid., 7–8.
46 Raby 1982b, 54–60; Rogers, in Levenson 1991–1992, 82.
47 Bianchi and Howard 2003, 241; Howard 2005–2006, 19–21.
48 For this, see Raby 1982b, esp. 61–2 and 81–2.
49 Schmidt Arcangeli 2007, 126.
50 Davies 1961, 327–8 (NG 1478); Baker and Henry 2001, 406. NG 1478 was purchased by the National Gallery in 1896.
51 Raby 1982b, 35–52.

a painting mentioned by Sansovino in the Venetian church of Santa Maria de' Crociecchieri,[52] but its provenance is uncertain before its documentation in the Manfrin Collection, Venice, in 1856.[53] In view of the date on the Louvre *Reception* it now seems to include the first accurate representation of Mamluk clothing in Venetian fifteenth-century painting, even predating the Lichtenstein *St Mark* and Cima's *St Mark healing the Cobbler Ananias* (Berlin, Gemäldegalerie), the two surviving paintings from the St Mark cycle for the Guild of the *Setaiuoli*, dated between 1496 and 1499. The National Gallery canvas presents the Trinity, with the two Maries, John, James, Peter, Nicodemus and Joseph of Arimathaea. Mamluk clothing is used, as it were, to label Nicodemus and Joseph as inhabitants of the Levant, and within this context, as Jews. Joseph bears the *tāqiyya* on his head, while round Nicodemus's neck are the thin strips of white cloth which are also characteristic of Mamluk dress. Significantly, Mansueti's much praised accuracy had its limits: this is generic Mamluk costume, not that specifically assigned to Jews within the Mamluk domains. The Lichtenstein painting, which is dated 1499, is more ambitious. It represents Mansueti's first attempt to integrate crowds of Mamluks into complicated architectural *capricche*, his other salient artistic characteristic.[54] Again, the clothing worn by the many Mamluks is impressive for its accurate details.

Should the Louvre *Reception* therefore be attributed to Mansueti? Given his fascination with Mamluk imagery, this may seem a compelling hypothesis. Indeed a drawing at Windsor generally attributed to him is often said – wrongly – to represent three of the Mamluk officials standing at the right of the Louvre painting (it is actually a conflation of figures from the *Arrest of Saint Mark* and the *Scenes from the Life of St Mark*, ca. 1518–1526).[55] This evidence has been used to give the *Reception of the Venetian Ambassadors* to Mansueti. There is little doubt that he knew the picture, as his later works make copious use of details from it. For example, the Archer in *Saint Mark healing Ananias* (Venice, Gallerie dell'Accademia, ca. 1518–1526) seems to be a copy of the same striking (and archaic) figure in the Louvre *Reception*. However, the emphatically methodical and ordered feel of the Louvre painting seems a world away from Mansueti's liking for more busy compositions, which was strongly criticised by Carlo Ridolfi in *The Marvels of Art*. One sees this in many pictures, but perhaps never so clearly as in the *Scenes from the Life of Saint Mark* (Venice, Gallerie dell'Accademia) where figures in Mamluk turbans are crammed incoherently into every available space.[56] The Louvre *Reception*'s internal organisation is far more akin to Gentile Bellini's characteristic integration of figures and architecture in harmonious horizontal planes, exemplified by the *Procession in Piazza San Marco* (Gallerie

---

[52] Sansovino 1663, 168–9.
[53] Davies 1961, 328.
[54] For Mansueti, see in particular Brown 1988, 200–203.
[55] Campbell and Chong 2005–2006, 23.
[56] Ridolfi 1914–1924, vol. 1, 50.

dell'Accademia, Venice, 1496) and most appropriately of all, his final painting, *Saint Mark Preaching in Alexandria*, brought to completion by his brother Giovanni (Milan, Pinacoteca di Brera, ca. 1507).[57] While the Louvre *Reception* is clearly by a follower of Gentile (who died in 1507), working in his manner of ca. 1500,[58] its figural and architectural composition suggest very strongly that this painter was not Giovanni Mansueti.

Which of Gentile's many followers was responsible for the Louvre *Reception*? The artist had a close familiarity with the work of Gentile Bellini. He must have at the very least have had access to the artistic material which could be consulted in the workshops of the Bellini brothers. This is demonstrated by the motif of the stooping doe in the right foreground of the picture, which is replicated in another drawing in the Louvre, attributed to an artist in the circle of Jacopo Bellini and his sons, and which seems to this author to date around 1500.[59] But rather than Mansueti, several other possible candidates, or at least ambiences, for the authorship of this painting spring to mind, including Girolamo da Santacroce, Vincenzo Catena and the artist(s) of the Bellinian *Adoration of the Magi* in the National Gallery. Like the Louvre *Reception*, the National Gallery's *Adoration of the Magi* from the Layard Collection (Plate 30) has been associated with Carpaccio, Gentile and Giovanni Bellini. Presently ascribed to Giovanni Bellini's workshop, the similarly flat organisation of the front plane of figures in the foreground could suggest a comparison with the Louvre *Reception*.[60] However, the National Gallery *Adoration* – whoever it is by – seems to belong to an earlier visual tradition. It has closer connections with works from the 1480s and 90s, while details like the sleeves of the Venetian consul demonstrate that the artist of the Louvre *Reception* (Plate 28) is at least familiar with the artistic transformation of Venetian painting by Titian and his contemporaries in the first two decades of the sixteenth century.

An interesting hypothesis is that the Louvre painting could be connected with Vincenzo Catena. Giles Robertson, in his 1954 monograph on the artist, rejected the idea that Catena was responsible for the *Reception*.[61] However, the association of Catena with this painting has something to recommend it. Although there is no work approaching its narrative scale in Catena's oeuvre, he is alleged to have produced paintings of this type. Both the range and clarity of the colours found in the Louvre canvas resembles much of Catena's surviving work, from portraits

---

[57] Brown 1988, 203.

[58] Campbell and Chong 2005–2006, 23.

[59] Musée du Louvre, Départment des arts graphiques, RF 43328 recto, black chalk and brown washes on grey prepared paper. For an image of this drawing, see the Louvre's website, at the following address: http://artsgraphiques.louvre.fr/fo/visite?srv=mfc&paramAction=actionChangePage&idFicheOeuvre=501455#ancre8.

[60] I would like to thank Jill Dunkerton for sharing with me her thoughts on this painting, which she presented to the National Gallery Renaissance Seminar Group in 2003.

[61] Robertson 1954, 70, n. 1.

like *Doge Andrea Gritti*, former Venetian consul in Constantinople (first attributed to Catena by Johannes Wilde), to smaller scale private devotional works like the National Gallery's *St Jerome in his Study*.[62] Another salient feature of Catena's work, and the *Reception of the Venetian Ambassadors*, is the placement of figures in somewhat unconvincing two-dimensional spaces, often before a wall or another plain architectural setting, seen in the St Jerome, but most notably, in Catena's mature masterpiece, the *Holy Family with a warrior adoring the Infant Christ* (Plate 31). This comparison draws attention to the affinities between Catena's manner of working and the narrative mode of the Louvre painting: however its artist belongs among the less distinguished associates of the Bellini family workshop.

The drawing in the Louvre (Figure 5.1) mentioned earlier, a study for a member of the Venetian delegation, provides the key to the attribution of the Louvre painting.[63] This blue paper sheet is clearly Venetian, and although it has been most recently associated with Carpaccio, its affinities with Gentile Bellini's workshop are clearer still. Its use of thick ink lines with the brush to reinforce the outlines of the figures particularly recalls the drawing of *Men from the Procession in Piazza San Marco* (Turin, Biblioteca Nazionale). This has been called one of Gentile's studies for the Accademia painting,[64] but it seems rather to be a copy after the composition, arguably by the same hand as the Louvre drawing.[65] In contrast the latter sheet is probably a study, since the young man it depicts is represented slightly differently in the painting (compare plates 28 and 31). The artist of these drawings, whose style reflects his training in the Bellini shop and familarity with Gentile Bellini's artistic manner, seems the most likely inventor of the Louvre *Reception*. However, both sheets, although the production of a not particularly skilful workshop member, are indisputably of higher quality than this painting. A large canvas, it exhibits no pentiments or changes of any sort, and the technical quality of the painting is low, almost mechanical.[66] There seem no reasons for doubting that this famous work is an early sixteenth-century replica, albeit the prime surviving one (there are at least three others),[67] of a

---

[62] Ibid., 59, cat. 20.

[63] I should like to thank Claire Van Cleave for bringing this little known sheet (inv. 4795) to my attention.

[64] Meyer zur Capellen, 1985, 166–7, cat. D7.

[65] I am very grateful to Alan Chong, with whom I have examined and discussed this drawing extensively.

[66] These observations are based upon a discussion with Jean Habert and Brigitte Arbus of the x-radiograph of the painting.

[67] Wace and Clayton, 1938; Raby, 1982b, 59–60 and 91, n. 74; Meyer zur Capellen, 1985, 143–5, cats B8, B8a-c. Two are paintings, last known in the Stern and Langlade Collections in Paris. The third is the aforementioned tapestry at Powis, dated 1545: the publication of Helen Wyld's new research on this is awaited eagerly. Very interestingly, all three pictures have early French provenances, and the tapestry is apparently of French manufacture.

lost work by a better artist. But even this figure was an inferior follower of the narrative mode associated with Gentile Bellini.

Could the artist who invented the Louvre *Reception* have been Girolamo da Santacroce (ca. 1488-1556), one of Gentile's most loyal but least talented followers? The Louvre *Reception* has affinities with several pictures of the *Martyrdom of St Lawrence* by Girolamo and his workshop. Girolamo, from a village near Bergamo, trained in Gentile Bellini's workshop, and he evidently remained close to him. Bellini's will of 1507 includes a bequest of drawings to Girolamo his *garzone*, including some of his drawings of oriental figures. These drawings must have included the studies which have been associated with Gentile's visit to Constantinople – and there were presumably others, now lost.[68] Girolamo's small-scale paintings of St Lawrence are notable for the number of Mamluks they contain. But rather than crowding the pictorial space claustrophobically like his fellow Bellini pupil Mansueti, Girolamo's figures disport themselves with greater control and decor. They are remarkably static, like the participants in the *Reception of the Venetian Ambassadors*. Three versions of Girolamo's *Martyrdom of St Lawrence* survive. Two, in now in the Museo di Capodimonte, Naples and the Dresden Gemäldegalerie, are of much higher quality, and must be autograph works: perhaps the Dresden painting is the prime version. The third painting (Plate 32), which belongs to the Nelson-Atkins Museum in Kansas City, is more two-dimensional.[69] It is likely to be by a member of Girolamo's workshop.

It is tempting to suggest that this same workshop assistant may also have been responsible for the Louvre *Reception of the Venetian Ambassadors*, or as it should more accurately be called, *The Reception of the Venetian Community in Damascus*. Regardless of its author and quality, the painting's significance and its complexity has been enhanced by its recent conservation, and in particular the revelation of the date 1511 on the canvas. The Louvre *Reception* remains a unique visual record of an early sixteenth-century Venetian's remembered experience of Damascus, and of Venetian diplomacy, celebrated for its entrancing depiction of the Levant since the seventeenth century. But although a work of enormous interest as a document of political history, and of transnational and cultural connections, this picture does not belong to the highest rank of painterly production in early sixteenth-century Venice. Most ironically, this 'icon' for modern Islamicists was not made by a painter with deep experience of the Eastern Mediterranean, but by a moderately talented artist who probably never left Italy.

---

[68] Campbell and Chong, 2005–2006, 98–105.

[69] My thanks to Ian Kennedy and Scott Heffley for enabling me to examine the Nelson-Atkins painting. For the painting, see Rowlands 1996, 189–95.

Chapter 6

Giacomo Gastaldi's Maps of Anatolia: The Evolution of a Shared Venetian-Ottoman Cultural Space?[1]

Sonja Brentjes

Giacomo Gastaldi (d. 1566) was one of the most influential map-makers in Venice between 1539 and 1566.[2] He produced some one hundred maps and introduced a new era in the cartographic representation of Asia, Africa and two major regions of West Asia (Anatolia, the Fertile Crescent). All of his maps of Asian territories were very successful in Venice, Rome, Antwerp, Amsterdam and elsewhere, as the many copies, re-editions and revised prints show. Examples are the copies and reproductions made by Paolo Forlani, Gian Francesco Camoccio, Michele Tramezzini, and Antonio Lafreri in Venice and Rome, as well as those that Abraham Ortelius, Gerard Mercator, Jodocus Hondius, Willem J. Blaeu and Joan Blaeu made in Antwerp and Amsterdam. It is no exaggeration to claim that Gastaldi's maps of Asia, Anatolia and Syria, and to a slightly lesser extent of Africa, shaped Western European geographic views of the Middle East far into the eighteenth century in respect to two points – the usage of oriental or orientalising toponymy and the study of oriental sources. But did Gastaldi study indeed oriental sources and if so, which can be traced in his maps and proven to have been available in Venice between 1546 and 1566? Did he apply different approaches to creating his maps of *Asia Minor, Natolia, Imperium Turcicum,* and other parts of Asia? Do his maps differ in respect to their elements and cultural perspectives? These are the three main questions that I am going to explore in this paper in order to answer the question formulated in the paper's title: do Gastaldi's maps of Anatolia represent the evolution of a shared Venetian-Ottoman cultural space?

I will discuss these questions in regard to three maps created by Gastaldi between 1548 and 1564. Two maps are part of the first Italian translation of Ptolemy's *Geography* made by the Venetian physician Pietro Andrea Mattioli and printed in Venice in 1548 – the *Tabula Asiae Prima* and the map titled *Natolia, Nova Tabula.* The map of 1564 is called in the secondary literature *Asia Minor* or *Natolia.*[3]

---

[1] I thank The Map Collection, The British Library, for the Harley Fellowship, which enabled me to start the research that finally led to this chapter.
[2] Busolini 1999.
[3] See Almagià 1948, 34, Tavola VIII.

In the copies of 1566 and 1570, available to me, the map carries no separate title. In the dedication of the 1566 copy, for instance, the map is said to 'represent the natural (space) of the province of Natolia and Caramania and a part of Soria together with the Archipelago and a part of Romania'[4] (see plates 33 and 34).

Gastaldi's Two Maps of 1548

Tabula Asiae Prima forms part of the ancient maps that illustrate Mattioli's translation of Ptolemy's *Geography*.[5] It is a copy of the corresponding map from Sebastian Münster's new rendition of the work.[6] This choice was appropriate since Mattioli translated Münster's Latin text. Münster's map itself is derived from an earlier edition of Ptolemy's work, most likely from the Ulm 1482 edition.

Natolia, Nova Tabula forms part of the newly added maps to Ptolemy's *Geography* that pretend to offer 'modern' knowledge. A close look at Gastaldi's map shows that its novelty consists primarily in its use of elements from portolan charts. Gastaldi appropriated knowledge enshrined in portolan charts in his portrayal of the territorial outline of Anatolia and in his usage of parts of the map's toponymy.[7] A portolan chart whose outline of Anatolian territory comes close to that of Gastaldi is Grazioso Benincasa's chart of 1482.[8]

In general, the toponymy of *Natolia, Nova Tabvla* is dominated by Ptolemaic concepts. Intruders are elements from Christian church history, portolan charts, Venetian or Genoese trade, and possibly Western travel accounts about Asia. The name *Natolia*, a derivation of the Greek *Anatole*, is given to the entire territory, first in the map's title and then repeated as the inscription *Natolia Per Tvto* on the mainland. In almost the same size and prominence, the territory is then divided into several ancient provinces such as *Galatia, Panphlia* (sic), *Licia, Cilicia, Armenia Menor, Armenia Mazor, Capadocia,* or *Siria*. A further province in Gastaldi's map was not recognised as such in ancient geographical and historical writings, but was important as the place where one of the church concilia met – *Calcedonia*. From all of Gastaldi's provincial or regional names only one points to the major ethnical, political and cultural shifts, which had taken place in Western Asia since this concilium – *Erizeli*. The majority of the place names are also of ancient origin,

---

[4] The British Library, London, The Map Collection, CXIV/63. Other copies of the map were made in 1570 in Bologna (Zaltieri) and Venice (anonymous) or are undated (Donato Bertelli). See The British Library, London, The Map Collection, CXIV/64; Almagià 1948, vol. II, Tavola VIII, Tavola XXX.

[5] Ptolemy 1548.

[6] Münster 1540. See http://www.maphist.com/artman/publish/munster_1540.html, Map 17 and Ptolemaeus 1966, vol. V, vii.

[7] Almagià suggested already in 1948 that Gastaldi had followed portolan charts when drawing the contours of Anatolia. Almagià 1948, vol. II, 34.

[8] Benincasa 1482.

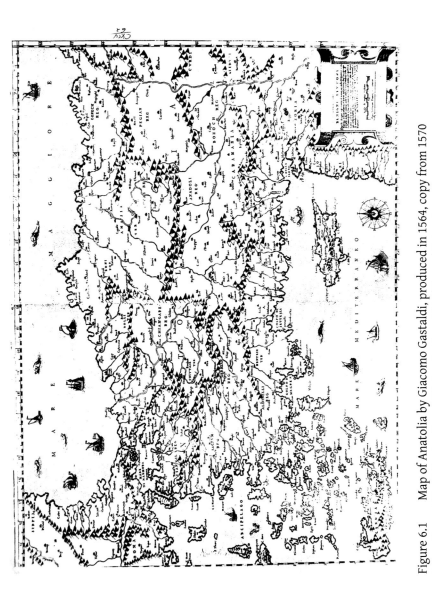

Figure 6.1　Map of Anatolia by Giacomo Gastaldi, produced in 1564, copy from 1570
Source: *Harvard Map Collection, Harvard University. Copyright of Harvard University.*

but some of them appear in vernacular Greek, Italian, or mixed forms such as *Laiazzo, Tarso, Apami, Setelia,* or *Caesarea Vechia*. Some of those names suffer under printing errors such as *Sanasta*. Other names are Western transformations of Arabic, Syriac or Turkish place names. Some of them can be already found in portolan charts such as *Soldino* in Syria. Others such as *Caraciafa, Casara, Cangre, Maras, Sis, Beida, Cageoy,* or *Antp* appear to have been borrowed from material available at the San Michele monastery.

When comparing Gastaldi's two maps of 1548 with each other, we find that ancient Greek concepts for structuring and dividing geographical space dominate Gastaldi's new *Anatolia* as they did in the case of his ancient *Asia Minor*. Hence, the novelty of Gastaldi's *Natolia, Nova Tabula* of 1548 is more a matter of declaration than a representation of new knowledge.

Gastaldi's Map of Anatolia of 1564

Things changed profoundly in the sixteen years that passed between 1548 and 1564. Gastaldi's new map of Anatolia differs substantially from the previous maps in several points. Its title describes the mapped territory by two components, *Natolia* and *Caramania*, rather than one, although the territory itself is again identified as *Natolia*. The margins have been extended to cover parts of *Soria, the Arcipelago, Romania, Candia,* and *Cyprus*. The longitudinal and latitudinal framing of *Natolia* and *Caramania* was extended towards the west and the east by approximately 1° in each direction and towards the north and the south by approximately 2° in each direction. In a sense, this enlargement of the mapped space allows the map-maker to inform the viewer about the new territorial changes in the east of the Ottoman Empire and about the standing of Venice within the Eastern Mediterranean sea and its adjacent lands. The inclusion of *Caramania* in the naming of the map may have served to alert the viewer precisely to these changes.

The extended framework indicates, on the other hand, that Gastaldi had no firm grasp of the geographical coordinates of Anatolia. This impression is confirmed by the additional modifications introduced by the map-maker with regard to geographical features such as rivers, lakes, and mountains. The relative position of Greek names in Gastaldi's new map of Anatolia has changed in comparison to his map of 1548 often by at least 1° either in latitude or in longitude, rarely in both directions. The change in the relative position towards a river, lake or mountain is occasionally even more remarkable. *Laranda*, for instance, is situated in the 1548 map slightly east of the lake, which surrounds *Acriotiri*. In the exemplars of Gastaldi's map of 1564 *Laranda* moved almost 2° to the south. It is now situated at the beginning of a river. While the river itself exists indeed, *Laranda* lies somewhere else. Such errors occur often in the exemplars of Gastaldi's map of 1564. Almost all names of provinces such as *Aidinelli, Mentese, Caramania, Bozoch, Alidvli,* or *Genech* are placed too far to the east and in a number of cases to the south. The provincial capitals often are situated outside the province's borders. The relative position of towns is rarely correct and occasionally even totally wrong as in the case of *Gerede* and *Bolli*. Exceptionally, such relative positions come close to reality as in the case of *Sinopi* (Sinop), *Ottomangiuch* (Osmancık), and *Amasia*. These observations indicate that Gastaldi had no clear understanding of the physical geography of Anatolia and no qualified help for checking errors. They also suggest that Gastaldi worked at least with two sets of sources: one for the Turkish names of towns, villages and rivers and their relative positions, another one for the names of provinces, territories and peoples.

The second major shift from the map of Anatolia of 1548 to the map of Anatolia of 1564 concerns the language used for names of regions, towns, villages and rivers. It has become more homogeneous in respect first to the public addressed by the map and second to the contemporary cultural and political conditions in the mapped territory. In the 1564 map, all classical names for regions and provinces have disappeared. The entire territory of Anatolia is now structured by Turkish 'regions, territories, and peoples' such as *Becsangil Reg:, Sarcvm Reg:, Aldinelli Reg:, Germian Reg:, Chivtaie Ter:, Bolli Ter:, Roni Pop:, Anadoli Reg:, Bozoch Reg:,* or *Pegian Reg:*.[9] Many of these names are easily identifiable as names of pre-Ottoman principalities such as Germiyan, Karaman, Menteşe, Aydın-eli, Saruhan, Turkish place names such as Kütahya, Çankırı, Bolu, or names of tribes, peoples, or rulers such as Besyan, Kurds, or 'Ala' ul-Din Dhu'l-Qadir, although several spelling errors as well as changes in Turkish orthography and pronunciation need to be considered in the process of identification. A few names remain ambiguous or unidentifiable such as *Becsangi(a)l* and *Roni*. The former may perhaps stand for *Begsancaq*, while the latter may be a slight misspelling of *Rūmī*.

The shift in names means that Gastaldi replaced his former classical approach to the Asian part of the Ottoman Empire by a description rooted in an Ottoman-Turkish identification of its various parts and regions and their pre-Ottoman and Ottoman histories. The same process can be observed with regard to many towns and villages that populate the map of 1564 and its numerous copies. Many of the Greek names found on Gastaldi's *Natolia, Nova Tabvla* did not make it into the new map. Gastaldi's shift in naming transformed *Asia Minor* as well as *Natolia* into *Anadolu* whose Greek past and present remained nonetheless visible.

A fascinating aspect of this transformation is that it happened through the working procedures applied by Gastaldi. Their conceptual consequences were not recognized by the mapmaker.[10] A close study of the new geographical terminology of Gastaldi's map of 1564 indicates that he was uncertain in his

---

[9] Several of these names taken from the copy of 1566 suffer under misspellings, which, while their spelling in the 1561 copy of Gastaldi's map of Asia, part 1 (original 1559) is either correct or better. Examples are Aidinelli and Sarcvm.

[10] Gastaldi also produced a map called *Turcicum Imperium* in 1555 which, however, I was not able to see and hence cannot judge for its conceptual features.

newly acquired knowledge of Anatolia. This uncertainty is reflected in a number of his choices. He integrated, for instance, several spellings of one and the same place name taken from different sources as different locations. Examples are the following four pairs of names – *Cunia, Cogno; Acsa, Acsara; Cangri, Cangria; Nigdia, Nigida*. He also interpreted names of rulers as place names as indicated by the following two examples – *Alidvli* and *Durgutoli*. The first name stands for 'Ala' ul-Din, a Dhu'l-Qadir ruler in eastern Anatolia. Gastaldi probably appropriated it from an anonymous Italian travel account whose author was identified as Domenico Romano who was in Iran from 1507 to 1510.[11] He derived the second name from Giosafatte Barbaro's letters written in 1472–1473, where the Venetian ambassador to Uzun Hasan talked about *Durgut Uguli*, a ruler of Konya.[12]

In addition to filling the territorial contours of Anatolia with hundreds of new place names, Gastaldi introduced further novelties into his new map. He changed the spelling and position of place names which he took from his previous maps. He increased the number of mountains and rivers noted and altered their positions. Finally, he modified the relative size of the mapped territory and its location in geographical coordinates. Most of the changes in physical space were not grounded in a greater familiarity with Anatolia's landscapes. The relative harmony and symmetry of the positions of new rivers and mountains rather seem to reflect shifts in ideas about what constitutes an ideal image of *Asia Minor* or *the lands of the Turks*.

Possible Sources of Gastaldi's Map of Anatolia

For more than a hundred years, the sources for Gastaldi's maps of Asia, but not that of Anatolia, have been debated time and again because Abraham Ortelius had remarked in his wall map of Asia (1567) on the authority of Guillaume Postel that Gastaldi had merely copied Abu'l-Fida's (d. 732 /1331) *Taqwīm al-buldān*.[13] In the secondary literature, two positions have been formulated. Historians of cartography such as Almagià pointed out that the number of towns from Abu'l-Fida's geography published by Gastaldi's friend and supporter Giovanni Battista Ramusio (1485–1557) in volume II of his *Navigazioni e viaggi* was too small to explain all the toponymy in Gastaldi's Asian maps.[14] The spelling of the names in Ramusio's extract and that in Gastaldi's maps did not always agree and the geographical coordinates differed between the two works. Most of the historians of cartography who engaged in this debate did not read any oriental language and

---

[11] Ramusio 1583, fols 78a–91a.
[12] See Anon 1543.
[13] See for a brief, albeit slightly faulty summary in David Woodward's review of Günter Schilder's *Monumenta Cartographica Neerlandica*, vol. 2: http://www.swaen.com/monumenta.html.
[14] Almagià 1948, vol. II, 65. Levi della Vida 1939.

hence had only one type of alternative sources to offer for explaining Gastaldi's rich oriental and orientalising toponymy – travel accounts and histories composed in Christian Europe. The prime candidate was Marco Polo's (d. 1324) *Divisament dou monde*, a variant version of which was also part of Ramusio's volume II. Additional options proposed were the accounts by the papal and royal envoys to the Mongol khans of the thirteenth and fourteenth centuries and to Timur in the early fifteenth century, the history of the Mongols by the Armenian emigrant and convert to Catholicism Hethum (1307), and the letters and reports by Venetian envoys to various Islamic dynasties in Western Asia. Already in 1901 Nordenskjöld pointed out that Marco Polo's text in Ramusio's version did not suffice as a source for all of Gastald'is names and coordinates.[15]

Scholars of the late twentieth and early twenty-first centuries, in contrast, have argued that Postel translated Abu'l-Fida's text and tables in 1553–1554 and that this translation was accessible to Gastaldi, but is lost today.[16] None of these scholars, however, included Gastaldi's map of Anatolia in the debate. Having checked Postel's manuscript of Abu'l-Fida's text in the Vatican, I cannot but support Almagià's claim in regard to Gastaldi's maps of Asia and extend it to his map of Anatolia.[17] Postel's manuscript carries in his handwriting a transliteration exactly of those place names that appear in volume II of Ramusio's *Navigazioni e viaggi*. This is insufficient for all of Gastaldi's maps. Furthermore, a good number of Gastaldi's Turkish place names are not found in the *Taqwīm* at all. The same is true for many of Gastaldi's Persian place names in the two maps of Asia mentioned above. Hence, Abu'l-Fida's geography cannot have served as a comprehensive source for Gastaldi's cartographic work.

Nordenskjöld's suggestion that Gastaldi could not have relied substantively on Medieval Latin or vernacular travel accounts and histories is also to be confirmed on the basis of the available philological and numerical evidence. As in the case of Abu'l-Fida's geographical work, the number of Arabic, Turkish and Persian place names used by Gastaldi surpasses substantially the nomenclature offered in Medieval Latin or vernacular sources. If we consider only Anatolia, the number of place names mentioned in this type of sources is less than a dozen. Since their spelling also differs from that used by Gastaldi it is highly unlikely that Medieval Latin or vernacular travel accounts and histories were his source.

In order to improve our understanding of the Gastaldi's working practices and sources of information I turned to other types of documents – Persian,

---

[15] Nordenskjöld 1910.

[16] Bellingeri 2003, 88–9; Fabris 1991, 58; Arbel 2002. This view is, in all likelihood, derived from Schilder's interpretation of Ortelius's statement on his wall map of Asia. See the link given in footnote 12.

[17] I thank the Vatican Microfilm Library at the Saint Louis University, Saint Louis, USA for the fellowship, which enabled me to study a number of microfilmed manuscripts among them the one mentioned here, i.e. ms. Città del Vaticano, Biblioteca Ambrosiana Vaticana, Arabe 266.

Arabic and Ottoman Turkish geographies and geographical tables; Italian letters and reports of ambassadors, merchants, and other travellers; Ottoman Turkish diplomatic letters; and Medieval world maps and portolan charts in various languages. The first set of documents did not yield convincing results. Italian diplomatic and commercial letters and reports of the late fifteenth and early sixteenth centuries occasionally provided Gastaldi with some information. Ottoman Turkish diplomatic documents may have confirmed his already available knowledge and added occasionally a new name. A few portolan charts gave Gastaldi specific Turkish, Greek and Italian names not found in the textual sources. A major source turned out to be one particular travel account which brought together information collected by a diplomat from Ottoman Turkish sources with the experience of a curious, young Italian traveller in the diplomat's entourage. However, all these identifiable sources do not suffice to explain the entire set of Ottoman Turkish and Greek toponyms used by Gastaldi. The only other assumption possible then is oral, personal collaboration between the map-maker and visitors to Venice. It is this combination of multiple sources of information and their diverse layers of access that turned Gastaldi's map of Anatolia into a cultural space inhabited by Venetian and Ottoman Turkish compatriots and their works. In the following sections, I will present the evidence for the specific forms of appropriation and adaptation that characterise Gastaldi's work.

Maps as Gastaldi's Sources?

Italian, Catalan, Spanish, Portuguese and French sea chart and world-map makers of the fourteenth and fifteenth centuries used three forms of naming Anatolia and its parts. They called it either by ancient names such as *Asia Minor* or simply *Asia* and listed its parts as *Bithynia, Pa<m>philia Capadocia, Ysauria*, etc. using Latin Medieval maps and texts as reservoirs from where to choose names and identities. A representative of this approach is Pietro Vesconte's world map in the various manuscripts of Marino Sanudo's *Liber Secretorum Fidelium Crucis* of 1320, 1321, and later years. A variant of this approach is constituted by sea charts and world maps of the fifteenth and early sixteenth centuries that use classical names, but lean rather on the now available Latin translation of Ptolemy's *Geography* than on Medieval Latin sources. An example for this variant is the sea chart by Diego Ribeiro of 1529.[18]

A second form consists in applying 'modern' names given in Catholic Europe to the region such as *Turchia, Natolia*, or in a Catalan variant *Naturi*, and combining these regional appellations with names for coastal towns, harbours, bays, caps, islands and a number of inland towns, rivers, and mountains of mixed ancestry – Greek, Italian, Catalan (?) and Turkish. Representatives of this approach are Guillelmus Soleri's sea chart of ca. 1385 and the copy of Juan de

---

[18] Mollat and de la Roncière 1984, no. 37.

la Cosa's sea chart of 1500 that clearly copies earlier Catalan charts.[19] A variant of this approach consists in suppressing a name for the region altogether and indicating only localities and the occasional river or mountain. A representative of this variant is the world map called Borgia V, a derivative of Fra Mauro's world maps ascribed to Gracioso Benincasa.[20] Greek names in Anatolia of Borgia V are for instance *acriotiri, sauastia de capadocia, cesaria capadocia, galati, amasia, laranda*, and *m. olinpo*. Turkish and Turkicised names are *boli, borli, belaçuch, calaçuch, hotmançuch, culasari, caraisar, ianisari, cogna, bursia*, and *iznich*. Italian and other vernacular names are, among others, *alto loco, follia uechia, Castelle comani, la roxa*, and *belueder*.

A third approach mixes classical and 'modern' concepts and regional names, independent of the origin of the latter. Angelino Dulcert, for instance, named in his sea chart of 1339 the region *TVRChIA*, explaining that this is the contemporary name of *Asia Minor* adding west of it and totally unconnected in much smaller letters *Naturi*. Vesconte Maggiolo identified in his world map of 1511 the region as *Asia minor turchia* and populated its south-eastern borderland with *turchimany*. Guillaume Brouscou, in his sea chart of 1543, kept as the only names for the region and its coasts *Natolie dit asie petitte*.[21]

A comparison of these three approaches to naming Anatolia and its parts indicates that Gastaldi followed in his 1548 map a variant of the first approach. He chose names mainly from classical and medieval sources with a clear preference for Ptolemaic names. While such a choice may seem appropriate for maps added to an edition of Ptolemy's *Geography*, it contradicts the claim to novelty in the map's title and its pretence to map Anatolia. In the map of 1564 Gastaldi chose a naming strategy very similar to that of Borgia V. In respect to the quantity of transliterated Turkish names, Gastaldi noted significantly more such names than the author of Borgia V. From among 47 names of towns in the interior of Anatolia on Borgia V, slightly less than a third appears to be either transliterated Turkish names or Turkicised forms of previous Greek names.[22] On Zaltieri's reprint of Gastaldi's map of Anatolia 347 names of places are found, seven of which belong to Syria. These seven names do not come from an oriental source, but were obviously taken from sea charts. Somewhat less than a fourth of the remaining 340 place names appears to be either of Turkish origin or Turkicised forms of former Greek names. In absolute numbers this means a more than fourfold increase in Turkish or Turkicised names in Zaltieri's copy of Gastaldi's map of 1564. The other exemplars of Gastaldi's map of Anatolia available to me differ from Zaltieri's reprint by showing a larger part of Syria and of the Aegean sea. Hence, they contain names not found in this reprint. The relative relationship between Turkish and Turkicised names versus Greek and other names does not

---

[19] Ibid., no. 9 and no. 22.
[20] Almagià 1948, vol. II, Tavola XIV.
[21] Mollat and de la Roncière 1984, no. 7 and no. 42.
[22] Almagià 1948, vol. II, Tavola XIV.

change significantly. In respect to the quality of transliteration, Gastaldi's choice is superior to the one by the author of Borgia V. Nonetheless, Gastaldi may have used information available at the monastery of San Michele where Borgia V is said to have been drawn in the second half of the fifteenth century. Not only names of more famous towns such as *Cogna* (Konya) or *Laranda* (Larende) appear in both maps. Both maps also share names of smaller towns, fortresses, or even camps such as *Osmancık, Külehisar, Beybazar,* or *Yenisaray*. However, Gastaldi did not appropriate every single name found on Borgia V. The transliteration of those he appropriated he improved. Since Gastaldi himself did not know Turkish, he probably had help in the process. The alternative assumption that Gastaldi used a source which contained already the Turkish and Turkicised place names in the way he spelled them is difficult to maintain. Not only is there no such single source known to me after having checked systematically a substantial number of maps and texts. The mixed character of Gastaldi's work and the repetition of several place names in deviant spellings speak against such an assumption.

Table 6.1   Similarities between Borgia V, Giorgio Sideri (1541) and Gastaldi's map of Anatolia[23]

Borgia V	Sideri	Gastaldi
Nigida		Nigida; Nigdia
ianisari/ianisar		
Silafchia		Seleschi; Seleucha
laranda (2)	laranda	laranda
Cogna	conia	cogna
Sidy		
Afimigraca		
Fijsari		
Nigroa		
Parati		Paterea
Cinabata	çinabaça	
Istaria	istaria	
Sourasari		Siurasar
Culasari		Culeisar
Acogis		
caraisar (?)	qarisar	caraisere
Acriotiri	acrotiri	Acrioteri

[23]   Tolias 1999, 90–91.

Borgia V	Sideri	Gastaldi
Ahasari	asari	Acsara
Tiria	tiria	Tiria
Pergamo	pergana	Pergama
Bursia		Bursia
Golia	golia	
Conrasa		
Hotmançuch	otinauçuch	Ottomangiuch
Bapasam		
Bol		Bolli
Belaçuch		
Calaçuch		
Çuedeta		
Borli		Borli
Isnic		Isnich
Toroncala		Roncala
Anguri	Anguri	Anguri
Galati	Galati	
cocia (2)	coria (?)	
Sultanasia	sultasit (?)	
Coimuas		
Marcariam		
Amasia	Amasia	Amasia
Vogala		
Comaria	coria (?)	
sauasti de capadocia		Suuas
cesaria capadocia		Caisaria
	Açilli	Azili
	Diçuas	
	Gianjsam	
	la cara casa	
	Efeso	
	Amatiria	
	Togata	Tocato
	Nicomedia	

Ottoman-Turkish Documents in the Venetian State Archives as Possible Sources for Gastaldi's Map of Anatolia 1564?[24]

In the end of the month of Shawwāl of the year 955 of the Hijra/mid-December 1548 (Venetian dating before the reform: late November, 1548), Sultan Süleyman sent from Aleppo a *Fethname* about his latest military campaign against the Safavid shahs to the Venetian Signoria. In the letter, he mentioned several names of towns, fortresses, and provinces mostly of the Asian domains of his empire as well as those he had conquered or battled against such as *Malāzkird, Arjīsh, Qaramān, Arz-i Rūm, Rūmelī, Anāṭūlī, Diyār Bakr, Rūm, Dhū'l-Qādir, Baghdād, Kirkūk, Vān, Shirvān,* or the fortress *Umaq*. Occasionally, the scribe of the Ottoman letter used a vernacular spelling, for instance *Ghazwīn* for *Qazwīn* or *Azarbayjān* for *Adharbayjān*. The *Fethname* was translated into Italian in November 24, 1548. When transliterating the Turkish, Persian, and occasional Arabic names, the translator followed mostly Turkish pronunciations. Hence, *Arjīsh* is rendered as *Erzis, Malāzkird* as *Melascherd, Diyār Bakr* as *Diarbechir, Arz-i Rūm* as *Arzrvm, Marant* as *Merent*, or *Azarbayjān* as *Edirbaizan*. Occasionally, the translator misread letters as when he rendered *Shirvān* as *Sirvan* or *Kirkūk* as *Chivrchi*. In the case of the two Persian towns *Iṣfahān* and *Hamadān*, the translator curiously opted for an altogether different sound, namely 'k' rather then 'h': *Isfechàn* and *Chemedan*. In a few instances, he chose not to transliterate the Turkish names, but to replace them by what he considered as cultural equivalents. Examples are *Romania* for *Rūmelī, Cappadocia* for *Rūm, Cilicia* for *Dhū'l-Qādir,* and *Tauris* for *Tabrīz*. In one case, the translator felt compelled to replace the Arabic *Āmid* by its original Greek form *Amida* and then to explain it by its Turkish variation *Carahemit* (Qara-Āmid).

The letter and its translation seem to have arrived in Venice in February 1549, if the date on the letter's envelope was meant in this manner. Hence, it was too late for being used in Gastaldi's map in Ptolemy's *Geography*. But was it used six years later? Almost all of the regions, towns and fortresses mentioned in Süleyman's *Fethname* are beyond the reach of Gastaldi'a map of Anatolia since it ends in a more western territory slightly east of the Euphrates. But what can be said about Gastaldi's map of Asia?

The first part of Gastaldi's map of Asia reprints a substantial part of his map of Anatolia. Then it extends further east as far as modern Afghanistan, Pakistan, and north-western India. Hence, Süleyman's *Fethname* may have been exploited for compiling information for this map. A comparison between the forms of transliteration in the Italian translation of Süleyman's *Fethname* and the forms used in Gastaldi's map of Asia speak to the contrary. The translator's *Diarbechir, Melascherd, Arzrvm, Carahemit, Erzis, Sirvan, Gasuin, Edirbaizan,* and *Isfechan* reappear as *Diarbech, Malagird, Erzervm, Arzervm,* and *Arxervm* in three different locations,

---

[24] I thank Maria Pia Pedani, Venice very much for presenting me copies of Turkish and Italian documents from the Venetian State Archives to help me in my research efforts.

Caramit, Ergis, Servan, Cazmin, Adilbegian, and *Ispaham.* Other names are absent such as *Marand* and *Hamadān.* Gastaldi obviously used several sources which he could not evaluate and hence integrated their different spellings and locations within one map. He took the spellings of his sources including substantial errors. The Italian translation of Süleyman's letter of success to the Signoria apparently was not among them.

Venetian Reports about the Ottoman Empire, the Aq-qoyunlu, and the Safavid Shahs

There were numerous Venetian reports about the Ottoman Empire sent from Istanbul or Aleppo to Venice from the early sixteenth century. Many of them contain place names. Some also list systematically names of provinces, districts and smaller administrative units. The Venetian documents about the Ottoman Empire report about the country's geography basically from four closely interrelated perspectives – the increasing territorial expansion of the Ottomans; the accumulation and distribution of wealth through military landholdings, taxation and tributes; the family affairs of the ruling Ottoman sultan; and military campaigns against the Safavids and Georgian principalities in the Caucasus mountains. A fifth issue is provided in Venetian documents from Iran reporting about the Signoria's efforts to forge alliances with the Aq-qoyunlu ruler Uzun Hasan and the Safavid shahs Ismail and Tahmasp.

The geographical concepts used to talk about these five points show similarities, but also marked differences. The presentation of the increasing territorial expansion of the Ottoman Empire relies mostly upon ancient geographical concepts, which occasionally are combined with contemporary local names in more or less apt spelling. The accumulation and distribution of wealth through military landholding and the system of taxation and tribute payments is discussed in a mixture of contemporary Ottoman and Italian terms, sometimes interspersed by ancient names. The geographical names needed when discussing the family affairs of the ruling Ottoman sultan are mostly taken from the small reservoir of transliterated names used by Ottoman sources. When the military campaigns against the Safavids are discussed, a mixture of ancient Greek and Latin names, contemporary misspelled and often truncated transliterations of Turkish, Arabic and Persian names, and correctly transliterated forms of local names in Turkish pronunciation appear. The documents about the negotiations with Uzun Hasan work mostly with local, contemporary names except for a few names of highly sensitive cultural meaning such as Constantinople. Travel accounts to the Safavid Empire mix ancient and contemporary local names, often using for the latter distorted transliterations. The analysis of the details of these differing approaches to geographical names and concepts shows that members of the educated elite tend to prefer ancient classical names for official, standard reports to the Signoria about a term of office in Istanbul or Aleppo, while letters reporting on political sensitive travels tend to prefer local names. Members of the elite even refer to Ptolemy in order to lend their geographical names and concepts the patina of age and the respectability of scholarship. Travellers outside the diplomatic service copy the behaviour of standard diplomatic reports, including quotations from Ptolemy, when their authors are young noblemen travelling in the retinue of the *bailos*. Anonymous documents and accounts by merchants tend to mix ancient and contemporary names without caring much for their spelling.

It is in diplomatic letters of the 1470s related to the negotiations with Uzun Hasan that a series of names appears, which resurfaces later in a deviant spelling on Gastaldi's maps. To this series of names belong for instance *Aydin, Sarchan, Malatia, Bir, Arzingan, Trapezonda*, or the region of *Caraman*.[25] Other names such as *Thocato Cesarea* or *porto de S. Thodaro de Charaman* do not appear in this form or even not at all on Gastaldi's maps.[26] This observation implies that Gastaldi did not use the letters' information in a systematic manner. That Gastaldi indeed used some of the letters is indicated by a set of place names, which the map shares with the letters by Giosafatte Barbaro mentioned earlier. To this set of names belong *Curco* (Korghos), *Seleucha* (Silifke), *Anguri* (Ankara), *Aidin, Cunia* (Konya), *Anamir, Arminico, Durgutoli, Candeloro, Pally*, and *Arcalach*. In Barbaro's letters these names appear occasionally in slightly different spellings such as *Animur, Arminiacho, Pallu*, and *Scandeloro* or in variable spellings such as *Cunia* and *Cogno, Curco* and *Colcos, Seleucha, Selefica*, and *Selefecha*.[27] Gastaldi was not only uncertain, which of the different spellings was preferable, he also thought that some of them indicated different towns. Hence, he marked *Cunia* and *Cogno* at two different localities. As already mentioned, Gastaldi used occasionally names of rulers to indicate a region or a town, misunderstanding obviously the information given by the author of the text he was reading. Such a misunderstanding occurred with regard to *Durgut Uguli*. Barbaro described this man as *Vaivoda nel ditto loco*, which in the context of the letter can only mean *Cogno*.[28] Gastaldi, however, added to *Cunia* and *Cogno* a third place called *Durgutoli*.

Gastaldi also had difficulties in identifying the position of several places mentioned by Barbaro. He situated, for instance, *Seleucha* and *Anamir* far into the interior of Anatolia, while both localities are ports on the Mediterranean coast. Several names of castles, villages, towns and mountains given in Barbaro's letters did not make it into Gastaldi's maps, even if they occurred more than once like *Charasaria* (Qarasaray), *Fora* (Euphrates), or *Selefica* (Silifke). The diplomatic letters about the negotiations with Uzun Hasan do not cover all the names found in Gastaldi's maps of Anatolia. Even when we combine them with the names borrowed from material available at San Michele, many names remain unaccounted for in Gastaldi's map of 1564.

[25] Cornet 1856, 28, 29, 41, 43, 80, 83, 126, 127.
[26] Cornet 1856, 60.
[27] Cornet 1852, 32, 34–5, 47, 52–5, 79, 123.
[28] Ibid., 52; Cornet 1856, 79, 121.

The material of Venetian visitors about Safavid Iran does not prove of more consequence for Gastaldi's map than that of their predecessors. Michele Membré (d. 1594), for instance, was one of the envoys sent by Venice to the Safavid dynasty. In the report about his diplomatic mission to Shah Tahmasp, which took place from 1539 to 1542, he talked of fifteen localities in Ottoman Anatolia, the spelling of only three of which agree with that used by Gastaldi as shown in the following table.

Table 6.2　Differences between Membré's travel account to Iran and Gastaldi's map of Anatolia

Membré	Gastaldi
Manissia	Magnesia
Caraissare	Caraisere
Anguri	Anguri
Suverrassar	Siurassar
Cancria	Cangria
Arzinjan	Arzingan
Namisso	
Marzinvan	Marzuan
Trapezonda	Trapezonda
Adana	Adena
Tarsus	Tarso
Sinop	Sinopi
Marand	

When we turn to Venetian documents from the Ottoman Empire, the situation is even worse. Among the many Venetian reports about the Ottoman Empire available to me and published before Gastaldi drew his map there is only one document that contains names relevant for Gastaldi's map of Anatolia of 1564. It is an enriched variant of the standard description of the Ottoman provinces found in reports by Venetian ambassadors to the Ottoman court. This variant is attached to a travel account called *Libri tre delle cose de' Turchi* by the Venetian gentleman Benedetto Ramberti. It was published in Venice in 1541. Three other versions of this account were published in Venice in 1539 and 1543, but only the print of 1541 contains the text mentioning the names that are of interest here. It is altogether unclear why this list can be found only in this particular edition and who decided to include it.[29] Ramberti embarked on 4 January 1533 at Venice travelling to Istanbul together with the secretary Daniello de' Ludovisi who took on the duties of the *bailo*.[30] Preto and Bellingeri highlighted the structural similarities between Ludovisi's report to the Signoria and Ramberti's travel account.[31] With respect to the information about Ottoman provinces, however, the two texts differ. The most important difference in respect to Gastaldi's later map is that Ludovisi does not list the names of the major districts within each of the Anatolian provinces, as does the 1541 edition of Ramberti's text. Additionally, there are some differences in spelling. Nonetheless, Ludovisi may well have been the ultimate source for the short list of districts given in the appendix to Ramberti's account. If indeed the 1541 edition of Ramberti's text was a direct source of Gastaldi's map of Anatolia, as it seems to be the case, then again the cartographer modified the spelling of several of the names substantially and ignored some of them. The information provided by Ramberti thanks to his travel to Istanbul allowed Gastaldi an indirect access to Ottoman Turkish sources on Anatolian geography and administration. Gastaldi's map of Anatolia of 1564 hence reflects a shared Venetian-Ottoman cultural space in more than one meaning.

Table 6.3   Names of Ottoman provinces, districts, and towns in Ramberti's *Tre Libri de cose de Turchi*, Gastaldi's map of Anatolia (1555 and later exemplars), and Ludovisis's report

Ramberti	Gastaldi (1566, 1570)	Ludovisi
Natolia che era anticamente Asia minor	Natolia	... la Natolia ..., che è l'Asia Minore, ...
Caramania, che era anticamente Cilicia	Caramania	Caramania, che è la Cilicia, ...
Amasia & Toccato, che era Cappadocia	Amasia, Tocato	... l'Amasia e Toccato, che è la Galazia e la Cappadocia, ...
Anadoule, che è loco tra la Soria, Caramania, et & (sic) Toccato, quale era anticamente Paphlagonia, & è la mità dell'Armenia minor	Anadoli	... il paese di Aliduli, nel quale ... è l'Armenia Minore

[29]   Bellingeri 2003, 92–3. I thank G. Bellingeri for his support and friendly help in clarifying the relationship between the various editions of the *Tre Libri delle cose de' Turchi* and in giving me information about Ramberti, Ludovisi, and other Venetian dignitaries in Istanbul.
[30]   Preto 1975, 326–7.
[31]   Ibid., 327. Bellingeri, letter to me, 14 July 2003.

Ramberti	Gastaldi (1566, 1570)	Ludovisi
Mesopotamia, sotto alquale è il resto dell'Armenia minore, & parte della maggiore	Alidvli	… il Diarbek, che è la Mesopotamia, con parte dell'Armenia Maggiore …
Damasco, & Soria & Giudea	Parte della Soria	… la Siria e la Giudea sotto il beilerbei di Damasco
Chiothachie	Chivtaie	
Chiogiaeli		
Boli	Bolli	
Castamoni	Castamoni	
Anguri	Anguri	
Cangri	Cangri	
Thechieli	Tachiali	
Matesseli	Menteseli, Mentese Ter.	
Aydineli	Aidinelli, Aldinelli Reg., Aiduaelli (sic, 1570)	
Hallayce	Alaser (?)	
Buga	Buga	
Magnesia	Magnesia	Magnesia
Amasia	Amasia	
Chiorme	Chiorme	
Gianich	Gianich	
Charaysser	Caraisere	
Sansum		
Trabisonda	Trabisonda	Trebisonda
Naranda	Laranda	
Ciogna	Cogno	
Axar	Assar, Azar	
Eschissar		
Versageli	Versageli	
Siurassar	Siurasar	
Maras	Marar (1566, 1570)	
Sarmussaeli	Sarmusada (1566, 1570)	
Albistaucrassi	Elbustan	
Adana	Adena	
Tersis	Tarso	
Malathia	Malatia	
Payburt (in Diarbakr)	Baiburt (in Canik)	

Oral Informants

The main argument for Gastaldi's use of oral information about Anatolia comes from the quality of the transliteration of the oriental toponymy found in his maps. The relationship, for instance, between the Turkish names and their Italian transliteration surpasses all forms of transliterated Turkish geographical names found in travel accounts, letters and reports by Venetian diplomats, merchants, gentlemen travellers, soldiers and adventurers of the period. This also holds true for transliterations in travel accounts, letters and reports by travellers from other Catholic, as well as Protestant, nations or towns in Europe during the sixteenth and seventeenth centuries. The sources of such a knowledge of Ottoman geography, history and language must be sought either in one or more Turkish texts, which were translated for Gastaldi, or in Latin or vernacular texts written by a Catholic or Protestant traveller or prisoner of war with excellent knowledge of Turkish or with access to an informant with excellent knowledge of both Turkish and Italian, or another Western language. However, no textual source which would satisfy most of Gastaldi's nomenclature could be found so far. An additional argument is derived from the differences between the transliterations of Ottoman Turkish place names in the Borgia V map as compared to Gastaldi's map of Anatolia of 1564. If Gastaldi indeed had access to this map or other material available at the monastery of San Michele, these differences cannot have been introduced by Gastaldi himself since he did not know Ottoman Turkish or any other oriental language. Hence, Gastaldi must have encountered someone with excellent knowledge of Turkish and Italian. The lesser quality of transliterations found in papers of the Venetian State Archives suggest that this person or persons was not one of the interpreters of the Signoria, but rather a foreign visitor to Venice. Other transliterated place names in Gastaldi's map such as *Ineiul* (Inegöl), *Felechedin* (Falak al-Dīn), *Cursunli* (Cursunlı), *Chiorlich* (Çorlu), *Mugla* (Muğla), *Acsu* (Aksu), *Genisar* (Yenihisar), *Desgnisli* (Denizli), *Chiutaie* (Kütahya), or *Chiarsamba* (Čaharşambe) support such an interpretation. Since Gastaldi was, as is well known, befriended with Ramusio and Membré with whom he dined occasionally in San Michele together with merchants from the Ottoman and Safavid Empires such as *Chaggi Memet* (Ḥājjī Muhammad) from *Chilan* (Gīlān), assuming oral help is not a far-fetched idea.[32]

Conclusions

Gastaldi, as we have seen, did not study any oriental source directly. But he accessed oriental knowledge through diverse indirect channels. As a result, a multilayered cultural space was inscribed into the different maps which he created of Western Asia and its regions. The most important feature of this

---

[32] Fabris 1993, 35.

multilayered cultural space is its slow transformation from a space that was dominated by one kind of culture to a space which several cultures inhabited. This shared cultural space was created through Gastaldi's eclectic mode of map-making which allowed him to approach sources of different kinds in his search for information. This eclecticism rested on the actual physical sharing of the geographical territories represented by Gastaldi through travelling for the sake of diplomacy, politics, commerce and leisure. Its ability to accommodate conflicting information as well as elements of an imagined nature stems from epistemic values and mechanisms of evaluation that privileged authorised sources, but downplayed the need for deciding which coordinate or which spelling was better than the other. The cultural space expressed in Gastaldi's maps is thus not only made possible by a shared physical presence in geographical space. It derived at the same time from a specific kind of intellectual space inhabited by early modern map-makers and printers. The single most important component of Gastladi's new knowledge represented in his map of Anatolia of 1564, the Turkish and Turkicised place names, imply a belief in the superior value of contemporary local knowledge over knowledge traded in books and maps alone. They also reflect a shrinking relevance of ancient geographical concepts and names for the Venetian map-maker, his successors and their customers. It is in these two elements that the cultural space inscribed in the maps of Gastaldi and his successors differed substantially from the one described in books. Gastaldi's decision in favour of contemporary Ottoman geographical and administrative terminology proved of great importance for the diversion that separated maps of and texts about the Ottoman Empire and Western Asia as made or written in Catholic and Protestant Europe for the next two and a half centuries. While the written word remained closely affiliated with ancient Greek perspectives, maps reflected primarily knowledge written down in Arabic, Persian and Ottoman Turkish geographies, histories and administrative documents, as well as inscribed in maps from those cultures. It is through this conceptual decision that Gastaldi managed to transform the broader culture that linked Venice and the Ottoman Empire in the sixteenth and seventeenth centuries into a shared cultural space portrayed in maps.

Chapter 7

Turning a Deaf Ear

Owen Wright

As this is the only chapter devoted to music it seems sensible to offer, rather than the detailed exploration of a specialist topic, some kind of marginal commentary draped around the more substantial and in-depth examinations of ideas and objects that constitute the core of the present volume. A brief general survey, in short, that attempts to outline, however sketchily, the trajectory of musical contacts and perceptions, to account for fluctuations in interest and comprehension, and also, incidentally, to take account of some of the ways in which music is represented visually. To be comprehensive, though, is out of the question; rather, a few representative instances will be considered, some of which, in relation to any conventional art-historical Renaissance time frame (say 1400–1600), will be impudently anachronistic. The justification for this is to be sought both in the exiguous nature of the evidence, which necessitates trawling rather more widely through time, and in the artificiality, for music, of whatever chronological slicing is standard for art.[1]

Nor should we expect, despite occasional points of comparison, that Ottoman-European musical relations, whether within or beyond the temporal confines of the Renaissance, will provide a close analogy to those that obtain in the visual domain. At first blush this might seem surprising, now that we have become conditioned to see the arts as unavoidably entangled in the same social and ideological webs, and hence to pursue parallels between them in relation to patronage, status, production and reception. We are accustomed to analyses of the intellectual strands tying together artists, writers, architects and composers at particularly propitious moments.[2] But these imply spatial as well as temporal compression: they are generally monocultural and effectively monolingual, and in the absence of such compacted overlapping, when one should speak, rather, as in the present case, not merely of conflict but of geographical separation, cultural and linguistic barriers, and of doctrinal hostility and fear undermining the human gains of diplomacy and commerce, the expectation, or at least the hope, that we might disinter equivalent musical counterparts to the reciprocal

---

[1] See e.g. the article 'Renaissance' in *Musik in Geschichte und Gegenwart* for a discussion of the problems involved, following on from the initial statement that the term has '*zwar weite Verbreitung erfahren, war und ist aber sowohl inhaltlich als auch methodisch umstritten*', and likewise Owens 1990.

[2] E.g. Schorske 1981 and Harvey 2003.

transfer of artefacts between Europe and the Ottoman world and the stylistic enrichment that flowed from them is as unreasonable as it is illusory, and this for the most obvious of reasons: music does not generate objects. It is, rather, a social activity and an experience, usually enjoyable and possibly profound, but still transient and impermanent, recuperable only from memory, so that except in the case of a score transferability is limited to what human contact allows, and it is worth emphasising that scores are highly specialised products of limited applicability. They may enable and up to a point control future realisation, but can only mediate between groups with a common cultural grounding, an insider command of their many conventions and, normally, of the style they imperfectly represent. Western notation can thus be used with varying degrees of approximation and efficiency (or inefficiency) to convey impressions of other idioms, but works much less well as a vehicle for exporting information about Western music to another culture ignorant of it, even if potentially receptive, while the partial equivalent of notation within the Ottoman and Persianate worlds during the fifteenth and later centuries, the annotated song-text, could not have served this purpose at all, for however detailed, it functions as a mnemonic aid to future realisation by someone who has already learned the piece, and could therefore never be used to communicate a repertoire to the uninitiated outsider.

How, then, between Europe and the Ottoman world, could musical communication occur? How could interest be provoked and transfers effected? Setting aside for the moment the world of ideas that can be conveyed at a distance by the written word, it is clear that direct and sympathetic human contact is required if there is to be any transmission of repertoires, styles or techniques, any real possibility of mutual appreciation and the consequent desire to borrow and absorb. Instruments could theoretically be regarded as potentially neutral, as inert exportable objects, but the impulse to acquire them can hardly have come just from an appreciation of the workmanship involved: exposure and receptivity to their use in performance is an obvious precondition. Thus whatever the degree of earlier European indebtedness to Islamic musical culture as it had evolved in al-Andalus, there can be no doubt that the enabling condition was the existence there, despite intermittent conflict, of sustained contact at the human level. The *Cantigas* miniatures, for example, can no doubt be variously read, but certainly accord with the notion of earlier musical *convivencia* surviving still at the thirteenth-century court of Alfonso el Sabio (Plate 35). Islamic decorative elements may be noted in later Spanish representations of lutes,[3] and the diffusion of borrowings from Arab musical culture is clear, above

---

[3] Matoušek 1994 notes 'oriental influences' in the design of rosettes and intarsia on a lute in a fourteenth-century altarpiece (of the castle church of St Coloma at Quaralt, now in Barcelona, Museo de Belles Artes de Cataluña). The scene in which it appears is the suitably 'oriental' one of Salome dancing before Herod.

all, from the enrichment of the range of instruments.⁴ This would be further reinforced by Crusading encounters, from the late eleventh century to the late thirteenth, with Middle Eastern military ensembles of trumpets, shawms and impressive percussion instruments. Joinville, for example, records the capture of kettledrums (*nacaires* < *naqqāra*) at the siege of Damietta in 1249,⁵ and the frightening impact of these ensembles, which Europeans were quick to imitate, is reflected in numerous Old French and Middle High German literary references.⁶ Within the established communities of the Crusader kingdoms military confrontation often yielded to more peaceful contacts with Islamic culture, resulting in the employment of a clearly Islamic visual language in the representations of court musicians flanking a ruler that are incorporated into the frontispiece of a late thirteenth-century *Histoire universelle*.⁷

If we turn now to Italy, the late fourteenth-century 'Intemperance' from the Genoese *Tractatus de septem vitiis*⁸ reverts to the Islamic military instrumentarium, but offers us an intriguing cross-cultural group serenading an evidently oriental as well as over-indulging potentate (Plate 36).

The, by now, quintessentially Western organ is here combined not only with trumpets but also with kettledrums carried by a black, presumably 'Moorish' musician playing cymbals (and to the modern eye the hierarchical layering of the pictorial arrangement is itself reminiscent of Islamic miniatures).⁹ Yet whatever the visual reading of this miniature, the very presence of the organ warns against a facile interpretation of the other instruments and their performers as indicators of morally suspect alterity. Indeed, we may assume that by the beginning of the Italian Renaissance any Arab elements that had been incorporated long before into the musical idioms of Spain (or Sicily, for that matter) and transmitted thence would have been fully integrated, and that both the instruments acquired during the Crusades and, especially, those that

---

⁴ For a general outline of developments in Muslim Spain see Wright 1992, and for a dispassionate assessment of the vexed question of the extent of Arab musical influence in Europe see Perkuhn 1976. Exemplary for the way in which the significance of this whole cultural encounter can be marginalised is its isolation within the first volume of *The new Oxford history of music* (Farmer 1957), while in the recent multivolume survey *The Oxford history of Western music* (Taruskin 2005) the emphasis on notated sources also allows it to be given short shrift.

⁵ Marcuse 1975, 281b–82b.
⁶ For an extensive survey of the field see Bowles 1971.
⁷ British Library MS Add. 15268, fol. 2. See Zeitler 1997.
⁸ BL. Ms Add. 27695, fol. 13r.
⁹ One of the frontispieces of the six-volume 1216–1219 *kitāb al-aghānī*, for example, has a princely figure placed centrally with attendants above and musicians segregated into a band at the bottom. However, there is no reason to assume access to such material, and earlier Christian art provided abundant models for the spatial disposition of the figures in this miniature.

Figure 7.1   Piero della Francesca, *Natività*, 1470–1475, oil on poplar
Source: London, National Gallery, NG 908. © The National Gallery, London.

had been diffused over the centuries from the Islamic cultural environment of Spain and had subsequently evolved further, such as the fiddles in Plate 38, had long lost any sense of strangeness: awareness of their ultimate origin had lapsed, and with it any possible association with Islamic culture. Hence Piero della Francesca's angels in the *Natività* can happily play rebec and lutes[10] (Figure 7.1), the Arab derivation of which would have been no more perceptible than that of the pseudo Kufic inscription that some years before had decorated the

---

[10]   For Vincenzo Galilei, writing in the late sixteenth century (Galilei 2003, 367), the lute originated in decidedly non-Islamic Pannonia (= Hungary).

angel's drum in Fra Angelico's Linaiuoli Tabernacle of 1433[11] (Plate 37). Musical iconography, accordingly, is happily eclectic, and in Fra Angelico's even earlier *Christ Glorified in the Court of Heaven* (1423–1424) the inclusion of instruments of Arab provenance again implies no awareness of their source. They have been fully domesticated and have none of the exotic aura that may have been associated with them on their first appearance: the angelic host simply exults in the joyous possibilities of celestial concord that their inclusion allows (Plate 38).

By the time of Fra Angelico one may surmise that at the level of art music an Italian and a Middle Eastern musician would have employed the lute to rather different effect, and with correspondingly different playing techniques: the increasing emphasis on polyphony in the West meant that the two cultures were simply growing further apart, to the extent that even if the opportunity presented itself they would now probably be unable to appreciate what the other had to offer. While resident in Naples in the early 1480s, Johannes Tinctoris (d. 1511) was able to hear a Turk play a *tanbur* (a type of long-necked lute that to him resembled 'a large spoon'), and was at least interested enough to describe its tuning in his *De inventione et usu musicae*.[12] But only towards the end of this treatise does he offer a reaction to the music, one in which his insight into human motivation – they play to express homesickness – is brushed aside by the curt comment that the performance just went to show how uncouth they are (*quod solum id ad eorum ostendendam barbariem*), a pallid reflection of the standard propagandistic view at that time of the Turks as savage invaders notorious for their cruelty and blood-lust.

The complete absence of sympathetic response in this particular instance, let alone of musical exchange or transfer, may be regarded as symptomatic of a wider Western indifference at the level of high culture to the Ottoman musical other, and one reciprocated by Ottoman attitudes to European music, that appears to typify the fourteenth to mid-seventeenth centuries. The ramifications of the Ottoman impact on military music are undeniable, and there must have been numerous unrecorded contacts and exchanges at the popular level, but although the literature available to the Renaissance readership contains several brief items of information and occasionally vivid personal reactions, the intellectual community provides scant evidence of willing engagement, let alone receptivity. At the same time, paradoxically, the Middle East is musically present throughout this period, albeit in comedic distortion, at first in the form of the *moresca*, a parody dance that by the sixteenth century had become an ingredient of Italian stage interludes,[13] and later through the emergence and increasing popularity of *turquerie*, a more generalised form of representation included in the ornate

---

[11] Or the Arab derivation of the shawm played by another angel in the Linaiuoli Tabernacle.

[12] Weinmann 1917.

[13] See Taylor 2007, 21 for a much earlier (1393) instance, an aristocratic entertainment that ended in tragedy.

tableaux integral to lavish ceremonies patronised by court circles. Indicative here is the presence of Turkish models in a Milanese tailor's stock book of the second half of the sixteenth century,[14] while Molière's inclusion of comic pseudo-Turkish elements in *Le bourgeois gentilhomme* (1670) provides just one of numerous instances of an Ottoman presence on the stage.[15] But however realistic the costumes may have been, there is nothing authentically Turkish in the music that Lully provided to accompany these scenes: although a language of musical exoticism would certainly emerge, its conventions were arrived at less by direct borrowing than by developing (or distorting or even suppressing) pre-existing elements within its own resources.

Objective information on Turkish music was in any case by no means easy to find. The general inquisitiveness of the educated reading public, which revelled both in strange tales and in more sober ethnographic reports of the East, had its appetite fed by the publication of numerous accounts of pilgrimages, gradually supplemented (and supplanted) during the sixteenth century by a more factual and somewhat less biased literature produced by travellers and returning diplomats that occasionally included illustrative woodcuts and reactions to, and observations about, music, performers and instruments, and even, in one or two exceptional seventeenth-century instances, brief samples of notation. However, these were too fragmentary and selective to build up a coherent, comprehensive knowledge base, and in any case the general message of what one might term the ethnographic discourse they rely on and perpetuate was hardly enticing: one way or another the impression conveyed was normally one of Turkish musical inadequacy, or if not inadequacy then unpleasantness of sound. One of the earlier witnesses, Guillaume Postel (1510–1581), already uses in his description of a wedding procession the simple but typical formula of factual report followed by denigratory comment that will recur in later accounts. The accompaniment, he informs us, consists of several percussion, wind and string instruments (*tabourins, cimballes, bassinets, haubois, flutes, luts*), the sound of which might be pleasant (*dous*) to the Turks, but for even the coarsest of French cowherds would be an ear-splitting din.[16]

There are, nevertheless, exceptions. Devoid of any equivalent visual bias are the early engravings, beginning in 1502 with the depiction of shawm and drum players on horseback given by Bernhard von Breydenbach,[17] and there are also

---

[14] Saxl 1987. More specifically, in 1589, Thoinot Arbeau (repr. 1980, 82–3) mentions a ballet devised for a court masquerade by the Knights of Malta in which both men and women wore Turkish costumes.

[15] A useful survey of representations of Turks on the French stage, and in French literature generally, is given in Rouillard 1938.

[16] *assés pour romper la teste & les oreilles au plus gros bouviers de France* (Postel 1560, pt. 1, 11).

[17] von Breydenbach repr. 1961. This and the following visual material is reproduced in Aksoy 1994, 242 et seq. By far the most thorough and detailed review of the sources, this

descriptions that are neutral or even positive in tone, for example the short but factual and informative mid sixteenth-century chapter describing various types of lute by Pierre Belon (1517–1564);[18] the account supplied by the same Guillaume Postel of a professional female ensemble (singing, dancing and playing harp, frame drum and castanets),[19] which is paralleled by the drawings made between 1555 and 1560 by Melchior Lorichs; and the later description of the Mevlevi ceremony by Pietro della Valle (1586–1652), which contains the comment: *la musica che fanno è galante, e degna d'esser sentita: e quei flauti, che chiamano* nai ... *non si può creder quanto dolce suono rendano*.[20]

Forming part of the increasingly ample and factually accurate ethnographic material on the Ottoman Empire, such information was no doubt welcome as part of a wider visual and textual panorama within which we can also situate the references to Turkish instruments in the *Harmonie universelle* by Marin Mersenne (1588–1648),[21] and the first brief samples of notation. The earliest, recorded by Salomon Schweigger (1551–1622) is, significantly, the outline of a military band melody,[22] but interesting as its inclusion is, his text is sufficiently negative in tone to stifle any nascent interest, despite the added documentary value of the engraving of a mixed group of instrumentalists on the previous page.

On its first appearance (p. 39), this engraving (Figure 7.2) is somewhat incongruously related to a reference to a military ensemble, the sound of which is sarcastically likened to the din of coopers at work.[23] When it reappears (p. 208), its composite nature is explained, accompanied by precise comments on the instruments,

---

invaluable study not only surveys the general descriptive material but also includes a rich selection of iconographical illustrations together with a full collection of the notations of Turkish music made by Western observers and scholars down to the beginning of the twentieth century.

[18] Belon 1553, 204–6, while elsewhere (p. 118) he described the Egyptian *rabāb al-shā'ir* ('viole').

[19] Postel 1560, pt. 1, 18–19. He also gives (pt. 3, 42–3) a clear description of drum, kettledrum and cymbals.

[20] della Valle 1843, 47–50. This positive evaluation is nevertheless preceded by stern condemnation of their indulgence in the vice of pederasty. Another neutral, informative description of a dervish ceremony from the seventeenth century, albeit one that says little about the music, is given in de Monconys 1973.

[21] Mersenne 1636, vol. 3, prop 18, 227–8. See Aksoy 1994, 250.

[22] Schweigger 1608, facsimile 1964, 209. It is described as a *Melodey eines Feldgeschreys*. This work also contains engravings of military ensembles. The other early examples of notation appear in Kircher 1650, which contains an oddly unconvincing religious chant ('Alla alla') and Du Loir 1654 (1639–40), part of a Mevlevi *selâm*. All are reproduced in Aksoy 1994.

[23] *Das war ein sehr holdselige liebliche Musica/als wenn die Bütner Fässer oder Schäffer binden.*

Figure 7.2   Turkish musicians – the ensemble of the governor of Belgrade
Source: Schweigger 1608, 39. Photograph by Glenn Ratcliffe.

identified by letters, but the quality of the music is again roundly dismissed as lacking in pleasing qualities: it is coarse, violent, without skill or refinement.[24]

Later in the seventeenth century the flow of written accounts increases, but even then the musical observations made continue to provide just one more small element within a general inventory of Ottoman culture and manners, and are thus doomed to be no more than brief glimpses, and ones, it must be stressed, that still rarely convey a positive reaction. A typical representative is Jean de Thévenot (1633–1667), who introduces the reader to the *tanbur* with the comment that the performers are happy to play on it all day long, even though the music is not very pleasant.[25] The potentially positive impression gained by learning that some Turks with sufficient leisure were keen amateur performers is thus immediately dispelled by disparagement of the results and by the implication of a deficiency of taste. A little later, in a rather similar vein, Rycaut

---

[24]   *Diese Music aber/im grund davon zu reden/hat nichts lieblichs oder holdseligs in sich/ sondern ist gar ungestüm unnd feindisch ... es ist in summa kein Verstand oder Geschicklichkeit darinnen zu finden.*

[25]   Thevenot 1664, 65: *ils en ioueront tout un iour sans s'ennuyer, quoy que la melodie n'en soit pas fort agreable.*

(or Rycault) (1628–1700), gives a brief description of a Mevlevi ceremony, and refers to the importance of the *ney*. But he conveys a far less positive impression than Pietro della Valle, for apart from mentioning cost he offers nothing beyond the back-handed compliment that 'It hath a doleful melancholy sound; but their constant exercise and application thereunto makes it as Musical as can be imagined in such an Instrument'.[26] But all this is still quite positive when compared with Praetorius and Febure. The former blames Islam in the severest terms for post-classical musical impoverishment,[27] while the latter is as scathing as the title of the relevant chapter (Article XI) would suggest: *Dell'ignoranza de' Turchi circa l'arti e scienze*. There follows the pointed (if absurd) remark that there are no performers of cultivated instruments such as spinet and lute, and the Turks are dismissed, essentially, as uncouth yokels: they have only *alcuni sonatori d'istrumenti rustici, come di zampogna, piva, fistula, e tamburino* (p. 64). There is more in the same bilious vein in his lengthier *Teatro della Turchia*, which almost suggests that their major merit is actually an appreciation of Western music[28] (Perrault, cited below, more convincingly suggests quite the contrary), and when he actually manages to go beyond the rustic instruments his tone is just as disparaging, pouring ridicule upon the exaggerated vocal responses to performances on the *tanbur*[29] and, again, on the uncouthness of those who are so enthusiastic about such inharmonious sounds: *a quel suono, e rumore concorrono tutti, lasciando i giuochi ed ogn'altroesercizio, per godere di quel disonante concerto, che ascoltano con grandissimo gusto, & applauso*.[30]

[26] Rycaut 1682, 263–4. Another brief description is given by Febure (1674, 21).

[27] Praetorius 1618, repr. 1884, 98: *Seider dem aber der Machomet daselbst sein Zelt aufgeschlagen, hat sich die Musik so gar verloren, dass man auch fast nichts mehr davon weiß: Ja man ist deren so gram und entgegen worden, dass nach Art und Natur der wilden Leut, mehr auf ein Satyrisch Pfeifflein und Päuklein, als auf ein recht geschaffene* Musica *gehalten wird.*

[28] Febure 1683, 213: *Godono però molto di sentire la dilettevole diversità de' nostri concerti, & ammirano l'armonia de' nostri strumenti musicali.* He then adds a fascinating anecdote: *Obbligarono, tre anni sono, certi Religiosi franchi di portare alla Città d'Adrianopoli i loro organi, per toccarli in occasione d'un matrimono, che si fece all'hora, della figliuola del Gran Signore con il Cuc Ogli*. Organs, of which more below, are almost a favourite theme (even if, or perhaps partly because, they are complex mechanical devices and sometimes particularly cumbersome objects) of regal diplomatic showmanship, although in the present case we are dealing with small portable examples. Credence is added to this somewhat surprising account when we learn from a tenth-century Byzantine text (Marcuse 1975, p. 608) of the 'custom of conducting a bride of noble birth to the bridegroom's house accompanied by the music of portable organs'.

[29] *E un divertimento de' piu curiosi, e riducoli l'udirli gridare a tutta voce, come spiritati, quando toccano un certo strumento a due corde, chiamato da essi tamburo.*

[30] Yet further such negative judgements are offered in his *L'estat present de la Turquie*, 1675, for which see Obelkevich 1977. This article provides a most valuable assemblage of textual material, but it is difficult to assent to the implication that Turkish music was quite often to be heard in Paris. It is much more likely that genuine Turkish sounds were

Apart from its obvious disincentive to curiosity, such material has evident limitations with regard to the quality and extent of the information it transmits. Very little is said about the manner of performance, still less about the nature of the repertoire, and above all, as it is inescapably silent it can convey nothing of the music itself. It is, then, hardly surprising that no one appears to have been sufficiently enthused to seek out performers to learn from or otherwise attempt to gain some familiarity with Ottoman practice. Yet European curiosity concerning Ottoman music is assumed by Giovanni Battista Donado, a contemporary of Rycaut and Febure, to whom we owe the first serious attempt at notating Turkish secular melodies. Included as an appendix to his pioneering study of Turkish literature,[31] they consist of transcriptions of three songs, but as before this positive contribution is undermined by being presented (as shown in Figure 7.3) together with a clear signal of cultural deficiency: a second, empty stave, a void deliberately embodying the absence of that most fundamental element of art-music, a bass line.[32]

The logic of this was to be carried through soon after by Chabert, who does indeed domesticate his notation of a Mevlevi piece by adding a bass accompaniment (see Figure 7.4).

Technically bland, its reassuring effect may be compared to the addition of gilt Corinthian capitals above the whirling dervishes dramatically portrayed in an impressive double-page depiction of a Mevlevi *mukabele* in the same volume[33] (Plate 39).

---

only to be heard, if ever, on the rarest and most exceptional occasions: we are dealing, rather, with the gradual creation, adjustment and reproduction of topoi constituting an imaginary soundscape. A striking contrast to the general hostility within which information about Ottoman instruments is framed is provided by the slightly later but wholly neutral account of the Persian instrumentarium in Kaempfer 1712.

[31] Donado 1688. The publisher's preface mentions respectfully earlier French descriptions of religion, ceremonies, dress, etc., but complains of the complete lack of any previous study of literature. As evidence of literary activity Donado gives a bibliographical survey of materials found in a variety of fields, followed by a heterogeneous selection of translated texts. Poetry comes at the end, and there is a brief discussion of songs, in which it is suggested that words are set to the music, rather than the reverse. He is particularly struck by the lack of notation, a theme taken up by later observers. A few poems and translations are followed by two fold-out pages with his own notations. For originals and transcriptions see Aksoy 1994, 289–94 (and also *Turkish Music Quarterly*, 4/3, 1991, 10–12).

[32] Avvertirò pur anco il Lettore, che se nella Musica non vi si vede il Basso, questo accade, per lasciar le Canzoni Turchesche nell'aria appunto, che stanno, & lo praticano I Turchi ; poiche loro nella Musica non hanno il Basso.

[33] de Ferriol 1715. The preface mentions M. de Ferriol (French ambassador at Istanbul 1699–1711), who commissioned the collection (as is clear from a second title page, which adds ... *tirées sur les Tableaux peints d'après Nature en 1707. et 1708. par les ordres de M. de Ferriol ... et gravées en 1712. et 1713. par les soins de M^r. le Hay*).

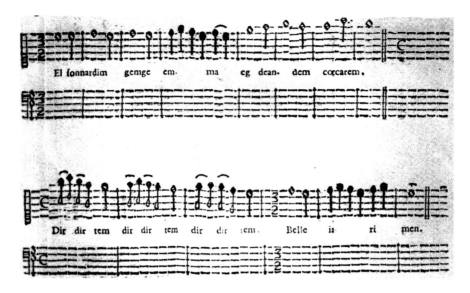

Figure 7.3   Notation of a Turkish song
Source: Donado 1688, final fold-out pages. Photograph by Glenn Ratcliffe.

European assessments of the deficiencies of Turkish music were matched by general Ottoman indifference to, or disdain for, European music. It is clear that each culture had a self-sufficient and constantly renewed repertoire, and possessed in addition a body of authoritative texts that not only provided theoretical backing to practice but also discussed more abstract concerns. Neither experienced a sense of inadequacy, and certainly no pressing need to learn from the other; if it overheard something, it usually judged it wanting, and certainly lacked sufficient stimulus to seek out and appropriate what might be on offer. Significant on the Ottoman side, for example, is the exclusion of any European musical ingredient from the policy of cultural pluralism pursued by Mehmed II after the conquest of Constantinople: no Italian musician was invited to entertain the sultan while Gentile Bellini was sketching his portrait.

This mutual indifference is equally apparent on the intellectual level, if not more so. In contrast to, say, medicine, where there was a renewed concern during the Renaissance with improving texts that had previously been translated from Arabic, music inherited no such theoretical corpus, for despite one or two minor and marginal borrowings the earlier European indebtedness to Arab scholarship, so marked in other domains, had never extended to music: there was no call upon the major texts of al-Kindi, al-Farabi and Ibn Sina, presumably because of the partial mediation of Greek theory already provided by Boethius and included

Figure 7.4 Notation of a Mevlevi melody, with bass line added by Chabert
Source: de Ferriol, 1715. Copyright of the British Library.

in the *quadrivium*.³⁴ In consequence, there was no pre-existing body of translated material for Renaissance scholars to react to.³⁵ Nor, despite the creation of university chairs in music and in oriental languages,³⁶ was there to be any later awakening of interest in the theoretical legacy of the Islamic world, for by this time original Greek sources were becoming available. Islamic theorists, on the other hand, were no longer directly concerned with these: the Greek legacy had already been partially, and for their purposes sufficiently, assimilated by their Abbasid predecessors, especially al-Farabi, from whom they were content to select what they occasionally needed as background or supplement to their accounts of contemporary systems. As a result, the two theoretical traditions evolved independently, despite the presence of a substratum of common elements and concerns, particularly regarding the ethical and cosmological domains and the overriding concept of harmony. But harmony was being played out horizontally in Middle Eastern monody, according to subtle modal rules, and vertically in Europe, where theorists such as Zarlino (1517–1590) considered that it had reached its apogee in the mid sixteenth-century vocal polyphony of Willaert.³⁷

For the Islamic world, then, the novel Western concept of harmony was irrelevant, and it is hardly surprising to find no trace of an awareness of European theoretical discourse. What we do encounter, after an apparent lull in theoretical writing activity following the *kitāb al-shifā'* of Ibn Sina (d. 1037) and the *kitāb al-kāfī* of his pupil Ibn Zayla (d. 1048), is the production from the mid-thirteenth century on of a series of texts, beginning with the influential *kitāb al-adwār* of Safi al-Din al-Urmawi (d. 1294),³⁸ that combine the mathematical analysis of intervallic relationships with a sophisticated categorisation of rhythmic and, especially, modal structures. This series culminates in the work of an older contemporary of Fra Angelico, al-Maraghi (d. 1435) who, despite spending the latter part of his long life in Samarkand and Herat, where opportunities to hear European music would have approached zero, did at least manage to note, in his catalogue of instruments, the existence of the portative organ that, travelling by quite different routes, would later reach Moghul India and appear in a miniature of Plato charming animals to sleep.³⁹ But although al-Maraghi's work was at least

---

34   Material on music was only transmitted when a section in an encyclopaedic or survey work was devoted to it, as in al-Farabi's *iḥṣā' al-'ulūm* (see Farmer 1934).

35   There is, accordingly, no mention of music in Burnett 1999.

36   At Bologna: the chair of music was instituted in 1450 (but not immediately filled), that in oriental languages in 1464.

37   Zarlino 1558, 1–2.

38   ed. al-Rajab 1986; facsimile in Publications of the Institute for the history of Arabic-Islamic science, series C, 29, Frankfurt 1986; tr. in D'Erlanger 1938, 185–565.

39   British Library Ms. Or. 12208, fol. 298a. Published in Woodfield 1990.

partially known to the Ottomans,[40] it failed to penetrate further westwards, and the various fifteenth-century Anatolian texts in Turkish, which have a rather different theoretical emphasis, with cosmological themes once again coming to the fore,[41] likewise failed to catch the European eye. When the fifteenth-century scholar Giorgio Valla (1447–1500) ventures forth to the Levant, it is specifically to search for Greek material:[42] the idea that there might be another textual tradition of musical theory worthy of exploration never surfaces.

What is implicit here becomes quite explicit in the dismissive remarks of the early sixteenth-century theorist Salomon de Caus. After an exposition of a fundamentally Greek-derived theory of intervals (parallels for much of which are to be found in early Arabic texts), he ends the first part of his *Institution harmonique*[43] with a brief fill-up section (quite literally: '*Pour remplir ceste Page*') that mentions other cultures, principally China, and includes a comment on Turkish music, possibly reflecting someone's unappreciative reaction to the sound of the *mehter*, the Janissary military band, that entirely disregards the possibility of a parallel theoretical discourse. It speaks of a lack of consonance – except by accident – and the pleasure taken in mere din,[44] providing in effect a slightly more technical and less brutal echo of Postel. But setting the derogatory tone aside, the lack of interest this betrays was, no doubt, only to be expected, given the general bias of humanist scholarship towards a creative re-appropriation of the classical world. It is true that there is a reference to a Middle Eastern tradition in the oration in praise of music by Beroaldo (1453–1505), professor of rhetoric at Bologna: but it is that of Biblical antiquity, and he otherwise predictably invokes only classical sources.[45]

Paradoxically, however, one might have expected this very bias to provoke investigative curiosity into contemporary phenomena in the Middle East, for one area of argument in Renaissance discussions of the great emotional power of music stressed in classical Greek sources concerned the extent to which it

---

[40] A copy of his *maqāṣid al-alḥān* (Leyden Or. 270–71) is dedicated to Sultan Murad II. Although there is some uncertainty about identities (see Fallahzadeh 2005, 179–81, 187–8) it appears that a son and grandson of al-Maraghi moved to the Ottoman court, and there produced further, derivative treatises. But whatever influence these may have had appears to have been short-lived. As composer, however, al-Maraghi is still held in high esteem, and has long been considered the founding father of the Ottoman tradition, linking it therefore to the Persianate cultural world in general and in particular to fifteenth-century Timurid Herat.

[41] See e.g. Seydī 2004.

[42] On his musical writings see Bellini 1988 and Palisca 1985.

[43] Caus 1614.

[44] *En Turquie il y a aussi plusieurs sortes d'instruments, avec lesquels ils iouent le plus souvent avec confusion, sans user de consonnantes, sinon de celles qui viennent accidentallement, & se contentent seulement d'ouir un grand bruit confus.*

[45] Beroaldo 1500.

had either been mediated by subtleties of intonation that only pure monody allowed, or implied the use of harmony as currently understood. But it is not until considerably later, in the second half of the seventeenth century, that we encounter any awareness that a parallel for the former might be sought in Ottoman practice.[46] As Perrault (1628–1703) puts it, in the mouth of a participant in an interesting debate, the music of the Ancients was monodic, as is the music of the whole world still today, except for part (an interesting restriction) of Europe, and multi-part music is as yet still unknown even in Constantinople.[47] There is an incredulous reaction to this, and the discussion then ranges wider, evincing curiosity, unprejudiced observation, but still mutual incomprehension:

> L'ABBÉ. Vous connoissez Mr. Petis de la Croix … Il vous dira que s'étant trouvé à Constantinople lorsque nostre amy Mr. de Guilleragues y étoit en Ambassade, il fut pleinement convaincu, non sans étonnement, de ce que je viens de vous dire. Mr. de Guilleragues avoit des Laquais & des Valets de chambre qui joüoient tres-bien du Violon, & qui composoient une bande complete. Lorsqu'ils joüoient quelques-unes de ces belles Ouvertures d'Opera, qui nous ont charmez tant de fois, les Turcs ne pouvoient les souffrir, traittant de charivary le meslange des parties auquel ils ne sont pas accoutumez.[48]

Despite this antipathy, the Turks were still able to appreciate the proficiency of the performers, while for his part Perrault's protagonist recognised the greater refinement of the single melodic line characteristic of the music of the 'Orientals' (Persians and Indians[49] as well as Ottomans) and the Ancients, and also lavished praise on the technical skill and power of memory of a Persian instrumentalist he had heard.[50] One might have expected such open-minded responses to echo earlier seventeenth-century testimonies and thereby contribute to the elaboration of a theme adumbrated already in the sixteenth

---

[46] Perrault 1688, 258–74 (although a premonition, not followed up, it seems, is found in Belon's *Observations* of a century before: *Qui vouldroit esclaircir quelquechose de la musique des instruments anciens, auroit meilleur argument de l'experience de ceux qu'on veoit en Grece & Turquie, que de ce que nous en trouvons par escript*).

[47] *Il est constant que la Musique des Anciens ne consistoit que dans un chant seul, & qu'elle n'a jamais connu ce que c'est qu'une basse, qu'une taille & qu'une haute contre … La Musique des Anciens est encore aujourd'huy la Musique de toute la Terre, à la reserve d'une partie de l'Europe. Cela est si vray qu'à Constantinople mesme ils ne connoissent point encore la Musique à plusieurs parties.*

[48] For further extracts from this dialogue see Obelkevich 1977.

[49] Obelkevich interprets *au Mogol* as referring to the Mongols; but presumably it is the Mogul Emperor who is intended.

[50] Even though it would be misleading to see a parallel in terms of underlying ideologies, it is interesting nevertheless to note here the similarity with the emergence of *vergleichende Musikwissenschaft*, pursuing a historicism that sought analogies to what was presumed to be the Western past in current phenomena in other cultures, viewed implicitly as static and non-progressive.

century by Vicentino (1511–1575/6)[51] and realised through the shift, associated particularly with Monteverdi and the rise of opera, towards monody and the need to express more directly the emotional content of the text.[52] But in the event Perrault's was a lone voice, and knowledge of the practice he mentions was virtually non-existent. All European musicians had to rely on up to that point was the limited information supplied by the reports of travellers, not normally as well informed as Perrault, who offered, as we have seen, some comments of substance but few that are at all sympathetic:[53] with only the occasional exception Western reactions to Turkish music (dance is a somewhat different matter) tended to be unenthusiastic at best, decidedly hostile at worst.

Turkish reactions to Western music, Perrault apart, are poorly documented. Ambassadors to Venice were generally lodged in the Giudecca, but had ample opportunities to mix socially, and one, as a result, is reported to have hosted, around 1570, a concert of harpsichord and violin.[54] However, the fact that it was noted at all suggests that it was an exceptional occurrence, and certainly nothing seems to have flowed from it. If, around 1600, an Ottoman emissary had been able to venture inside St Mark's, he might have encountered a polychoral (*cori spezzati*) setting by Giovanni Gabrieli, and been mightily puzzled: the antiphonal style and polyphonic texture would have been quite alien, the rhythm unclear, while if he could have picked out a melodic line he might have found it uncouth and bare. In short, he would have encountered nothing worth emulating, and it is entirely understandable that no Venetian musician should have been invited to Istanbul. In any case, inquisitiveness about European music could have been satisfied locally, among the diplomatic and mercantile communities in Pera and Galata, and if a reference surfaces to a European musician (or, more precisely, a musician of European origin), it is one who has mastered the Ottoman idiom.[55] The one Turkish traveller with something positive to report is the ever-curious if not always wholly reliable Evliya Çelebi, who was struck by the vast size and sound of the organ of the Stephansdom in Vienna, and even if his reactions have more to do with technology than music he does also comment favourably on the choir of *castrati*.[56]

---

[51] Another Willeart student, Nicola Vicentino, introduces a shift of balance to express better the passions of the words (Vicentino 1555).

[52] See Galilei 2003.

[53] In addition to Aksoy 1994 a useful and perceptive general survey is provided in Cavallini 1986.

[54] Pedani 1994.

[55] There is e.g. a seventeenth-century reference to a composer called Firenk Mustafa (see Feldman 1996, 67–8). A number of Greek composers also contributed to the Ottoman tradition, but the circumstances here are quite different, as they were essentially native to the idiom.

[56] Evliya equates the Western major mode, quite reasonably, with the *makam rehavi*. Particularly fascinating, and odd enough to verge on the plausible, is his description

The reception of European ambassadors to the Porte involved a different kind of sound, that of the ceremonial band, loud, raucous and designed to impress: they do not appear to have relished the experience. But as European sovereigns jostled to seek Ottoman alliances, they too could enable their diplomatic envoys to call upon musical instruments as ancillary tools to create an effect. Fittingly, the beginning of the lengthy alliance between France and the Ottomans was singled out in later historical accounts for the first such episode, dated to 1543, when French musicians were said to have been sent by François I to perform for Süleyman the Magnificent. This proved, however, to be a diplomatic miscalculation, for we are told that the sultan, fearing potentially deleterious effects on his subjects, sent the unfortunate musicians packing. Although this story, with its most unconvincing pedigree, is clearly apocryphal,[57] there is, on the other hand, no doubt that in 1599 Elizabeth I sent an organ to Mehmed III. But, as is made clear by the vivid account of its transport and delivery written by its builder, Dallam,[58] this was less a musical instrument – although it was certainly playable, and performed on by him for the sultan – than a complex piece of clockwork machinery, to be understood culturally in the first instance within the context of the Ottoman taste for ornate clocks that the Habsburgs were required to satisfy,[59] and in a broader historical perspective as another in the long line of stunning mechanical and often sound-producing devices used for diplomatic effect that had been begun long before by the Byzantines and Arabs. Although Mehmed III himself was suitably impressed by this elaborate gift, whatever musical potential it had was secondary, and whether or not it soon broke down it certainly did not survive him for long, being destroyed by his successor, Ahmed I.[60]

We are thus no nearer to any deeper mutual understanding of idiom, still less to any productive exchange. If Islamic artefacts could be appreciated and

---

of the bellows mechanism, which consisted of *castrati* choirboys swarming up ladders to jump onto a wooden platform that then compressed the inflated bellows beneath to power the organ—*tavâşî gulâmlar nerdübânlardan enüp körüklerin tahtalarına binüp körükler ile aşağı bile enerken körüklerden bir gûne rîh-ı sarsar zâhir olur* (Evliya Çelebi 2003, 104; see also Kreutel 1957, 111–14).

[57] There appears to be no contemporary reference that might substantiate it, and the circumstantial evidence speaks strongly against it. It first surfaces in Praetorius 1618, repr. 1884, 98. In the nineteenth century it becomes contaminated with another, equally obviously fabricated story in which Süleyman's reaction is now positive, so much so that he asks his own musicians to imitate the rhythm of a particular piece, thus leading to the invention of the rhythmic cycle *frenkçin* (see Rauf Yekta Bey 1922, 3044, and Reinhard 1984, 209, both of whom give credence to this later twist).

[58] Recounted in Mayes 1956.

[59] See Rogers 1993.

[60] For a vivid and instructive description of the manner in which it was disposed of, and of the motivation, see the Prologue in MacLean 2004. For the possible connections between these various episodes see Wright 2011.

Ottoman rugs, fabrics and metalwork acquired and their designs imitated and assimilated, responses to literature and music, in stark contrast, remain muted or absent, and part of the reason is to be sought in the very proximity and power of the Ottoman state: it could not be reduced and assimilated to the category of the barbarous and alien typified by the various cultures of the Americas that were gradually being explored, presented and theorised.[61] But these, crucially, belonged to the conquered, which partly explains the difference in the tone of Torquemada's account of the facility with which the subject peoples were able to master aspects of Western culture, music included.[62] The indigenous population was considered potentially malleable not just theologically but also culturally,[63] thus providing a sharp contrast with the obduracy of the Ottomans, who continued to present an immediate and pressing problem, a religious challenge and a military threat, unmitigated, as far as music was concerned, by the material advantages that commerce could bring. It is thus hardly surprising to find, in contrast to the multifarious traces left by the musical contacts and influences that mark both the earlier period of Muslim ascendancy in Spain and, more obviously, the later period of European domination, both that their musical culture is generally considered inferior and that what is taken from them derives above all from the domain of violent conflict: the sounds that percolate are those inescapable on the battlefield, so that the instruments that impress and are urgently sought after are those of the Janissary band, made up of shawms, trumpets and assorted percussion.[64] A group of three dramatically if improbably flared shawms, with drum, appears at the beginning of the sixteenth century in Carpaccio's *St. George Baptising*, and although the particular source for these is unknown,[65] representations of the Janissary band appear later, as has been noted above, in sixteenth-century woodcuts, while texts contain descriptions of the main percussion types. As for the instruments themselves, some were obtained as battlefield trophies, others as diplomatic gifts, but however acquired they were to have a profound influence. As with the similar process of acquisition and imitation of Islamic military instruments – percussion in particular – that

---

[61] See Taylor 2007.

[62] Torquemada 1615, a work largely relying on sixteenth-century sources. Relevant extracts are given in Harrison 1973.

[63] But there was also a recognition that the process might be arduous and that the demonic was not easily overcome: see Tomlinson 1999, repr. in Tomlinson 2007, 197–230 (see 201–4).

[64] There is no record of European battlefield sounds having any such impact. One may note, however, a pleasant if barely credible story reported by Jean d'Auton (1466–1528) of besieged Turks (during the unsuccessful attack on Mytilene in 1501) listening appreciatively to French musicians performing songs and motets at night under the walls (see Cazaux 2002, 39).

[65] See Raby 1982, 73 and 76. Ivanoff 1994 suggests, though, that they may be shawms of Dalmatian origin that Carpaccio could have observed.

had occurred earlier during the Crusades,[66] the Janissary *mehter* was to exert, from the fifteenth century on, a decisive impact on the constitution of European military bands and the kinds of sound they produced. Particularly important was the kettledrum: in 1542 Henry VIII asked for kettledrums to be sent from Vienna, to be played 'in the Hungarian manner' – a clear indication of the route through which Ottoman influence was spreading[67] – and other European nations also began to use them: even the mnemonic syllables used to define sequences of drum strokes may have been transmitted along with them.[68] Other percussion instruments incorporated into the military band include bass drum, cymbals and Jingling Johnny, and the increasing importance of oboes no doubt reflects the central role in the *mehter* of the *zurna*. Eventually, Jan III Sobieski of Poland (1629–1696) was to be granted a complete *mehter* ensemble by the sultan, other European rulers sought to follow and, as is well known, the eventual infiltration of this particular military soundworld into the realm of European art music was to result in the late eighteenth-century Turkish march style of the Viennese classical school.

More difficult to trace, because undocumented, is the wide area of social contact that includes conflict and capture but goes beyond it to encompass the more peaceful interactions of traders and sailors. We can only guess at the extent of exchange, but must certainly allow for the possibility that material as diverse as lullabies, dance melodies and sea shanties could travel between cultures.[69] Moreover, musicians are notoriously mobile, and therefore likely conduits for the diffusion of exotic features, although here, too, evidence is disappointingly elusive. One potentially promising case would seem to be that of Giorgio de Modon, alias Zorzi Trombetta,[70] a fifteenth-century trumpeter who eventually became head of the civic ensemble of Venice, for as well as being a professional musician he was a seafaring man, and thus perfectly positioned to

---

[66] See Farmer 1941 and 1949, both repr. in 1997 (679–86 and 693–9 respectively).

[67] Ibid. See also Farmer 1946, repr. in 1997, 687–92.

[68] The case for this has been argued in Neubauer 2008. In particular, this draws attention to, and provides an explanation for, the resemblances between the representations of rhythmic groupings given by Thoinot Arbeau in the first part of his *Orchésographie* (fn. 10), which is devoted to military music, and the earlier Islamic formulations, which are most fully expounded by al-Farabi.

[69] A tantalising hint of such possibilities is provided by Guillaume Joseph Grelot (1680, 226), who describes an impromptu intercultural exchange thus: *Un autre de la bande voyant que nous estions assez pour former une petite dance en rond, commença à entonner une chanson Turque ... & nous mettre en train par la nouveauté de sa chanson; mais après que chacun eût dit la sienne, qui en Turc, qui en Arabe, ils m'obligerent aussi d'en dire une en François; à quoy ayant satisfait, ils se prirent tous à rire si fort de ce qu'ils ne pouvoient repeter ma chanson, comme je répetois la leur, qu'ils aimerent mieux quitter la dance, & achever la garde au-tour d'un qui prit son taboura, & qui chantoit dessus un air nouveau, que de suivre le mien, & répeter des paroles qu'ils n'entendoient pas.*

[70] See Strohm and Blackburn 2001, 117–18.

come into contact with practitioners of other traditions and transmit something of what he had heard. But the records he kept suggest that he did nothing of the sort: although he certainly travelled the eastern Adriatic, he was employed entertaining well-to-do Venetians along the coast, and the songs he notated are French, and were clearly not learned in port taverns.

Nevertheless, for all that the documentary record is lacking, it is hardly to be doubted that occasional contacts took place, and it is generally assumed that at least one instrument, the *colascione*, known principally in South Italy and Sicily, was a sixteenth-century borrowing, despite Tinctoris's scorn for Turkish *tanbur* players, of a similar form of Turkish long-necked lute, and where the Turks were a more permanent presence, in the Balkans, such borrowing naturally occurred with greater frequency.[71]

Two centuries after Zorzi Trombetta we encounter a much better documented European musician who this time does acquire a mastery of an Ottoman musical idiom, Wojciech Bobowski (1610?–1675). A captive who converted to Islam and is generally known by the name Ali Ufki, he became a member of the Ottoman court ensemble, performing on *santur*, and as he was familiar with notation from his earlier Western musical training he began to record items from both the instrumental and the vocal repertoires.

Figure 7.5, from a manuscript now in the Bibliothèque Nationale,[72] shows a sample of one of his earlier efforts, with a transliteration of the text and, below, the Arabic script version of the original Ottoman Turkish verse in another hand.[73] A second collection, now in the British Library, is much fuller, much more assured. But the point here, rather than to comment on the undoubted importance of this material for the history of Ottoman music, is to note that these manuscripts remained personal documents without repercussions: the second was acquired by John Covel (1638–1722) and was destined after its arrival in London to become part of the Sloane collection and gather dust on library shelves.[74] To speak of contact in the case of Ali Ufki would thus be a misnomer, and of transfer there is no trace: originating in one musical culture, he was simply ingested by another.[75]

---

[71] It is interesting to note that Schweigger's material derives from a visit to Belgrade. However, the effects of the Turkish presence in the Balkans lie outside the concerns of the present chapter.

[72] Ms. Turc 292.

[73] A routine bacchic piece beginning *sāqiyā son bāde-ye ḥamrā'i bir nūş edelim* ('Wine pourer, let us just carouse with the last of the red wine').

[74] British Library Ms. Sloane 3114. See Behar 1991 and Behar 2005, 17–55. The British Library ms. has been published in a rather poor facsimile (Elçin 1976) and in a modern transcription (in Cevher 2003).

[75] A curious reflection of this enculturation appears in his ascriptions of the melodies of the psalms he translated to Ottoman *makams* (see Behar 1990 and Haug 2010).

Figure 7.5   Notation of a song from an untitled collection made by Ali Ufki
Source: Paris, Bibliothèque Nationale de France, Ms Turc 292. Courtesy of the Bibliothèque Nationale de France.

The description of musical activities he includes in his account of the social structure of the Palace, and especially the strict eyes-down etiquette required when the musicians performed in the harem,[76] was doubtless an exotic element of incidental interest to European readers. But it did not lead them towards any of his own compositions, which are in Ottoman idiom: they were never transmitted to European musicians, and his collections mediated nothing, despite being contemporary with an increasingly common Turkish musical presence on the Italian stage. Representations such as that in Figure 7.6 perpetuated a stereotype

---

[76] *Saray-i enderun*. The publication of the original Italian version within Magni 1679 was preceded by a German translation that appeared two years earlier.

Figure 7.6   Burlesque Turks dancing
Source: Lambranzi 1716. Photograph by Glenn Ratcliffe.

that emerged out of the post-Renaissance evolution of opera, or, to be more specific, the elaborately costumed and choreographed balletic interludes that formed a prominent feature of lavish seventeenth-century productions.

In these, whatever musical codes may have been called upon to signify Turkishness failed to include any direct imitation of elements of Turkish art-music,[77] and the *alla turca* style as it developed during the eighteenth century conveyed deficiency by the exaggerations and imbalances resulting from a deliberately reductive selection within the range of indigenous resources.[78] But it could equally be said that crucial to this strategic choice, whatever its ideological import, was lack of access to the original, and at this negative point the gap between musical and visual representations narrows somewhat. For Venice, at least, Raby speaks tellingly of 'the continuing limitations of the Ottoman *exempla* accessible to artists',[79] thereby resulting in the reduction of representation to types, or to marking identity by the inclusion of elements of a conventional dress code. But perhaps even more telling is the parallel with literature: European writers deployed a particular set of tropes to set the Turk apart, all the while being unable or unwilling to scale the language barrier sufficiently to gain better purchase on their subject. They thus remained profoundly ignorant of Ottoman poetry and the way the *gazel* encapsulated a view of the world and the emotions not fundamentally alien to that found in the Renaissance and mannerist lyric,[80] while their musical counterparts remained just as unaware of the subtle and complex world of melodic modes and rhythmic cycles that Ottoman composers used for the songs that would be performed in the palace settings typified in Plate 40. European composers contented themselves with incorporating partial and distant impressions or imaginations of the *mehter* sound to develop a parallel set of imaginary representations, bellicose or burlesque. They remained as essentially oblivious, and deaf, to Ottoman art music as Ottoman composers were to European.

---

[77] As Cavallini 1986 puts it: *questo tipo di produzione operistica si limita a parodiare il fracasso delle bande giannizzere, evocando sonorità orientali che hanno legami blandi* (or, one might add, none at all) *con le arie turche.*

[78] On the later development of these conventions see Meyer 1973–1974. As this makes clear, the particular language of musical exoticism involved was one that developed its own conventions, and failed to seek out genuine Turkish material even when more accurate representations began to make themselves available.

[79] Raby 1982, 83.

[80] See Andrews and Kalpaklı 2005.

Plate 1 Astrolabe with Arabic and Latin inscriptions, Fez, dated 699/1299–1300. Florence, Museo di Storia della Scienza, inv. no. 1109. After Curatola 1993, 179.

Plate 2 Arabic-Latin dictionary, Spain, end of thirteenth – early fourteenth century. Florence, Biblioteca Riccardiana, no. 217, fol. 115r and fol. 226v. Copyright of the Biblioteca Riccardiana.

ALPHABETVM ARABICVM

Cum licentia superiorum.
ROMAE.
In Typographia Medicea.
M. D. XCII.

Plate 3 Title page. Giovan Battista Raimondi, *Alphabetum Arabicum*, Rome, 1592. The Arcadian Library, www.arcadian-library.com.

Plate 4 Cup with one handle – from the ambo of Henry II, Iraq or western Iran, tenth century (?). Aachen, Palatine Chapel. Photo: Anna Contadini.

Plate 5 Dish, from the ambo of Henry II, Fatimid Egypt (?), late tenth – early eleventh century (?). Aachen, Palatine Chapel. Photo: Anna Contadini.

Plate 6 Lothar cross, c. 1000. Aachen, Chapel's Treasury. Copyright Marburg Archive.

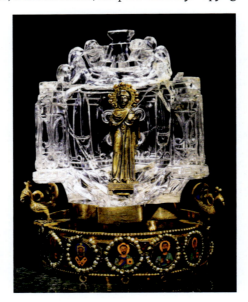

Plate 7 *Grotta della Vergine* (The Virgin's Grotto), rock crystal, Fatimid Egypt (?), eleventh century (?); crown: silver-gilt, enamels and precious stones, Constantinople, ninth-tenth century; statuette of the Virgin: silver-gilt, Venice, thirteenth century. Venice, Treasury of St Mark, Tesoro, inv. no. 92. Courtesy of Tesoro di San Marco, Venice.

Plate 8 Rock crystal ewer, Fatimid Egypt, late tenth – early eleventh century; European silver gilt and enamelled mount, early seventeenth century. Fermo, Treasury of the Cathedral. Photo: Simone Piazza.

Plate 9 Small-pattern Holbein carpet, West Anatolia, third quarter of the fifteenth century. Florence, Museo Bardini, inv. no. 7865. After Boralevi 1999, 46, cat. 10.

Plate 10 Gentile da Fabriano, *Madonna of Humility*, c. 1420. Pisa, Museo Nazionale di San Matteo. Photo: Anna Contadini.

Plate 11 Dish, sheet brass incised and inlaid with silver and gold, Egypt or Syria, 1300–1350. Aron Collection. Photo: Valerio Ricciardi.

Plate 12 Ottoman silk (*kemkha*), second half of sixteenth century.
Prato, Museo del Tessuto, inv. no. 75.01.316. Courtesy of Museo del Tessuto.

Plate 13 *Çatma* (brocaded velvet), Ottoman, late sixteenth – early seventeenth century. Prato, Museo del Tessuto, inv. no. 75.01.33. Courtesy of Museo del Tessuto.

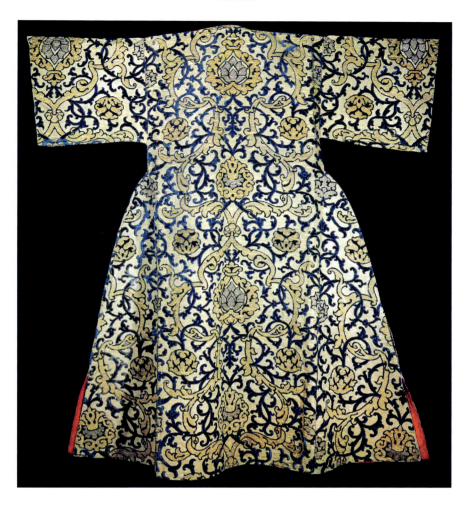

Plate 14 Short-sleeved kaftan, probably belonging to Osman II (1618–22), European, probably Italian. Istanbul, Topkapı Sarayi, inv. no. 13/360. After Rogers 1986, cat. 42.

Plate 15 Velvet, Florence, sixteenth century. Venice, Museo di Palazzo Mocenigo, inv. no. 491/191. Copyright of the Fondazione dei Musei Civici di Venezia.

Plate 16 Agnolo Bronzino, *Eleonora of Toledo with her son Giovanni de' Medici*, c. 1545. Oil on panel. Florence, Galleria degli Uffizi, inv. no. 748. Copyright of the Polo Museale della città di Firenze.

Plate 17 Velvet, probably Venice, sixteenth century. Florence, Museo Nazionale del Bargello, inv. Franchetti 639. Photo: Anna Contadini.

Plate 18 Mahmud al-Kurdi, bowl-shaped box with cover of engraved brass inlaid with silver, disputed provenance, fifteenth century. London, Courtauld Institute, O.1966.GP.204. Courtesy of the Courtauld Institute.

Contadini

Plate 19 Bookbinding, *dogal commission* to Michele Foscarini, 1587. Venice, Biblioteca Nazionale Marciana, Cod. It. VII, 1724 (=8126). Courtesy of the Biblioteca Marciana, Venice.

Plate 20 Gilded and varnished hanging leather with a horizontal band in Ottoman style, Venice (?), sixteenth century. Bologna, Museo Civico Medievale, inv. no. 2014. Copyright of the Museo Civico Medievale, Bologna, Italy.

Contadini

Plate 21 Gilded leather shield and detail of the arms of the Foscarini family, Venice, 1550–1600. Venice, Armeria del Palazzo Ducale, No. Inv. 65/Sala E. Photos: Anna Contadini.

Plate 22 Hans Memling, *The Virgin and Child with Saints and Angels*, Donne triptych, centre panel, 1478. Oil on panel. London, National Gallery, inv. no. 6275.1. © The National Gallery, London.

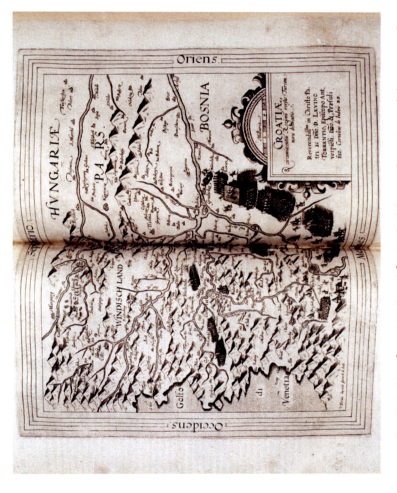

Plate 23 Cornelius de Iudaeis [Cornelis de Jode], 'Newly delineated, Croatia and the surrounding region against the Turk', undated. British Library Board. All Rights Reserved. Maps. C.7.c.13.

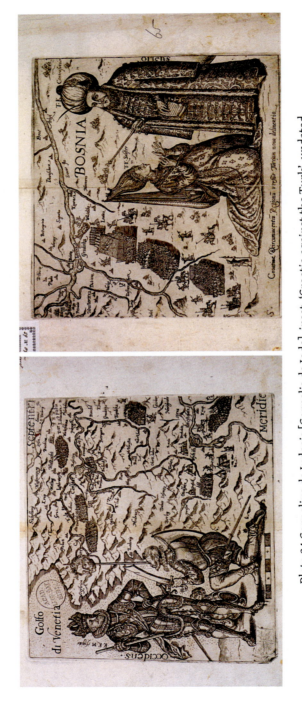

Plate 24 Cornelius de Iudaeis [Cornelis de Jode], inset, 'Croatia against the Turk', undated. Leiden University Library, COLLBN Port 123 N 138 and COLLBN Port 168 N 65. Copyright University Library, Leiden.

Plate 25 Ioani Bussemechers [Johan Bussemacher], 'Thrace and Bulgaria and Surrounding Territory' [Cologne], 1596. British Library Board. All Rights Reserved, Maps, C.39.c.1.(67).

Plate 26 *Pyramids at Giza*, 1560, from the travel diary of Alessandro Magno.
Folger Library, Washington DC, ms V.A. 259 (1317/1), f. 131.
Copyright Folger Shakespeare Library.

Plate 27 *View of Alexandria*, from Archivio di Stato di Venezia, Cinque Savii alla Mercanzia, 'Capitolare cottimo Alessandria', busta 844 bis (neg. no. 306). Copyright Archivio di Stato di Venezia.

Plate 28 Follower of Gentile Bellini (Girolamo da Santacroce?), *The Reception of the Venetian Ambassadors in Damascus*, after 1511. Oil on canvas. Paris, Musée du Louvre. © RMN / Thierry Le Mage.

Plate 29 Giovanni Mansueti, *Symbolic Representation of the Crucifixion*, probably around 1492. Oil on canvas. © The National Gallery, London.

Plate 30 Workshop of Giovanni Bellini, *The Adoration of the Magi*, 1475–80. Oil on canvas. © The National Gallery, London.

Plate 31 Vincenzo Catena, *Holy Family with a warrior adoring the Infant Christ*, after 1520. Oil on canvas. © The National Gallery, London.

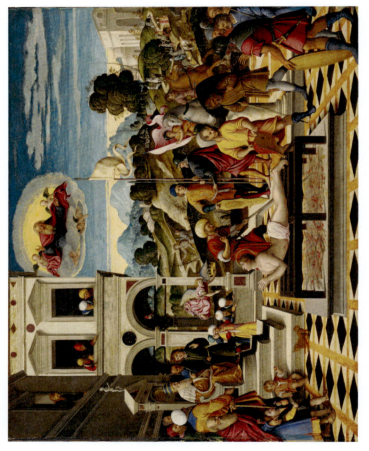

Plate 32 Girolamo da Santacroce, *Martyrdom of Saint Lawrence*, c. 1550. Oil on panel with tempera highlights. The Nelson-Atkins Museum, Kansas City. Gift of Mrs. Mary Evans and Mrs. John Wheeler in memory of Harry Martin Evans, 40-44/1. Photo: John Lamberton.

Plate 33 *Tabula Asiae Prima*, from the first Italian translation of Ptolemy's *Geography* prepared by Pietro Andrea Mattiolo, Venice, 1548. Harvard Map Collection, Harvard University. Copyright of Harvard University.

Plate 34 *Natolia, Nova tabula*, added to the first Italian translation of Ptolemy's *Geography* by the cosmographer Jacopo or Giacomo Gastaldi. Harvard Map Collection, Harvard University. Copyright of Harvard University.

Plate 35 Muslim and Christian musicians playing the same instrument. *Cantigas de Santa Maria* for Alfonso X, Spain, thirteenth century. Madrid, Biblioteca Real, San Lorenzo del Escorial, MS T.I.1. Courtesy of the Biblioteca Real, San Lorenzo del Escorial.

Plate 36 *Intemperance*, Anon. *Tractatus de septem vitiis*, Genoa, late fourteenth century. London, British Library, Ms Add. 27695, fol. 13r. Copyright of the British Library.

Plate 37 Fra Angelico (Guido di Pietro), detail of 'Angel beating a drum', from the Linaiuoli Tabernacle, 1433. Florence, Museo di San Marco. Copyright of the Polo Museale della città di Firenze.

Plate 38 Fra Angelico (Guido di Pietro), detail from *Christ Glorified in the Court of Heaven*, 1423–4. London, National Gallery, NG 663.1.
© The National Gallery, London.

Plate 39 Depiction of the ending of the dance during a Mevlevi *mukabele* (*Les Dervichs dans leur Temple de Péra, achevant de tourner*), de Ferriol, 1715. Copyright of the British Library.

Plate 40 Detail of musicians from the painting of the circumcision festival of Bayezid and Cihangir, Arifi, *Süleymanname*, Ottoman, 965 AH / 1558 AD. Istanbul, Topkapı Palace Museum, H. 1517, fol. 412r. After Atıl 1986, 181, cat. 40.

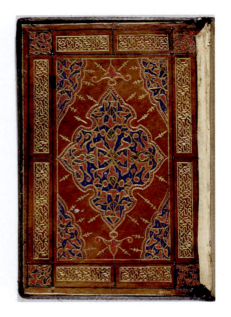

Plate 41 (top left) Upper cover, *Commission*, Venice, 1500. Venice, Biblioteca Marciana Ms.It.VII, 597 (=7820), 26 × 17.7 cm. Courtesy of the Biblioteca Marciana, Venice.

Plate 42 (top right) Doublure, L. Bruni, *Commentarius rerum in Italia suo tempore gestarum*, Bologna?, 1464–5. Venice, Biblioteca Marciana, Lat.X, 117 (=3844) 19.7 × 11.9 cm. Courtesy of the Biblioteca Marciana, Venice.

Plate 43 (left) Upper cover, *Commission*, Venice, 1571. Venice, Biblioteca Marciana, Ms.It.VII, 1366 (=8092), 23.4 × 15.4 cm. Courtesy of the Biblioteca Marciana, Venice.

SECTION III
Renaissance Thought

Chapter 8

Old and New Demarcation Lines between Christian Europe and the Islamic Ottoman Empire: From Pope Pius II (1458–1464) to Pope Benedict XVI (2005–2013)[1]

Zweder von Martels

Over the last century, relations between Europe and Turkey have gradually improved and reached a point when Turkey's admission to the European Union looks nearer than ever. At least, this is what many are hoping who value Turkey's strategic position and its contribution to Europe's defence. Others wish to delay the process. They require that first the country fully complies with the rules of the European convention on human rights, the key to Europe's integration since World War II. In short, the question of Turkey's place within Europe still remains a difficult subject. There are many other sensitive issues related as well to the tensions between Christian Europe and the Muslim world. These need to be treated with care and tact. This even applies to examples taken from the past, such as the crusades propagated by Christian popes and princes against Muslims in Asia and Africa. Pope Pius II,[2] who tried to unite Christian Europe for a holy war against the Ottomans in the fifteenth century, is no exception. No matter whether his wish to counter their advance in Europe and regain Constantinople and all the Christian provinces taken by the Ottomans was justified, for many, the mere thought of a crusade is revolting. Pius's writings, though, offer other aspects that are fascinating because of their relevance to the modern discussion. This is especially true for the pope's letter to Sultan Mehmed II (1461/2), in which an imperial crown is offered to that conqueror of Constantinople. Pius's aim was the 'unification' of Mehmed's Empire and 'Christian Europe'; but like the EU today, Pius stipulated one condition: that the sultan exchanged his Muslim for the Christian faith and allow himself to be baptised. A little water would make him the greatest, mightiest and most famous man.[3]

---

[1] I am indebted to Prof. Arjo Vanderjagt of the University of Groningen for reading this text and his helpful comments.

[2] Pope Pius II was born as Aeneas Silvius Piccolomini, as I will call him when there is mention of events before his papal election in 1458.

[3] Glei and Köhler 2001, 142 (9).

For pope Pius in the fifteenth century to find a solution to the almost irreconcilable differences of religion between Christian Europe and the Islamic Ottoman Empire was a task as hard as sailing between Scylla and Charybdis. In the early twenty-first century, it has, in my view, become easier to build bridges between these antagonistic worlds! While the Renaissance pope saw a unity of faith as the condition for concord and peace, the European Union has replaced this by putting human rights centre stage. Among other things, the idea of the separation of Church and State caused this change; moreover, as a result of the radical reversal of the hierarchy of divine and human laws, the modern focus is on general ethical and human problems, less on thorny and 'subjective' religious ones. Within the new political framework, freedom of religion is permitted, as long as it is in harmony with the other human rights. The practical advantages of this new demarcation line are recognised by the Vatican, not in the least as a persuasive instrument in safeguarding Christian interests within the Islamic world. Proof of this is the recent declaration of its secretary of state, Cardinal Tarcisio Bertone, in which he hinted that Vatican would not oppose Turkey's admission to the European Union, as Turkey 'had come a long way' and 'respected the fundamental rules of coexistence'.[4]

It is tempting to place Pius's epistle to Mehmed in the long tradition of efforts of seeking peace and unity between worlds of different religions by persuasion rather than arms. At the same time it is worth considering that the letter was never actually sent to the sultan and did not contribute to an immediate rapprochement. It had, in fact, quite the opposite effect because it helped Europeans to define those values, which separated them from the Ottomans.[5] Pius's letter was not a misguided and short-lived attempt, but as much as his failed crusade, a strong reminder that sacrifices were needed for the defence of what had shaped Europe's unique identity.

Before examining the demarcation lines which Pius stipulated in his letter to Mehmed, I shall describe the background of hostility and religious discord which formed the backdrop against which Pius and later generations operated. After this the pope's policy will be briefly compared to the diplomacy of the Austrian ambassador Augerius Busbequius, who resided in the Ottoman capital between 1554 and 1562. He will serve as an illustration of the growing importance of diplomacy which saw an adherence to international law, and not a unity of religion as the necessary condition for lasting settlements. Mediation based on international law is an important step to the situation today in which human rights have become the leading principle of guidance for the relationship between nations. This paper will be concluded with a short comparison of the approaches of Pope Pius II and Pope Benedict XVI to the relation of Christian Europe and Muslim Turkey.

---

[4] *La Stampa*, May 30, 2007 (*Interni*, 15).
[5] Glei and Köhler 2001, 98.

The dramatic fall of Constantinople on 29 May 1453, was neither the first nor the last Ottoman triumph of Mehmed the Conqueror. Soon the Morea, a number of Greek islands and Bosnia followed as trophies of his restless military campaigns, but he did not succeed in carrying out a threat mentioned by Pope Pius II in the thirteenth book of his *Commentaries*. Pius explained that as soon as Mehmed learned that the pope, the doge of Venice and the duke of Burgundy were girding themselves up for a crusade, had answered: 'I will spare those weak old men the trouble of sailing; I will take the field first and seek them out in their own homes. There, if they will, they shall contend with me over the empire.'[6] There is little doubt that the Ottoman sultan desired to be regarded as the legitimate successor of the Byzantine emperor killed during the final days of the siege of Constantinople. Coins with his image reveal his imperial aspirations.[7] Mehmed and his successors eagerly looked forward to new conquests in Europe and Afro-Asia. Under Süleyman the Magnificent (1494-1566), the power of the Ottoman Empire reached its zenith. In 1521, he took Belgrade, but three years later, he was thrown back from Vienna. With France as her main ally, the Ottoman Empire became a major player in the struggle for power around the Mediterranean.

Bloodshed and looting had accompanied Constantinople's fall, but soon afterwards the depopulated city against everyone's expectations began to benefit from Ottoman rule. The imperial city now styled Istanbul was made Mehmed's new capital. In the following years, new people were recruited to repopulate the place, and restoration work soon commenced. Piccolomini, who waxed eloquent about the slaughter of 1453, remained silent about these new signs of prosperity.[8] Alarmed by the imminent prospect of an Ottoman domination of Europe, he time and again pressed for a crusade against an enemy he saw as especially horrific. Themes such as the barbarous background and culture of the 'infidels' return in most of his writings which were meant to mobilise support for his plans.[9] An exception, however, to this general trend is his epistle to Sultan Mehmed, an extensive treatise in which arguments rather than the threat of weapons prevail. This was meant to be Pius's humanist contribution to the discussion on what conditions the unity and peace between Europe and the Ottoman Empire should be based.

---

[6] Bellus and Boronkai 1993-1994, vol. I, 628. On Mehmed's ambitions, see Babinger 1978, 494-508.

[7] Babinger 1978, picture facing 388.

[8] Indeed, Piccolomini did not like the idea of a prosperous Constantinople under the Ottomans. Writing to pope Nicholas in 1453, he remarked: 'Furthermore in his time the royal city of Constantinople was taken and looted by the Turks. Perhaps one might even say: destroyed and set ablaze, even though the destruction of the city would suit us more than that it had fallen into the hands of the enemies undamaged.' See Wolkan 1909-1918, vol. 4, 200-201.

[9] Meserve 2008, 101-5.

In the course of time, European images of the Ottoman Empire were gradually changing. A case in point of this long process is found in the letters of the earlier mentioned Augerius Busbequius, who like other contemporary travellers not surprisingly compared Ottoman society to European contexts. He praised the Ottomans for their – comparatively speaking – religious tolerance, for the order and discipline of their society, and for a number of other fine qualities.[10] Yet despite such positive signals, a constant and much larger stream of anti-Ottoman/Islamic writings continued to be printed as long as the Ottoman Empire remained a threat.[11] These writings unremittingly hammered home the message that the 'Turkish' religion, barbarity, its slave mentality and the refusal to live by the rules of international law were alien to European institutions and ideas.

'Faith is dead apart from works'

The concentrated and polished form of Pius's letter to Mehmed (1461/2) leaves little doubt about the author's serious intention. It must be read against the background of his long dealings with the Turks.[12] At the time of Constantinople's fall in the spring of 1453, Piccolomini had already become an outspoken advocate of a crusade. In each of his orations on behalf of Emperor Frederick III he followed similar patterns of arguments, based on three central issues: how just, how useful and how easy the crusade against the infidel would be – arguments that returned in a different form in his letter to Mehmed.[13] From the start, Piccolomini expected little from these political gatherings, because he realised how much the various factions and nations distrusted one another: 'Christians are without a leader whom all would like to obey. Neither the pope, nor the emperor is conferred what belongs to them, there is no respect, no obedience. ... Each nation has its own king.'[14]

After his election as pope in the summer of 1458, Pius set his hopes on an international council which convened at Mantua. As few had come to Mantua, practical decisions about a crusade had to be postponed until 1462. In the years after Mantua, Pius was torn apart by a plethora of urgent matters at home, which drew heavily on the financial reserves of the Church. As a consequence, only sporadic and limited support could be given to the combatants against the Turks. Yet, Pius not prepared to forget his duty, eventually opted to try a political solution. This was not a new approach for him, not even in religious affairs, as his long argument with George of Podiebrad, the leader of the Bohemian sect of the Hussites, demonstrates. As bishop of Siena, he had urged Pope Nicholas to

---

[10] Rouillard 1938; von Martels 2011.
[11] Göllner 1961–1968.
[12] Helmrath 2000, esp. 89.
[13] Blusch 1979, esp. 84–8; Helmrath 2000, esp. 92–5.
[14] Letter to Leonardo Benvoglienti of 5 June, 1454 in Silvius 1967, 656–7.

be lenient in his dealings with him and to put trust in the force of arguments. With his oratorical talent he might lure Podiebrad away from his friends. But in 1464, he admitted its failure by excommunicating his opponent, the one and only way left in his view to bring the man to his senses and to save the unity of the Church.[15]

Disheartened by the continuous wars in Italy and the political division of Europe, Pius was more inclined to listen to his cardinals, Cusanus and Torquemada, and others who favoured a dialogue with the enemy. Both men had written comparative studies on the sacred texts of Christianity and Islam and they had come to the conclusion that the Christian belief in the Holy Trinity was the main obstacle for agreement between both faiths.[16] A brief journey by Pius to Subiaco on invitation of Torquemada in September 1461 must have been the start of Pius's attempt to convince Sultan Mehmed by reason instead of force.[17] The letter to Mehmed was written in the course of the following months.[18]

The epistolary genre suited Pius's aim to create an atmosphere of discussion about the truth which is inherent in Christianity and Islam. The first sentence of his letter is of crucial significance. The sultan is invited to listen carefully as the salvation of his soul, his glory and the common solace of many peoples and peace were at stake.[19] In general, the pope addresses his opponent as an intelligent prince longing for the glory of just leadership and receptive to the truth, and he encouraged him to 'leave darkness and follow the light'.[20] From the start, he was aware that theological arguments alone would be insufficient to convince the Turkish conqueror who was known to be inspired by the deeds of Alexander the Great.[21] Therefore, he claimed that it would be extremely difficult for the Turks to prevail over Europe's military strength and above all over that of Italy with the best soldiers in the world. After this plain introduction, Pius dared to touch upon the main condition by which Mehmed could achieve his imperial dreams:

> A small thing can make you the greatest, mightiest and most famous man of all who live today. ... it is a little bit of water to baptise you, so that you bring yourself by it to Christian worship and belief in the Gospel. When you have

---

[15] Kaminsky 1959.

[16] For a discussion on Cusanus *Cribratio Alkorani* and Juan de Torquemada's *Tractatus contra errores perfidii Machoheti*, see Glei and Köhler 2001, 35-61.

[17] Bellus and Boronkai 1993-1994, vol. 1, 320-23.

[18] See Glei and Köhler 2001, 25. Torquemada's *Tractatus* (see note 16) was used as basis for the second part of Pius's letter to Mehmed, the comparison between both religions.

[19] See Glei and Köhler 2001, 130.

[20] Ibid., 322-3 (147).

[21] See Piccolomini 1454, in Enea 1967, 687 A/B.

done this, there is no prince on earth who will be superior to you in glory, or who may reach up to you in power.[22]

Mehmed's conversion would not be something uncommon or new after the examples of Clovis King of the Franks and a number of other sovereigns. But none was greater than Emperor Constantine, whom Mehmed was urged to follow. Then imperial power would be transferred to him to the benefit of himself and his people and he would receive the crown of the last Byzantine emperor who had, along with Constantinople, fallen in 1453.[23] As earthly pleasures unfortunately do not last, the sultan should now while it was still possible take care of the salvation of his soul. Pius invites Mehmed to give heed to his exposition why the Christian truth is to be preferred to Islam.[24]

In short, as already implied in the first sentence, the letter is not only about the truth of faith, but also just leadership. Both aspects remain until today fundamental concepts in discussions about European identity. Though it is uncertain whether Mehmed would have interpreted these notions in the way Pius expected from him, we need to ask how Pius used them and how they were related to each other in his view? First then, what did Pius mean by faith?

From early on, Pius had seen his Christian faith as more than merely a strong belief in God. In his age, cultural and ethical values and laws were brought together under the umbrella of religion, much as they are today brought together in constructions of a secular nature.[25] Faith, in turn, was strongly connected with ancient Greek and Latin learning, which had played such an important role in the development and maintenance of Christianity. His awareness of the tight connection between faith and learning received a new meaning as a result of the menace from the East. In a letter to Pope Nicholas V shortly after the loss of Constantinople, Piccolomini expressed his fear that with the extinction of this Greek source of the Muses, faith and learning would also be destroyed.[26] In another letter to Cardinal Cusanus, he stressed that the preservation of ancient learning was hanging on a thin thread, now that Constantinople, monument to ancient wisdom, had been captured. Its future now depended on Rome: 'As long as the Holy See thrives, Latin literature will thrive; if it disappears all learning will disappear with it.'[27]

These views about faith and learning return in the letter to Mehmed. Its second part elaborates on the differences between Christian and Islamic teaching. In accordance with tradition, Pius treats Islam as a heretical sect of Christianity, which itself had remained loyal to the traditions of the Old and New

---

[22] Glei and Köhler 2001, 142–3 (9).
[23] Ibid., 158–65 (22–6).
[24] Glei and Köhler 2001, 164 (27).
[25] von Martels 2003.
[26] Letter to Nicholas V of 12 July, 1453 in Wolkan 1909–1918, vol. 4, 200.
[27] Letter to Cardinal Cusanus of 21 July, 1453 in Wolkan 1909–1918, vol. 4, 211.

Testament.²⁸ He reminds the sultan of the numerous Christian church fathers, philosophers and theologians who spent much of their lives reflecting on the truth of their faith.²⁹ By contrast, Pius criticised Muhammad's interdiction to discuss the teaching of the Qur'an, which was not correct, as the prophet had known.³⁰ Among the absurdities of Islamic teaching, the pope mentions the promise of the Qur'an of a paradise overflowing with milk, honey, delicious spices, many women and concubines and carnal unions of virgins and angels acting in shameful obedience, and all else that the flesh might desire.³¹

Pius claimed that with Mehmed's conversion to Christianity, a new era of Augustean peace would ensue, which Islam would never be able to achieve.³² As a man open to reason and in search of the truth, the sultan is urged to pursue this goal, but warned not to place too much trust in the ignorant masses of Muslims. The other Turks would not allow their sultan to abandon the faith of their fathers. Still, there was no reason to be frightened by them. He might give positions of power to his subjects who were of Christian origin, even when they were circumcised. There were many of them, so that they would protect him against the wrath of his Muslim brethren.³³

This apparently Machiavellian feat of political calculation brings us to the second fundamental concept present in Pius's letter to Mehmed, that of just leadership. What did the pope understand by this turn of phrase, and what did it mean for his own conduct and that of his opponent? In Mehmed's case, he may have thought of the definition of leadership developed in his period of service to Emperor Frederick III. In an oration (1452) on the emperor's behalf for Pope Nicholas, he held that princes are elected so that their peoples may enjoy the benefits of justice; that it is their task to ward off injuries, and that they must try to manage the state not with a view to their own interest but to that of those who had entrusted it to them.³⁴ These remarks were meant to encourage Frederick to use his imperial rights to unite the Christian nations and to lead their united armies against the Ottomans. Next to Frederick, Piccolomini looked up to the pope as the second pillar on which Europe's defence could rest. Shortly after the loss of Constantinople, he summoned Nicholas V to avenge this humiliation. What will future historians write when they come to the glory (*gloria*) of Nicholas's reign? In laudatory terms they would mention among other things his birth in Tuscany and construction of the palace of St Peter's – beautiful and fitting things, indeed, but a last addition, the conquest and looting of

---

28   Glei and Köhler 2001, 260–322 (102–46).
29   Ibid., 318–22 (145–6).
30   Ibid., 292–6 (125–7).
31   Ibid., 238 (85).
32   Ibid., 146–50 (12–14).
33   Ibid., 150–58 (15–21).
34   Kollarius 1762; Piccolomini 1685, 308. Piccolomini's words derive from Cicero 2001, 2.41, 3.74 and 1.85.

Constantinople, will spoil his reputation.[35] The list of Nicholas's deeds is nothing less than a model for an *ante-mortem* epitaph of which Piccolomini composed several others on various popes and even an interesting one on himself in the final years of his papacy![36] The latter is jotted down on an empty sheet in the middle of the first book of the manuscript of his *Commentaries*; it first lists Pius's achievements as pope and then concludes with the mention of his death during a war led against the Turks.[37]

In his *Commentaries* Pius preferred to speak of his own leadership of the Church not in Ciceronian terms – as in his oration to Nicholas – but in Biblical ones as those in his praise of St Ambrose in a sermon given on the saint's name day in Basel in 1436. On that occasion he called the holy man a true shepherd who had cared for his sheep.[38] All in all, Pius expected Mehmed to share with him his view of leadership which was of an aristocratic, monarchical, and not obviously of a democratic kind. His was a leadership based upon hereditary rights, divine predestination and personal merit – in short, a heady mixture of medieval ideas of hereditary imperial power and of predestination together with humanist conceptions of merit, and indeed even of *gloria*. Through the ethical connotation, the concept of Christian faith was also narrowly connected with that of just leadership. In his letter to the sultan, Pius noted that for Mehmed more was needed than 'a little water' were he to become a Christian, for 'faith is dead apart from works'.[39] A little earlier he had reminded him in Cicero's words that according to the most learned philosophers all will receive a place in heaven who have served their country. Pius added that if this is true for the classical thinkers, he believed it would certainly be true for those who worked for the preservation and expansion of the teaching of Christ. He expected Constantine to be in heaven and urged Mehmed to follow his example.[40]

Though the project of his letter was apparently abandoned as unrealistic, the pope remained loyal to this idea of Christian leadership by works. This became spectacularly clear shortly after he had finished his letter to Mehmed. In the spring of 1462 he suddenly announced that he himself would lead the crusade necessary for the protection of Christian Europe. At first his preparations went according to plan, but a late refusal by the Duke of Burgundy, Philip the Good, to fulfil his commitment to take up the cross thwarted all hopes for success. Pius

---

[35] Letter to Nicholas V of 12 July 1453, Wolkan 1909–1918, vol. 4, 200–201.
[36] Bernetti 1971, 47–52.
[37] Ibid., 42–6; Piccolomini 1994, 171–2. It is little surprise that the idea of good leadership and fame was also a subject of the preface of his *Commentaries* commenced in the Spring of 1462 or shortly thereafter.
[38] Mansi 1755–1759, vol. 1, second oration.
[39] Glei and Köhler 2001, 176–7 (35).
[40] Ibid., 162–5 (26); Cicero 1928, 6.13.

then decided to continue even if it were to kill him: all would lose confidence in him and the institution of the Church if his actions deviated from his promises.[41]

Augerius Busbequius: International Law as a New modus vivendi

In the age after Pius's death, Biblical studies, the influence of ancient literature and the widening of the horizon as a result of new discoveries were to lead to self-reflection, and this in its turn led to a changing European image of the Ottomans. A single line from Erasmus's adage *Dulce bellum inexpertis* suffices to underscore the changed mood: 'Whom we call Turks are to a large extent semi-Christians and probably nearer to true Christianity than most of us.'[42] Such modesty suited the period after the Reformation even more: Europe was being torn apart by religious wars, and many who were persecuted on grounds of their religion fled to the Ottoman Empire to find a place of refuge. The old dream of a unified Europe under an emperor or pope, fighting the infidels to restore the ideal of universal faith, had lost its meaning. Europe's internal division demanded prudent diplomacy to withstand Ottoman aggression at the borders. Already in Pius's age, diplomacy had grown in importance. For an ambassador what counted were the interests of his sovereign.[43] Eloquent examples of this are found in the four letters Augerius Busbequius wrote about his stay in the Ottoman capital from 1554 to 1562. They demonstrate to us some other changes in approach as part of a longer development continuing into the twenty-first century, in which human rights play a dominant role in international relations.

Busbequius's letters describe his years at Süleyman's court. King Ferdinand of Austria (1563–1564) had resorted to the art of diplomacy so as to avoid wars with the Ottomans. His envoys were welcomed within the Ottoman Empire, but they were not always free to return. In general, the Ottomans demonstrated little respect for the traditional rights of envoys. For any envoy to Constantinople, there was always uncertainty. Much depended on the way the envoy comported himself. Busbequius was deeply aware of this.

Busbequius owed his own success to his moderate, consistent and prudent behaviour, which after many years paid off well. A friendship flourished up between him and Grand Vizier Ali Pasha, a 'thorough gentleman' with 'a kind and feeling heart'.[44] With him he could discuss the matters of his master in an honest way. Ali Pasha strenuously urged that each of them should advise his own master to take the course he considered most appropriate for his interests.[45]

---

[41] For this episode see Bellus and Boronkai 1993-4, vol. I, 634-635; see also von Martels 2005.
[42] Erasmus 1999, 39, lines 828–30.
[43] Mattingly 1955, 109.
[44] Forster and Blackburne Daniell 1881, vol. 1, 157.
[45] Ibid., vol. 1, 346.

There is an incident which illustrates that Ali Pasha and Busbequius perfectly well understood that Europe and the Ottoman world, as a result of differences in religion, were separated from each other by a great distance. The event happened against the background of the internal struggle for power between Süleyman's sons Selim and Beyazid. All along Busbequius had hoped that these dangerous developments for the Ottomans would continue to benefit his negotiations, but when the news of Beyazid's death arrived he was alarmed that his negotiations would come the nothing. Ali Pasha warned him not to wait any longer for other concessions from the Ottomans, for 'old friendship can be restored between two princes who share the same faith more easily than a new one can be cemented between two Sovereigns of different religions'.[46]

These words made a deep impression on Busbequius and convinced him to agree with the terms negotiated so far. Thus his embassy ended with a peace treaty between Ferdinand and Süleyman. The outcome showed that Ferdinand's unilateral decision to establish an expensive permanent embassy in Constantinople was an investment that had paid off well.

This may provide an impression of the conditions in which Busbequius had to operate. Pius's short-lived dream of a converted Ottoman sultan ruling as a new Byzantine emperor for this reason meant little to nothing for Busbequius, whose priority was, rather, attaining a form of consensus with the Ottomans on common issues. To him, the practical nature of Roman law and a shared respect for fairness offered the best perspectives for the protection of the rights of envoys and for international treaties. Moreover, whereas Pius had grown up with the ideal of a universal Christianity, Busbequius was accustomed to the harsh reality of a divided Christian world. This opened his eyes to the different religious groups coexisting within the Ottoman Empire, and as a result he regarded the various religions which he encountered in the Ottoman empire with some detachment. This is clearly seen in his remarks on Metropolitan Metrophanes, the abbot of a monastery in Chalcis in Greece. Metrophanes, he writes, was 'a polite and well-educated man, who was most anxious for a union of the Latin and Greek Churches. In this he differed from the views entertained by Greeks generally, for they will hold no communion with members of the Latin Church, which they consider an impure and profane sect.' And Busbequius concludes meaningfully: '*Adeo suus cuique mos placet*', which can be interpreted as: 'This shows how strong is each man's conviction of the truth of his own faith.'[47]

By putting the differences between religions into perspective Busbequius's words have a modern ring.[48] His allusion to the subjective, personal, character of faith may serve as bridge between Pius's firm belief in the need of political

---

[46] Ibid., vol. 1, 385.

[47] Ibid., vol. 1, 341–2.

[48] This is not to say that Busbequius was indifferent to which faith he adhered: he declined an honourable offer from Roostem Pasha to convert himself to Islam, ibid., vol. 1, 235.

Christian unity in the known world and the modern global world of interreligious dialogue in which popes of our age, such as Benedict XVI, and their cardinals must find their way. A few final marginal notes about the contrast between Pius's and Benedict's position are in place.

Pope Benedict XVI: In the Footsteps of Pope Pius II?

Pius's intention of offering an imperial crown to his great adversary in return for his conversion was quite in harmony with the medieval view that nothing could compete with the Christian faith as ultimate truth. His step may therefore be regarded as a logical step. The pope must have realised, though, that his plan, if carried through, would cause great embarrassment in Europe. For decades, many Christian writers, among whom Pius took a prominent place, had depicted the Ottomans in demonising ways as barbarians from dark corners of the world like Scythia. In addition, he understood that it would not be easy to convert someone from one religion to another. Even when his letter assumes implicitly the impression that the theological doctrine of the Holy Trinity was based on invincible arguments, Pius was well aware that Christian theology is full of uncertainties and unresolved questions. Bartolomeo Platina, one of his biographers, interestingly passes down his aphorism that divine nature can be better understood by *belief* than by debate and that even if miracles had not confirmed the truth of the Christian faith, it would have to be accepted on the basis of its moral integrity (*honestas*).[49]

Down through the centuries moral values, such as those of universal human rights, considered by Pius as an integral part of faith, have been adopted by modern, secular, institutions. These rights, which have their roots in the philosophical idea of natural rights common to all people and therefore more readily accepted,[50] have now become a useful instrument to popes today. It is used by them, for instance, to encourage states to protect the freedom of religion, such as in cases where Christians are threatened by violence and discrimination. It is not by accident that Cardinal Tarcisio Bertone (mentioned earlier) underscores the observance by the modern, secular, Turkish state of these human rights. He added that fundamental rules for human coexistence are developed through dialogue and evolution,[51] a humanist view and very similar to the one which once convinced Pius that Mehmed's acceptance of the truth of Christian faith would have a humanising effect on the actions of that conqueror.

Bertone's positive evaluation of Turkey's political conduct has now placed Pope Benedict in a position similar to Pius's towards the Ottoman state then at Europe's borders. He must decide whether he is going to make the next,

---

[49] Zimolo 1964, 120.
[50] Ishay 2004.
[51] See n. 4.

logical, step of more openly supporting Turkey's entry into the European Union. He might then emulate Pius, but this would no doubt stir great indignation. Opponents of Turkey's entry have been already pointing out Turkey's long history *outside* Europe. Indeed, such historical arguments have always played a role in discussions about the Turks, even in Pius's age. It is to be found in his opinion of their barbaric origin but also in his refusal to regard the teaching of Muhammad as the foundation of the Islamic faith. Pius preferred to consider the prophet's words as a continuation of the heresy of Arius and others who had opposed the doctrine of the Holy Trinity formulated by the Council of Nicea (325).[52] The mere repetition of this old point of view could well cause tremendous upheaval. Pope Benedict's badly received quotations of the Greek emperor Manuel II Palaiologos at Regensburg (2006) remind us of the friction which exists between traditional approaches and modern aspiration which requires new accents and appropriate answers.[53] In this particular case, the pre-eminence of human rights has enabled Rome to avoid speaking of Islam in terms of 'heresy'. Instead, Islam is seen as one of the great world religions with which Rome wants to enter into dialogue. Yet, this transformation of policy will not mean that the Roman Catholic Church is abandoning its belief in the Holy Trinity,[54] nor will it give up its traditional claim of universal primacy.[55]

---

[52] Glei, *Epistola ad Mahumetem*, 204–7 (56–8).

[53] See Benedict's lecture 'Faith, Reason and the University: Memories and Reflections (12 September 2006) http://www.vatican.va/holy_father/benedict_xvi/speeches/2006/september/documents/hf_ben-xvi_spe_20060912_university-regensburg_en.html (last accessed: July 18, 2012).

[54] Jukko 2007.

[55] This has recently been reasserted by the Vatican's Congregation for the Doctrine of the Faith: Responses to some questions regarding certain aspects of the Doctrine on the Church from the Offices of the Congregation for the Doctrine of the Faith, 29 June 2007. See http://www.vatican.va/roman_curia/congregations/cfaith/documents/rc_con_cfaith_doc_20070629_responsa-quaestiones_en.html (last accessed: 18 July 2012).

Chapter 9

Turco-Graecia: German Humanists and the End of Greek Antiquity – Cultural Exchange and Misunderstanding

Asaph Ben-Tov

On the 7 June 1597 an elderly professor of Greek at Tübingen, Martin Crusius (1526–1607), recorded a dream in his diary:

> A dream: 3rd hour before sunrise. We were seated at a table in Constantinople. The Turk drank to my health (kindly and with seemly merriment), and I, rising to my feet, said: Most gracious Emperor (*Allgnaedigster haerr Kaiser*), after which he spoke in German to some people [seated] at another table, while still seated with us; I do not know what he said. I therefore said humbly: Most gracious Emperor, where did your Imperial Majesty learn German? He replied: "From people around me." Then I awoke. I later got up at the 4th hour. This too did I ask: "Most gracious Emperor, is there not something, perhaps an old Greek book, I could take home with me (to Germany)?" He replied: "Oh yes, let us have a look among our books." So much for this.[1]

In his waking hours, needless to say, Crusius never met the sultan; in fact, he rarely ventured outside Tübingen, and while Mehmed III is often mentioned in Crusius's diary, it is in a matter of fact vein, concerning his military exploits, usually his prolonged struggle with the Habsburgs, and yet, in a way, this dream reflects more reality than is evident at first glance.

Since the 1540s we find a growing interest among German Lutherans in Byzantine writings and a curiosity as to the post-Byzantine fate of the Greeks and their Church. Crusius, whose academic career spanned from the 1540s to the first years of the seventeenth century, stood at the centre of this 'discovery' of post-Byzantine Greeks.

Modern Byzantinists tracing the history of their profession have paid considerable attention to its sixteenth-century roots. While the editing and

---

[1] I am grateful to Reinhard Flogaus for his comments on an earlier version of this paper. Needless to say, I am alone responsible for any remaining errors and misconceptions. This curious entry in Crusius's diary, written in a mixture of Latin, German and Greek is printed in Crusius 1927 and 1931, vol. 1, 348.

translation of Byzantine sources since the 1550s was by no means a German or Lutheran preserve, Lutheran scholars' predominance in the field is patent. Suffice it here to mention Hieronymus Wolf (1516–1580) and his *editio princeps* of Zonaras and Choniates (1557), to which he added Nicephorus Gregoras five years later to form the *Corpus Universae Historiae Byzantinae*, Wilhelm Xylander (1532–1576) and his erstwhile student in Heidelberg Johannes Löwenklau (1541–1594),[2] and Wolf's student and successor in Augsburg David Hoeschel (1556–1617).

The same studies of German Late Humanism and Byzantine letters also make the convincing argument that the philological activity of the day did not make a clear distinction between Byzantine and ancient Greek texts, and that a clear dividing line between Greek antiquity and Medieval Greek did not yet exist.[3] At the same time these studies have discerned an ambivalent stance of German Humanists towards Byzantines and contemporary Greeks; while not being clearly distinguished from their ancient predecessors, neither were they distinctly opposed to their Ottoman adversaries and later lords.[4]

A different, though related, approach has been to view sixteenth-century interest in Byzantine history and contemporary Greece as an early phase of Philhellenism, in a sense, as a sixteenth-century precursor to the better known Philhellenism of the Romantic age.[5] Such interpretations tend to focus on the life and opinions of the above-mentioned Crusius, who entertained an enthusiastic interest and sympathy for almost anything related to Greek, and was among the few 'Latins' of his day to acquire a command of contemporary Greek (*barbarograeca* as he termed it).

A third strand of interpretation concentrates on the growing interest of sixteenth-century Lutheran theologians in the Greek Orthodox Church of their day; an engagement which has its roots with the Wittenberg Reformer Philipp Melanchthon (1497–1560) in his later years and the following two generations of Lutheran theologians.[6] This interest culminated with the ecumenical correspondence (1573–1581) between Lutheran theologians of Tübingen and the patriarch of Constantinople, Ieremias II, which was initiated and kept going by a group of Tübingen theologians. Convinced at first that they shared most essential beliefs and practices with their Greek contemporaries, Lutheran theologians were soon proven wrong yet persistently kept up the correspondence until

---

[2] Johannes Löwenklau (Leuncavius) was Reformed rather than Lutheran and was thus barred from a professorship in Heidelberg. While he shares several traits with his Lutheran counterparts, he occupies an ambivalent position at the fringes of the milieu considered here, with considerable differences of world-view. See Burtin 1990.

[3] E.g. Beck 1958, esp. 66–72; Reinsch 1994, 47f.

[4] Ibid., 49.

[5] See e.g., Pfeiffer 1968. For Crusius see: Suchland 2001.

[6] See especially Benz 1952; Benz 1971. For a study of sixteenth-century Lutheran views on Byzantium in the context of universal history see Ben-Tov 2009, esp. ch. 2.

the patriarch finally put an end to it in 1581. Here too Crusius, who served as translator, played a pivotal role.[7]

While the present inquiry is greatly indebted to the above-mentioned interpretations, I wish here to offer a different context for this interest in Byzantium and 'discovery' of contemporary Greeks: that of a confessionalised humanist engagement with Antiquity. I wish to argue that the very nature of this milieu's understanding of later Greek history went through a subtle yet significant and traceable change during the latter half of the sixteenth century, which reflects both the growing availability of Byzantine texts and a concurrent change in their understanding of the history of the later Greek world, which is not directly derived from Byzantine sources.

As Crusius's dream demonstrates, Greeks and the capital of their fallen empire were still associated with Greek manuscripts. That Greek scholars were still conduits of Greek manuscripts at this late stage is exemplified by the career of the poet and manuscript dealer Antonios Eparchos (1492–1571), who was active both in Venice and in his native Corfu.[8] In 1544 Eparchos sold the imperial city of Augsburg a large collection of Greek manuscripts.[9] The evaluation of the manuscripts was entrusted to the staunch Reformer Wolfgang Musculus (1497–1563). Yet, while Eparchos's (not altogether felicitous) dealings with the city of Augsburg are a case of genuine cultural commerce, if not cultural exchange, his German contacts of the following year are a classic example of fundamental cultural misunderstanding. While modern historians have been eager to celebrate the former, the latter has occasionally been tactfully played down, though cultural exchange and profound misunderstanding here, as is often the case, went hand in hand.

Having dealings with the city of Augsburg and Wolfgang Musculus probably brought the idea of contacting Philipp Melanchthon to Eparchos's mind the following year. In a verbose letter composed in Atticised Greek, Eparchos urged the Wittenberg Reformer to put aside the 'trifling wrangle' with the Catholic Church, which was, he explained, a gratuitous impediment to Christian unity in the West and, most importantly, diverting energy and attention, which could be better employed organising a united Christian Crusade against the Turks. If the religious strife continued, Eparchos warned Melanchthon, Germany's fate would be sealed. For all his lavish compliments to the addressee, Eparchos crassly misunderstood the religious and political situation he believed he was addressing: Melanchthon and his colleagues should give up the folly of squabbling over definitions of things in heaven and address the urgent needs on earth, i.e. a Christian crusade against the Ottomans. That Eparchos supposed such argumentation would convince even a relatively conciliatory Reformer is evidence of the single mindedness of his hopeless appeal and the religious and

---

[7] See e.g. Schaeder 1958; Wendebourg 1986; Runciman 1968, 238–58.
[8] For Eparchos' career see Legrand 1885, ccx–ccxxvii.
[9] See Zäh 1997.

mental chasm between addressor and addressee. That Eparchos should have chosen to address Melanchthon may be an indication of the latter's standing as champion of Greek studies and, as Eparchos states in his letter, due to his reputation as a conciliatory figure. Melanchthon, expectedly, disapproved of the appeal, which to him smacked of preference of secular concerns over Christian doctrine, and was to his mind an unfair rebuke aimed at Lutheran politics, which he believed posed no obstacle to a crusade against the Ottomans. He preferred not to reply himself, and asked his friend, Joachim Camerarius (1500–1574) to do so for him.[10]

While this first encounter with a living Greek was for Melanchthon an awkward embarrassment it marks a watershed in his attitude to the fate of contemporary Greeks. In the latter decade and a half of his life (Melanchthon died in 1560) we find a growing awareness of the fate of contemporary Greeks and their Church.[11] A case in point is a short biographical declamation on Basil the Great that Melanchthon composed in 1545.[12] The biographical narration opens with the following statement:

> When I observe Basils' homeland and abode with my mind's eyes, the consideration of the devastation the Turks have wrought upon that most flourishing and beautiful region causes me immense grief. [...] But who would now refrain from grieving, when we hear that those churches and towns have been turned into Turkish stables and huts abounding with impiety, lechery, and cruelty; considering which, not only should we grieve Asia's calamity but should also be perturbed by the peril looming over ourselves. If we wish to beat the Turks, and fear a disaster similar to the Asian one, the causes should be removed. God's wrath is to be assuaged by true offices of piety [...].[13]

The association of a prominent member of Christian Antiquity with the sad contemporary state of affairs is in my opinion a clear indication that later Greek affairs, and the fall of Constantinople were on Melanchthon's mind at the time. The final argument according to which the 'Turkish peril' could only be encountered through an adoption of true religious practice, may be understood as an indirect riposte to Eparchos; not only was the Reformation not responsible for lack of substantial aid to the vanquished Greeks, it in fact offered, to Melanchthon's mind, the only possible remedy to the Ottoman menace.

Significantly, in *De Basilio Episcopo* (1545) the picture we get is of total devastation and no mention is made of any 'remnants of the Church', an otherwise common phrase in his writings. Melanchthon's interest in contemporary Greeks culminated in the realisation that a Greek Church still existed through the

---

[10] Benz 1971, 18–22.
[11] Ibid., passim; Benz 1952, 17–20.
[12] Melanchthon *Corpus Reformatorum* (CR) xi, 657–84.
[13] Ibid., 677.

prolonged sojourn in Wittenberg in 1559 of a Serb by the name of Demetrius, who served as deacon in Constantinople and was sent to Wittenberg to learn at first hand about the nature of the Protestant movement. When he departed Demetrius was handed a Greek translation of the Augsburg Confession as well as a letter by Melanchthon (in Greek) for the patriarch of Constantinople, Ioasaph II. Melanchthon died some months later, and the patriarch, if he indeed received the letter, never replied.[14] The letter itself, however, is extant. In it Melanchthon assures the patriarch that the Greek Orthodox and Protestants share all essentials, and beseeches him to pay no heed to Catholic slurs. Melanchthon assures the Patriarch that both Churches adhere to Scripture, the prophetic and apostolic writings, are heirs to the teaching of the (Greek) Fathers, and adhere to the first Synods.[15]

Three years before this encounter with the 'remnants of the Greek Church' Melanchthon composed a declamation on the fall of Constantinople, which was probably inspired by the publication of a Latin translation in March 1556 of Laonicus Chalcondyles's *De origine et rebus gestis Turcorum* (*On the Origin and Deeds of the Turks*). The Athenian historian Laonicus Chalcondyles (ca. 1430–1490) offered Renaissance readers a contemporary's account of the fall of Constantinople and other remnants of Byzantine sovereignty in an historical account which is full of admiration for Mehmed II and the great achievements of the Ottomans, whose rise from obscurity to greatness it chronicles. The Zurich born pastor Konrad Clauser (ca. 1520–1611) translated the history into Latin. The work was printed in Basel by Johannes Oporinus (1507–1568), who was later to publish the *Corpus Universae Historiae Byzantinae*. It is worth noting that while Clauser's Latin translation seems to have enjoyed considerable popularity, and a French translation followed in 1577, the Greek *editio princeps* only appeared in Geneva in 1615.[16] This general context of a growing awareness to the fate of later Greeks without yet a clear idea of the nature of the contemporary Greek Church sets, in my opinion, the general context of Melanchthon's *De capta Constantinopoli* ('On the Capture of Constantinople'), which was delivered at the university of Wittenberg in 1556.[17]

Melanchthon opens the account of the fall of the capital of the 'Greek Empire' (*imperium graecum*)[18] thus:

---

[14] Benz 1952, 18f.

[15] Printed by Martin Crusius in Crusius 1584, 557; found also in CR ix, 922f.

[16] See F. Hieronymus in *Griechischer Geist aus Basler Pressen* www.unibas.ub.ch/kadmos/gg *ad loc* (retrieved 17.5.2012).

[17] CR xii, 153–61.

[18] Melanchthon and his contemporaries repeatedly refer to Byzantium as the 'Greek Empire'. 'Byzantium' for most sixteenth-century writers was no more than a geographical term designating the site of the Dorian colony founded by the Bosporus in the seventh century BC.

This year is the hundred and third after the Turks, on the twenty-ninth of May, after a fifty-four day siege, forcefully captured Constantinople, which was not only the stronghold of the Greek Empire but also an abode of learning and an ancient residence of the Church, following the most cruel murder of the emperor, his wife, daughters and sons and that of many noble families and many of the common folk.[19]

This opening statement is a good indication of Melanchthon's sympathy for the subject matter, but equally of the limits of his information on Byzantine history. Whether he truly believed the last Byzantine emperor, Constantine XI, had perished with his wife, daughters and sons, or whether it was a guess or convenient rhetorical flourish (*facta caede crudelissima imperatoris, coniugis, filiarum et filiorum*)[20] a better informed writer would have realised this to be impossible since Constantine XI was twice widowed, unmarried and without issue at the time of the city's fall.[21]

More important perhaps is Melanchthon's repeated acknowledgement here of Constantinople's standing as a centre of learning as well as an 'ancient residence of the Church'. A sombre sense of urgency pervades since the Turks are now devastating Hungary and not just Greece, Melanchthon admonishes his audience, a consideration of Constantinople's fate offers a dismal foretaste of what Germany itself is about to suffer.

At the outset Melanchthon posits two prophecies as a basis for his sombre prediction: Ezekiel's prophecy (Gog and Magog) and prophecies by the Franciscan monk Johann Hilten (ca. 1425–1500), who predicted the conquest of Germany and Italy by the Ottomans by 1600.[22] Hilten's prophecy coincides with Melanchthon's expectation that the end of the world would occur in 1600, as set out in the preface of his universal history, the *Chronicon Carionis* (1558/60), where he expounds the Talmudic *Traditio Domus Eliae*. According to Hilten the conquest of the Holy Roman Empire in 1600 would be a preamble to the renewal of Christianity and the final destruction of Islam, to be followed by the end of the world in 1651 – Melanchthon, however, passes this prophetic apodosis in silence. It is worth noting that among the writers discussed here Melanchthon is the only one to posit the fall of Constantinople within a prophetic and possibly apocalyptic context.

Before turning to the fate of Constantinople, he expounds, by way of preface, the fall of Athens to the Ottomans. This in itself is misleading since he does not give the date of Mehmed II's conquest of the Florentine duchy of Athens. The

---

[19] Ibid., 153.

[20] Ibid.

[21] See Nicol 1992, 13, 17f., 44f.; Runciman 1963, 54f.

[22] Predictions of the subjugation of Germany to the Ottomans based on Ezekiel 38, 39 and Hilten's vision were fairly widespread among Lutherans. See Barnes 1988, esp. ch. 2.

lower city was occupied by the Ottomans in 1456. The duke of Athens, Franco II, and many of the citizens fled to the palace on the Acropolis, where they remained until their surrender in June 1458 – i.e. five years after the fall of Constantinople.[23] Paraphrased, Melanchthon's account of the fall of Athens runs thus: The Florentine ruler of the city died leaving behind a widow and a young son. The widow fell in love with a married Venetian who poisoned his own wife in order to marry her and rule the city. Mehmed was called on to intervene. He executed the Venetian and entrusted the city to a relative of the young heir who in turn had the Florentine widow murdered. The young heir called on Mehmed to intervene, fearing this relative was taking possession of what was rightfully his. The sultan, his patience exhausted, put an end to all this by ordering the governor of Thessaly to conquer the city. Athens was later further devastated following a rebellion. All these events are understood by Melanchthon as forms of divine retribution.[24] He then summarises:

> Now naught is left but ruins, fishermen's shacks and a rabble of wanderers of barbarian stock, who have converged there by chance. This is the fall of the city, which erstwhile displayed remarkable instances of virtues, was the abode of learning and achieved great and worthy feats against the Persians with prudence and valour, and in its rule was more moderate than either the Spartans or the Thebans. Two thousand years separate Solon and this Mehmed the destroyer of Athens.[25]

Such praise, however tempered, of the Athenian empire of the fifth century BC, is absent from Melanchthon's account of ancient history in the *Chronicon Carionis*. Melanchthon, furthermore, does not seem to appreciate the significance of Latin rule in the Peloponnese since the Fourth Crusade, which can hardly be taken as a continuation of ancient or any other Greek rule. Yet more revealing is the choice to preface his Fall of Constantinople with the chronologically misleading account of the later Ottoman conquest of Athens. This, as his final praise of Athens implies, is to set the fall of Constantinople within the context of Greek Antiquity, positing it within the framework of the two millennia, which separate Solon, its founder in Melanchthon's eyes,[26] and Mehmed II, its devastator.

The Athenian episode is also revealing since it is clearly a synopsis of Chalcondyles's account of the fall of his native city.[27] Unlike Melanchthon,

---

[23] Babinger 1978, 159f.; and Runciman 1963, 171.
[24] CR xii, 154f.
[25] Ibid., 155.
[26] For Melanchthon's understanding of Solon's legislation as a founding moment in Greek history see Melanchthon CR xii, 788f.
[27] References to Clauser's Latin translation of *De origine et rebus gestis Turcorum* is to the second edition by Oporinus as supplement to Hieronymus Wolf's 1562 *editio princeps*

Chalcondyles's account is written in a matter of fact vein, despite the piquant nature of the story. Furthermore, the fall of Athens appears in Chalcondyles in its correct chronological position. There is nowhere in his account an attempt to give the fall of his native city the tragic significance attributed to it by Melanchthon.[28] In stark contrast to the Reformer, Chalcondyles's account is not hostile to Mehmed II, and immediately following the account of the fall of Athens Chalcondyles tells us of the sultan's visit to the city and his great admiration for its ancient monuments, which he ordered to be preserved. Melanchthon, who follows Chalcondyles's account of the fall of Athens and in all likelihood read the paragraph immediately following, in which Chalcondyles describes Mehmed's admiration for the monuments of Greek Antiquity, passes the latter in silence and instead offers the historical epitome of Athenian history from Solon to Mehmed II.

While Melanchthon in his later years showed a growing awareness and interest in the fate of latter-day Greeks, it was his erstwhile student, the Rostock theologian and humanist David Chytraeus (1531–1600) who in 1569 first offered a detailed account of the contemporary Greek Orthodox Church in his frequently reprinted *Oratio de Statu Ecclesiae hoc tempore in Graecia Asia, Austria, Vngaria, Böemia & c.* ('An Oration on the current State of the Church in Greece, Asia, Austria, Hungary, Bohemia, etc.').[29]

Chytraeus was summoned to Vienna in 1568 by the emperor Maximilian II to draft a church ordinance for the Protestant communities of the Habsburg lands of Lower Austria. This endeavour was thwarted by strong Catholic opposition at the Habsburg court.[30] Being neither able to return home to Rostock nor to work on the ordinance to any effect Chytraeus spent much of his time travelling in Austria and Hungary and got as far as the Hungarian border with the Ottoman empire. He himself never ventured into Ottoman lands but used his newly acquired acquaintances in Austria and Hungary to compose an account on the state of the Orthodox Churches – mostly but not exclusively, Greek Orthodox.

The tone at the outset of the work is of surprise and excitement at the survival of a Church in the remote south-eastern extremities of Europe, as well as wonder at their survival at the very centre of Turkey; and these, Chytraeus stresses, are by no means meagre remnants, but fairly elaborate ecclesiastical institutions – a sure sign of divine benevolence and a source of comfort.[31]

---

of Nikephoros Gregoras: *Nicephori Gregorae, Romanae, hoc est Byzantinae historiae Libri XII* (Basel, 1562) hence Chalcondyles 1562.

[28] Chalcondyles 1562, I5r.
[29] Chytraeus 1569. For a discussion of the work and its background see: Engels 1939–40; and Benz 1952, 21–4; Benga 2001, available at: http://www.opus.ub.uni-erlangen.de/opus/volltexte/2004/86/ (retrieved 17.5.2012).
[30] Benz 1952, 21; Fichtner 2001, 148–54.
[31] Chytraeus 1569, A2v–A3r.

The detailed account itself, while pervaded by sympathy for fellow-Christians under Ottoman rule, is remarkably sober and void of the 'Romantic' delusions about the discovery of Christian Antiquity. In fact, considering the fact that the first systematic and protracted Protestant-Orthodox exchange came four years later, the degree to which Chytraeus was informed is remarkable. Thus, for instance, apart from being aware of the elaborate Marian worship in Greece,[32] he is aware of Thomas Aquinas's translation into Greek and his popularity among many Greek scholars, as well as the Orthodox practice of celebrating mass for the dead, which he describes without passing judgement.[33]

Chytraeus's sober description of contemporary Athens makes it clear that he thinks its days of glory are gone. And yet he stresses that unlike reports to the contrary, the city still stands and even hosts a church of modest size. Like Melanchthon he too culls part of his information from Chalcondyles; yet while Melanchthon is careful to avoid Chalcondyles's admiring observations about the sultan, Chytraeus repeats the latter's account of how Mehmed II was struck by the ancient monuments of the city.[34]

A clue as to the Byzantine Empire's relation to Antiquity, and correspondingly the significance of the Ottoman conquest can be found in Chytraeus's detailed account of contemporary Athens:

> But let us return now to Athens, which was once the abode of all philosophy and eloquence, and later also of religious doctrine and all finer arts. These arts were renewed in Italy a hundred years ago thanks to the exile of Greeks [such as] Theodorus Gaza of Thessaloniki, the Athenian Demetrius Chalcondyles, Georgius Trapezuntius and Marcus Musurus of Crete, and before them Manuel Chrysoloras who died in Germany at the time of the Council of Constance. Now, however, the study of ancient philosophy and more learned teaching has come to a halt in Athens and in the rest of Greece, and I hear that most priests and monks are even ignorant of Ancient Greek. Furthermore, I have heard that in some places reading the ancient poets, orators, philosophers, or any of the other pagan writers is prohibited by episcopal laws.[35]

The decline of learning is then epitomised in a pithy statement about the prayer books recited by Greek priests and monks: 'They read but do not understand.' As a natural consequence of the quenching of pristine teaching Chytraeus goes on to discuss contemporary Greek 'superstition'.

Another channel of information about contemporary Greeks was offered by travellers to the Ottoman Empire. While the best known is the Flemish imperial emissary to the High Porte, Ogier Ghislain de Busbecq (1522–1592), several

---

[32] Ibid., C3v–C4r.
[33] Ibid., C4r.
[34] Ibid., B8v.
[35] Ibid., C2v–C3r.

German Lutheran travellers are of more immediate relevance in the present context. One such traveller was a retired Fugger agent, Hans Dernschwam (1494–1568), who in 1553 joined an Imperial delegation to Constantinople and Asia Minor out of sheer curiosity and at his own expense. Two decades later, two young Lutheran chaplains and former students of Martin Crusius, Stefan Gerlach (1546–1612) and Salomon Schweigger (1551–1622), stayed in Constantinople for several years as Lutheran chaplains to Imperial delegations. Dernschwam in the 1550s and Gerlach and Schweigger a generation later, kept a detailed account of their journey, which reflect changing perceptions of contemporary Greeks – a change, I would argue, closely related to questions of historical periodization i.e. defining the contours of Greek Antiquity.

Dernschwam, embarking on his voyage in 1553, kept a diary during his journey to Constantinople and Asia Minor, which remained in manuscript until its publication by Franz Babinger in 1923.[36] During his stay in the East Dernschwam purchased a manuscript of the *Epitome of Histories* by the twelfth-century Byzantine chronicler Ioannes Zonaras. On his return he persuaded his former employer Anton Fugger to commission his librarian Hieronymus Wolf to edit and translate the work.[37]

Dernschwam's diary also affords us a view of Lutheran expectations of the Greeks and echoes, in layman's terms, a typical reaction to post-Byzantine reality. Shortly after arriving in Constantinople Dernschwam dwells at length on the Greeks' adherence to the apostolic faith, but this, significantly, before he had any contact with Greeks in the city:

> [..] and so the Pope holds no sway over the Greeks, for even now under oppression they remain obedient to their Patriarch throughout Greece, Egypt etc. and they adhere to their ancient Christian faith, which was handed down from the Apostles, more truly and steadfastly than the seductive Pope with all his monastic orders.[38]

This is followed by further anti Papal invectives and praise of the Patriarch of Constantinople.[39] The Greeks, with whom Dernschwam was not yet acquainted, are portrayed as a Protestant idealisation of the Early Church, in stark contrast to a corrupt Papacy, and are described as the source of all Christian teaching.[40] Dernschwam concludes this lengthy excursus by postulating the purification of

---

[36] Dernschwam 1986.

[37] Testimony to the significance of this publication are the repeated pirate editions which offered the Latin translation without the Greek (e.g. Paris 1567 and Cologne 1567) and the fact that by 1560 both a French and Italian translation were available. See Krumbacher 1897, 374 n. 1; and Husner 1949.

[38] Dernschwam 1986, 78.

[39] Ibid., 79.

[40] Ibid., 81.

Western Christianity as a precondition for the liberation of Constantinople by a pious (Holy Roman) emperor.

During his stay in the city Dernschwam became aware of the discrepancy between his idealisation and the actual practices of contemporary Greeks. That such a sober disenchantment should take place is hardly surprising, yet the crucial point for understanding Dernschwam, and, I would argue, Crusius later in the century, is the way he explains this discrepancy between his expectations and observations about three months after arriving in Constantinople:

> It is no wonder that Christianity has deteriorated in Turkish lands. An indication for this is the fact that the Greeks make do with the mass, and otherwise know little about the Word of God, since the laymen are not preached to in the churches, and [the Word of God] is not presented to them. Even the tolling of bells is not allowed them in the whole of Turkey, nor are clocks to be found anywhere. Small wonder that the Italians and their like are such godless Christians. This is because they are only seldom preached to, mostly during fasts, and their priests are predominantly mass performers like all papist monks and so too are the Greek monks, as I have come to know them. They are hermits who live in solitude, abstain from meat, fast a lot but drink wine; and the Patriarch of the Greeks is such a monk. Nor do they preach in their Greek language, which would be intelligible to the poor simple folk.[41]

It is no wonder that Christianity has deteriorated in Turkish lands. Once Dernschwam realised the chasm between his prior expectations and the reality of Greek Orthodox practice, which for him was a form of Papism, it did not cause him to question his prior convictions about the Greek Church in Antiquity or in later times, but to dwell on the degenerate character of Christian worship under Ottoman rule.

Stefan Gerlach and Salomon Schweigger were both theology students in Tübingen and served consecutively as Lutheran chaplains to the first two Imperial delegations at the High Porte, and became Lutheran ministers on their return. Both kept a German travel diary, which in both cases were published decades later. Both corresponded with their former teacher Martin Crusius during their travels in the Ottoman Empire. Crusius in turn published some of these letters as sources on the state of affairs in the Greek world and enthusiastically publicised his former students' exploits in the East in his own books, and even composed his own account of Schweigger's travels in 1584, more than two decades before Schweigger himself published his travel diary.[42]

Gerlach and Schweigger, unlike Dernschwam two decades earlier, arrived in Constantinople after the 'discovery' of the Greek Church in Lutheran circles. Their views on the Greek Church are critical from the outset. Writing in the 1570s (and

---

[41] Ibid., 144.
[42] This was appended to Crusius 1584b.

probably editing their work at a later date), they were far better acquainted than Dernschwam with the reality of Greek Christianity before setting off on their journey. Their descriptions of Orthodox practice is by far better informed than Dernschwam's, but void of sympathy. The differences between the two young theologians and Dernschwam can, of course, be explained as a professional and generational gap between a Protestant layman born in 1494 (and formerly employed by the Catholic Fuggers) and confessionalised Lutheran divines – Gerlach was to spend his later years inveighing against Calvinist doctrine. But though this is clearly part of the answer, a closer look at their former teacher, Martin Crusius, suggests a more complex and interesting shift in attitude.

Crusius closely followed his students' exploits in the East, and was eager to draw as much information about contemporary Greeks as he could. The famous ecumenical correspondence with the patriarch failed and left the Lutheran theologians disenchanted, and embarrassed.[43] Yet for Crusius it was also the starting point for establishing contact with Greek scholars, among whom was the patriarchal protonotary Theodosios Zygomalas (1544–1614). Long after the theological correspondence had run its course Crusius and Zygomalas were still exchanging letters. Zygomalas supplied the Tübingen professor with sources on the political and ecclesiastical history of the Greeks since 1453, most important perhaps was a political history of the Greeks, compiled by Zygomalas himself, which Crusius translated into Latin and published in 1584. Zygomalas was forced to sever his ties with the Germans by the Ottoman authorities, who suspected him of seditious dealings.[44] In 1597 we find Crusius writing to various Greek dignitaries wondering whether his former correspondent was still alive.[45] He was, however, for several years an invaluable source of information for Crusius and a broader readership on the fortunes of post-Byzantine Greeks. The latter also had ample opportunity to hear demotic Greek since he hosted several Greeks in Tübingen, though in his later years he seems to have grown weary of the petitions of destitute Greeks, and finally wrote to the patriarch of Constantinople, stating he would only receive petitioners whose pleas were authenticated by him.[46] All this has earned Crusius in modern times the accolade of Philhellenist, a term he himself used. But a celebration of his enthusiasm for all things Greek has often obscured an interesting ambivalence.

The main scholarly result of Crusius's interest in post-Byzantine Greeks is an extensive compilation of sources concerning post-Byzantine ecclesiastical and secular history published in 1584. Fifteen years later, in letters to two Greek Bishops resident in Venice, Gavrielos Severos (1541–1616) and Maximos

---

[43] The correspondence was published in 1584 by unnamed Tübingen theologians: Anon. 1584.

[44] See Fatouros 1998, vol. XIV, cols 675–6.

[45] See e.g. Crusius's letter of 18 July 1597 to the (by then deceased) Patriarch of Constantinople Ieremias II in Crusius 1927 and 1931, vol. 1, 368.

[46] Ibid.

Margounios (1549–1602) Crusius apologised profusely for the offence he realised he had caused by the work's title: *Turco-Graecia*. In these letters of apology he professed anew his sympathy for contemporary Greeks and their plight.[47] This may well have been genuine, but to understand Crusius and his contemporaries' view of Greeks under Ottoman rule we must turn to the *Turco-Graecia* itself in which Crusius explains the book's unlikely title:

> I have given [my work] the title TVRCO-GRAECIA since it contains accounts of affairs since the fall of the Greek Empire under Turkish rule. Greece has been thoroughly turkified: Greece is subjugated to Turkish servitude and, moreover, Greece is now guilty of many errors in religion and superstitions of which we were not at first aware. It is therefore with good reason that her misery should be lamented.[48]

Crusius goes on to stress his great achievement in bringing this hitherto unknown chapter of Greek history to his readers; but this is a sad achievement. Athens, once the radiant centre of learning is reduced to the destitution of a fishing village, and the Greeks are immersed in error and superstition.

Revealingly, Lutheran laments for the changed fortunes of Athens often appear within the context of the fall of Constantinople. Since Melanchthon in the 1550s, in rounding up laments of the fall of Constantinople, the chronological framework discussed is usually from Solon to Mehmed II. Crusius explains the nature of the contemporary Greek Church as a 'turkification', despite his continued sympathy for Greece and the Greeks. This and countless similar utterances suggest that he understood the Ottoman conquest of Constantinople to be the closing of Greek Antiquity. That Crusius was not alone in this view is made clear by some of the poems written for him by several well-wishers and printed on the opening pages of the *Turco-Graecia*. Apart from fulsomely praising Crusius's achievement, these poems address the subject of post-1453 Greece. Hellas, we are told in florid Neo Latin and pseudo-Homeric Greek, once the envied abode of the Muses (etc.) fell to the hands of the Turks (through her own fault) and is since piteous and barren. Lorenz Rhodomann (1546–1606), a Lutheran pedagogue and authority on Greek Letters expressed this view in a Greek poem he composed in Crusius's honour. An abridged prose translation of lines 1–18 runs thus:

> Hellas, exulting in the Muses' revered eloquent monuments, was the most conspicuous and fragrant in all the land. From Parnassus' stream she sent to the entire world the Hermes like waters of wise eloquence. Happy would she have been but for her love of internal strife. She who had achieved greatness through the possession of great wealth (abundance, it is known, breeds

---

[47] Crusius 1927 and 1931, vol. 2, 386.
[48] Crusius 1584, 2v.

hubris) by her own hands forfeited her might, having acted foolishly she lost her sovereignty to the Turks. Thereupon the Muses (Aonids) having left their shrines took headlong flight beyond the snow-capped Alps to the valiant land of the Teutons [..] and shall converse with to the Germans instead of the Castalians. You, children of the beautiful land of Germany, pray to Christ for wisdom in addition to good fortune (worldly happiness). Now the migrant Muses adorn the abode of the German land with the far shining spark of wise men.[49]

The motive of German inheritance is important and has an interesting confessional context,[50] but for the present inquiry what is most important is the claim that Hellas herself was dead, and that she had died in 1453.

An echo of this view we can find three years later, in a textbook by one of Crusius's friends and a former student of Melanchthon's, Michael Neander (1525–1595) in his handbook on universal history, *Chronicon sive Synopsis Historiarum* (1582), where he makes the following observation about contemporary Athens:

In recent years Martin Crusius, an illustrious man, professor of rhetoric and Greek at the University of Tübingen, and a great old friend of ours has had letters sent to him by Christian Greeks written in Turco-Greek, Scythian and a mixture of Ancient and vulgar Greek (*mixobarbara*). Whereby the following too is worthy of mention: nowhere in Greece nowadays do people use a more barbarous idiom than in Athens. Athens, which was once the common school of mankind and the workshop of all instruction [...] it was by no means in vain that the following was announced to the Athenians by Oracle: "Do not praise the Athenians to me, they shall [one day] be [but] oxen hide." That is, they shall be wineskins, and shall one day fall from their forefathers' nobility, virtue, learning, refinement, eloquence and wisdom.

Two thousand years separate Solon, that wise governor of the Athenian state and celebrated legislator, and Mahomet (Mehmed II), the destroyer of Athens.[51]

The conquest of Constantinople by Mehmed II put an end to Athenian glory, begun with Solon's legislation. The remaining Greeks for Neander are a strange people speaking a semi-barbarous idiom, Turco-Greek and Scythian. Neander nowhere writes of 'Christian Spaniards' or 'Christian Italians', whose Christianity is taken for granted. In referring to Crusius's correspondents as 'Christian Greeks' it is clear that for Neander, and possibly his readers, with the fall of the "Greek Empire" the very identification of Greeks as Christians could no longer be taken for granted.

---

[49] Ibid., 9r.
[50] See Ben-Tov 2009, ch. 5.
[51] Quoted from the later extended edition: Neander 1586, 162r.

Greek Antiquity was over, and as Lutheran scholars' idealised vision of Greeks as a latter-day personification of Christian Antiquity was dashed, the Greeks' fall from Ancient learning and pure Patristic doctrine became yet another instance of the mutability of worldly affairs as history approached its end.

Chapter 10
Positive Views of Islam and of Ottoman Rule in the Sixteenth Century: The Case of Jean Bodin

Noel Malcolm

The sixteenth century saw a transformation in West European thinking about the Ottoman state and Ottoman society. Not everything changed, of course; Western ideas about Islam were still largely determined by the long tradition of medieval anti-Muslim polemics, and popular culture maintained the image of the 'Turk' as an embodiment of cruelty, ferocity and lust. But any literate person could, by the second half of the century, gain access to a substantial body of information about the conditions of life and government in the Ottoman world – information provided by writers who had been there and seen it for themselves. Broadly speaking, these authors divided into two categories: former captives on the one hand, and those who travelled there in connection with diplomatic missions (whether as ambassadors or as scholars in the envoys' entourages) on the other.[1]

In the first category the most important writers were George of Hungary (or 'of Transylvania'), who had been enslaved by the Turks for twenty years, and whose *Tractatus de moribus, condictionibus et nequicia Turcorum* was first published in 1481; Bartholomeus Georgewitz [Djordjević], from southern Hungary or Slavonia, who had spent thirteen years as a captive, and whose *De turcarum ritu et caeremoniis* was published in 1544; Luigi Bassano, from Zadar, who had been seized in ca.1530 and returned in 1541, publishing his *I costumi, et i modi particolari de la vita de' Turchi* in 1545; and Giovanni Antonio Menavino, from Genoa, who was captured by corsairs in 1505, and published his *I cinque libri della legge, religione, et vita de' Turchi* (also issued under the title *Trattato de' costumi et vita de' Turchi*) in 1548. All of these works went through many editions; and there were also popular compilations, such as Francesco Sansovino's *Dell'historia universale dell'origine et imperio de' Turchi* (1560), in which most of them were reprinted.[2] The key accounts by diplomats and travellers, on the other hand, were mostly written by Frenchmen: this was a consequence of links forged by the pro-Ottoman policy

---

[1] In the summary of this material which follows, I recapitulate some points made in Malcolm 2003, 48–51.

[2] On Sansovino's influential work see Yérasimos 1997.

of François I and his successors. These authors included Christophe Richer, whose short treatise appeared in both Latin (*De rebus turcarum*) and French (*Des coustumes et manieres de vivre des Turcs*) in 1540; Antoine Geuffroy, whose *Estat de la court du grant Turc* was published in 1542; Pierre Belon, the naturalist who accompanied the French ambassador in 1547 and published his *Les Observations* in 1553; Nicolas de Nicolay, a member of a subsequent French mission, whose *Les Quatre Premiers Livres des navigations* was published in 1568; and the scholar, Arabist and visionary religious universalist, Guillaume Postel, whose *De la République des Turcs* was published in 1560. One other important text was produced by a Habsburg diplomat: the *Epistolae* of Ogier Ghiselin de Busbecq, published in two instalments, in 1581 and 1589, and frequently reprinted thereafter.

All of these writers expressed both a fundamental hostility to the Turks, which could be extremely bitter in the case of the former captives, and a belief that Islam was an inferior and false religion. But their writings were based on observation, not on blind prejudice (even if they sometimes misunderstood what they observed, and even though they did occasionally borrow material or arguments from previous writers). And what emerged, overall, from this body of writings was a coherent and quite detailed picture of a well-ordered society and state – a society which not only was efficiently administered, but also embodied virtues that seemed to be comparatively lacking in Western Europe.

One of the things that most impressed these writers was Ottoman military discipline. George of Hungary commented on the extraordinary silence that reigned in the Ottoman army camp; Busbecq, likewise, wrote that in the camp 'Everywhere order prevailed, there was perfect silence, no quarrels, no bullying ... no drinking, no gambling.'[3] Georgewitz and Postel remarked on the absence of stealing by soldiers, even from the local population when on campaign.[4] The explanations offered by these authors for these striking features of military life included the influence of Islam (in the prohibition of drinking and gambling); a general ethos of sobriety, simplicity, good order and the lack of luxury (for example, in dress – a point strongly emphasised by George of Hungary); severe and peremptory justice (the punishment of theft); and, above all, military virtue, instilled by strict and thorough training. All writers commented on the system of the *devşirme* (boy-tribute), and on the way in which the youths thus removed from their parents could be moulded into Janissaries loyal only to the sultan.

Another positive feature of Ottoman life on which most writers commented was the administration of justice. Georgewitz was struck by its impartiality; Menavino was impressed by the sheer speed with which justice was meted out by the 'kadi' (judge).[5] Postel expressed his admiration for the 'diligence de

---

[3] Georgius de Hungaria 1993, 222; Forster and Blackburne Daniell 1881, vol. I, 288. For a classic account of the discipline that reigned in Ottoman army camps by another influential author, see Coccio 1560, vol. II, col. 1049.

[4] Georgewitz 1544, sig. D2r; Postel 1560b, 31, 47.

[5] Georgewitz 1544, sig. D3v; Menavino 1548, 54.

Iustice' of the Ottomans, declaring that 'it makes me ashamed to describe such great diligence in a people who have been proclaimed wicked [by us]: it is this diligence that, undoubtedly, makes them rule, conquer and keep their conquests as they do.' He also attributed the speed and honesty of their judicial procedure to the absence of lawyers: 'there', he wrote, 'they have no lawyers to put false appearances on things.'[6]

Another common theme was the equality and meritocracy of Ottoman society, in the absence of a hereditary nobility. George of Hungary emphasised that officials were promoted 'according to proven virtue', not according to birth, 'From which it follows that all the magnates and princes of the whole kingdom are like office-holders, not lords or owners of estates ... And hence it follows that in the Sultan's realm, although there is an innumerable mass of people, no contradiction or resistance can arise; they act like a single person in all things.'[7] Postel made a similar point about promotion based on merit, and Busbecq waxed rhapsodic about it: 'Among the Turks, therefore, honours, high posts and judgeships are the rewards of great ability and good service ... This is the reason that they are so successful in their undertakings.'[8]

Also given great emphasis in these accounts was the theme of welfare – both private charity and public provision. Georgewitz praised the 'imarets' (public kitchens that dispensed food to paupers and travellers); Menavino devoted three pages to imarets and 'hans' (inns, at which, he noted, a traveller would be given food and lodging for three days, free of charge); and Bassano commented on the higher standards of private and public hygiene, noting that there was organised street-cleaning and describing the 'hamams' (public baths) in great detail.[9] Postel spent eight pages describing their hospitals, imarets and hans, lamenting the fact that private charity was much greater among Turks than among Christians, and commenting that Turks who visited Venice were shocked by the sight of sick people begging there in the streets.[10] Geuffroy grudgingly declared that 'the only good thing about them, if there is any at all, is that they are charitable, and great founders of hospitals', and Nicolas de Nicolay, in his otherwise rather hostile account of the Ottomans, repeated both Bassano's admiring account of their public baths and Postel's praise of their humane treatment of the sick, the mad and the indigent.[11]

Finally, one other aspect of the Ottoman system attracted special comment: the toleration shown towards the practice of both Christianity and Judaism. George of Hungary noted that 'the Turks never force anyone to renounce his

---

[6] Postel 1560, 36, 127.
[7] Georgius de Hungaria 1993, 212–14.
[8] Postel 1560, 121; Forster and Blackburne Daniell 1881, vol. I, 154–5.
[9] Georgewitz 1544, sig. C1r; Menavino 1548, 48–50; Bassano 1568, fols 48–52, 65v, 66v.
[10] Postel 1560, 56–63.
[11] Geuffroy 1543, fol. 4r; de Nicolay 1989, 134–40.

religion; nor, in this matter, do they try very hard to persuade anyone either'.[12] Pierre Belon commented as follows: 'Each of the Christian faiths active in Turkey is allowed to have its own separate Church. For the Turks do not force anyone to live as they do. This is what has always sustained the great power of the Turk: for, whatever country he conquers, he takes it as sufficient that he be obeyed, and so long as he receives the taxes they pay, he does not bother about people's souls.'[13] This essentially *politique* explanation of Ottoman religious toleration became the dominant one in Western writings in this period, and could sometimes be given a more negative twist: thus François de La Noue would write that the Turk tolerated Christians 'just as we permit cows and sheep to live in our fields – because they are useful to us'.[14] But it was not the only explanation. Menavino declared that the Muslims believed that Christians and Jews could also reach paradise: 'they say that there will be no distinction [there] between Christians and Muslims, or between Jews and Moors, but that all those who have practised good works towards God will be equally beautified and equally blessed.'[15] And Busbecq, similarly, quoted a senior pasha as saying that all virtuous people would be saved, regardless of their religion (though he noted that this view, while held by other Turks as well, was nevertheless heretical).[16]

II

Jean Bodin was one of the first Western theorists to assimilate this new body of information. His reading was very wide, and seems to have encompassed many of the works mentioned above. In his guide to the reading of history, the *Methodus ad facilem historiarum cognitionem* (1566), he recommended the works by Richer and Postel, as well as a number of historical studies of the Ottomans.[17] He also recommended a short anonymous treatise on the Ottoman state, *Ordinatio politiae Turcorum domi et foris*, which was printed among the mass of supplementary materials accompanying the second edition of the medieval Latin translation of the Qur'an issued by Theodore Bibliander; he had certainly studied some of the anti-Muslim theological treatises (by Nicholas of Cusa, Juan de Torquemada and Ricoldo da Montecroce) that were included there, so it can be assumed that he had read the works by George of Hungary and Bartholomeus Georgewitz which

---

[12] Georgius de Hungaria 1993, 244.
[13] Belon 2001, 464.
[14] de La Noue 1587, discours 22, 459. De La Noue's comment was in fact in line with the original meaning of the term 'reaya' ('flocks'), used for the Ottomans' subject peoples – though it is highly unlikely that he was aware of this.
[15] Menavino 1560, fol. 17r.
[16] Forster and Blackburne Daniell 1881, vol. I, 235.
[17] Bodin 1572, 608. When giving references to the original I cite the 1572 edition, which incorporates some minor revisions by Bodin. For a translation see Bodin 1955, 378.

Bibliander also reprinted.[18] It is clear that Bodin was also familiar with Pierre Belon's *Observations*.[19] Among the other sources of his knowledge, one book should be singled out for the frequent use he made of it: the treatise on northern Africa by 'Leo Africanus'.[20] And it should be noted that books were not his only sources; he also gathered information from diplomats and merchants.[21]

In his writings on history, politics, and society, Bodin echoed many of the positive comments on Ottoman life that were briefly summarised above. That the Turks were a warlike people, with a natural aptitude for military affairs, was one of his constant themes; but he went further, describing the military organisation and discipline of the Turks as the only system that now matched that of the ancient Romans. In his major political treatise, the *République* (1576), he wrote:

> it shall be fit to erect some legions of foote and horse according to the estate and greatnes of euery Commonweale, that they may be bred vp in martiall discipline from their youth in garrisons [and] vpon the frontires in time of peace, as the antient Romans did, who knew not what it was to liue at discretion, and much lesse to rob, spoile, and murther, as they do at this day, but their camp was a schoole of honor, sobrietie, chastitie, iustice, and all other vertues, in the which no man might reuenge his owne iniuries, nor vse any violence. And to the end this discipline may be obserued, as they do at this day in the Turks armie, it is necessarie that good Captaines and souldiers be recompenced ... after the manner of the Romans.[22]

Earlier in the same work he commented quite positively on the *devşirme* system, noting that some of its intake went on to obtain the highest offices of

---

[18] Bodin 1572, 608 and Bodin 1955, 378. The first edition was published in Basel in 1543; on the materials added to the second edition (Basel 1550) see Bobzin 1995, 262–3. On Bodin's sources see Berriot 1985; and Bobzin 1996. As Bobzin points out, Bodin's citations of the Qur'an sometimes diverged from the Bibliander edition; in these cases Bodin (who did not know Arabic) had taken his information from Postel.

[19] See Bodin 1580, fol. 100r.

[20] Bodin knew both the original Italian text, Leo Africanus 1550, and the French translation by Jean Temporal 1556, *Historiale Description de l'Afrique*, Lyon, Jean Temporal: see Turbet-Delof 1974. On Leo Africanus (Hasan al-Wazzan) see Davis 2006.

[21] Berriot 1985, 172 (diplomats); Bodin also referred to conversations with French merchants who traded in Egypt, in Bodin 1580, fol. 100r.

[22] Bodin 1962, 613D-E. I cite this translation (which includes passages added in the later Latin translation by Bodin), not only because it is generally accurate, but also because, in the absence of standard modern editions of the French and the Latin, this is the most widely available version of the full text. For the original French I give references to Bodin 1583, which incorporates minor revisions made by Bodin; here Bodin 1583, 780.

state; and in the Latin text he expanded this passage, adding strong praise of the Ottoman system for its meritocracy and reward of virtue:

> For as concerning the Turkes Pretorian souldiors, and those youths which are taken from the Christians as tribute, and are called tribute children, I neuer accounted them for slaues; seeing that they are enrolled in the princes familie, and that they alone enioy the great offices, honours, priesthoods, authoritie and honour; which nobilitie extendeth also vnto their [grandsons] ... and all their posteritie afterward beeing accounted base, except by their vertue and noble acts they maintaine the honour of their grandfathers: For the Turkes almost alone of all other people measure true nobilitie by vertue, and not by discent or the antiquitie of their stocke.[23]

Another major theme treated in Bodin's political writings was the Ottoman practice of religious toleration. In book 4 of the *République* he observed:

> The great emperour of the Turkes doth with as great deuotion as any prince in the world honour and obserue the religion by him receiued from his auncestors, yet detesteth hee not the straunge religions of others; but to the contrarie permitteth euery man to liue according to his conscience: yea and that more is, neere vnto his pallace at Pera, suffereth foure diuerse religions, *viz*. That of the Iewes, that of the Christians [*sc*. Roman Catholics], that of the Grecians, and that of the Mahometanes.[24]

The main argument which Bodin put forward here for religious toleration was a prudential one: if a significant part of the population of a state followed a different religion from the majority, the ruler should tolerate at least the private practice of that religion, since any policy of total suppression might have worse consequences, reducing the minority first to atheism and then to rebellion.[25] For a similar reason – the danger that religious conflict would lead to civil strife – he commended the policy of 'all the kings and princes of Affricke and of the East', who 'doe most straitly forbid of all men to dispute of their religion'.[26] But, as

---

[23] Bodin 1962, 44G-H; Bodin 1586, 43; cf. Bodin 1583, 64. For another passage added in the Latin on the theme of the Turks measuring nobility by virtue, see Bodin 1962, 396K; Bodin 1586, 357.

[24] Bodin 1962, 537E; this combines Bodin 1583, 654–5 and Bodin 1586, 483.

[25] Bodin 1962, 539; Bodin 1583, 655.

[26] Bodin 1962, 536F; Bodin 1583, 653 (adding that the application of this principle in the Peace of Augsburg had brought an end to years of bitter fighting in Germany). The charge that Muhammad had made such a prohibition – in order to ensure the success of his own teachings – was one of the points traditionally made in Christian anti-Muslim polemical works; Bodin's commendation of such a ban was unusual.

we shall see, his reasons for advocating religious toleration extended some way beyond the merely prudential.

Elsewhere in the *République* Bodin commented approvingly on other aspects of Ottoman statecraft. He recommended that kings should not show themselves too frequently to their people, and that they should maintain a strong sense of their 'majesty' – like 'the great kings of Aethiopia, of Tartarie, of Persia, or of Turkie, who suffer not their subiects so much as to looke directly vpon them'.[27] He also gave his approval to the Ottoman policy of disarming the population, noting that 'The Turkes herein go yet farther, not onely in punishing with all seuerity the seditious and mutinous people, but also by forbidding them to beare armes, yea euen in time of warre, except it bee when they are to giue battell.'[28] And another feature of the Ottoman system that won his praise was the method of gathering taxes, which he portrayed as both efficient and uncorrupt. His scorn was reserved for the French method of tax-farming: 'it is a strange thing and very absurd in this realme, to see so many men giue money to their maister to pick his purse. The Emperour of Turkie doth otherwise, for he neuer sels office ...'[29]

Of the various positive themes mentioned above, the only one at which Bodin appears to have baulked was that of the speedy and comparatively informal administration of justice at the hands of an individual *qadi*. He had evidently studied Postel's account of the Ottoman judicial system, and he included in his text some details of the role of the *qadi* (whom he confused, to a certain extent, with a mufti).[30] But Bodin's own *formation professionnelle* as a lawyer led him to insist both that speedy justice was often bad justice ('For right hard it is for a judge pressed with choller and desire of reuenge, hasted by some, and thrust forward by others, to doe good iustice'), and that judges did better when sitting in a panel than when acting individually. In Cairo, he observed, appeals were decided by a judge sitting on his own, 'whom it is no great matter for him to winne, that standeth in his good grace, or that hath the greatest presents to giue him'. And he went on to criticise the fact that in the Ottoman Empire the judges could be dismissed and replaced, at will, by the sultan or his senior officials.[31] This is one of the very rare points on which one finds Bodin making a general or structural criticism of the Ottoman regime.

Thus far, Bodin's views have been drawn from a political treatise in which he stated his own opinions. But some of his strongest statements about Ottoman society – and, in particular, about the values and beliefs of Islam – are to be found in a more literary text, the interpretation of which is therefore less

---

[27] Bodin 1962, 507A; Bodin 1583, 618.
[28] Bodin 1962, 542F–G; Bodin 1583, 658. (In fact this prohibition was only on non-Muslim subjects, and it was in practice ignored in many areas.)
[29] Bodin 1962, 686G; Bodin 1583, 912.
[30] Bodin 1962, 279C–D; Bodin 1583, 374.
[31] Bodin 1962, 515C, 487E–488F; Bodin 1583, 629, 596.

straightforward. This is the *Colloquium heptaplomeres*, one of Bodin's last works (written probably in the period 1590–1592), which circulated in manuscript from the early seventeenth century onwards and was eventually printed in 1857.[32] The work is presented as a discussion on religious and philosophical themes between seven characters: a Catholic, a Lutheran, a Calvinist, two non-religious figures (who have traditionally been taken to represent 'Deism' and sceptical naturalism), a Jew and a Muslim. The last of these, called Octavius, describes himself as a Sicilian who was seized by pirates and sold into captivity in Syria, where he converted to Islam.[33] His fervent commendations of Muslim beliefs and practices are, therefore, those of a character in a literary work, and not necessarily those of Bodin himself; nevertheless there are some significant congruences between his statements and the views expressed by Bodin elsewhere. Thus it is not surprising to find that the passage in which Octavius commends the religious toleration practised by Muslim rulers is followed by a more general discussion of religion and politics in which Bodin recycles material first presented in the equivalent discussion in the *République*.[34] And, in the light of Bodin's endorsement of most of the positive themes to be found in the accounts of Ottoman life by Postel and the other authors, it seems reasonable to suppose that Bodin agreed with the sentiments expressed by Octavius on the one other major theme mentioned above, that of the Muslims' attitude to charity and welfare:

> They are amazed that Christian men are able to bear with equanimity so great a multitude of needy people, such want and poverty of their own people, since among the Muslims there are more homes for the needy and strangers than people who need them. Often you could see Turks in this city [*sc.* Venice] throwing coins freely to the poor who were chasing everywhere after the money ... Also educated men have provided numerous homes near the shrines

---

[32] Bodin 1857. There is a modern English translation, Bodin 1975. Doubts have recently been raised (mistakenly) about whether Bodin was the author of this text; for a study of the issue, which includes an account of the early history of the text, see Malcolm 2006.

[33] Octavius says that he was influenced by two things: discussions with his owner, 'Paracadius', and reading 'a little book in defense of the Mohammedan faith, written in the Arabic tongue by a certain Dominican who had deserted the Christian faith' (Bodin 1975, 225; Bodin 1857, 171–2). Some modern writers take 'Paracadius' to be a personal name; it was in fact intended as the title of a type of *qadi*, mentioned by Bodin in the *République* (Bodin 1583, 374; Bodin 1962, 279D). Berriot 1985, 175, has suggested that the 'little book' was the treatise known as the *Tuḥfa* by the Catalan ex-Dominican and convert to Islam Anselmo Turmeda (d. 1424). If this is correct, it is further testimony to Bodin's information-gathering about the Islamic world; the most authoritative modern study finds only one brief mention of the *Tuḥfa* in Arabic before the seventeenth century, and no mention of it in this period by any Western writer: de Epalza 1971, 43–8.

[34] Bodin 1857, 121–3 (Bodin 1975, 157–60); Bodin 1962, 536–8.

and very ample provisions for food. There is hardly any rich man who is not responsible for consecrating either a temple or a public lodging.[35]

III

It is clear, then, that Bodin had studied the recent accounts of life in the Ottoman world, and had drawn from them positive ideas on a number of different themes. But his interest in the Ottoman Empire was more far-reaching than that, going some way beyond any mere accumulation of favourable opinions on disparate topics. In the classificatory system which his political theory expounded, the nature of the Ottoman regime was given, at the outset, an exemplary role to play – even if, when one inspects it more closely, its precise place in that scheme of things becomes quite hard to assess.

Bodin distinguished between three types of monarchy: 'royal' monarchy (where the monarch's actions were bound by the laws of nature); 'lordly' or 'seigneurial' monarchy (where the monarch enjoyed plenary power over the lives and properties of his subjects); and tyranny.[36] It was an important feature of his argument that the second of these types was not the same as the third. Lordly monarchy was, he insisted, a valid form of rule: it proceeded from victory in legitimate warfare (when all rights to the lives and properties of the conquered passed to the conqueror), and it involved not a purely selfish exploitation of the subjects by the monarch, but rather a paternalistic system of rule, in which the monarch governed his subjects 'as doth the good housholder his seruants or slaues'.[37] And the classic example of a lordly monarch – an example to which Bodin turned repeatedly in his treatise – was the Ottoman sultan.[38]

Many earlier writers had been content with a two-fold scheme, in which the king was simply contrasted with the tyrant: such a distinction could be based on statements by both Plato, who argued that the king rules morally and the tyrant immorally, and Aristotle, who said that the king rules willing people in their interest, while the tyrant rules the unwilling in his own interest. But a third category had emerged in the Western tradition, based on Aristotle's comments in Book 3 of the *Politics* on a type of rule that was modelled on the 'despotes' or master of a household (a household conceived, significantly, as containing both family and slaves): 'There is another sort of monarchy not uncommon among the barbarians, which nearly resembles tyranny. But even this is legal and hereditary...' When sixteenth-century writers such as Louis Le Roy developed this category as a description of the sultan's rule, they gave it a very negative

---

[35] Bodin 1975, 219–20 (emended); Bodin 1857, 167–8. ('Hospitium' here, translated by Kuntz as 'lodging', could mean either an inn or a hospital.)
[36] Bodin 1962, 199D–200G; Bodin 1583, 272–3.
[37] Bodin 1962, 200F-G, 201A-B; Bodin 1583, 273, 274; Bodin 1586, 190.
[38] See Le Thiec 2004.

coloration: Le Roy described seigneurial rule as 'a strict form of rule, in which the lord commands absolutely and at will, with complete power of life and death over his subjects ... as is today the authority of the Sultan ... whose subjects are obliged to obey him like animals.'[39] From this notion of lordly or 'despotic' rule, indeed, there sprang the whole subsequent tradition of Western theorising about 'oriental despotism'.

Bodin, however, gave the concept of seigneurial monarchy a much more positive intepretation. He strongly emphasised the difference between this type of monarchy and tyranny, exclaiming: 'If we will mingle and confound the Lordly Monarchie, with the tyrannical estate, we must confesse that there is no difference in warres, betwixt the iust enemie and the robber; betwixt a lawfull prince and a theefe; betwixt warres iustly denounced, and vniust and violent force.'[40] On the face of it, there is a contradiction between his emphasis here on the 'lawful' nature of such rule and his description of 'royal' monarchy as the 'legitimate' or 'lawful' form of rule: 'Wherefore a lawfull or royal Monarchie is that where the subiects obey the lawes of a Monarque, and the Monarque the lawes of nature, the subiects inioying their naturall libertie, and proprietie of their goods.'[41] But Bodin is talking about two different types or levels of law: natural law where the royal monarchy is concerned, and the *ius gentium*, the law of nations, in the case of seigneurial rule. That the latter type of rule had this sort of legal basis was something he emphasised more strongly in successive versions of his text. In the first French edition he wrote: 'for it is not unfitting that a sovereign prince, having defeated his enemies in a good and just war, should make himself lord of their goods and persons by right of war, governing his subjects as slaves, just as the head of a family is lord of his slaves and of their goods, and disposes of them as he pleases'; in the revised version of the French he added, after that last phrase, 'in accordance with the law of nations'; and in the Latin translation this passage became: 'for it is not wrong [or: 'not iniquitous'] that he who has defeated and subdued men in a just and legitimate war should be the lord of their persons and goods, while he treats his subjects just as a good head of a family treats his slaves, as indeed we see to be accepted in the customs and laws of almost all peoples.'[42]

---

[39] Le Roy 1568, 46.

[40] Bodin 1962, 204F; Bodin 1583, 278. Such explicit statements run counter to the interpretation of Bodin put forward by Mesnard: 'Seigneurial monarchy and tyranny are thus false governments, non-juridical adminstrations of sovereignty. In fact they have their origin in a state of affairs that is prior to any law' (Mesnard 1969, 499–500).

[41] Bodin 1962, 200F; Bodin 1583, 273.

[42] Bodin 1583, 274 (cf. 235 in the Paris, 1576 edition); Bodin 1586, 190: While emphasising his claims about the *ius gentium* (law of nations), Bodin seems to have been retreating somewhat from the position he took on the natural character of lordly rule in the *Methodus*, when he wrote that it was 'not contrary to nature or to the law of nations' (Bodin 1955, 204; Bodin 1572, 313).

Near the end of his treatise, Bodin declared that royal monarchy was best.[43] He did not argue the point in detail; but, given the emphasis on respect for 'naturall libertie' and 'proprietie' in his account of royal rule, there could be little doubt that he regarded that form of rule as preferable – even though there is nothing like a worked-out theory of natural-law jurisprudence (still less a theory of natural rights) to be found in the *République*. Nevertheless, while the superiority of royal over seigneurial rule seems clear, in Bodin's theory, where the abstract categories are concerned, it would not be such a simple task to judge between the actual nature of the Ottoman state, as Bodin understood it, and the nature of the contemporary monarchical states in Western Europe. For he appears to have believed that in many ways the objectionable features of lordly rule had, in the Ottoman case, been modified and rendered tolerable.

Where slavery was concerned, Bodin did not of course deny that slaves were to be found in the Ottoman Empire: he gave examples of Christians captured by the Ottomans in recent wars being sold there as slaves.[44] But he was also aware that Muhammad had 'proposed liberty for all who followed him', which meant that Muslims did not – at least, officially did not – enslave Muslims.[45] (Indeed, in the *Methodus* he wrote that the Christian emancipation of slaves took place merely as an imitation of the emancipation by Muhammad and his followers.)[46] As for the Christian subjects of the sultan who were seized in the *devşirme*, and who were declared slaves (before being converted to Islam), Bodin explicitly denied, as we have seen, their slave-like status: 'as concerning the Turkes Pretorian souldiors, and those youths which are taken from the Christians as tribute, and are called tribute children, I neuer accounted them for slaues …'.[47] So it is hard to see in what sense, if any, he regarded all the people of the Ottoman Empire as slaves of the sultan.

Where the sultan's lordship over property was concerned, the facts (as Bodin understood them) offered more support for the 'seigneurial' theory. In the *Methodus* he reported, on the strength of information given to him by two French statesmen and diplomats, that in the Ottoman Empire 'all lands, with the exception of only a few', were entrusted as feudal holdings ('*timars*') to knights ('*timariots*'). 'When a *timariot* dies, the military office is arbitrarily awarded by grace of the prince, as once fiefs and benefices used to be given.' This system of strict military feudalism, together with the 'praetorian legions' paid from the state treasury, rendered the Ottoman state 'invincible'.[48] In the *République* he returned to this theme, writing that the *timariots* 'hold all their

---

[43] Bodin 1583, 972; Bodin 1962, 721C.
[44] Bodin 1583, 64; Bodin 1962, 44F-G.
[45] Bodin 1857, 176–7; Bodin 1975, 231: 'he summoned those in servitude to freedom and proposed liberty for all who followed him and his teaching'.
[46] Bodin 1572, 343; Bodin 1955, 222. Cf. also Bodin 1583, 58; Bodin 1962, 39D-E.
[47] See n. 23.
[48] Bodin 1955, 262; Bodin 1572, 413–14.

possessions in fealtie of the Prince, as it were during pleasure, renewing their letters patents from ten yeares to ten yeares: neither when they dye can they leaue their children heires of their possessions, but of their moueables onely'. But in the Latin version he added a qualification showing that he understood that the system was rather less strict in practice: 'except by the gift of the prince they keepe the possession of their fathers lands, as they doe of his goods.'[49] In another discussion of the *timar* system in the *République* he noted that it had been imposed only in areas conquered by the Ottomans 'by the law of armes'; so the 'auntient subiects' of the Ottoman heartland had not been affected by it.[50] In any case, the great majority of the sultan's subjects were not *timariots*; and while Bodin supposed that they could not own land outright in those territories where the *timar* system operated, he also stated that the Sultan took only 10 per cent of the non-*timariots*' wealth when they died.[51] So it seems that, once again, the notion of a sultan enjoying absolute ownership of both the persons and the property of his subjects did not match the reality of the Ottoman system as Bodin saw it: if the ownership existed in theory, it was not exercised, or exercised only very partially, in practice. This disparity was clearly sensed by Bodin himself, by the time he wrote the Latin version of his political treatise: there, after the phrase 'The Emperour of the Turkes styleth himself *Sultan*, that is to say Lord ... for that he is lord of their persons and goods', he added the phrase: 'whom for all that he gouerneth much more courteously and freely, then doth a good housholder his seruants.'[52]

Bodin's praise of various aspects of the Ottoman state has already been noted. But it should be emphasised, in addition, that there was one fundamental criterion on which he clearly regarded seigneurial rule as better or more effective than royal rule: that of the stability and durability of the regime or state. Given the practical concerns of this *politique* theorist, who set a high value on civil peace and declared that even the worst tyranny was preferable to anarchy, this must have been, for him, an important consideration.[53] As he put it when introducing the subject of seigneurial monarchy, 'The Lordly Monarchies haue bene both great and of long continuance ... the Lordly Monarchie is more durable than the royall.' The reason he gave for this was 'for that it is more maiesticall'. Only when he went on to explain this point did a note of moral criticism creep into the argument: he wrote that such a regime endured because each subject,

---

[49] Bodin 1962, 201D; Bodin 1583, 275; Bodin 1586, 191.
[50] Bodin 1962, 656H; Bodin 1583, 866.
[51] Bodin 1962, 65A: 'the Grand Signior ... is heire ... to his other subiects for the tenth'; Bodin 1583, 94.
[52] Bodin 1962, 201C-D; Bodin 1583, 274–5; Bodin 1586, 190.
[53] Bodin 1962, 539D: 'the greatest tyranny is nothing so miserable as an Anarchie'; Bodin 1583, 655.

having been reduced to the status of a slave, 'becommeth humble, abiect, and hauing as they say a base and seruile hart'.⁵⁴

However, elsewhere in his writings Bodin suggested that servility was a vice against which Muslims were to some extent protected or fortified by their religion. Commenting acerbically in the *Methodus* on the historian Paolo Giovio (who had accused the French of worshipping their kings), he exclaimed: 'all his life he did not blush to kiss more than servilely the feet of his master [sc. the Pope]. Not only the kings of the Persians and of the Turks, but even the most haughty caliphs of the Arabs always abhorred that kind of worship.'⁵⁵ In the *Colloquium* Octavius likewise states, of the Islamic peoples, that 'no nation is any farther removed from the suspicion of idolatry'.⁵⁶ So, while Muslim subjects of 'lordly' rule might well be cowed, for all practical purposes, by the power and majesty of the monarch, they would not make the mistake of engaging in the sort of self-abasement towards their ruler that was appropriate only towards God. And there is another way in which Bodin believed that 'lordly' rule was attemperated by Islam, at least in the case of the Ottoman Empire: in the *Methodus* he wrote that 'The man who is mufti, or chief priest, is indeed regarded as interpreter of the divine law to this extent, that no one may introduce legislation which violates religion.'⁵⁷ In the Latin version of the *République* he declared that 'the Turkish and Arabian princes ... honour and obserue their Mufties, or high Bishops, with the greatest honour and respect possibly to bee giuen vnto them, still referring vnto them the greatest and most doubtful questions of their law, to be by them decided.'⁵⁸ While the suggestion that irreligious law-making was prohibited to the sultan may have been quietly dropped in the latter work, the claim that religion operated as source of norms external to the sultan was clearly maintained.

It seems, then, that if 'lordly' monarchy was to be thought of as occupying a spectrum, the rule of the Ottoman sultans was placed by Bodin not at the extreme end of that spectrum but rather towards the end that came closest to 'royal' monarchy. The vice of servility was moderated; some check or control was supplied by superior (or, at least, independent) norms; and besides, as we have seen, the whole system of rule worked not to crush the people into an undifferentiated mass, but to elevate and reward those of them who displayed virtue. Indeed, at one point in his argument Bodin came close to suggesting that the sultan's rule shared one of the essential characteristics of 'royal' monarchy. When he presented his famous distinction between the nature of the sovereign and the nature of the government, he wrote that a monarchical sovereign might have a popular government if he distributed offices and honours indifferently

---

54 Bodin 1962, 204G-I; Bodin 1583, 278–9.
55 Bodin 1955, 258; Bodin 1572, 406.
56 Bodin 1975, 219; Bodin 1857, 167.
57 Bodin 1955, 211–12; Bodin 1572, 326.
58 Bodin 1962, 393D; Bodin 1586, 353–4.

among the people; 'But if the prince shall giue all commaund, honours, and offices, vnto the nobilitie onely, or to the rich, or to the valiant, or to the vertuous onely, it shall be a royall Monarchie, and that simple and pure, but yet tempered in maner of an Aristocracie.'[59] Since Bodin had already praised the sultan for awarding high office on the basis of 'vertue and noble acts', this comment could easily have been taken to imply that the Ottoman system combined essential features of both lordly and royal rule.

Similarly, if the 'royal' monarchy of north-western Europe, as portrayed by Bodin in the *République*, were placed on its own spectrum, it would be situated somewhere towards the 'lordly' end. Bodin described the origins and development of the feudal system in north-western Europe as a kind of penumbral version of lordly rule. When 'Northern' people such as the Goths, Lombards, Franks and Saxons had 'tasted the maners and customs of the Hunnes' (an Asiatic people who did practise lordly rule), 'they began to make themselues Lords, not of the persons, but of all the lands of them whom they had vanquished'; the feudal estates which they gained in this way 'for this cause are called Seigneuries, or Lordships; to show that the shadow of the auncient lordly Monarchie as yet remayneth, although greatly diminished.'[60] Perhaps, indeed, those two spectrums should be seen as sections of one larger continuum, with a central area in which the distance between a feudally-based royal monarchy on the one hand, and a well-managed and Islam-fortified version of lordly rule on the other, was not so very great – in which case, the task of deciding which was better might not be so simple after all.

Bodin's remark about 'Northern people' supplies a clue as to how this issue might have been resolved in his mind. For it brings us to a major feature of his political theory, as set out in both the *Methodus* and the *République*: his climatic (or, more strictly speaking, zonal) theory of human nature. Different parts of the world were subject not only to different effects of temperature and atmosphere, but also to different astrological influences. These factors, while not absolutely determining human characteristics, had a large influence upon them: so people with different qualities and tendencies, both physical and mental, would be found in different zones of the habitable earth.[61] Bodin divided that territory into three zones. In the North, people were naturally warlike; they were good at seizing territory but not good at holding it, since they lacked wisdom. In the South, people were contemplative, and could be spiritual or indeed fanatical; they had a talent for religion and philosophy, but were bad at practical organisation. And in the Middle zone the people had characteristics between those two extremes, with more of a talent for the practicalities of human life.

---

[59] Bodin 1962, 199E: combining Bodin 1583, 272, and Bodin 1586, 189.
[60] Bodin 1962, 202I; Bodin 1583, 276.
[61] For a classic study of Bodin's views on these matters, emphasising the degree to which he was merely synthesising a large body of medieval doctrines, see Tooley 1953.

The people therfore of the middle regions haue more force than they of the South, & lesse pollicie [sc. cunning]: and more wit than they of the North, & lesse force; and are more fit to commaund and gouerne Commonweales, and more iust in their actions. And if we looke well into the histories of all nations, we shall find, That euen as great armies and mighty powers haue come out of the North; euen so the [occult sciences,] Philosophie, the Mathematikes, and other contemplatiue sciences, are come out of the South; and the politike sciences, lawes, and the studie thereof, the grace of well speaking and discoursing, haue had their beginnings in the middle regions.[62]

As Bodin went on to explain in the *République*, the principles of government of the three zones were force (for the North), equity and justice (for the Middle) and religion (for the South).[63] And the virtues naturally possessed by the three types of people were as follows: mechanical skill and force to execute (in the North), ethical wisdom (in the Middle), and philosophical wisdom (in the South). From which it followed that each had a role to play in what Bodin called 'the vniuersall Commonweale of this world': the southerners were made to instruct others in 'occult sciences' and religion; the northerners were made 'for labour and manuall artes'; and those of the middle zone were designed by God 'to negotiat, traffique, iudge, plead, command, establish Commonweales; and to make lawes and ordinances for other nations'.[64]

While Bodin's views were not completely deterministic, he did argue that these characteristics must be taken into account when designing suitable forms of rule for different populations: a system suitable to the people of Spain could not simply be imposed, for example, on the people of the Netherlands. The Northerners, 'being fierce and warlike, trusting in their force and strength, desire popular Estates, or at the least electiue Monarchies; neither can they easily endure to be commaunded imperiously.'[65] The Southerners (and people of the East, who have a natural affinity with them) were better suited to living under lordly rule; 'But the people of Europe more couragious, and better souldiers then the people of Africke or Asia, could neuer endure the lordly Monarques.'[66] As Bodin's comments on the origins of feudalism showed, however, while the Northerners might have been inclined to resist lordly rule, they were at the same time apt to impose it, as their warlike propensities often put them in the position of successful conquerors. Hence, perhaps, the 'shadowy', half-and-half nature of seigneurial power in those parts of Europe where the Northerners had played a significant role.

---

[62] Bodin 1962, 550G; Bodin 1583, 671.
[63] Bodin 1962, 559B; Bodin 1583, 686. In the *Methodus* the principle for the Middle zone was described as 'law and legal decision', Bodin 1955, 115; Bodin 1572, 167.
[64] Bodin 1962, 561C; Bodin 1583, 690.
[65] Bodin 1962, 563C-D; Bodin 1583, 694.
[66] Bodin 1962, 202H; Bodin 1583, 276.

This whole pattern of argument supplies a way of explaining why, in Bodin's opinion, a country such as France (a Middle-zone territory, strongly touched by Northern influences) had been and should continue to be a 'royal' monarchy. For any individual country, located in a particular zone, the theory would suggest an appropriate form of government – something to be commended not in absolute terms, but because it was relatively most suited to the nature of that particular population. This does not mean, it should be noted, that Bodin was necessarily committed to simple relativism. It does seem that (as some commentators have suggested) he regarded the people of the Middle zone as possessing superior qualities; in which case it might be true to say that the perfect Middle-zone state – which would have to be a royal monarchy – was the 'best' state of all.[67] The point is merely that the 'best' model might not be applicable to human kind more generally.

But what of the Ottoman Empire, a polity that encompassed many countries and peoples, covering large parts of the Southern and Middle zones and even, at its furthest extent, touching the Northern zone too? This was a different sort of state, something quite unlike the small kingdoms of contemporary Europe, and comparable only to past empires such as that of the Romans. In the *Methodus*, indeed, Bodin ridiculed the claims of the Holy Roman Empire to represent a continuation of the *imperium* of ancient Rome. 'What has Germany to oppose to the sultan of the Turks?', he asked. 'This fact is obvious to everyone – if there is anywhere in the world any majesty of empire and of true monarchy, it must radiate from the sultan. He owns the richest parts of Asia, Africa and Europe, and he rules far and wide over the entire Mediterranean and all but a few of its islands.'[68]

The Ottoman Empire may not have covered all three zones equally; it largely lacked territory in the North. But, on the other hand, Bodin constantly emphasised the point that the Turks were themselves a northern people, who had originally moved southwards thanks to their successes in war against their southern neighbours. (Here his views were influenced by two things: the common sixteenth-century identification of the Turks with Scythians, which had replaced an earlier humanist theory that they were 'Teucri' or Trojans; and his attentive reading of the medieval Armenian historian Hayton or Hetoum, who located the origin of the Turks in Turkestan.[69]) Gradually, what emerges from his portrayal of the Ottoman Empire is a picture of a polity which – unlike, perhaps, any other polity in recorded history – is structured in such a way as to create a successful combination of the virtues and abilities of people from all three zones. The Turks themselves, as people from the North, are suited to fighting and labour; they have taken their religion, Islam, from the South, relying on 'priests' and philosophers imbued with Arabic culture; and for the

---

[67] See, for example, Allen 1928, 431–8.
[68] Bodin 1955, 292; Bodin 1572, 463.
[69] See Pertusi 1970; Heath 1979; Hayton 1529, esp. sigs. B3v, D4v.

practical tasks of state administration they have selected, through the *devşirme*, talented people (mainly Greeks, Slavs and Albanians) from their Middle-zone territories. One might almost describe this as an 'optimal' combination of the qualities of all three zones; but it should be emphasised that this is an optimum which works on a very different basis from that of the 'best' state (i.e., the perfect royal monarchy). The 'best' state is too good for most people, as it requires the best subjects; whereas this model can encompass all of humanity, including both the belligerent Northerners and the timid and/or fanatical people of the South.

It is true, of course, that the theoretical fit here is not a perfect one. Law, as applied by the muftis, is drawn from the religious culture of the South, not from traditions of the people of the Middle zone (it may be relevant that, as we have seen, the legal system was the one area in which Bodin did not echo the positive appraisals found in the recent literature); and Bodin must also have been aware that the *devşirme* supplied Janissaries as well as administrators. It is also true that Bodin nowhere made this connection explicitly between the division of tasks in the Ottoman state and his tri-zonal scheme of human aptitudes. But that scheme was so fundamental to his thinking that he must surely have given some thought to the idea of a state in which the three elements were optimally combined; and, when he did so, he could hardly have failed to notice the resemblance with the Ottoman Empire. For in many ways, the Ottoman system of government and society, as described by Bodin, could be seen as satisfying the general principles of harmony in multiplicity, *concordia discors*, which had for him a cosmological, as well as a political, significance. As he put it in the *Methodus*:

> If we refer all things to nature ... it becomes plain that this world ... consists of unequal parts and mutually discordant elements and contrary motions of the spheres, so that if the harmony through dissimilarity is taken away, the whole will be ruined. In the same way the best republic, if it imitates nature, which it must do, is held together stable and unshaken by those commanding and obeying, servants and lords, powerful and needy, good and wicked, strong and weak, as if by the mixed association of unlike minds. As on the lyre and in song itself the skilled ears cannot endure that sameness of harmony which is called unison; on the contrary, a pleasing harmony is produced by dissimilar notes, deep and high.[70]

IV

Finally, what of Bodin's views on Islam? Here, as mentioned above, some of the most striking evidence is to be found in the *Colloquium heptaplomeres*, in the speeches made by Octavius – which do not necessarily express Bodin's own opinions. But when those statements are considered in the light of the whole

---

[70] Bodin 1955, 268; Bodin 1572, 423–4.

pattern of argument of that work, and correlated with comments in Bodin's other writings, a distinctly Bodinian view of the nature and significance of Islam does begin to emerge.

A useful starting-point is the question of religious toleration. This is the one issue on which, in the final section of the *Colloquium*, the views of the speakers converge: they agree that religious persecution is bad not only because it leads to civil unrest, but also because genuine religious belief cannot be produced by coercion. However, it is clear that renouncing intolerance involves, for the Catholic, the Lutheran, the Calvinist and the Jew, detaching themselves from the practices and traditions of their faiths; the only religion which is presented here as accepting a norm of toleration is Islam. As Senamus (the so-called 'sceptical naturalist') puts it: 'If all people could be persuaded as the Muslims, Octavius, and I are that all the prayers of all people which come from a pure mind are pleasing to God, or surely are not displeasing, it would be possible to live everywhere in the world in the same harmony as those who live under the emperor of the Turks or Persians.'[71] Senamus is echoing here a statement of fundamental principle made a few pages earlier by Octavius: 'The prayer of the multitude is efficacious if it has beseeched eternal God with a sincere mind.'[72] This was a principle which Bodin himself endorsed – and, at the same time, associated with the Ottomans – in his discussion of religious toleration in the Latin version of the *République*. In that discussion he not only emphasised the point that coerced worship could not be pleasing to God; he also gave the example (quoted above) of the toleration of different religions by the sultan, comparing his policy to that of Augustus and concluding: 'For why the people of auncient time were persuaded, as were the Turks, all sorts of religions which proceed from a pure mind, to be acceptable vnto the gods.'[73]

This concept of authentic religion ran through all of Bodin's writings, having been stated quite clearly by him in his earliest major work, the *Methodus*, where he defined religion as 'the direct turning of a cleansed mind toward God'.[74] The implications of such a view were potentially radical: one possible conclusion might have been that all forms of organised religion were superfluous, and that it was sufficient for individual human beings to worship and 'turn to' a God whose existence and nature they had worked out for themselves on more or less Deist grounds. That was not Bodin's own position, however. While he appears to have thought that individuals untouched by divine revelation (pagans, for example) could turn towards God in a rudimentary but acceptable way, he did not think that man's knowledge of God must be limited to the conclusions of abstract reasoning. He believed that God intervened actively in human affairs, and that God had imparted to mankind a special revelation: the Hebrew Bible.

---

[71] Bodin 1975, 467 (emended); Bodin 1857, 355.
[72] Bodin 1975, 464; Bodin 1857, 353.
[73] Bodin 1962, 538F; Bodin 1586, 484.
[74] Bodin 1955, 33; Bodin 1572, 40.

At the heart of the discussion of religious matters in the *Colloquium* is the close agreement that springs up between Toralba, the so-called 'Deist', and Salomon, the devout Jew. The fundamental principle on which they agree is that, as Toralba puts it, 'the best religion is the oldest'; Salomon concurs that 'that the best religion is the most ancient one, which has been handed down from the best Parent of the human race; this religion devotes itself to the purest worship of one eternal God, shunning the throng of gods and divinities and all created things.'[75]

The best religion, then, was a kind of pure monotheism which not only embodied the self-evident truths of philosophical theology, but also conformed to the religion of the patriarchs as described in the Bible. That religion, it should be noted, was a kind of proto-Judaism or palaeo-Judaism, not identical with the Mosaic Judaism which Salomon himself would have practised. As Salomon explains, the children of Abraham lost the original pure religion when they were corrupted by Egyptian idolatry and polytheism; Moses' task (given to him by God) was 'to call the people back to their natural and God-inspired religion which had almost become obliterated from their souls'.[76] This he did not only by re-asserting the basic demands of monotheism, but also by adding a large body of ritual law – the rituals being imposed not because they were in themselves necessary for true religion, but in order to replace or counteract the false sacrifices of the heathen cults.[77] Moses effected a vital reformation and restoration; but he could not restore the pristine religion of Adam, Seth and Noah. The form of Judaism which he instituted was a religion which, in order to protect the core principles of true belief, had to make some compromises with the frailty of human nature.

In a remarkable passage in Book 5 of the *Colloquium*, when Salomon recapitulates this argument (declaring that Moses renewed the observance of the laws of nature, which had been shamefully neglected and defiled), he is followed immediately by Octavius, who makes just the same claim about the prophet of Islam: 'Muhammad imitates Moses. When he realized that natural laws, that is, divine laws, had fallen into ruin and dead men were worshipped in place of eternal God, he renewed the law of nature concerning the worship of one eternal God and removed the most harmful worship of the dead. Thus the fourth Sura clearly witnesses that he worships the God of Abraham and recalls the life of Abraham for use.'[78] According to Octavius, Muhammad had not only removed the most important post-Mosaic corruption of religion (namely, the worship of the dead Christ); he had also dispensed with some of the Mosaic innovations, thereby developing a form of religion that was in some ways closer to the original true faith. Octavius emphasises the similarities between Islam

---

[75] Bodin 1975, 173, 183 (emended); Bodin 1857, 133, 141.
[76] Bodin 1975, 184; Bodin 1857, 142.
[77] Bodin 1975, 186–9; Bodin 1857, 143–5.
[78] Bodin 1975, 249 (emended); Bodin 1857, 191.

and Judaism, but he also insists that Islam is purer and stricter in its rejection of images and superstitions. He reacts with scorn to a description of the Jewish 'tefillin', exclaiming that 'The Muslims abhor all those amulets, and feigned images, so that they may embrace true piety'; later, commenting on the small but significant differences between the two faiths, he says that 'We have only necessary rites and ceremonies, none useless.'[79] Insofar as Islam diverges from Judaism, according to Octavius, it does so by agreeing with the more purely philosophical theology of Toralba: 'The Muslims differ not at all with Toralba, and only a little with Salomon.'[80]

This does not mean, however, that Muhammad restored the ancient religion in all its pristine purity. Two of the other speakers, Curtius (the Calvinist) and Salomon, bring up the standard accusation that Muhammad 'tried to entice wicked men to the worship of his religion by the foulness of the basest pleasures' – that is, by offering them the prospect of a sensual paradise. Octavius's reply is that it was necessary for Muhammad to make this compromise with human psychology: 'Since, however, people of the southern regions are most of all inclined towards Venus, Muhammad thought up those rewards so that he might draw men though unwilling to true honor.'[81] This, he says, is merely an application of the principle laid down by Plato and Xenophon, that magistrates and physicians may tell lies to those in their charge in order to bring about good effects – a principle which Bodin himself endorsed, using almost the same words, in the *République*.[82]

This emphasis on adapting to the psychological needs of people in the South might give the impression that Bodin was portraying Islam as a religion suited only to that zone. But no such geographical limitation is implied by the other comments on Islam in Bodin's writings. The argument presented by Octavius is not merely that Islam is better adapted to human psychology, but also that it produces better human behaviour – better, that is, by universal standards, on a comparison made with people anywhere else in the world: 'They by far surpass all people not only in the purest worship of one eternal God but also in humanity and kindness.'[83] Stating his reasons for this in the last book of the *Colloquium*, Octavius observes that 'I think the Muslims are far superior to Christians, especially in acts of virtue, that is, in piety, justice, love, courage and temperance, because they have been instructed in such a way that they believe the summit of salvation has been placed in virtuous acts.'[84] His claim against the Christians was that they linked salvation to what he called 'faith and empty credulity about

---

[79] Bodin 1975, 211, 228; Bodin 1857, 163, 174.
[80] Bodin 1975, 227 (emended); Bodin 1857, 174.
[81] Bodin 1975, 229, 230; Bodin 1857, 175, 176.
[82] Bodin 1975, 230 (Bodin 1857, 176); Bodin 1962, 531E (Bodin 1583, 649).
[83] Bodin 1975, 219; Bodin 1857, 167.
[84] Bodin 1975, 426; Bodin 1857, 323–4.

Christ's death'.⁸⁵ On this point, at least, his argument might have suggested that Islam and Judaism were in exactly the same position. But it is worth noting that in his treatment of one other important issue Bodin emphasised the difference between them. Discussing the issue of religious toleration in the Latin version of the *République*, he drew a sharp distinction between the charitable attitude of the Islamic Turks and the position taken historically by the Jews: 'Onely the Iewes of all people detested straunge ceremonies; whereby they prouoked the hatred of all people against them.'⁸⁶ Once again, Octavius's claims about the peculiar moral excellence of Islam receive at least a partial and implicit endorsement from Bodin himself.

Notwithstanding this whole pattern of argument, there is no reason to suppose that Bodin was in any sense a crypto-Muslim. His writings do not supply the slightest evidence that he regarded the Qur'an as divine revelation – whereas he evidently did grant that status to the Hebrew Bible. The precise nature of his religious beliefs has always been hard to pin down; he has sometimes been portrayed as a sort of auto-convert to Judaism, but it would surely be more accurate to say that what he believed in was not the Judaism of the contemporary synagogue, but the ancient philosophical Judaism – the religion of the patriarchs – which emerges in the *Colloquium* from the discussion between Salomon and Toralba. This, they agreed, was 'the best religion', and Bodin himself seems to have thought so too.⁸⁷

To say this, however, is not to deprive Islam of a special significance in his thinking. For here too, just as in the case of the Ottoman system of government, a distinction must be made between that which is best absolutely and that which is most suited to the generality or totality of the human race. Exceptional individuals, such as Bodin himself, might aspire to the highest form of religion; but something more adapted to human psychology, with formal rites and ceremonies reduced to a bare minimum but not altogether excluded, was needed for mankind in general. Once again, the metaphor of *concordia discors* seems appropriate: the task was not to isolate the single most perfect note or consonance, but to bring together both the finer and the coarser sounds, from the whole range of human aptitudes and tendencies, into an overall harmony. That, it seems, is how Bodin regarded the achievement not only of the Ottoman system of government, in the realm of politics, but also of Islam, in the realm of religion.

---

[85] Bodin 1975, 422; Bodin 1857, 320.
[86] Bodin 1962, 538G; Bodin 1586, 484.
[87] The best studies of Bodin's religious ideas are Roellenbleck 1964; Baxter 1973; Rose 1980.

SECTION IV
The Renaissance and the Ottoman Empire

Chapter 11

Binding Relationships: Mamluk, Ottoman and Renaissance Book-Bindings

Alison Ohta

In the fifteenth century, new techniques and decorative elements were introduced into the Italian book-binder's repertoire that were eventually to permeate throughout Europe. The work of the distinguished book-binding scholar, Anthony Hobson has shown how the humanist binders of Renaissance Italy drew inspiration for these 'new' bindings from the styles and techniques used by Ottoman and Mamluk binders.[1] By the middle of the fifteenth century, decorated bindings were being produced in Italy for manuscripts which celebrated the revival of classical literature and learning, written in a new style of handwriting, 'the humanistic script'. The techniques of gold tooling,[2] filigree work and pressure-moulding were now used for their decoration. Pasteboard replaced wooden boards for the covers and the Islamic layout of ornament, concentrated at the centre and the corners within a frame, replaced the old all-over Gothic type patterns.[3] Prior to this, bindings had been covered in plain leather or textiles over wooden boards with metal clasps or were decorated with horizontal or vertical rows of repeated small tools derived from French Gothic style of binding practised in Paris from the 1370s.

Within the Islamic context, the technique of gold tooling and pasteboard had long been used for bindings. Pasteboard had begun to replace wooden boards on Islamic bindings by the tenth century. The treatise of Bakr al-Ishbili, a bookbinder from Seville, entitled *the Art of Bookbinding* dateable to between 1185 and 1198 CE, describes how heated tools were used for the application of gold and distinguishes between bindings with wooden boards and pegs for fastening and bindings with pasteboards and flaps.[4] However, in the mid-fifteenth century

---

[1] Hobson 1989b, 33–59.

[2] Powdered gold in suspension had been used prior to this on European bindings but it was painted on. Hobson 1989b, records the earliest use of gold tooling in Europe on the binding of Guarino of Verona's translation of Strabo's *Geographia* presented by the Podestà of Padua, Jacopo Antonio Marcello to King René of Anjou dated 13 September 1459, produced in Padua.

[3] Pasteboard had been known in the West from the fourteenth century but was considered only suitable for cheap and unimportant books. Hobson 1989b, 37, n. 1.

[4] Gacek 1990–1991.

other innovative techniques – the use of stencils, polychrome filigree work, panel-stamping and pressure-moulding were added to the Mamluk and Ottoman binder's repertoire as the result of developments noted on bindings produced in Iran during the first quarter of the fifteenth century and were then developed to new heights of virtuosity in the Timurid and later Turkmen ateliers. It was these changes that contributed to the development of the *alla islamica* style of binding of the Renaissance.

Additions were also made to the decorative vocabulary of the Ottoman and Mamluk binders with the introduction of floral arabesques, cloud-collar profiles[5] and cusped corner pieces. It is the aim of this paper to provide a brief survey of styles and techniques of Italian Renaissance bindings and examine their relationship with developments in Mamluk and Ottoman binding during the fifteenth century, looking at how these were then adopted and adapted by the binders of Renaissance Italy.

First of all, it has to be said that although the Italian binders adopted Islamic styles and techniques for decorating the bindings, they did not include the flap, a distinguishing feature of Islamic bindings. Also, Islamic covers were glued to the text block not sewn and block-printed leather doublures were not used for Renaissance bindings, a common feature of Mamluk and Ottoman bindings during the fourteenth and fifteenth centuries.

Decorated bindings with gilt ornament began to be produced using simple tools to create composite knot/rope-work patterns in the first quarter of the fifteenth century in Florence, styled in inventories as *alla fiorentina* or *modo fiorentina*. These knot and rope-work patterns often enlivened with gold punches were used extensively to fill the interstices of the central patterns and as border decoration on Mamluk and Ottoman bindings of the fourteenth and fifteenth centuries. However, the gilt dots of the Florentine bindings were attached with gesso and then fixed with a reddish varnish and painted in gold rather than being gold tooled. These bindings also continued to use wooden covers with metal clasps and bosses.

We should also note that the Italian binders in the middle of the fifteenth century restricted themselves to creating knotwork borders that were used to decorate Mamluk bindings of the fourteenth and Ottoman bindings of the fifteenth century made up of the impressions of pallet and punch tools. The more complex patterns which commonly occur in the borders of Ottoman and Mamluk bindings either through the use of one small tool or a design built up through a selection of different tools were not replicated by the Italian binders.

The fifteenth century saw increased trade between the Levant and the Italian states of Venice, Florence, Genoa, Naples and Ancona and by 1450 Venice had become the leading power in the Eastern Mediterranean. With this development came greater opportunities for exposure to contemporary binding developments

---

[5] This term was used by Raby and Tanındı 1993, 37 to refer to the cruciform cartouche which resembles the 'cloud- collar' of Chinese Yuan robes.

in the Ottoman and Mamluk realms. From the end of the fourteenth century Venetian consuls (*baili*) were present in Alexandria, Cairo, Damascus and Beirut and commercial treaties were agreed with the Mamluks and Ottomans. This period marks active interaction between Venice and the East and the imitation and the adoption of Eastern techniques by Venetian craftsmen is to be noted in the production of glassware, textiles and leather.[6] This interest extended to manuscripts and Hobson notes King René of Anjou owned Arabic and Turkish manuscripts for which he employed a translator and the 1481 inventory of the Vatican lists twenty-two manuscripts in Arabic.[7]

Examples exist of Italian manuscripts bound in Islamic bindings. The Marciana Library in Venice has a volume containing two manuscripts, one dated 3 December 1453 which once belonged to Marino Sanudo the Younger (1466–1533), the diarist, entitled *De vita et moribus philosophorum*.[8] The binding, with a flap, is worn and has at its centre a tooled 10-pointed star extending into geometrical interlace, very much in keeping with Mamluk or North African bindings of the fourteenth and fifteenth centuries.

A manuscript dated to between 1460 and 1470 of Petrarch's *Canzoniere and Trionfi* in the Bodleian Library is Florentine but was bound by an Ottoman or Mamluk binder without a flap and the Islamic style of sewing can still be seen although it has been rebacked.[9] The doublures of a binding of a manuscript copied for the Mamluk sultan Qaytbay (1468–1496) in 1484 can be compared to those of the *Canzoniere* and *Trionfi* manuscript.[10] Both doublures are in pale brown morocco leather and the Mamluk binding has a silver medallion filled with blue and silver knotwork while the other is decorated similarly except in gold instead of silver. Comparable Ottoman examples exist dated to between the 1460s and 1470s.

Likewise, the cover of this Florentine manuscript (Figure 11.1) can be closely compared to the binding of another manuscript prepared for Sultan Qaytbay in two volumes dated by a *waqf* inscription to 1473 of Dimyati's *Mashāri' al-ashwāq ilā maṣāri' al-'ushshāq*[11] (Figure 11.2). The medallions are filled with fine arabesques which are repeated in the cusped corner- pieces. The segmented borders of the Mamluk binding are filled with quatrefoil stamps while the binding of the Florentine manuscript contains finely tooled knotwork. Segmented borders

---

    6   Carboni 2007.

    7   Hobson 1989b, 22.

    8   W. Burley, *De vita et moribus philosophorum*, 1453, Biblioteca Marciana, Lat.VI 270 (=3671), 14 × 20 cm.

    9   Petrarch, *Canzoniere and Trionfi*, Florence, 1460–1470, Oxford, Bodleian, Ms.Canon. Ital.78, 21.8 × 13.8 cm, Hobson 1989b, figs 15 and 16.

    10   Yusuf bin Abd al-Hadi (Ibn al-Mabrid), *Al-Durrat al-muḍiyya wa'l-'arūs al-marḍiyya*, Cairo, 1484, Topkapı Palace Library, Ms.A.2829, 32 × 21.5 cm; Karatay 1966, no. 6032.

    11   Dimyati, *Mashāri' al-ashwāq ilā maṣāri' al-'ushshāq*, Cairo, 1490, Topkapı Palace Library, Ms.A.649/1, 36.5 × 26 cm; Karatay 1964, no. 2995; Raby and Tanındı 1993, fig. 21.

Figure 11.1 Upper cover, Petrarch, *Canzoniere and Trionfi*, Florence, 1460–1470. Oxford, Bodleian, Ms.Canon.Ital.78, 21.8 × 13.8 cm
Source: Courtesy of the Bodleian Library.

were generally abandoned by Ottoman binders by the middle of the fifteenth century which suggests that this manuscript was bound in the Mamluk realm.[12]

This shows that contemporary examples of Ottoman and Mamluk bindings were available to serve as models for the changes in Renaissance binding that were to take place after 1500.

The earliest representation of Islamic type bindings in painting is to be found on Andrea Mantegna's (1431–1506) San Zeno altarpiece painted in Padua

---

[12] Raby and Tanındı 1993, 11.

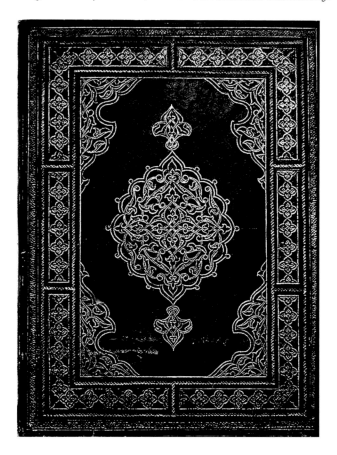

Figure 11.2 Upper cover, al-Dimyati, *Mashāri' al-ashwāq ilā maṣāri' al-'ushshāq*, Cairo, 1490. Topkapı Palace Library, A.649/1, 36.5 × 26 cm
Source: Courtesy of the Topkapı Palace Library.

in 1456–1459. The covers on the books held by the Saints, John the Baptist and Zeno, have Mamluk style rosette centrepieces that must reflect styles found on contemporary Italian bindings.[13] Likewise, Carpaccio's (1465–1525) representation of St Augustine in his study in the Scuola di San Giorgio degli Schiavoni in Venice painted ca. 1502–1508 shows an Islamic type binding featured prominently on his desk and several gilt bindings displayed on a shelf nearby.[14]

By the 1490s, the innovations that had taken hold in the Mamluk and Ottoman realms of book-binding began to appear in the Italian book-binder's repertoire

[13] Mack 2002, fig. 132.
[14] Brown 1988, plates XIII and XIV.

and develop into what Hobson terms the fully developed 'humanistic style' which he believes began in Padua sometime before 1460.[15] Hobson has sought to attribute these developments to a group of antiquaries in Padua who included Andrea Mantegna the artist, Giovanni Marcanova (ca.1418–1467) the academic, Bartolomeo Sanvito (1435–1518) the renowned calligrapher and Felice Feliciano (1433–1479), a poet and book-binder.

The developments quickly spread to Venice and by the 1470s Venetian binders were producing bindings which included all these new techniques.

A copy of Cicero's *Epistolae ad familiares*, bound for Peter Ugelheimer (d.1489), the German owner of Deutches Haus Inn, and printed by Nicolas Jenson (1420–1480) on parchment in Venice in 1475, exhibits many features found on Mamluk bindings of the fifteenth century.[16] The centre of the cover is decorated with a large lozenge which was widely used on Ottoman and Mamluk bindings and unusually, floral escutcheons which are found more normally on Mamluk and Ottoman lobed medallions are attached at either end. A segmented knotwork border surrounds the central panel. The use of the Y-shaped stamps which fill the central lozenge appear out of place as they are found on metal work do not usually occur on Ottoman or Mamluk bindings. Ugelheimer was a well-known bibliophile who commissioned several other bindings in this style. These constituted fine or 'extra' bindings produced for the wealthy élite.

Many of these *alla islamica* bindings are most commonly found on certificates of appointment by the Venetian doges. Although commissions for senior positions were sponsored by the state those for lower level posts such as captains or governors were left to the recipients who had their *Commissioni* manuscripts copied, illuminated and bound by artists working in Venice.

A binding of a commission dated 1500 for three captains going to Beirut[17] has a cloud-collar profile which was first used in the Timurid context in illumination in a *Shāhnāma* produced in Shiraz in about 1397 and makes its appearance on Ottoman bindings produced in Amasya, Bursa and Edirne in the 1450s and 1460s[18] (Plate 41). The border decoration is in the classical style. On many of these bindings, classical elements of decoration such as Roman vases and cherubs are often contained in roundels which have their origins in Mamluk rosette centre-pieces and have lobed corner-pieces with split palmettes constituting variations and adaptations of what is found on Mamluk and Ottoman covers.

In addition to the incorporation of decorative elements to the binder's vocabulary, new techniques were introduced such as filigree leather work and pressure-moulding. The technique of filigree is an ancient one and was used

---

[15] Hobson 1989b, 39–53.
[16] Cicero, *Epistolae ad familares*, Venice, 1475, Paris, Bibliothèque National, Vélins 1149, 29.3 × 18.8 cm; Hobson 1989b, 40–41, fig. 34.
[17] Commission dated 1500, Biblioteca Marciana Ms.It.VII, 597 (=7820), 26 × 17.7 cm.
[18] Raby and Tanındı 1993, 42.

to decorate both Coptic and Manichean codices of the tenth century.[19] Filigree leather-work begins to appear on covers in Mamluk Cairo in some numbers at the end of the fourteenth century in spite of its susceptibility to damage. It is generally only on Mamluk bindings that filigree work is used for the covers; Persian and Ottoman bindings usually confine the use of filigree to the doublures. Within the Mamluk context, the earliest known filigree binding of this type contains a manuscript dated to 1391 entitled *Al-Shifā' fī ta'rīf ḥuqūq al-Muṣṭafā* copied by Ahmad b. Muhammad al-Balisi.[20]

The central panel is tooled with large floral forms outlined in gold which also appear on Ottoman bindings of the 1460s. The technique of placing filigree work on textile seems to have been discontinued by the Mamluk binders by the middle of the fifteenth century and when the technique of filigree reappears again it is used for the doublures of fine bindings. Now, the textile backing has been replaced by pasteboard which allowed for firmer fixing and for the use of several colours to highlight different parts of the pattern.

The binder of the Codex Lippomano which contains a collection of Latin poems by Jacopo Tiraboschi and was written in Padua in or soon after 1471 must have been aware of the earlier Mamluk bindings which employed filigree for their covers described above.[21] The corners of the cover of this binding are laid down on a green silk background and its central panel contains a large lobed lozenge. The cover has a filigree border for which there is no Mamluk exemplar. However, the centre contains a profile portrait of Antinous producing an odd combination of classical and Islamic styles. Hobson attributes this binding to Felice Feliciano, the Paduan scribe and antiquarian, who is also thought to be the binder of the Marcanova codex and a volume by Leonardo Bruni which will be discussed later.[22]

Filigree doublures are first found on fine or 'extra' Mamluk bindings at the end of the fifteenth century and on Ottoman bindings by the 1460s. They closely followed the style and techniques used on filigree doublures on a pasteboard backing on manuscripts copied for Sultan Ahmed Jalayir who ruled in Baghdad and Tabriz between 1382 and 1410.[23]

---

[19] For Coptic examples see Hobson 1939, 210–11; British Library 1978, nos 142, 147, 148. For fragments from Turfan see Gulácsi 2005.

[20] Qadi Ayyad, *al-Shifā' fī ta'rīf ḥuqūq al-Muṣṭafā*, Cairo, 1391, Topkapı Palace Library, Ms. A. 317, 27 × 17.5 cm; Karatay 1964, no. 2744, Tanındı 1990, 149, n. 13.

[21] Codex Lippomano, Jacopo Tiraboschi, *Carmina*, Padua, ca.1471, Private Collection, 17.3 × 11.8 cm; Hobson 1989b, 46, fig. 41.

[22] G. Marcanova, *Collectio Antiquitatum* a Bologna, ca. 1464–1465, Modena, Biblioteca Estense, Cod. Alfa, L.5.15; L. Bruni, *Commentarius rerum in Italia suo tempore gestarum*, Bologna?, 1464–1465, Venice, Biblioteca Marciana, Lat.X, 117 (=3844), 19.7 × 11.9 cm; Hobson, 1989b, fig. 37, 43; Granzotto 1995; Mack 2002, 129.

[23] Ohta 2004. See the doublures of *Divān of Sultan Ahmed Jalayir*, 1406, Museum for Turkish and Islamic Art, Ms. 2046, 27.1 × 18.3 cm published in Sakisian 1934, 188; Brend

On his demise, his calligraphers, binders and illuminators went on to find employment with the Timurid courts – particularly that of Iskandar Sultan in Shiraz (1395–1399) (1409–1414) and Sultan Baysunqur in Herat (1399–1433) where further developments took place in the development of filigree with the use of polychromy and increased tooling in gold. Bindings of this type are usually distinguished by an oval centrepiece filled with arabesques and cusped corner pieces.

The binding of *Commentarius rerum in Italia suo tempore* of Leonardo Bruni in the Biblioteca Marciana and the *Collectio Antiquitatum* of Giovanni Marcanova in Modena (wooden boards) are the earliest European bindings with filigree and the earliest with filigree doublures.[24] Both these doublures are decorated with a cloud-collar profile with cut-away filigree work on a red, blue and green painted ground which is sprinkled with tiny glass-like beads (Plate 42). Both these bindings are attributed to Felice Feliciano who copied the Marcanova codex for Giovanni Marcanova, another of the Paduan antiquaries group in Bologna to provide a record of the antiquities Marcanova had seen and the inscriptions he had copied. Feliciano also copied the beginning of the Bruni while in Bologna between 1464–1465, so it is supposed that both these bindings were done there.[25]

By the beginning of the sixteenth century Venetian binders were producing bindings that can be closely compared to Ottoman rather than Mamluk examples. From 1516 with the defeat of the Mamluk sultanate by Selim I (r. 1465–1520), the production of 'extra' bindings declined in Cairo as binders and other craftsmen were transferred to Istanbul.

We now turn to the technique of pressure-moulding which used large stamps to produce decoration in relief of the covers usually in the form of a lobed centrepiece with a defined gilded outline and accompanying corner pieces, all filled with delicate floral decoration.[26] This technique was used extensively on Turkmen bindings in the fifteenth century and was to dominate Ottoman bindings of late fifteenth century. Within the Mamluk context there are only a few examples of bindings that utilise this technique for their decoration. Raby and Tanındı have shown that the technique of pressure-moulding was introduced to Ottoman bindings with the introduction of influences from the Turkmen-held cities of Shiraz, Isfahan and Tabriz when Sultan Mehmed (1432–1481) profited from his defeat of the Aq-qoyunlu in 1473 by removing the artists and binders to Istanbul.[27]

1989, 236 and those of Hamza b. Hasan al-Isfahani, *Tārīkh-i Iṣfahān* copied for Baysunqur in 1431, British Library, Or. 2773, 23 × 14 cm; Arts Council of Great Britain 1976, no. 559.

[24] See n. 22.
[25] Hobson 1989b, 43.
[26] For a full description of the technique of pressure-moulding see Raby and Tanındı 1993, Appendix 1, 216.
[27] Raby and Tanındı 1993, 69.

Figure 11.3   Upper cover, Fra Giocondo, *Sylloge*, Venice, ca. 1520–1530, Chatsworth, 25.1 × 15.9 cm
Source: Courtesy of the Trustees of the Chatsworth Settlement.

The decoration of the upper cover of the binding of Fra Giocondo's *Sylloge* at Chatsworth bound in Venice between 1520–1530, copied by Bartolomeo Sanvito, another member of the Paduan antiquaries, is pressure-moulded[28] (Figure 11.3). The central medallion on a gold ground can be directly compared with

---

[28]   Fra Giocondo, *Sylloge*, Venice, ca. 1520–1530, Chatsworth Library, Chatsworth House, Derbyshire, 25.1 × 15.9 cm; Hobson 1989b, fig. 119.

Ottoman examples of the late fifteenth century[29]. The Chinese scrolls appear on contemporary Ottoman and Persian bindings and an Ottoman lacquer Qur'an with this form of decoration in the Biblioteca Marciana dated 1536 suggests that ready examples were available for the binders.[30] The doublure has arabesque filigree work within a lobed medallion on a blue ground and the central cruciform medallion is in a paler turquoise.

In conclusion, it has to be remembered that the binders of Renaissance Italy drew their inspiration from a variety of sources and those that include Persian, Ottoman and Mamluk decorative elements constituted very small part of those produced for the Venetian élite. However, the impact of these influences was long-lasting and far-reaching. A group of bindings from the latter part of the sixteenth century which contain commissions dated between 1530–1571 and bound by the 'Arabesque outline tool binder' as named by Hobson still bear traces of their indebtedness to Mamluk and Ottoman bindings.[31] The groupings of three small dots are to be found as a detail on Ottoman and Mamluk pasteboards of filigree work and also occur in Turkmen illumination. Also, the large open palmette corner pieces are a studied development of their Eastern forebears[32] (Plate 43). However, all these elements have been adapted and transformed into another style which was to spread throughout Europe decorating the bindings prepared for the library of François I (1494–1547) at Fontainebleau and beyond.

---

[29] See for the example the cover of a copy of the *Sūrat al-an'ām*, ca. 1480, Topkapı Palace Library, Ms. B.29, 21 × 14 cm; see Raby and Tanındı 1993, cat. 36.

[30] Qur'an, 1536, Biblioteca Marciana, Orientali 68.

[31] Commission, Venice, 1571, Biblioteca Marciana, Ms.It.VII, 1366 (=8092), 23.4 × 15.4 cm. An identical cover is found in the British Library, Egerton Ms.757 cm, 23.4 × 15.4 cm also dated 1571; see Nuvoloni 2000; see also Hobson and Culot 1991, 47.

[32] The corner pieces with their wide tendrils can be directly compared to those on the binding of a Mamluk Qur'an most probably made for Qansuh Khamsmiyya who held the position of *Amir Akhur* (Master of the Stables) between 1481–1496, Museum of Turkish and Islamic Art, Istanbul, TIEM 508, 62 × 38 cm; see Ohta 2004, fig. 12; Tanındı 2012.

Chapter 12
Ottoman Textiles in European Markets

Suraiya Faroqhi

When historians have discussed the import trade in textiles from the Ottoman realm to western or southern Europe, until quite recently they have focused on the importation of raw fibers. The cottons *'en laine'* from Syria or western Anatolia that filled the holds of Venetian ships in the 1400s have been studied in detail, and the same applies to the wool from Balkan sheep that, throughout the sixteenth and early seventeenth centuries, traders from Dubrovnik marketed in Italy.[1] Before about 1400, finished fabrics from the Middle East had played an important and sometimes decisive role in European markets. To mention but one example among many, textile experts have long acknowledged the impact of Mamluk designs upon medieval European silk weaving.[2]

However, beginning with the early 1400s and certainly in the sixteenth century, the current was reversed. Fabrics of Italian and later English origin now entered the markets of the Eastern Mediterranean in sizeable quantities, partly because of the trade connections established by late medieval Venice, the dominant player in Mediterranean commerce at this time. Venice has been described as exercising a virtual trade monopoly in this region, even though proto-colonial power continued to elude the Serenissima.[3] For in the political realm Ottoman sultans from the reign of Mehmed the Conqueror onwards rapidly established a dominant position and by the mid-seventeenth century if not earlier, completely evinced Venice.

Venetian imports of raw cotton and later of wool from the Eastern Mediterranean were in part paid for by the exportation of manufactured textiles. At first this involved mainly silks and velvets, but by the second half of the sixteenth century, woollens were a significant export item as well.[4] On the other hand by the late 1400s the demand in European markets for silks and velvets from the Eastern Mediterranean seems to have contracted. Apart from rugs and carpets, finished textiles manufactured in the Ottoman lands now appeared much more rarely in the markets of the West.[5]

---

[1] Ashtor 1978; Carter 1972, passim.
[2] Schmidt 1963; von Wilckens 1991.
[3] Ashtor 1978b.
[4] Sella 1968.
[5] Jacoby 2004. I am grateful to the author for allowing me to read his important text, and also for his enlightening discussion of the late medieval silk trade.

Certainly the vogue for Italian textiles in the regions bordering the Eastern Mediterranean was real and not a figment of twentieth-century 'orientalist' imagination: when in Ottoman official records of the early 1600s the activities of Venetian merchants are referred to, it is routinely assumed that the latter brought in 'woollen cloth and [other] fabrics'. And when during those same years a dragoman in the service of the Venetian permanent ambassador in Istanbul, known as the *bailo*, was accorded a special privilege in recompense for his services, it was a small quantity of silks and velvets that he was permitted to import free of customs duties every year.[6] Even in the Ottoman palace of the sixteenth century, Bursa silks and velvets were supplemented by albeit limited quantities of Venetian imports.[7]

On the other hand, decreasing exportation from the Ottoman lands did not mean that in the 1400s and 1500s, Middle Eastern silks disappeared from wealthy homes in western and southern Europe, as we will see after a brief overview over recent publications. After all the similarity between certain Ottoman and Venetian textiles during this period can only be explained by continuing and intensive contacts between workshops in Istanbul and Venice. Moreover mohair cloth, delicate and perishable and therefore of no great interest to textile collectors, materially contributed towards keeping the westward flow of textiles moving. Where Bursa and Istanbul fabrics did not go, those of Ankara might find a market.

Of Humanism and Consumption: Valuable Fabrics as a Site of Historiographical Debate

Beyond being simple statements of fact, why are these observations significant? In the context of intensive debates among Renaissance historians, early modern currents of trade across the Mediterranean have taken on special meaning. During the last decade scholars such as Lisa Jardine, Deborah Howard, Rosamund Mack and Jeremy Brotton have pointed out that far from disappearing as the impact of Greco-Roman art became more prominent, Middle Eastern luxuries with inherent artistic qualities such as riding gear, majolica and carpets, continued to fire the imaginations of European painters and designers.[8]

Jeremy Brotton especially has downplayed the impact of Greco-Roman antiquity in comparison to the various kinds of inspiration that fifteenth-century artists derived from the contemporary Middle East and also the Iberian peninsula: after all in the art of the territories forming the incipient Spanish kingdom, the Islamic component remained clearly visible throughout the

---

[6] Başbakanlık Arşivi-Osmanlı Arşivi (BOA), *Düvel-i ecnebiye Defterleri* 13/1, p. 93, no. 460 (Cemaziyelevvel 1021/ July 1612).

[7] Mackie 2004.

[8] Jardine 1996; Howard 2000; Jardine and Brotton 2000; Brotton 2002; Mack 2002; Spallanzani 2007.

fifteenth century.⁹ Brotton's metaphor of the 'bazaar' emphasises the mixity and heterogeneity of the world inhabited by Renaissance artists and patrons, a conglomerate that included numerous borrowings from the Islamic world. In addition as the author has emphatically pointed out, artists and their sponsors in the 1400s were perfectly well aware of the debt owed to artifacts from the Islamic world. They thus were much more realistic – or honest – than many scholars active in the nineteenth and twentieth centuries.

These revisionist statements have certainly been inspired by the 'orientalism' debate: Renaissance humanism is now seen as a most ambiguous heritage.¹⁰ In Brotton's perspective humanist training in Greek and Latin philology, in evident contradiction to the claims of its promoters, emphasised rote learning and submissiveness to authority. Even more seriously humanism encouraged the 'otherisation' of all those to whom the ever more intensive assimilation of the Greco-Roman heritage had little meaning. In other words, Muslims were now not only infidels as they had been in earlier times, but were also cast as barbarians in Greco-Roman terms.¹¹

If on the other hand Renaissance art was to a considerable extent inspired by Middle Eastern artifacts, then as the saying goes, it becomes possible for the modern historian to kill two birds with one stone. On the one hand, Middle Eastern models for Renaissance artifacts are usable in scholarly polemics; previous research is laid open to criticism due to its conscious or unconscious neglect of the Middle Eastern and Islamic component of European Renaissance culture. As a result the scholars under attack are seen to adhere to an 'orientalist' discourse that many of their colleagues today are trying their level best to shed. But viewed from a different perspective, if Middle Eastern artifacts were so important to early modern art in Italy and elsewhere, it becomes possible to assume that 'orientalism' was not as pervasive throughout European Renaissance culture as had once been claimed. Going yet a step further it may even be suggested that a degree of multi-culturalism existed within the Renaissance context, even though it was during this very same period that writers voicing claims to cultural and even 'racial' superiority first came out into the open. In so far as artists, artisans and their patrons refused to completely 'buy' into the humanist discourse they may be regarded as having formulated statements that were not 'exclusivist'; in other words they remained relatively untainted by the 'superiority complex' that affected so much European writing about the outside world after about 1550.

---

⁹ Brotton 2002, 34 and elsewhere.
¹⁰ Said 1978.
¹¹ For a well-known sixteenth-century author see Busbequius 1994, 125. While Busbecq is relatively moderate in his expressions, his travelling companion Hans Dernschwam, who at his death left a major library peppered the diary covering his travels in the Ottoman Empire with remarks of this kind: Babinger 1986, passim.

Yet there are more mundane reasons for the recently reviving interest in Middle Eastern goods that once circulated in the markets of Renaissance Europe. For a long time historians have regarded the economy as being driven by investment and technological innovation, both of which unambiguously belong to the 'supply' side. All aspects of demand, including especially consumption were devalued in consequence. Yet during the last twenty years or so there has been a turnaround. First of all the distribution sector, that is the retail trade which mediates between supply and demand, has come in for a good deal of attention: thus in early modern England itinerant traders offered textiles at low prices that allowed even farm-workers to acquire a few shirts. And once fabrics had become accessible to different classes of consumers, the latter used them not only for comfort but also for display. As a result we have seen a massive expansion of studies concerning consumption and the identity-building so often connected with the possession of worldly goods.

Admittedly in the period between 1400 and 1700, on which we focus in the present paper, consumption as a mass phenomenon was only beginning to emerge, remaining basically limited to England and the Netherlands. Elsewhere the process only began well after 1700 and will not concern us here; thus in France something like a 'mass' consumption of textiles could first be observed during the eighteenth century. Further east the beginnings of mass consumption are even more recent, often dating back only to about 1850.

When focusing on consumption during the early modern period we therefore are obliged to limit our studies to the wealthy and privileged, especially princely courts, and to some extent, country gentlemen and rich merchants. On occasion this select group may include a handful of Italian artists. Though often from an artisan milieu the latter might, if very successful indeed, come to claim the status of gentlefolk. All these people, and not least the artists, were possible consumers of more or less valuable fabrics imported from the Middle East; in other words we are dealing with luxury consumption. In the 1960s and 1970s such a research enterprise might have been considered as rather futile and even frivolous by many members of the historical profession. But for better or for worse, in our present-day world nobody needs to be ashamed of studying luxury and privileged consumption. To sum it all up the imports of valuable Ottoman fabrics into Christian Europe have emerged as a topic of study because the importation of these artifacts can be linked to the 'orientalism' debate, and also because in our present-day world, notable for its sharp differentiation between rich and poor, examining the consumption of the upper classes has regained legitimacy among historians.

A Brief Glance at Ottoman Silks in the Hands of European Consumers

Some silks, velvets and brocades came to early modern European markets from Istanbul, Bursa or Damascus, either by way of trade or else as diplomatic gifts.[12] However the number of surviving examples is quite limited; thus Venice, the transit point for many of these items, today has very little to show for its long involvement in the textile trade with the Middle East. In part this is doubtless due to the fact that by the sixteenth century, Ottoman silks were having a hard time competing with Italian fabrics; but we also need to take the vicissitudes of later history into account. For when Napoleon abolished the ancient Republic in 1797, precious textiles in public collections were mostly burnt in order to retrieve the gold and silver that so many of them contained; and that these items were associated with the defunct state and with the Catholic church also must have done little to endear them to the revolutionaries.[13]

Comparable losses are on record for Prague. Wealthy inhabitants of this city, in the late sixteenth and early seventeenth centuries the imperial residence of the noted collector Emperor Rudolf II, also favoured both Italian and Ottoman brocades. But today, only painted portraits document this type of conspicuous consumption: for as the city was repeatedly plundered already during the 1600s, no examples of such textiles survive today. Jewish embroiderers active in the ghetto of Prague worked Italian and Ottoman textiles into curtains for their synagogues; the designs they employed were often of Ottoman origin, and the same also applies to certain vestments manufactured for Catholic churches of the period.[14]

Of course this kind of indirect evidence tells us nothing about the quantities of silk imported; on the contrary painters could keep a very few pieces of foreign silks in their workshops and use them in more than one painting. In the same fashion, designs could be copied by several local manufacturers even if there were only a few genuine Bursa or Istanbul fabrics available. But viewed from the perspective of the Renaissance cultural historian, a decline in the quantity of imported silks does not invalidate their argument; as long as Ottoman pieces were available for copying and actually were being copied, Renaissance art still was nourished by Middle Eastern, as well as by classical, traditions.

As for Florence and the surrounding region, Ottoman silk fabrics have been preserved in appreciable numbers in the Bargello Museum and elsewhere. Already in the late fifteenth century, Florentine merchants were present in Bursa.[15] Two hundred and fifty years later in the early 1600s, the acquisition of valuable goods of Ottoman provenience was partly linked to the fact that the Medici family, now grand dukes of Tuscany, were establishing a free port in

---

[12] The basic reference work is Atasoy et al. 2001.
[13] Davanzo Poli 2003.
[14] Kybalova 1997.
[15] For an example see Halil İnalcık 1980–1981, 78; and recently İnalcık 2008.

Leghorn/Livorno in order to facilitate commerce with the Middle East. Princely ostentation also had a role to play: in the late sixteenth and early seventeenth centuries, the Medici acquired two huge carpets that are still preserved in a Florentine museum. In addition, fine cottons and sashes from the Ottoman lands were acquired for the Medici wardrobe, while silk fabrics were usually not bought for their own sakes but because they formed part of elegant weaponry or fancy horse-gear. Rather less peacefully, the Medici grand dukes cast themselves in the role of latter-day 'crusaders', in other words as freebooters who had founded the Order of St Stephen, a small-scale copy of the Knights of Malta.[16] This warlike stance probably explains why Ottoman armory formed an important part of the Medici collection; some of the pieces recorded in the grand-ducal inventories, textiles included, may well have been booty.[17]

Moreover in spite of the numerous misfortunes that Poland has suffered during the nineteenth and twentieth centuries, textile historians have located quite a few Ottoman silks and brocades in Cracow and other towns. Thus in 1992 an exhibition in the former capital of the Polish-Lithuanian Commonwealth showed items from church treasuries that are of interest for our purposes. The catalogue featured a sixteenth-century Ottoman silk fabric that had been reused as a chasuble and an early seventeenth-century item that had ended up as a dalmatic; unfortunately we have no clue as to the place(s) of manufacture. Elaborately decorated cushion covers also appeared in wealthy Polish houses. These latter items were probably imported from Bursa, where cushion covers were produced in such great quantities that the available supply was not monopolised by sultans and viziers, but available for local consumption on the part of well-to-do townspeople and also for export.[18]

Some Ottoman silks also were used for church vestments in Hungary. Unfortunately the relevant catalogue entries do not tell us whether this transformation is supposed to have occurred in those parts of Hungary that were under direct or indirect Ottoman control, or else in the strip of land known as 'Royal Hungary', ruled by the Habsburgs.[19] Only in this latter case can we postulate an earlier exportation into Christian Europe; it thus remains doubtful whether the Hungarian church treasures do in fact qualify for inclusion in the present survey. But with respect to a piece of figured silk manufactured in the second half of the sixteenth century that, after tailoring, became a child's jacket, we can be fairly sure that exportation had occurred at one point in time, either commercially or else because the fabric in question had been given to

---

[16] Damiani et al. 2003.

[17] Orsi Landini 2006.

[18] National Museum in Cracow 1992, Ill. 28, 29 and 38. I am much obliged to Dariusz Kołodziejczyk who has presented me with a copy of this publication. The new Benaki Islamic Museum in Athens contains an impressive array of Bursa cushion covers.

[19] Gerelyes 1995, items no. 98 and 100 – thanks to Ipolya Gerelyes for sending me a copy; Schuckelt and Schnitzer 1995, item no. 161, p. 152.

a Hungarian dignitary as a diplomatic present. For this piece of Ottoman silk belonged to the once-famous collection of the princely family of Esterházy that had risen to prominence in Royal Hungary during the seventeenth century.[20]

Given all this evidence – and new items are constantly being published – it is surprising that the early modern vogue for Ottoman silks and velvets has only been studied during recent years. Things might have been different if the designs of Ottoman silks and brocades had been as 'peculiar' as those of rugs and carpets; after all importation of the latter has been in the public eye for quite a long time already. But unfortunately from our point of view, Ottoman textile designers sometimes adopted motifs known from Italian silks, such as the crown, while certain Venetian workshops catered for the Ottoman market and therefore produced designs that closely imitated Ottoman silks and damasks. As a result only textile experts who are able to evaluate technical characteristics are able to tell these silks apart and that only if they see the originals and not merely paintings or engravings.[21]

Moreover even if the originals do survive, in some cases the place of manufacture, either Venetian or else Ottoman, remains disputed. Thus a late fifteenth-century red velvet today in the Bargello Museum has been catalogued as 'probably' Italian, but the cataloguer admits that an Ottoman workshop might also have produced such an item with a view to the European market.[22] In consequence while Renaissance paintings have been a reasonably helpful source for scholars trying to piece together the history of Ottoman carpets, the same does not apply where silks and velvets are concerned, and the peregrinations of these textiles among European consumers remain quite opaque.

Manufacturing Precious Mohair Cloths

Our ignorance is exacerbated by the fact that some luxury fabrics from the Ottoman realm had smooth surfaces without any design and thus even if depicted may not be recognisable to the modern viewer. This is particularly true of the cloth known in Ottoman sources as *sof*, *zambelotti* in Venice and *zamlot* in German; to date I have not seen any catalogue entries showing holdings of this fabric in any museum collection. However due to its special 'watered' surface, *sof* was so much appreciated in its time that in spite of the obvious difficulties involved, a few European illustrators did attempt to render it pictorially.

Sof/zambelotti were woven from the hair of the Angora goat that during the fifteenth to seventeenth centuries flourished only in the region of Ankara;

---

[20] Gerelyes 1995, item no. 94. After restoration much of the Esterhazy treasure is now in the Museum of Applied Arts in Budapest.

[21] This was especially apparent in the exhibition held in Prato during the summer of 2006. See Contadini 2006b.

[22] Suriano and Carboni 1999, 80–81.

if transplanted the animals no longer grew the silky coats from which this desirable fabric was woven, but only the rough hair usable for sacking and little else. There has been a good deal of speculation concerning the origins of the Angora goat. Some authors have pointed to depictions of this creature in Greco-Roman imagery, while others have suggested that it was brought into the region by shepherds who migrated from Central Asia into Anatolia during the medieval period. The French cultural geographer Xavier de Planhol has come up with yet a third solution, proposing that spontaneous mutations produced Angora goats every now and then throughout recorded history, but that these animals were only consciously bred once Ankara had become a commercial centre of some importance, in all likelihood during the fifteenth century.[23]

Within the Ottoman borders by the mid-1500s, Ankara had acquired a reputation for the production of *sof*. This must have increased when Süleyman the Lawgiver (Kanuni) (r. 1520–1566) who became more pious as he grew older, started to wear this fabric instead of the silk that according to Islamic religious law males are not supposed to wear. However the ruler did not cease to appear as the 'Magnificent' as European authors were accustomed to call him, and at least in winter *sof* with its lustrous sheen could serve as an appropriate substitute. However the sultan's palace by no means monopolised mohair cloth and moreover after Süleyman's death, Ottoman rulers were no longer greatly interested in it: from Selim II (r. 1566–1574) to Ahmed I (r. 1603–1617) the sultans were once again mainly attracted by the silks, brocades and velvets of Istanbul and Bursa which reached a peak of sophistication at just this time.

As a result fine mohair fabrics were available for export. In the 1550s Hans Dernschwam who had long served the Fugger and thus acquired the wherewithal to accompany the Habsburg ambassador Ogier Ghislain de Busbecq on his travels to Istanbul and Amasya, noted the work of village women in the pay of Ankara merchants who spun the yarn to be worked up by local weavers. Dernschwam commented on the simplicity of the implement these peasant women used in order to wind the thread, and was much surprised that the spinners were able to produce very fine yarn with such an elementary tool. He also described the *cendere*s or presses that only operated in major towns, especially in Ankara itself. Since, to my knowledge, he was the only observer to ever do so, his description is worth recounting in some detail.

Treatment in the *cendere* was preceded by washing the dyed fabrics in clean water – in its natural state the Angora fibre was white. Dyeing was a job for specialised artisans, who turned over their completed handiwork to the presses. At some point in the process the manufacturers also seem to have pounded the fabric with their feet, and this made the finished material denser; the process was probably comparable to the treatment that woollen cloth was given in Europe, in some places as late as the eighteenth century.[24] Once this had been completed 70

---

[23] de Planhol 1975–1977.
[24] Braudel 1979, vol. 3, 515.

lengths of mohair cloth were piled one on top of the other in copper kettles, with reeds separating each layer. This latter device ensured that water could evenly penetrate every piece of cloth. Only fabrics of one and the same colour were treated together; the lot of textiles that Dernschwam had information about happened to be black. As the next step, the kettle that had previously been set over a ditch in which a fire could be lit was filled with water and was then heated. At the end of the day, the fabrics were removed and the reeds pulled out. Then all 70 pieces together were placed under a press, and the water was allowed to run off; this step shows that the fabric in question must have been quite delicate, otherwise seventy layers of textile could never have been treated together. After separation of the layers, each piece of *sof* was folded lengthwise and placed under another press, this time individually. Once again Dernschwam thought that the press was not at all well constructed, and could have been worked with much less manpower if the technology had been more sophisticated. As it was, seven men were employed in its operation.

This sequence of treatments was what gave the finished fabrics their silky 'watered' appearance. Dernschwam's travelling companion Busbecq, as a courtly humanist was not interested in the details of manufacture. But he knew a thing or two about the 'value added' by pressing *zambelotti*. According to Busbecq the most highly prized design consisted of large-scale, regularly shaped 'waves'. If smaller and irregular waves were also present this was considered a defect even if the fabric and the dyeing were otherwise of high quality. As a result, such items fetched a few gold pieces less than those with a perfectly regular design.[25]

Dernschwam's travelogue was only published in the twentieth century.[26] But it is perfectly possible that the oral reports of his more prominent companion Busbecq aroused curiosity about this textile, hitherto probably little known in Europe. With respect to the 1580s and 1590s Ottoman records concerning the exportation of *sof* to Venice and Poland are reasonably frequent, and have been thoroughly analysed by Özer Ergenç.[27] Some Polish and Venetian merchants came to Ankara to make their purchases in person, while others used the services of professional middlemen.

However our discussion of the export trade in mohair textiles is made more difficult by the fact that Ottoman sources seem to use the same term, namely *sof* for both the raw material and the finished fabric. By the mid-seventeenth century if not earlier, European traders also were exporting yarn; this was demanded especially by the manufacturers of the Dutch city of Leiden. For in addition to the well-known *Leidse lakens* made of sheep's wool, Leiden also had a reputation for its *greinen* that were woven out of the hair of Angora goats, entirely or at least in part.[28] It was probably due to Dutch demand that Ankara weavers began to

[25] Busbequius 1994, 91.
[26] Babinger 1986, 186–91.
[27] Ergenç 1975.
[28] Israel 1989, 262–3.

complain about a decreasing supply of raw material. In 1645–1646 a prohibition on exporting raw *sof* was confirmed by the Ottoman centre; thus an earlier one must have been issued as well, but unfortunately we know nothing about its date or the circumstances that had prompted it.[29] However, the Dutch only began to play a significant role in Ottoman markets in the early seventeenth century, and thus the original edict may well have been issued under Ahmed I. To date I have not found any references to the manufacture of mohair textiles either in Venice or in Poland; and since merchants from these two places were the main foreign purchasers of *sof* in the late sixteenth century, we can assume that before the Dutch entered the market, Ankara mainly exported finished cloth.

Sof found purchasers in Venice during the sixteenth century and even later, the trade being on record down to the Cretan war which began in 1645. Among other sources numerous complaints on the part of merchants involved in the business that survive in the Venetian archives, make the importance of the trade in *zambelotti* perfectly clear. For on the long haul from Ankara to Venice there were plenty of occasions for trouble. 'At source' we hear from producers in small places near Ankara such as Ayaş and Yeregömü, to the effect that they were being paid in debased coin by the correspondents of the firms that undertook to transfer their mohair to Venice; this got them into difficulty when dealing with outsiders and especially with tax collectors.[30]

Jewish merchants were particularly active in the export of *sof*; after all in the late sixteenth century many of them were based both in Istanbul and in Venice, and thus possessed more local knowledge than most of their Christian rivals.[31] Hayyim Saruq whose bankruptcy caused a major incident in sixteenth-century Veneto-Ottoman relations, dealt in *sof* among many other things.[32] Thus the trade in *zambelotti* was a major reason why so many Ottomans, Christians and Muslims as well as Jews, found their way to Venice.

From Venice to Ankara and Back Again

Quite often our sources mention *sof*-merchants who were robbed at sea, particularly by the notorious Uskoks from Segna (in Ottoman: Seng or 'rock'). This small community of diverse origins was loosely subjected to a Habsburg border commander; in theory they guarded the Habsburg-Ottoman frontier. But in real life the Uskoks with their small rapid boats preyed on Muslims and Christians alike; as to Uskok attacks on the latter, the 'ideological' justification was that people who traded with the Ottomans or else recognised the sultan

---

[29] Faroqhi 1984, 142. See also Kadi 2012.
[30] Faroqhi 1984, 143.
[31] Ergenç 1975, 155 gives a list of the people who took *sof* out of Ankara in 1599–1600; the vast majority were Jews.
[32] Arbel 1995, 100 and 115; I thank the author for his discussion of the issue.

as their overlord did not deserve any better treatment than 'infidels'.³³ As a relatively well-documented example of such problems the trader Seyyid Abdi, apparently a man of substance, in 1586 petitioned the doge and asked for redress: his cargo of *sof* had been plundered and a servitor assassinated by pirates, presumably Uskoks once again. The losses of this trader amounted to thirty-six loads of mohair.³⁴

Moreover apart from the source texts hitherto known, additional primary material has recently been unearthed in the 'Registers of foreign states' (*Düvel-i ecnebiye Defterleri*), located in the Prime Minister's Archives in Istanbul. This series was inaugurated in the very first years of the seventeenth century in order to keep track of the increasingly numerous sultanic commands issued in response to petitions presented by foreign ambassadors. Probably because Ottoman-Venetian trade had such a long history, *Düvel-i ecnebiye Defterleri* relating to the Venetians are among the oldest that have come down to us.³⁵ In October–November 1612 a ruling that dated originally from April–May 1600 was confirmed, permitting Venetian traders in Ankara to reside in one of the town quarters which had established themselves within the fortified enclosure of the citadel.³⁶ Non-Muslim subjects of the sultan previously had been accorded the same privilege, and the admission of the Venetians into this protected area was explained by the merchants' concern about their security. After all those town quarters of Ankara located outside the citadel's massive walls had recently been plundered by rebellious mercenaries.³⁷

From the same year, 1612, there survives the official Ottoman response to petitions from two Venetian merchants called Agostino Perulio (?) and Francesco (surname illegible): these two men – and others who remained unnamed – complained that the local collector of the *kasabiye* tax had told them that they could not remain in Ankara for more than two years without becoming liable for payment of the tax in question.³⁸ However the capitulations granted to the Signoria (*ahidname* in Ottoman parlance) explicitly exempted Venetian traders from this due, intended to finance the Janissary meat supply. The two merchants also complained that they had been forced to hand over goods – probably to well-connected purchasers – on credit (*veresiye*), but then had never received their money. As the Ottoman central administration at this time was greatly concerned with domestic problems, good relations with Venice were accorded high official priority. As a result local administrators were told that as long as the merchants 'behaved themselves and concerned themselves with their trade [alone]' they should be permitted to reside in Ankara as long as they wished.

---

33   Bracewell 1992.
34   Faroqhi 2002.
35   Faroqhi 1986; Goffman 2002.
36   BOA, *Düvel-i ecnebiye Defterleri* 13/1, p. 97, No. 481 (Ramazan 1021).
37   Ergenç 1980.
38   BOA, *Düvel-i ecnebiye Defterleri* 13/1, p. 88, No. 436 (Safer 1021).

We can thus assume that in the early seventeenth century, there were a few Venetians who were long-term residents of this town, and the only business that could have brought them there was the *sof* trade.

While these two texts must be interpreted with the help of what we already know before their value becomes apparent, a third document, dated to February 1612, is much more explicit.[39] This sultanic edict introduces us to the trials and tribulations of a caravan of Muslims, Jews and Venetians that travelled from Istanbul to Venice carrying *sof*. In the Ottoman province of Kilis/formerly Venetian Clissa the traders were attacked by robbers and one of the Muslims was killed. The men in charge of the caravan were able to salvage some of the dead man's *sof* which they carried to the Venetian fortress of Spalato (Ottoman İspilit). As prescribed by the capitulations the local commander took the goods into safe-keeping and prepared an inventory; this must have been a preliminary to dispatching the *zambelotti* to the dead man's heirs on Ottoman territory.

In addition, the attack on the caravan had apparently furnished an occasion for an Ottoman tax collector (*voyvoda*) stationed in the region to appropriate two *tahta* of *sof* belonging to a Venetian named Agostin (family name illegible) and recognizable by the latter's particular mark; all in all Venetian traders had lost a total of 43 *tahta*. Now the *bailo* proposed an exchange, which the Ottoman side found acceptable. The commander of Spalato was to send the *sof* belonging to the dead Muslim to Ottoman territory and the governor-general of Bosnia, the governor of Kilis and the local *qadis* were to ensure that on the return journey, the property of the Venetian merchants could be conveyed home by the messenger. This must have left the Bosnian authorities with the unenviable task of retrieving the *sof* from the hands of a fellow official.

Intriguing in this tale is the measurement of the *sof* in *tahta* (originally: plank, slab of wood). Normally this unit was used for fur; but apart from our text, some Ankara *qadi* records also document that *sof* might occasionally be measured in *tahta*.[40] From our point of view this custom is a real godsend: for while bales might contain raw wool or else finished cloth, *tahta* can meaningfully refer only to the fabric itself. Thus the misfortunes of our caravan show that the trade in *zambelotti* was alive and flourishing even in the troubled 1610s.

In Conclusion: 'A Shared World'

Another aspect of the merchants' tale of woe that is of interest to the social historian concerns the composition of the caravan, which included Muslims, (Christian) Venetians and Jews. Whether the latter were Ottoman or Venetian subjects unfortunately remains unclear. Nor does the text tell us what the losses

---

[39] BOA, *Düvel-i ecnebiye Defterleri* 13/1, p. 86, No. 420 (Zilhicce 1020).

[40] Ergenç 1995, 115; from this text we learn that a load (*yük*) of *sof* was equivalent to two *tahta*. For furs see Tezcan 2004.

of the Jewish merchants may have been. However, our story demonstrates that members of these three groups, subjects of different rulers, might travel together in the same caravan. This observation confirms Benjamin Arbel's judgement that even though religious and political divisions were crucial components in the identities of early modern people, when it came to questions of commercial advantage, these same men might stand together and thus show how as traders, they were part of the same mercantile world.[41]

As we have seen, a much larger quantity of valuable fabrics of Ottoman origin must have reached Venice or Poland than the limited number of Bursa or Istanbul silk fabrics today preserved in museums would let us believe. For at least in the sixteenth and early seventeenth centuries *sof/zambelotti* were numerous, and to us they form a 'submerged' part of the East-West trade in costly fabrics. To understand just how luxurious these *zambelotti* could be, it is sufficient to recall Busbecq's remark that a slight irregularity in the wavy design of the pressed fabric would decrease the price of the item in question by several gold pieces. It is difficult to imagine that a defect of this type would have had such an impact on the monetary value of everyday cottons or woollens.

Moreover if it is correct to assume that few if any *zambelotti* were produced in either Poland or Venice, the appropriateness of Molly Greene's remark that Ottomans and Venetians shared the same commercial space is confirmed in yet another fashion.[42] For when the English, the Dutch and the French entered Mediterranean trade in force, beginning in the late sixteenth century and continuing during the 1600s, the rules of the game were completely altered. English merchants seem to have experimented briefly with mohair cloth and then considered it not worth their while.[43] As to French traders they bought small quantities of mohair fabrics but were mainly interested in the yarn, which in the seventeenth and eighteenth centuries was used first in the manufacture of buttons and later on, in the woollen industry of Amiens.[44] But the major purchasers of non-woven mohair were the Dutch, and their demand gave the trade an entirely new complexion.

Certainly we are not greatly informed to what extent Ankara manufacturers were protected by the seventeenth-century export prohibitions we have just encountered. It does in fact appear that local artisans were able to hold on to the highest qualities of mohair even during the second half of the eighteenth century. Thus I am not so sure that a scarcity of raw material alone was responsible for the decline of the local weaving industry during the 1700s. Social factors also had a role to play: by the end of our period, in other words in the second half of the seventeenth century, taste and fashions were changing both in Europe and in the Ottoman Empire itself, and among rich consumers *sof* seems to have declined in

---

[41] Arbel 1995, 188–91.
[42] Greene 2000, 171–5, 205.
[43] For an example see Ergenç 1975, 159.
[44] Paris 1957, 521–2.

popularity. For the rich or at least the well-to-do, there were Kashmir shawls and imported French woollens, to say nothing of the Bursa silks now being produced for a wider market; and as to the poor, delicate mohair cloths with regular wavy designs must have been completely beyond their reach in 1700, as they had been during the sixteenth century.

Thus the exportation of luxury mohair cloths from Ankara to Venice and Poland was characteristic of a set of economic relationships and consumer preferences that after 1650 was being made obsolete by the activities of new players. Dutch merchants exported mohair to satisfy the demand of the manufacturers of *greinen*. And at the same time Ottoman court demand had disappeared; the fur-obsessed Sultan Ibrahim (r. 1640–1648) was hardly inclined to emulate his illustrious ancestor Süleyman by publicly showing himself draped in Ankara's *zambelotti*.

Chapter 13

Mehmed II as a Patron of Greek Philosophy: Latin and Byzantine Perspectives

Anna Akasoy[1]

In his *Balance of Truth* (*Mīzān al-ḥaqq*), the famous Ottoman writer Katib Çelebi (1609-1657), also known as Hajji Khalifa, discussed among other topics the subject of singing:

> Songs definitely have an influence on bodies and play a great part in stirring up soul and spirit. For this reason the sages have said that the person whose spirit prevails over his soul should overcome his brute soul and should give the reins of government, in the kingdom of the body, into the hands of Sultan Spirit. (...) For this reason Aristotle invented the *Organon* and had it played while giving instruction to the Peripatetics.[2]

This interpretation of the *Organon* was obviously inspired by its literal meaning, 'instrument', and suggests that Ottoman scholars of the seventeenth century were misinformed about significant aspects of Aristotle's work. This seems to confirm the conventional historiography of the philosophical tradition of Islam, which claims that its productive phase ended in the year 1198, the year Ibn Rushd died. According to this reckoning, later centuries witnessed little philosophical originality, and as a reflection of this abating intellectual grandeur, the medieval translations from Arabic into Latin came to a standstill towards the end of the thirteenth century. Baghdad, the vibrant capital of Arabic philosophy, patronised by the Abbasid caliphs, was nothing but a distant memory. The Latin West had recovered its Greek heritage and declared its independence of Aristotle's Muslim custodians. Renaissance philosophers, with the confidence of possessing the original Greek sources, criticised the Arab authorities as part of the scholastic tradition which characterised the dark ages.

About a decade ago, scholars started to challenge this paradigm. Dag Nikolaus Hasse, for example, has shown that Petrarca's statement, 'I will hardly be persuaded that anything good can come from Arabia', is hardly representative of

---

[1] I would like to thank Charles Burnett, Guido Giglioni and Dag Nikolaus Hasse for their helpful comments.

[2] Kātib Chelebi 1957, 40; Kātib Chelebi 1972. For the following see Zarcone 1988.

Renaissance attitudes.[3] Hasse demonstrated that Arabic influences prevailed and translations continued until well into the sixteenth century, when some trends actually only developed or culminated. In other respects, however, the historian confirmed the conventional historiography. He concluded that the Renaissance was indeed 'the time when the West began to forget its Arabic heritage.'[4] Furthermore, there was little awareness of or interest in more contemporary developments in Islamic thought. The reduced influx of philosophical ideas from the Muslim world to the West may thus have resulted not primarily from the source running dry, but rather from a more exclusive occupation of Europe with itself or, as we shall presently see, from a changed frame of Eastern-Western interactions.

In the Renaissance, Muslim-Christian relations were overshadowed by the growing military threat of the Ottoman Empire, which culminated in the conquest of Constantinople in 1453. Greek emigrants in Italy reinforced the martial image of the Ottoman Turks which would soon embody the Muslim in general. They depicted the Ottoman Turks as barbarians and destroyers of European culture, who had no stake in its intellectual legacy. These views were shared by most Italian writers. Marsilio Ficino, for example, expressed his disdain for the Turks in drastic terms: 'They [Greek scholars] have fallen down into darkness under the ferocious Turks. Alas what pain! Stars, I say, have fallen into darkness under savage beasts.'[5] Even though Western Europe eventually discovered a certain interest in and esteem for Persian culture, the image of the Ottoman Turks as brutes persisted.[6] It is only in recent times that scholars have examined this Renaissance historiography of European and Middle Eastern intellectual history more critically and to uncover chapters which had remained neglected. Nowadays, the Asian side of the Greek legacy is more widely acknowledged, and developments in Arabic and Islamic philosophy after the medieval translations into Latin receive more attention.[7] Much work remains to be done in the area of Ottoman intellectual history, but there is a promising trend in recent research, for example by M. Sait Özervarlı and Haşim Koç.[8]

---

[3] Burnett 1997, 49; see also Bisaha 2001.

[4] Hasse 2004, 5. On the use of Arab authorities among humanist medical writers see Hasse 2001.

[5] Bisaha 2004, chs 2 and 3; p. 75 for Ficino.

[6] For Western perceptions of Turks and Persians see Brentjes 2005.

[7] Strohmaier 1998; Gutas 2002; Wisnovsky 2004.

[8] The former is working on the Ottoman *Tahāfut*-tradition. The latter currently a research fellow at the Max Planck Institute (Gottingen), writing his PhD thesis under the title 'Die Antikenwahrnehmung der Osmanen im 17. und 18. Jahrhundert'.

Intellectual Culture at the Ottoman Court

In the medieval Middle East, courts were important centres of philosophical patronage and learning, often determined by the rationalist interests of rulers.[9] It was here more than anywhere else that financial resources and linguistic skills were accumulated in a uniquely fertile environment. According to conventional historiography, the Ottoman court, unlike that of the Abbasids, had little to offer in this respect. Neither the Islamic heritage of the sultans, nor the traditions of the newly acquired lands inspired any significant developments. Accordingly, Babinger depicted the philosophical endeavours of Mehmed II in a fairly bad light and all intellectual activity as caught in the narrow routine of daily monotony.[10] Inalcık, on the other hand, regarded science at the Ottoman court as part of a larger, Islamic heritage and suggested that the sultan's personal interest in sciences led to 'a real distinction (of the Ottomans) in mathematics and astronomy within the Islamic world.'[11] Even from a 'traditional' point of view, one can imagine that the Ottomans had a certain distinction in the technical side of the sciences given their obvious successes on the battlefield. The only example for an engagement with philosophy which has received attention among modern scholars is the resumption of the *Tahāfut*-debate at Mehmed's court, interpreted by Inalcık as a courageous attempt to re-open a debate which had only seemingly ended with a clear result.[12]

Cosmopolitan milieus are among the characteristic features of intellectual patronage at courts in the medieval and early modern Middle East. This particular aspect of scholarly activity at the Ottoman court has received some attention from academics, often from art historians. Julian Raby, for instance, ventured into the area of philosophy and science with his research on Mehmed's Greek scriptorium.[13] Exploring the presence of Greek culture in the sultan's surroundings, Raby and other scholars have studied texts such as Ptolemy's world map or Pletho's *Laws*, translated from Greek into Arabic, as well as the role of individuals, in particular high-ranking Byzantine intellectuals.[14] Attention has also been paid to Mehmed's contacts with Italy and the presence of Italian

---

[9] The most conspicuous example is the patronage for philosophy under al-Ma'mūn (r. 819-833) whose promotion of rationalism was supposed to increase the authority of the Abbasid caliphs in matters of religion, cf. Gutas 1998.

[10] Babinger 1978, 478.

[11] Inalcik 1973, 176.

[12] Ibid., 177.

[13] Raby 1983 and 1987.

[14] For cartography see Brotton 1997 (reissued edition 1998), 87–118. For the Arabic translations of Pletho cf. Nicolet and Tardieu, 1980 and Tardieu's edition of the Arabic version of Pletho's *Chaldean Oracles* in Tambrun-Krasker 1995, 157–71.

artists at his court. Little progress, however, has been made since the works of Babinger and Raby.[15]

In the history of medieval philosophy it has become quite common to combine Eastern and Western, Arabic and Latin perspectives, but little has been done in this respect for the early modern period.[16] As a contribution to filling this gap, I will focus in what follows on the court of Mehmed II and explore the sultan's role in intellectual contacts between the Ottoman Empire and the West. Did Mehmed's contemporaries in the Christian East and West consider him a patron of Greek philosophy and science? Were the Ottomans perceived as heirs to medieval Arabic Aristotelianism? In what follows I would like to use three prominent testimonies to discuss some elements of a very tentative answer to these questions.

Pius II

Aeneas Silvius Piccolomini (1405–1464), since 1458 Pius II, a well-known humanist writer, was also a fervent advocate of a crusade against the Turks.[17] One of Pius's texts, however, has given rise to speculations about a change in his attitude during the last years of his life.[18] In 1461 he wrote a letter to Mehmed II and tried to persuade him to convert to Christianity.[19] Nowadays, most scholars agree, and probably rightly so, that Pius's letter was never intended to be sent to the sultan, but rather composed with a Christian audience in mind. The same applies in all likelihood to many other 'inter-religious' documents of the pre-modern period such as Amirutzes's *Dialogue of Faith*.

Pius's letter includes arguments derived from a variety of sources. Nancy Bisaha listed these as 'doctrine, Scripture, history, classical literature, political thought, and "reason".'[20] The last element, reason, is of interest for the present purpose. Pius claims that Islam has a hostile attitude to reason and finally dealt the death-blow to a long tradition of philosophy and science in the region. One of the first victims was, according to Pius, the school of Alexandria:

> There was once a great and flourishing school of philosophers in Alexandria; many of its learned men whose names have come down to us were known throughout Syria and Asia. But ever since the Law of Mohammed won the day, few have attained renown for revealing the secrets of nature. This is

---

[15] Babinger 1951; Raby 1981 and 1980. For a summary Akasoy 2004.
[16] A good selection of recent research is available in Speer and Wegener 2006.
[17] For Pius's attitude to the Turks see Helmrath 2000.
[18] Piccolomini 1990; Bisaha 2002; Bisaha 2004, 86–7, 147–52, and 166–70.
[19] During the Middle Ages this was not an uncommon behaviour as is evident in several cases discussed in Lupprian 1981.
[20] Bisaha 2002, 183.

because neither your prophet nor your law, which is founded on pleasure and maintained by the sword, imparts wisdom to those lacking it.[21]

According to Pius, Muhammad used this hostility as part of a perfidious plan:

> A clever man, he saw that his teaching could be overthrown by two things, authority and reason. (...) He opposed the authority (...) by contending that the Old and New Testaments have been corrupted and that the only truths they contain are to be found in the Koran. Against reason he raised arms.[22]

Medieval Christian polemicists had already brought forward similar criticisms and explained the success of Islam as achieved by violence and compulsion. In Byzantium, the emperor Manuel II (reg. 1391–1425) presented a similar argument in his seventh 'dialogue' with a 'Persian', the text which was mentioned by Benedict XVI in the controversial lecture delivered in Regensburg in 2006.[23] Pius's argument differs from the medieval tradition when he appeals to the Sultan's ethnic identity, a typical argument of a humanist writer.[24] As a Scythian, Mehmed is superior to 'the effeminate Egyptians' and 'the unwarlike Arabs'. Pius exclaims:

> It is a cause for wonder, how the Arabs fascinated and lured the bold, great Scythians into an alliance. But how can we call it an alliance when it is not that but rather slavery since you, (Mehmed), are subject to their law? If only it were law and not deception and sorcery! An alliance with Christians will better suit you because the brave can be easily brought into alliance with the brave. Courage attracts courage.[25]

The use of female attributes to discredit the Easterners as unreasonable is a typical 'orientalist' topos.[26] Pius's attitude, however, seems to reveal more than a simple East-West divide.

Pius discussed the Scythian legacy of the Ottoman Turks in other documents too. The matter is also crucial in his geographical treatise on Asia, written in 1461/2, where he displayed a very different attitude. As Margaret Meserve has shown in detail, Pius's main intention in this text was to 'vilify the Turks

---

[21] Piccolomini 1990 (§184).
[22] Piccolomini 1990, 76 (§147).
[23] For Manuel's 'dialogues' see Manuel II. Palaiologos 1993, i, 238/9–242/3. Again, the dialogues were fictitious. For the medieval tradition see Daniel 1962, 145–50.
[24] Pius did not support the claim that the Turks were Trojans. For the debate see Meserve 2000 and 2003.
[25] Piccolomini 1990, 74 (§143).
[26] See Said 1978, which correctly pointed out some of these patterns, despite the criticism raised against it by, among others, Irwin 2006.

as barbarian Scythians and thus strengthen his case for mounting a military expedition against them'.[27] While his description of northern Asia is – again in a typically humanist fashion – mainly based on classical authors, his choice of information was also rather tendentious. The classical notion of the Scythians as noble savages, for example, is absent.[28] In Pius's letter to Mehmed, on the other hand, he emphasises the primitive greatness of the Scythians and does not suggest, for example, that they were hostile to reason. On the contrary, at least their leader must have possessed a naturally rational disposition.

It is by exposing Mehmed to the philosophical contradictions of Islam that Pius tries to alienate him from his faith. He argues, for example:

> Philosophers state that God is pure act, the beginning of all things, possessed of a completely simple, eternal nature. If God were corporeal [as, according to Pius, the Muslims believe], these things could not be attributed to Him and He would be composed of elements of other matter.[29]

If Mehmed only acknowledged the common ground of Islam and Christianity and employed his reason, he would understand the errors of the Muslims and see the truth of the Christian faith.

When Pius discusses the Trinity, an issue particularly sensitive in Christian-Muslim dialogue, he employs a philosophical terminology to render this element of Christian faith understandable to Mehmed and suggests an analogy with the human soul, a comparison which can be traced back to Augustine and was also used by Thomas Aquinas. Thomas, an influential author among Italians and Byzantines, had used the language of reason in a similar manner to defend his beliefs against the claims of non-believers. His *Summa contra gentiles* is a milestone in a more general development in which an internal dynamics and the confrontation with non-believers led to a more rational approach to religion and faith. Georgios Gennadios Scholarios, translator of Aquinas into Greek and first patriarch in Constantinople after 1453 also embraced the analogy with the human soul as a way of explaining the Trinity in his dialogue with Mehmed.[30]

Reason in Medieval Inter-Faith Encounter: A Retrospect

We do not know whether Pius had any confidence in Mehmed's susceptibility to philosophical arguments, but even if his letter was intended for a Christian readership, it must at least have made some sense to them that such arguments

---

[27] Meserve 2003, 25.
[28] Ibid., 26. For the classical notion of Scythians as noble savages see Lovejoy and Boas 1935, 287–362.
[29] Piccolomini 1990, §125.
[30] Turner 1969; Papadakis 1972; Hering 1961; Arnakis 1952.

should be presented to the Muslim sultan. One of the great positive outcomes of medieval Christian encounters with Islam was the discovery of reason as a common link between the two religions. A crucial ingredient in this development was the transmission of Aristotelian and Arabic philosophy from the Islamic world to the Latin West. Even though this situation had changed substantially in the fifteenth century, the discourse of reason as a common link continued, albeit as part of different strategies. Pius, for example, was keen on persuading Mehmed to accept the Christian doctrines immediately, whereas Ramon Llull (1232–1316), a Catalan missionary and native of Majorca, breached the subject in a more indirect manner. Llull, whose thought was deeply influenced by the Arabic intellectual tradition, had come to the conclusion that the missionary endeavours of the Christians would remain futile as long as they based their arguments on their own authorities which were not recognised by Muslims and Jews. As a solution to this problem he developed a rational and universal system which allowed a comprehensive approach to everything in reality. Already in the twelfth century, Peter the Venerable and Peter Abelard had presented an intellectual response to other faiths – but the Catalan missionary developed a uniquely original and elaborate system. This system, the *Ars*, was based on quasi-mathematical principles in which individual elements or aspects of reality are represented by letters. It supposedly demonstrated the truth of the Christian faith in a neutral language. Ramon Llull's reputation is also owed to the literary expression he gave to his ideas. The most famous of his narratives is *The Book of the Gentile and the Three Wise Men*, in which representatives of Judaism, Christianity and Islam try to convince a pagan of the truth of their respective religions. Their dialogue is guided by a 'Lady Intelligence', who instructs them in the use of five trees and their blossoms which represent the Llullian principles. The remarkable result of the debate is that the pagan declares he knows which religion is the true one, but he does not reveal which one it is. The message of the text is rather that reason provides the best means of communication between the religions. In his version of the logical part of al-Ghazali's 'Intentions of the Philosophers' (*Maqāṣid al-falāsifa*), Llull recommended a similarly gentle and open-minded approach which operates with different stages. One should first consider the claim of the other as possible and then become eventually convinced of its truth (at least as far as non-Christians are concerned).[31] Pius, on the other hand, demanded an instant conversion. In both cases, however, it is reason which serves as a universal means of communication, rather than a specific philosophical tradition as part of a common heritage.

It is hardly possible to mention Llull and Pius in such a context without including a third person who was a link between these two men: Nicholas of Cusa (1401–1464). Nicholas, since 1450 Bishop of Brixen and a close ally of Pius, had a great interest in Llull, as the large number of manuscripts of his works

---

[31] Fidora 2004, 121.

in Cusanus's library reveals.³² His approach to inter-faith relations was very much determined by the shock of the Ottoman conquest of Constantinople in 1453 and the need to establish a peaceful relationship with the neighbour. In the same year, Nicholas wrote his 'On the Peace of Faith' (*De pace fidei*), an irenic and utopian blueprint for uniting the different confessions under a Christian umbrella. In *De pace fidei*, Islam is represented by an Arab and a Persian. A Turk appears only briefly to ask a short question. The Scythian represents Eastern Christianity. Not unlike Llull, Nicholas uses these figures as advocates of different doctrines rather than as representatives of ethnic and political groups.

In the winter of 1460/61, i.e., around the same time that Pius wrote his letter to Mehmed, Nicholas composed his famous 'Sifting of the Koran' (*Cribratio Alkorani*) which bears the hallmarks of a more critical attitude. While both of his texts partake in the endeavour to refute Islamic doctrines in a rational manner, they also borrow material from the polemical missionary tradition. Neither of them would have received a positive response from Muslim readers and probably neither was written with such an audience in mind. Instead of adopting Nicholas's irenic approach, Pius in his letter made use of Cardinal Juan de Torquemada's *Contra principales errores perfidi Machometi*³³ which has a far less diplomatic tone.

Georgios Amirutzes

Little is known about my second example, Georgios Amirutzes, the 'little *amīr*' of Trebizond. His acquaintance with Mehmed seems to date back to the conquest of his home city in 1461 (the same year that Pius wrote his letter and Nicholas his *Cribratio Alkorani*), but Georgios was also in the fortunate position of being a relation of the Ottoman grand vizier Mahmud Pasha. Mehmed's Greek biographer Critoboulos describes the encounter between the sultan and Georgios as follows:

> Among the companions of the ruler of Trebizond was a man named Georgios Ameroukis, a great philosopher, learned both in the studies of physics and dogmatics and mathematics and geometry and the analogy of numbers, and also in the philosophy of the Peripatetics and Stoics ... The Sultan learned about this man and sent for him ... He gave him a suitable position in his court and honoured him with frequent audiences and conversations, questioning him on the teachings of the ancients and on philosophical problems and their

---

³² For different perspectives on Llull's influence on Nicholas cf. Bidese et al. 2005. Much ink has been spilled on Nicholas's attitude to the Muslims. See, for example, the articles by Izbicki and Biechler in Christianson and Izbicki 1991 and the publications by Hagemann 1976 and 1983. For a comparison see Euler 1995.

³³ Bisaha 2002, 193 with reference to Gaeta 1965, 161–74.

discussion and solution. For the Sultan himself was one of the most acute philosophers.[34]

Critoboulos repeats the idea of the sultan as a philosopher several times in his biography of Mehmed.[35] Naturally, these remarks need to be taken with a pinch of salt. Critoboulos is notorious for his flattery of the sultan, and his claim that Mehmed had a keen interest in philosophy might be simply due to the literary model of Alexander the Great. Fortunately, our evidence for Mehmed's interest in philosophy (or at least the perception that he had such an interest) is not limited to this biography. Georgios's contribution to the scientific life at court, as described by Critoboulos, is corroborated by the fact that he and his sons made Arabic maps for the sultan which were based on Ptolemy's geography.[36] Georgios himself confirms Mehmed's regard for his philosophical knowledge in his *Dialogue of Faith*, which is preserved in a Latin translation of 1518.[37] In this dialogue, Aristotelian philosophy serves as a common ground between the Muslim sultan and the Christian philosopher, even more markedly than in Pius's letter. Even though this document (like Pius's letter) was directed at a Christian audience, the sultan's familiarity with Aristotelian doctrines must have seemed plausible to them. Mehmed challenges for instance the Christian doctrine of Incarnation by offering an interpretation of Aristotle's doctrines in the *Metaphysics*.[38] Amirutzes responds duly with an exposition of his own interpretation of the Aristotelian philosophy. Whether or not this reference to the *Metaphysics* might reveal actual knowledge on the part of the sultan, is a question worth considering. In common with many others Mehmed would have relied for his knowledge not necessarily on the original text in Arabic translation, but rather on summaries, commentaries or more independent interpretations, e.g. by al-Farabi or Ibn Sina. The text refers, after all, to the notion of the 'necessary/necessarily existent' characteristic of Avicennian metaphysics. Manuscript collections in Istanbul contain several codices which include the part on the *Metaphysics* from Ibn Sina's *Kitāb al-shifā'*,[39] even though none of them can be linked more specifically to Mehmed II.

[34] Critoboulos 1954, 177.
[35] See, for example the short paragraph on 'how the Sultan was also a philosopher,' in which Critoboulos states that Mehmed was familiar with philosophical texts in Arabic and Persian as well as Greek philosophy as far as it had been translated into those languages, Critoboulos 1954, 14.
[36] See Brotton 1997 (reissued edition 1998), 87–118.
[37] The text has been edited and translated into Spanish by Óscar de la Cruz Palma: Jorge Ameruzes de Trebisonda 2000; and de la Cruz Palma 1999. See also Argyriou and Lagarrigue 1987 for an earlier edition and French translation .
[38] Jorge Ameruzes de Trebisonda 2000, 8 and 10. See also there for parallels in the *Metaphysics*.
[39] Bertolacci 2008 and Bertolacci 2006, 669 for a list of manuscripts.

Mehmed and Georgios appear as the pair of learned emperor and court-philosopher familiar from the Middle Ages: Frederick II and Michael Scot for example, or Ibn Rushd and the Almohad caliph, Abu Yaʻqub Yusuf. In all these cases, the interpretation of Aristotle's works was at the heart of intellectual discussions and patronage. Equally, in all these cases the ruler was already familiar with the key doctrines of these works, when his philosopher arrived at court. The obvious difference between these two medieval pairs on the one hand and Mehmed and Georgios on the other hand is that in the latter case the interpretation of Aristotle's works took place in an inter-religious encounter.

George of Trebizond

George of Trebizond (1396-1486), our third case, is a rather controversial case.[40] As early as in July 1453, two months after the fall of Constantinople, he composed in Naples a treatise directed to Mehmed II. He inundated the young sultan with noble titles which are – among Greek authors – typical only of the notorious Critoboulos's blandishments. Not unlike Pius, George tried to convert Mehmed to the Christian faith by proving the truth of its doctrines and by pointing out a glorious future, once Christians and Muslims united under the sign of the cross. George went in his endeavours far beyond letter-writing, and John Monfasani has discovered in George's eschatological ideas a convincing explanation for his repeated offers to serve the sultan.[41] In November 1465, George even travelled to Constantinople where he tried in vain to meet the sultan and dedicate his Latin translation of the *Almagest* to him. In his own preface for the *Isagoge* to Ptolemy's book, George reveals the highest admiration for Mehmed and appeals to his spirit as a man experienced in both military and scientific skills:

> Your Mightiness is also said to study Aristotle even more than those who have a professional responsibility to study Aristotle. Your nature exceeds that of all other kings by so great a degree that you are able to unite with extraordinary perfection the two extreme opposite goods of human nature, I mean the loftiness of kingship and the profundity of philosophy, bringing together as one military leadership and scientific learning.[42]

The conviction that Mehmed was familiar with Aristotelian philosophy is even more striking in a treatise George wrote on his way back from Constantinople to Italy in 1466. *On the Eternal Glory of the Autocrat and his World-Dominion* is an elaborate attempt to sketch a glorious future for Mehmed, once he accepts his

---

[40] For the following interpretation see Monfasani 1976, especially 131–6 and 179–94.

[41] Eschatological interpretations of the Turkish success were hardly uncommon at that time. See Meserve 2003, 28–9 for Pius's apocalyptic vision of the Turks.

[42] Translation from Monfasani 1984, 281–2.

historical role as a Christian world-leader.⁴³ George discusses several Christian doctrines which are problematic from an Islamic point of view, and explains how they are supported by Aristotelian ideas. The religious themes in this treatise are not very different from the ones chosen by Pius II, but while in the former, references to Aristotle abound, Pius decided on a more general language of reason.

When George returned to Rome, Cardinal Bessarion had got hold of Latin letters from George to the sultan in which he again declared his eagerness to serve the conqueror of Constantinople. In one of these letters, George described Mehmed as possessing *justitia, prudentia, peritia philosophiae peripateticae, doctrina in multis disciplinis* (i.e., justice, prudence, being learned in terms of peripatetic philosophy and various other sciences).⁴⁴ George had sent this letter together with his *The Difference between Plato and Aristotle* which probably means that he was convinced the sultan would appreciate such a gift. A statement regarding Mehmed's familiarity with Aristotelian philosophy can also be found in George's *On the Divinity of Manuel* (i.e., Mehmed after his conversion), written in 1467, in which he says about Mehmed that 'not only has he accurately mastered the works of Aristotle, but he is also firmly grounded in the mathematical sciences'.⁴⁵

In these texts, Mehmed appears as the very embodiment of the philosopher-king. George had to pay a high price for his praise. On Bessarion's order he was arrested and despite of his advanced age of 71 years, he remained incarcerated in prison for four months.

Conclusion

The authors we have discussed very briefly here were in very different positions when they approached the Ottoman sultan. Pius II was one of the most powerful men in Europe with little expectations of ever encountering Mehmed in person. George of Trebizond jeopardised persistently his own safety with his futile attempts to gain access to the sultan's court. Georgios Amirutzes and Critoboulos were Byzantine intellectuals on the sultan's payroll. Whereas they seem to have accepted their positions more or less voluntarily, Gennadios Scholarios tried several times to resign from his unwelcome post as a patriarch.⁴⁶ For all of them, the Ottomans were very real people, not theoretical or literary figures.

Greek philosophy and science play different roles in the ways these men addressed Mehmed. Pius assumed a general susceptibility of Mehmed for

---

⁴³ Edition and translation in Monfasani 1984, 492–563.
⁴⁴ Mercati 1943, 93 (M 366).
⁴⁵ Translation from Monfasani 1984, 566–7. Monfasani suggests that Mehmed was interested in George of Trebizond because of his knowledge of astrology, see Monfasani 1976, 188.
⁴⁶ See the articles mentioned in footnote 29.

philosophical arguments, similarly Gennadios Scholarios. In Amirutzes's *Dialogue*, the sultan displayed familiarity with Aristotle's writings. For Critoboulos and George of Trebizon, Mehmed appeared as an ideal patron and even 'practitioner' of Greek philosophy and science. To be sure, these examples hardly reflect the general attitude of Renaissance writers to the Turks, an attitude which was more often than not overshadowed by the military threat posed by the Ottoman Empire.

Pius, Gennadios Scholarios and Amirutzes continued medieval discourses which used philosophical arguments to persuade Muslims of the Christian faith. In the Middle Ages, the development of a philosophical interpretation of religion and inter-religious dialogues were deeply intertwined, and we can see from these examples that a similar relation persisted in the Renaissance, even though the two developments had begun to take separate paths. With the insistence on Mehmed's ethnic identity, for example, Pius introduced an argument typical of a humanist writer.

Another interesting feature of these uses of philosophy is the lack of references to the established authorities of the Arabic tradition, Ibn Sina (for both the Islamic world and the Latin West) and Ibn Rushd (primarily in for the West as Averroes).[47] The arguments of Renaissance writers were based on what they may have expected an Ottoman ruler learned in philosophy believed, but they were also shaped by internal Western debates.

In the cases surveyed here, the 'other' did not remain a distant enemy. Amirutzes and Critoboulos had immediate experiences of Mehmed's interest in Greek philosophy and science. Their testimonies are corroborated by a vast amount of material evidence. It is not by coincidence that Topkapı Palace library remains until today one of the most important sources for any historian of medieval philosophy and science.

---

[47] The only exception I have found so far is a short characterisation of Mehmed's successor Beyazid II (1481–1512) in Sansovino 1573. Sansovino says of the sultan that he 'enjoyed peace, as he had a serene soul and a pleasurable nature. He was intelligent and used to study philosophy and especially he liked the works of Averroes.' Quoted from Soykut 2001, 124.

Bibliography

Abulafia, David 2003, 'What is the Mediterranean?', in David Abulafia, *The Mediterranean in History*, London: Thames & Hudson, 11–27.
——— 2011, *The Great Sea: A Human History of the Mediterranean*, London: Allen Lane.
Agius, Dionisius A. and Richard Hitchcock (eds) 1994, *The Arab influence in Medieval Europe*, Reading: Ithaca Press.
Ágoston, Gábor 2007, 'Information, ideology, and limits of imperial policy; Ottoman grand strategy in the context of Ottoman-Habsburg rivalry', in Aksan and Goffman 2007, 75–103.
Ajmar-Wollheim, Marta and Flora Dennis (eds) 2006, *At Home in Renaissance Italy*, London: V&A Publications.
Akasoy, Anna 2004, 'Die Adaptation byzantinischen Wissens am Osmanenhof nach der Eroberung Konstantinopels', in Carsten Kretschmann, Henning Pahl and Peter Scholz (eds), *Wissen in der Krise, Institutionen des Wissens im gesellschaftlichen Wandel*, Berlin: Akademie Verlag, 43–56.
——— 2013, 'Mehmed II as a Patron of Greek Philosophy: Latin and Byzantine Perspectives', in Anna Contadini and Claire Norton (eds), *The Renaissance and the Ottoman World*, Farnham: Ashgate, 245–56.
Aksan, Virginia 1999, 'Locating the Ottomans Among Early Modern Empires', *Journal of Early Modern History* 3, 21–39.
——— 2004, *Ottomans and Europeans: Contacts and Conflicts*, Istanbul: Isis Press.
Aksan, Virginia and D. Goffman (eds) 2007, *The Early Modern Ottomans: Remapping the Empire*, Cambridge: Cambridge University Press.
Aksoy, Bülent 1994, *Avrupalı gezginlerin gözüyle Osmanlılarda musıki*, Istanbul: Pan Yayıncılık.
Albrecht Dürer, Master Printmaker (no author) 1971, Department of Prints and Drawings, Museum of Fine Arts, Boston, MA.
Alcouffe, Daniel and Margaret E. Frazer 1986, 'Grotta della Vergine', in Renata Cambiaghi (ed.), *Il Tesoro di San Marco*, Milano: Olivetti, 125–31, cat. 8.
Alcouffe, Daniel and D. Gaborit-Chopin 1991, 'Vase d'Aliénor', in Daniel Alcouffe et al., *Le trésor de Saint-Denis: Musée du Louvre, Paris, 12 mars–17 juin 1991*, Paris, 168–72, no. 27.
Ali Ufki 1976, *Mecmûa-i sâz ü söz*, facsimile in Elçin, Şükrü (ed.), *Ali Ufkî, hayatı, eserleri ve mecmûa-i sâz ü söz*, Istanbul: Kültür Bakanlığı.
Ali Ufki transcribed in Cevher, M. Hakan, 2003, *Hâzâ mecmûa-i sâz ü söz*, Izmir: Self-published.

Allan, James W. 1979, *Persian Metal Technology 700–1300 A.D.*, London: Ithaca Press for the Faculty of Oriental Studies and the Ashmolean Museum, University of Oxford.

——— 1986, *Metalwork of the Islamic World: The Aron Collection*, London: Sotheby's.

——— 1989, 'Venetian-Saracenic Metalwork: The Problems of Provenance', in Grube, Carboni and Curatola 1989, 167–83.

Allen, W. 1928, *A History of Political Thought in the Sixteenth Century*, London: Methuen.

Almagià, Roberto 1948, *Monumenta cartographica Vaticana*, Città del Vaticano: Biblioteca Apostolica Vaticana.

Andaloro, Maria (ed.), 2006, *Nobiles Officinae: Perle, filigrane e trame di seta dal Palazzo Reale di Palermo*, 2 vols, Catania: Giuseppe Maimone.

Andrews, Walter G. and Mehmed Kalpakli 2005, *The Age of Beloveds: Love and the Beloved in Early-modern Ottoman and European Culture and Society*, Durham and London: Duke University Press.

Andrews Reath, Nancy 1927, 'Velvets of the Renaissance, from Europe and Asia Minor', *The Burlington Magazine for Connoisseurs* 50, no. 291 (June), 298–304.

Anon 1543 (and again in 1545), *Viaggi fatti da Vinetia, alla Tana, in Persia, in India et in Costantinopoli, con la descrittione particolare di città, luoghi, siti, costumi et della Porta del Gran Turco et di tutte le intrate, spese et modo di governo suo et della ultima impresa contra Portoghesi*, Vinegia: nelle case de'figlivoli di Aldo.

Anon 1584, *Acta et Scripta Theologorum VVirtembergensium, et Patriarchae Constantinopolitani D. Hieremiae: quae vtriq; ab Anno M. D. LXXVI. vsque ad Annum M. D. LXXXI. De Augustana Confessione inter se miserunt: Graecè et Latinè ab ijsdem Theologis edita*, Wittenberg.

Appuhn, Horst 1966, 'Das Mittelstück vom Ambo König Heinrichs II. in Aachen', *Aachener Kunstblätter* 32, 70–73.

Arbeau, Thoinot 1980, *Orchésographie, et traicté en forme de dialogue, par lequel toutes personnes peuvent facilement apprendre et pratiquer l'honneste exercice des danses*, Langres, 1589 repr. Hildesheim, New York.

Arbel, Benjamin 1995, *Trading Nations, Jews and Venetians in the Early Modern Eastern Mediterranean*, Leiden: E.J. Brill.

——— 2002, 'Maps of the World for Ottoman Princes? Further Evidence and Questions Concerning "The Mappamondo of Hajji Ahmed"', *Imago Mundi* 54, 19–29.

Archer, John Michael 2001, *Old Worlds: Egypt, Southwest Asia, India and Russia in Early Modern English Writing*, Stanford: Stanford University Press.

Argyriou, Astérios and Georges Lagarrigue 1987, 'Georges Amiroutzes et son *Dialogue sur la Foi au Christ tenu avec le Sultan des Turcs*', *Byzantinische Forschungen* 11, 29–222.

Arnakis, G. Georgiades 1952, 'The Greek Church of Constantinople and the Ottoman Empire', *Journal of Modern History* 24, 235–50.

Arts Council of Great Britain 1976, *The Arts of Islam*, London: Arts Council of Great Britain.

Ashtor, Eliyahu 1978, 'The Venetian Cotton Trade in Syria in the Later Middle Ages', in Eliyahu Ashtor, *Studies on the Levantine Trade in the Middle Ages*, London: Variorum, VII.

——— 1978b 'The Venetian Supremacy in Levantine Trade: Monopoly or Pre-colonialism?', in Ashtor 1978, VI.

Atasoy, Nurhan, Walter Denny, Louise Mackie and Hülya Tezcan 2001, *İpek Osmanlı Dokuma Sanatı*, ed. Julian Raby and Allison Effner, Istanbul: TEB.

——— 2001b, *İpek: The Crescent and the Rose: Ottoman Imperial Silks and Velvets*, London: Azimuth Editions.

Atasoy, Nurhan and Julian Raby 1989, *Iznik: The Pottery of Ottoman Turkey*, ed. Yanni Petsopoulos, London: Alexandria Press in association with Thames and Hudson.

Atıl, Esin 1986, Süleymanname: The Illustrated History of *Süleyman the Magnificent*, Washington, DC, New York: National Gallery of Art, Harry N. Abrams.

——— 1987, *The Age of Sultan Süleyman the Magnificent*, Washington, DC, New York: National Gallery of Art, Harry N. Abrams.

Auld, Sylvia 1986, 'Kuficising Inscriptions in the Work of Gentile Da Fabriano', *Oriental Art* XXXII, no. 3 (Autumn), 246–65.

——— 1989, 'Master Mahmud: Objects fit for a Prince', in Grube, Carboni and Curatola 1989, 185–201.

——— 2004, *Renaissance Venice, Islam and Mahmud al-Kurd: A Metalworking Enigma*, London: Altajir World of Islam Trust.

——— 2007, 'Master Mahmud and Inlaid Metalwork in the 15th Century', in Carboni 2007, 212–25.

Austin, April 2006, 'A Cultural Exchange that Benefited East and West', *Christian Science Monitor* March 6, 19.

Babinger, F. 1951, 'Mehmed II., der Eroberer, und Italien', *Byzantion* 21, 127–70.

——— 1951b, 'Bajezid Osman (Calixtus Ottomanus), ein Vorläufer und Gegenspieler Dschems-Sultāns', *La Nouvelle Clio* 3, 349–88.

——— 1961, 'G.M. Angiolello', *Dizionario biografico degli Italiani*, vol. 3, Rome: Enciclopedia Italiana, 275–8.

——— 1978, *Mehmed the Conqueror and his Time*, trans. Ralph Manheim, ed., with a preface, by William C. Hickman, Princeton: Princeton University Press.

Bacci, Michele 2008, 'Byantinum and the West', in Robin Cormack and Maria Vassilaki (eds), *Byzantium 330-1453*, London: Royal Academy of Arts, 275–305.

Bacon, Francis 1985, *Essays* (1st edition 1595, final form first pub. 1625), ed. John Pitcher, London: Penguin Books.

Baer, E. 1989, *Ayyubid Metalwork with Christian Images*, Leiden, New York, København, Köln: Brill.

Bagnera, Alessandra 1988, 'Tessuti islamici nella pittura medievale toscana', *Islam - storia e civiltà* no. 25, VII, 4, 251–65.

Baker, Christopher and Tom Henry 2001, *The National Gallery Complete Illustrated Catalogue*, revised edition, London: The National Gallery.

Baker, P.L. 1995, *Islamic Textiles*, London: British Museum Press.

Baker, Patricia, Jennifer Wearden and Ann French 1990, 'Memento Mori: Ottoman Children's Kaftans in the Victoria & Albert Museum', *Hali* 51 (June), 13040, 151–2.

Baker, Patricia, Hülya Tezcan and Jennifer Wearden 1996, *Silks for the Sultans: Ottoman Imperial Garments from Topkapi Palace*, Istanbul: Ertug & Kocabiyik.

Balbi, Gasparo 1590, *Viaggio dell'Indie orientali*, Venice: Camillo Borgominieri.

Baracchini, Clara 1986, 'Sculture del XII secolo pertinenti al Duomo', in Guglielmo de Angelis d'Ossat (ed.), *Il Museo dell'Opera del Duomo a Pisa*, Milan: Silvana Editoriale, 65–75.

Barasch, Mosche 1997, *The Language of Art: Studies in Interpretation*, New York: New York University Press.

—— 1989, 'Some Oriental Pseudo-Inscriptions in Renaissance Art', in Claude Gandelman (ed.), *Visible Language*, volume XXIII, no. 2/3, 171–87.

Barleti, Marin 1596, *The historie of George Castriot, surnamed Scanderbeg, King of Albania. containing his famous acts, his noble deedes of armes, and memorable victories against the Turkes, for the faith of Christ*, 'newly translated out of the French' edition by Jacques de Lavardin, by Z.I. gentleman. London: for William Ponsonby.

Barnes, R. 1988, *Prophecy and Gnosis: Apocalypticism in the Wake of the Lutheran Reformation*, Stanford: Stanford University Press.

Barucca, Gabriele 2004, 'Reliquario a brocchetta in cristallo di rocca', in Paolo Dal Poggetto (ed.), *I Della Rovere*, exh. cat., Milan: Electa, IX.9, 369.

Basile, G. 1992, *Giotto – La Cappella degli Scrovegni*, Milan: Electa.

Bassano 1568, 'Costumi ... de' Turchi', in F. Sansovino (ed.), *Historia universale dell'origine et imperio de Turchi*, Venice: fols 48r–80r.

Baxter, C.R. 1973. 'Jean Bodin's Daemon and his Conversion to Judaism', in H. Denzer (ed.), *Jean Bodin: Verhandlungen der internationalen Bodin Tagung in München*, Munich: Verlag C. H. Beck, 1–21.

Beck, H.G. 1958, 'Die byzantinischen Studien in Deutschland vor Karl Krumbacher', in ΧΑΛΙΚΕΣ: *Festgabe für die Teilnehmer am XI. internationalen Byzantinistenkongreß München 15.-20. September 1958*, Freising: Datterer, 66–119.

Beech, George T. 1992, 'The Eleanor of Aquitaine Vase: Its Origins and History to the Early Twelfth Century', *Ars Orientalis* 22, 69–79.

—— 1993, 'The Eleanor of Aquitaine Vase, William IX of Aquitaine, and Muslim Spain', *Gesta* 32, no. 1, 3–10.

Behar, Cem 1990, *Ali Ufkî ve mezmurlar*, Istanbul: Pan Yayıncılık.

—— 1991, 'Wojciech Bobowski (Ali Ufki)'nin hayatı ve eserleri hakkında yeni bilgiler', *Tarih ve toplum*, 16/94, 17–22/209–14.

—— 2005, 'Wojciech Bobowski (Ali Ufkî): Hayatı ve Eserleri (1610?-1675)', *Musıkiden müziğe. Osmanlı/Türk müziği: gelenek ve modernlik,* Istanbul: Yapı Kredi Yayınları, 17–55.

Behrens-Abouseif, Doris 2005, 'Veneto-Saracenic Metalware, a Mamluk Art', *Mamluk Studies Review* 9 (2), 147–72.

Bellingeri, Giampiero 2003, 'Turco-Veneta', *Analecta Isisiana* LXV, 83–100.

Bellini, L. 1988, '"Ars Musica" e umanesimo musicale nell'enciclopedia di Giorgio Valla', *Quadrivium* 29/1, 25–51.

Bellus, I. and I. Boronkai (eds) 1993-4, *Pii secundi pontificis maximi Commentarii*, 2 vols Budapest: I. Budapest: Balassi Kiadó.

Belon, Pierre 1553, *Les observations de plusieurs singularitez et choses memorables, trouvées en Grece, Asie, Iudée, Egypte, Arabie, & autres pays estranges*, Paris: G. Corrozet.

——— 2001, *Voyage au Levant (1553): les Observations de Pierre Belon du Mans*, A. Merle (ed.), Paris: Chandeigne.

Benga, D. 2001, *David Chytraeus (1531–1600) als Erforscher und Wiederentdecker der Ostkirche. Seine Beziehungen zu orthodoxen Theologen, seine Erforschungen der Ostkirchen und seine ostkirchlichen Kenntnissen* University of Erlangen, PhD Thesis also available at:_http://www.opus.ub.uni-erlangen.de/opus/volltexte/2004/86/ (last retrieved 17.5.2012).

Benincasa, Grazioso 1482, *Carta nautica*, Ancona, Biblioteca Universitaria di Bologna, Rot. 3.

Ben-Tov, Asaph 2009, *Lutheran Humanists and Greek Antiquity: Melanchthonian Scholarship between Universal History and Pedagogy*, Leiden: Brill.

Benz, E. 1952, *Die Ostkirche im Lichte der protestantischen Geschichtsschreibung von der Reformation bis zur Gegenwart*, Freiburg and Munich: Alber.

——— 1971 *Wittenberg und Byzanz: Zur Begegnung und Auseinandersetzung der Reformation und der östlich-orthodoxen Kirche*, 2. edn., Munich: Fink.

Bernardini, Michele 1999, 'Un'iscrizione araba in una vetrata nella chiesa della SS. Annunziata a Firenze', in Antonio Cadei et al. (eds), *Arte d'Occidente - temi e metodi*, Studi in onore di Angiola Maria Romanini, Rome, 1023–30.

Bernetti, G. 1971, *Saggi e studi sugli scritti di Enea Silvio Piccolomini, Papa Pio II (1405-1464)*, Florence: Le Monnier.

Beroaldo 1500, *Orationes Multifariae et Poemata*, Bononiae, Benedictus Bibliopola Hectoris.

Berriot, F. 1985, 'Jean Bodin et l'Islam', in *Jean Bodin: actes du Colloque Interdisciplinaire d'Angers, 24 au 27 mai 1984*, Angers: Presses de l'Université d'Angers, 171–82.

——— 1996, 'Islamkundliche Quellen in Jean Bodin's *Heptaplomeres*', in G. Gawlick and F. Niewöhner (eds), *Jean Bodins Colloquium Heptaplomeresi*, Wiesbaden: Harrasowitz, 41–57.

Berti, Luciano 1961, 'Masaccio 1422', in *Commentari rivista di critica e storia dell'arte*, 12 (April–June), 84–107, tavv. XXXI–XLI.

Bertolacci, Amos 2006, *The Reception of Aristotle's* Metaphysics *in Avicenna's* Kitāb al-shifā'. *A Milestone of Western Metaphysical Thought*, Leiden: Brill.

——— 2008, 'On the Manuscripts of the *Ilāhiyyāt* of Avicenna's *Kitāb al-shifā*", in Anna Akasoy and Wim Raven (eds), *Islamic Thought in the Middle Ages: Studies in Text, Translation and Transmission in Honour of Hans Daiber*, Leiden: Brill, 59–75.

Bianchi, Francesco and Deborah Howard 2003, 'Life and Death in Damascus: The material culture of Venetians in the Syrian capital in the mid-fifteenth century', *Studi veneziani* 46, 233–300.

Bidese, Ermenegildo, Alexander Fidora and Paul Renner (eds) 2005, *Ramón Llull und Nikolaus von Kues: Eine Begegnung im Zeichen der Toleranz – Raimondo Lullo e Niccolò Cusano: Un incontro nel segno della tolleranza*, Turnhout: Brepols.

Birchwood, Matthew and Matthew Dimmock (eds) 2005, *Cultural Encounters Between East and West: 1453-1699*, Newcastle-Upon-Tyne: Cambridge Scholars Press.

Bisaha, Nancy 2001, 'Petrarch's Vision of the Muslim and Byzantine East', *Speculum* 76, 284–314.

——— 2002, 'Pope Pius II's Letter to Sultan Mehmed II: a Reexamination', *Crusades* 1, 183–200.

——— 2004, *Creating East and West, Renaissance Humanists and the Ottoman Turks*, Philadelphia: University of Pennsylvania Press.

Blusch, J. 1979, 'Enea Silvio Piccolomini und Giannantonio Campano. Die unterschiedlichen Darstellungsprinzipien in ihren Türkenreden', *Humanistica Lovaniensia*, 28, 78–138.

Bobzin, H. 1995, *Der Koran im Zeitalter der Reformation: Studien zur Frühgeschichte der Arabistik und Islamkunde in Europa*, Beirut, Franz Steiner Verlag.

——— 1996, 'Islamkundliche Quellen in Jean Bodin's *Heptaplomeres*', in G. Gawlick and F. Niewöhner (eds), *Jean Bodins Colloquium Heptaplomeres*, Wiesbaden: Harrassowitz, 41–57.

Boccaccio, Giovanni 1987, *Elegia di Madonna Fiammetta*, ed. Maria Pia Mussin Sacchi, Milan: Mursia.

Bodin, Jean 1572, *Methodus ad facilem historiarum cognitionem*, Paris.

——— 1576, *Les six livres de la république*, Paris: Jacques Du Puys.

——— 1580, *De la Démonomanie des sorciers*, Paris.

——— 1583, *Les Six Livres de la république*, Paris, photo-reproduction, Aalen: Scientia Verlag, 1977.

——— 1586, *De republica libri sex*, Paris.

——— 1857, *Colloquium heptaplomeres de rerum sublimium arcanis abditis*, ed. L. Noack, Schwerin: Friedrich Wilhelm Bärensprung.

——— 1955, *Method for the Easy Comprehension of History*, tr. B. Reynolds, New York Columbia University Press.

——— 1962, *The Six Bookes of a Commonweale*, tr. R. Knolles, ed. K.D. McRae, Cambridge, MA, Harvard University Press, originally translated by Knolles in 1606 and published by G. Bishop.

——— 1975, *Colloquium of the Seven about the Secrets of the Sublime*, tr. M.L. Kuntz Princeton, NJ: Princeton University Press.

Bonfiglio Dosio, Giorgetta (ed.), 1987, *Ragioni antique spettanti all'arte del mare et fabbriche de vasselle, Manoscritto nautico del sec. XV*, Venice: Fonti per la Storia di Venezia.

Boralevi, Alberto 1993, 'Tappeto da tavolo annodato in lana', in Curatola 1993, 396–8, cat. 247.

Boralevi, Alberto (ed.) 1999, *Geometrie d'Oriente. Stefano Bardini e il tappeto antico*, Livorno: Sillabe.

Boschini, Marco 1966, *La carta del navegar pitoresco Venice*, edizione critica, ed. Anna Palluchini, Rome: Istituto per la collaborazione culturale.

Bowles, E.A. 1971, 'Eastern influences on the use of trumpets and drums in the Middle Ages', *Anuario Musical*, 26, 1–28.

Bracewell, Catherine Wendy 1992, *The Uskoks of Senj: Piracy, Banditry, and Holy War in the Sixteenth Century Adriatic*, Ithaca: Cornell University Press.

Brasca, Santo 1966, *Viaggio in Terrasanta, con l'itinerario di Gabriele Capodilista 1458*, ed. Anna Momigliano Lepschky, Milan: Longanesi.

Braudel, Fernand 1949, *La Méditerranée et le Monde Méditerranéen à l'Epoque de Philippe II*, 3 vols, Paris: Armand Colin.

——— 1979, *Civilisation matérielle, économie et capitalisme*, 3 vols. Paris: Armand Colin.

——— 1995, *The Mediterranean and the Mediterranean World in the Age of Phillip II*, 2 vols, Siân Reynolds, trans., Berkeley: University of California Press (French 1st ed., 1949).

Brend, B. 1989, 'The Arts of the Book', in R.W. Ferrier (ed.), *The Arts of Persia*, New Haven, Yale University Press, 232–42.

Brentjes, Sonja 2005, 'Pride and Prejudice: The Invention of a "Historiography of Science" in the Ottoman and Safavid Empires by European Travellers and Writers of the Sixteenth and Seventeenth Centuries', in John Brooke and Ekmeleddin İhsanoğlu (eds), *Religious Values and the Rise of Science in Europe*, Istanbul: IRCICA, 229–54.

——— 2013, 'Giacomo Gastaldi's Maps of Anatolia: The Evolution of a Shared Venetian-Ottoman Cultural Space?', in Anna Contadini and Claire Norton (eds), *The Renaissance and the Ottoman World*, Farnham: Ashgate, 123–41.

Bretschneider, C.G. (vols 1–14) and H.E. Bindseil (vols 15–28) (eds) 1843–1860, *Philippi Melanthonis Opera quae supersunt omnia: Corpus Reformatorum*, Halle: C. A. Schwetschke.

Breydenbach, Bernhard von 1961, *Die Reise ins Heilige Land: ein Reisebericht aus dem Jahre 1483*, repr. Wiesbaden: G. Pressler.

Brilliant, Richard and Dale Kinney (eds) 2011, *Reuse Value: Spolia and Appropriation in Art and Architecture from Constantine to Sherrie Levine*, Farnham: Ashgate.

British Library 1978, *The Christian Orient*, London: British Library.

Brotton, Jerry 1997, *Trading Territories: Mapping the Early Modern World*, London: Reaktion Books (reissued by Ithaca: Cornell University Press, 1998).

——— 2002, *The Renaissance Bazaar, From the Silk Road to Michelangelo*, Oxford, New York: Oxford University Press.

Brown, Patricia Fortini 1988, *Venetian Narrative Painting in the Age of Carpaccio*, New Haven and London: Yale University Press.

——— 2004, *Private Lives in Renaissance Venice: Art, Architecture, and the Family*, New Haven and London: Yale University Press.

——— 2006, 'The Venetian Casa', in Ajmar-Wollheim and Dennis 2006, chapter 3, 50–65.

Brummett, Palmira 1994, *Ottoman Seapower and Levantine Diplomacy in the Age of Discovery*, Albany: SUNY Press.

––– 2007, 'Imagining the Early Modern Ottoman Space, from World History to Piri Reis', in Aksan and Goffman 2007, 15–58.

––– 2008, ' Turks" and "Christians": The Iconography of Possession in the Depiction of the Ottoman-Venetian-Hapsburg Frontiers, 1550–1689', in Matthew Dimmock and Andrew Hadfield (eds), *The Religions of the Book: Coexistence and Conflict, 1400-1660*, Houndsmills: Palgrave Macmillan, 110–39.

––– 2013, 'The Lepanto Paradigm Revisited: Knowing the Ottomans in the Sixteenth Century', in Anna Contadini and Claire Norton (eds), *The Renaissance and the Ottoman World*, Farnham: Ashgate, 63–93.

––– (ed.) 2009, *The 'Book' of Travels: Genre, Ethnology, and Pilgrimage, 1250-1700*, Studies in Medieval and Reformation Traditions, no. 140, Leiden: Brill.

Burke, Peter 2007, 'Translations into Latin in Early Modern Europe', in Peter Burke and Porchia Hsia (eds), *Cultural Translation in Early Modern Europe*, Cambridge: Cambridge University Press, 65–80.

Burnett, Charles 1979–1980, 'The Impact of Arabic Science on Western Civilisation in the Middle Ages', *Bulletin of the British Association of Orientalists* 11, 40–51.

––– 1997, 'Petrarch and Averroes: An Episode in the History of Poetics', in Ian MacPherson and Ralph Penny (eds), *The Medieval Mind: Hispanic Studies in Honour of Alan Deyermond*, Woodbridge: Tamesis, 49–56.

––– 1999, 'The Second Revelation of Arabic Philosophy and Science: 1492–1562', in Burnett and Contadini 1999, 185–98.

Burnett, Charles and Anna Contadini (eds) 1999, *Islam and the Italian Renaissance*, London: Warburg Institute.

Burnett, Charles and Benno van Dalen (eds) 2011, *Between Orient and Occident: Transformation of Knowledge*, special issue of *Annals of Science* 68, no. 4, Abingdon: Taylor and Francis.

Burtin, M. P. 1990, 'Un Apôtre de la Tolérance: l'Humanist Allemand Johannes Löwenklau, dit Leunclavius (1541–1593?)', *Bibliothèque d'Humanisme et Renaissance* 52, 561–70.

Busbequius, Augerius Gislenius 1994, *Legationis Turcicae epistolae quatuor*, ed. by Zweder von Martels, Dutch translation by Michel Goldstein, Hilversum: Verloren.

Busi, Giulio 2007, *L'enigma dell'ebraico nel Rinascimento*, Turin: Nino Aragno.

Busolini, D. 1999, 'Gastaldi, Giacomo', in *Dizionario Biografico*, Istituto della Enciclopedia Italiana, Roma, 52, 529–32.

Çagman, Filiz (ed.) 2000, *The Sultan's Portrait: Picturing the House of Osman*, Istanbul: İşbank.

Cambini, Andrea 1529, *Libro d'Andrea Cambini fiorentino della origine de Turchi et imperio delli Ottomanni*, Florence: heredi di Philippo di Giunta.

Cambini, Andrea 1562, *Two very notable commentaries the one of the originall Turcks and Empire of the house of Ottomanno..*, London: Rouland Hall.

Cameron, Averil 2012, *The Mediterranean World in Late Antiquity AD 395-700*, 2nd ed., London and New York: Routledge.
Campbell, Caroline and Alan Chong 2005–2006, *Bellini and the East*, exh. cat., Isabella Stewart Gardner Museum, Boston and National Gallery, London.
Campbell, Caroline 2005–2006b, 'The Bellini, Bessarion and Byzantium', in Campbell and Chong 2005–2006, 36–65.
––– 2005–2006c, 'Italian Images of Mehmed the Conquerer', in Campbell and Chong 2005–2006, 66–79.
––– 2011, 'Un Vénetien à Damas: représentations de Pietro Zen et relations entre Vénetiens, Mameluks et Ottomans', in Sandro G. Franchini, Gherardo Ortalli, Gennaro Toscano (eds), *Venise et la Méditerranée*, Venice: IVSLA, 83–101.
Capponi, Niccolò 2006, *Victory of the West: The Great Christian-Muslim Clash at the Battle of Lepanto*, Cambridge, MA: Da Capo Press.
Carboni Stefano (ed.) 2006, *Venise et l'Orient*, exh. cat., Institut du Monde Arabe, Paris and Metropolitan Museum, New York.
––– (ed.) 2007, *Venice and the Islamic World, 828-1797*, New York and New Haven: The Metropolitan Museum of Art and Yale University Press (French 1st ed., 2006).
Carletti, Lorenzo 2003, *Grifo*, in Tangheroni, Marco (ed.), *Pisa e il Mediterraneo: uomini, merci, idee dagli Etruschi ai Medici*, Milan: Skira, 408, cat. 116.
Carrié, Jean-Michel 1999, 'Commerce', in G. W. Bowersock, Peter Brown and Oleg Grabar (eds), *Late Antiquity: A Guide to the Postclassical World*, Cambridge, MA, London: Belknap Press of Harvard University Press, 386–88.
Carter, Francis W. 1972, *Dubrovnik (Ragusa) A Classic City-state*, London: New York: Seminar Press.
Carruthers, Mary J. 2009, 'Varietas: A Word of Many Colours', *Poetica: Zeitschrift für Sprach- und Literaturwissenschaft*, Munich, Fall, 33–54.
Casola, Pietro 1855, *Viaggio a Gerusalemme verso la fine del 1400*, Milan.
Castiglione, Sabba da 1554, *Ricordi*, Venice: Paolo Gherardo.
Caus, Salomon de 1614, *Institution harmonique*, Heidelberg.
Cavallini, I. 1986, 'La musica turca nelle testimonianze dei viaggiatori e nella trattistica del sei-settecento', *Rivista italiana di musicologia*, 21, 144–69.
Cavazzana Romanelli, F. 1983, 'Ambrogio Contarini', *Dizionario Biografico degli Italiani*, vol. 28, Rome: Enciclopedia Italiana, 97–104.
Cazaux, Christelle 2002, *La musique à la cour de François Ier*, Paris: École Nationale des Chartes – Programme «Ricercar».
Chakrabarty, Dipesh 2000, *Provincializing Europe: Postcolonial Thought and Historical Difference*, Princeton: Princeton University Press.
Chalcondyles, L. 1562, *De origine et rebus gestis Turcorum libri decem, nuper a Graeco inLatinum conuersi: Conrado Clausero Tigurino interprete*, in Hieronymus Wolf (ed.), *Corpus Universae Historia Byzantinae*, Basel: Opporinus.
Chambers, Iain 2000, *Culture After Humanism*, London: Routledge.

Chong, Alan 2006, 'Gentile Bellini in Istanbul: Myths and Misunderstandings', in Campbell and Chong 2005–2006, 106–29.

Christianson, Gerald, and Thomas M. Izbicki (eds) 1991, *Nicholas of Cusa in Search of God and Wisdom*, Leiden: Brill.

Christie, A.H. 1942, 'Two Rock-Crystal Carvings of the Fatimid Period', *Ars Islamica* 9, 166–168.

Chytraeus, David 1569, *Oratio in qua de statu Ecclesiarum hoc tempore in Graecia, Asia, Austria, Vngaria, Böemia & c. narrationes verae & cognitu non iniucundae exponuntur*, Rostock.

Cicero 1928, *De re publica*, The Loeb classical library, 213, Cambridge, Mass.: Harvard University Press.

—— 2001, *De officiis*, The Loeb classical library 30, Cambridge, MA: Harvard University Press.

Coccio, Marcantonio ('Sabellico') 1560, *Enneades* X, Book 9, in Coccio M. *Opera omnia*, 4 vols, Basel.

Coco, Carla and Flora Manzonetto 1985, *Baili Veneziani alla Sublime Porta. Storie e caratteristiche dell'ambasciata veneta a Constantinopoli*, Venice: Stamperia di Venezia.

Contadini, Anna 1988, 'Due pannelli di cuoio dorato nel Museo Civico Medievale di Bologna', *Annali di Cà Foscari*, Facoltà di lingue e letterature straniere, serie orientale 27, 3, 127–42.

—— 1989, '"Cuoridoro": tecnica e decorazione di cuoi dorati veneziani e italiani con influssi islamici', in Grube, Carboni and Curatola 1989, 231–51.

—— 1993, 'La Spagna dal II/VIII al VII/XIII Secolo', in Curatola 1993, 105–32.

—— 1995, 'Islamic Ivory Chess Pieces, Draughtsmen and Dice in the Ashmolean Museum', in *Islamic Art in the Ashmolean Museum - Oxford Studies in Islamic Art*, vol. X, part 1, Oxford, 111–54.

—— 1998, *Fatimid Art at the Victoria and Albert Museum*, London: V&A Publications.

—— 1999, 'Artistic Contacts: Current Scholarship and Future Tasks', in Burnett and Contadini 1999, 1–60.

—— 2006, 'Middle Eastern Objects', in Ajmar-Wollheim and Dennis 2006, 308–21.

—— 2006b, 'Le stoffe islamiche nel Rinascimento italiano tra il XV e il XVI secolo', in Daniela Degl'Innocenti (ed.), *Intrecci Mediterranei: Il tessuto come dizionario di rapporti economici, culturali e sociali*, Prato: Museo del Tessuto, 28–35.

—— 2010, 'Translocation and Transformation: Some Middle Eastern Objects in Europe', in Lieselotte E. Saurma-Jeltsch and Anja Eisenbeiss (eds), *The Power of Things and the Flow of Cultural Transformations*, Munich: Deutscher Kunstverlag, 42–64.

—— 2013, 'Sharing a Taste? Material Acquisitions and Intellectual Curiosity from the Eleventh to the Sixteenth Century', in Anna Contadini and Claire Norton (eds), *The Renaissance and the Ottoman World*, Farnham: Ashgate, 23–61.

Contadini, Anna, Richard Camber and Peter Northover 2002, 'Beasts That Roared: The Pisa Griffin And The New York Lion', in W. Ball and L. Harrow (eds), *Cairo to Kabul – Afghan and Islamic Studies presented to Ralph Pinder-Wilson*, London, 65–83.
Contarini, Ambrogio 1524, *Itinerario del Magnifico et Clarissimo messer Ambrosio Contarini, dignissimo Orator della illustrissima Signoria de Venetia, mandado nel anno 1472 ad Usuncassan Re di Persia*, Venice: Francesco Bindoni & Mapheo Pasini.
Cornet, Enrico (ed.) 1852, *Lettere al Senato Veneto di Giosafatte Barbaro Ambasciatore ad Usunhasan di Persia*, Vienna: Libreria Tendler & Comp.
——— 1856, *Le Guerre dei Veneti nell'Asia 1470-1474*, Vienna, Libreria Tendler & Comp.
Cortelazzo, Manlio 1976, 'La cultura mercantile e marinesca', in *Storia della cultura veneta I: Dalle origini al Trecento*, Vicenza, 671–91, reprinted in Manlio Cortelazzo, *Venezia, il Levante e il Mare*, Pisa: Pacini, 1989.
Cotrugli Raguseo, Benedetto 1990, *Il libro dell'arte de mercatura*, ed. Ugo Tucci, Venice: Arsenale Editrice.
Cressier, Patrice 2004, 'Historia de capiteles. ¿Hubo talleres califales provinciales?', *Cuadernos de Madīnat al-Zahrā'*, 5, 355–75.
Critoboulos 1954, *History of Mehmed the Conqueror*, trans. Charles T. Riggs, Princeton: Princeton University Press.
Crusius, Martin 1584, *Turco-Graeciae libri octo*, Basel: Henricpetrus.
——— 1584b, *Aethiopicae Heliodori Historiae Epitome. Cum Obseruationibus eiusdmem*, Frankfurt.
Crusius 1927 and 1931, *Diarium Martini Crusii 1596-1597*, ed. Göz, W. and E. Conrad, 2 vols, Tübingen, H. Laupp'schen Buchhandlung.
Curatola, Giovanni (ed.) 1993, *Eredità dell'Islam – Arte islamica in Italia*, Milan: Silvana Editoriale.
——— 2004, 'A Sixteenth-Century Quarrel about Carpets', in Doris Behrens-Abouseif and Anna Contadini (eds), *Essays in Honor of J.M. Rogers*, Muqarnas 21, 129–37.
Damiani, Giovanna, Selmin Kangal, Mary Işın (eds) 2003, *Medicilerden Savoylara, Floransa Saraylarında Osmanlı Görkemi*, Istanbul: Sakip Sabancı Müzesi.
Daniel, Norman 1962, *Islam and the West: The Making of an Image*, Edinburgh: Edinburgh University Press.
Davanzo Poli, Doretta 2003, 'Il tesoro tessile di San Marco', in Irene Favaretto and Maria Da Villa Urbani (eds), *Il Museo di San Marco*, Venice: Marsilio, 116–23.
Davids, Adelbert (ed.) 1995, *The Empress Theophano: Byzantium and the West at the Turn of the First Millennium*, Cambridge: Cambridge University Press.
Davies, Martin 1961, *National Gallery Catalogues: The Earlier Italian Schools*, London: The National Gallery.
Davis, Natalie Zemon 2006, *Trickster Travels: A Sixteenth-Century Muslim between Worlds*, New York: Hill and Wang.

da Montalboddo, Francazio (ed.) 1507, *Paesi novamente retrovati et Nuovo Mondo da Alberico Vesputio Florentino intitulato*, Vicenza: Enrico da Ca' Zeno.

——— (ed.) 1517, *Paesi novamente ritrovati per la Navigatione di Spagna in Calicut. Et da Alberitio Vesputio Fiorentino intitulato Mondo Novo*, Venice: Zorzi de Rusconi milanese.

de' Conti, Nicolò 1929, *Viaggi in Persia, India e Giava*, ed. Mario Longhena, Milan: Alpes.

de Epalza, M. 1971, *La Tuhfa, autobiografía y polémica islámica contra el Cristianismo de 'Abdallah al-Taryuman (fray Anselmo Turmeda)*, Rome, Accademia Nazionale dei Lincei.

de Ferriol, Charles 1715, *Explication des cent estampes qui representent differentes nations du Levant avec de nouvelles estampes de ceremonies turques qui ont aussi leurs explications* [commissioned by Charles, Marquis de Ferriol], Paris: Jacques Collombat.

de Groot, Alexander 2003, 'The Historical Development of the Capitulatory Regime in the Ottoman Middle East from the Fifteenth to the Nineteenth Centuries', *Oriente Moderno*, special edition, *The Ottoman Capitulations: Text and Context* (eds) Maurits van den Boogert and Kate Fleet, XXII (LXXXIII), n.s., 3, 575–604.

de la Cruz Palma, Óscar 1999, 'El *Dialogus de Fide* de Jorge Ameruzes de Trebisonda. Un mensaje político en el proemio', *Hispania Sacra* 51, 101–118.

de la Noue, F. 1587, *Discours politiques et militaires ... nouvellement recueillis & mis en lumiere*, Basel.

de Nicolay, Nicolas 1989, *Dans l'Empire de Soliman le Magnifique* [*Les Navigations et pérégrinations en la Turquie*], M.-C. Gomez-Géraud and S. Yérasimos (eds), Paris: Presses du CNRS, originally published in 1568.

de Planhol, Xavier 1975–1977, 'Rayonnement urbain et sélection animale: une solution nouvelle du probléme de la chevre d'Angora', in Secrétariat d'État aux Universités, Comité des travaux historiques et scientifiques, *Bulletin de la Section de Géographie* LXXXII, 179–96.

de Torquemada, Juan 1615, *Los veintiún libros rituales y Monarchia Indiana, con el origen y guerras de los indios occidentales*, Seville.

Degenhart, Bernhard and Annegrit Schmitt 1984, *Jacopo Bellini, the Louvre Album of Drawings*, translated from the German by Frank Mecklenbur, New York: George Braziller.

Degl'Innocenti, Daniela 2006, 'Velluto a maglia moresca', in Degl'Innocenti, Daniela (ed.), *Intrecci Mediterranei. Il tessuto come dizionario di rapporti economici, culturali e sociali*, Prato: Museo del Tessuto, 80–81, cat. 14.

Delcorno, Carlo 2000, *La tradizione delle 'Vite dei Santi Padri'*, Venice: Istituto veneto di scienze, lettere ed arti.

Denny, Walter 1982, 'Textiles', in Yanni Petsopoulos (ed.), *Tulips, Arabesques & Turbans: Decorative Arts from the Ottoman Empire*, New York: Abbeville Press, 121–67.

——— 2007, 'Oriental Carpets and Textiles in Venice', in Carboni 2007, 174–91.

Dernschwam 1986 (reprint) *Hans Dernschwam's Tagebuch einer Reise nach Konstantinopel (1553/55)* ed. F. Babinger, Berlin, Duncker & Humbolt, first published in 1923.

Dijk, Arjan van 2005, 'Early Printed Qur'ans: The Dissemination of the Qur'an in the West', *Journal of Qur'anic Studies* 7, Issue 2, 136–43.

Dimmock, Matthew 2005, '"Captive to the Turke": Responses to the Anglo-Ottoman Capitulations of 1580', in Matthew Birchwood and Matthew Dimmock (eds), *Cultural Encounters Between East and West: 1453–1699*, Newcastle-upon-Tyne: Cambridge Scholars Press, 43–63.

——— 2005b, *New Turkes: Dramatizing Islam and the Ottomans in Early Modern England*, Aldershot: Ashgate.

Doberer, Erika 1957, 'Studien zu dem Ambo Kaiser Heinrichs II. im Dom zu Aachen', in *Karolingische und ottonische Kunst: Werden, Wesen, Wirkung*, Wiesbaden: Franz Steiner, 308–359.

Dodds, Jerrilynn Denise, María Rosa Menocal and Abigail Krasner Balbale 2008, *The Arts of Intimacy: Christians, Jews, and Muslims in the Making of Castilian Culture*, New Haven, London, Yale University Press.

Donado, Giovanni Battista 1688, *Della letteratura de' Turchi*, Venice: Andrea Poletti.

Dooley, Brendan 2001, 'The wages of war: battles, prints and entrepreneurs in late seventeenth-century Venice', *Word and Image*, 17/1–2, 7–24.

Du Loir 1654, *Les voyages du Sieur du Loir*, Paris: Clouzier.

Dunbar, B. L. 1992, 'A Rediscovered Sixteenth Century Drawing of the Vatican with Constructions for the Entry of Charles V into Rome', in *The Sixteenth Century Journal* 23/2, 195–204.

Dursteler, Eric 2006, *Venetians in Constantinople: Nation, Identity, and Coexistence in the Early Modern Mediterranean*, Baltimore: Johns Hopkins University Press.

Edler De Roover, F. 1966, 'Andrea Bianchi, Florentine Silk Manufacturer and Merchant in the Fifteenth Century', in *Studies in Medieval and Renaissance History*, III, 223–85.

Engels, W. 1939–40, 'Die Wiederentdeckung und erste Beschreibung der östlich-orthodoxen Kirche in Deutschland durch David Chytraeus (1569)', in *Kyrios: Vierteljahresschrift für Kirchen und Geistesgeschichte Osteuropas* 4, 262–85.

Erasmus 1999, 'Adagium 3001: Dulce bellum inexpertis', in R. Hoven (ed.), *Opera omnia Desiderii Erasmi Roterodami. Vol. II.7: Adagiorum chilias quarta (pars prior)*, Amsterdam, North-Holland Publishing.

Erdmann, Kurt 1940, 'Islamische Bergkristallarbeiten', *Jahrbuch der Preussischen Kunstsammlungen*, 61, 125–46.

——— 1951, '"Fatimid" Rock Crystals', *Oriental Art* III, no. 4, 142–46.

Erdmann, K. and H.R. Hahnloser, 1971, 'Reliquiario del sangue miracoloso', in Hahnloser 1971, 116–18, cat. 128.

Ergenç, Özer 1975, '1600–1615 Yılları Arasında Ankara Iktisadi Tarihine Ait Araştırmalar', in Osman Okyar and Ünal Nalbantoğlu (eds), *Türkiye İktisat Tarihi Semineri, Metinler-Tartışmalar..*, Ankara: Hacettepe Üniversitesi, 145–68.

—— 1980, 'XVII. Yüzyıl başlarında Ankara'nın Yerleşim Durumu üzerine bazı Bilgiler', *Osmanlı Araştırmaları* 1, 85–108.

—— 1995, *Osmanlı Klasik Dönemi Kent Tarihçiliğine Katkı, XVI. Yüzyılda Ankara ve Konya*, Ankara: Ankara Enstitüsü Vakfı.

Esch, Arnold 1969, 'Spolien. Zur Wiederverwendung antiker Baustücke und Skulpturen im mittelalterlichen Italien', *Archiv für Kulturgeschichte*, 51, 1–64.

Euler, Walter Andreas 1995, *Unitas et Pax. Religionsvergleich bei Raimundus Lullus und Nikolaus von Kues*, Würzburg: Echter.

Euw, Anton von and Peter Schreiner (eds) 1991, *Kaiserin Theophanu: Begegnung des Ostens und Westens um die Wende des ersten Jahrtausends: Gedenkschrift des Kölner Schnütgen-Museums zum 1000. Todesjahr der Kaiserin*. 2 vols, Köln: Das Museum.

—— 1993, *Kunst im Zeitalter der Kaiserin Theophanu: Akten des internationalen Colloquiums veranstaltet vom Schnütgen-Museum, Köln, 13.-15. Juni 1991*, Köln: Locher.

Evliya Çelebi 2003, *Evliya Çelebi Seyahatnâmesi: Topkapı Sarayı Bağdat 304 yazmasının transkripsiyonu*, vol. 7, ed. Y. Dağlı, S.A. Kahraman and R. Dankoff, Istanbul: Yapı Kredi Yayınları.

Fabris, Antonio 1991, 'Artisanat et culture: recherches sur la production venitienne et le marché ottoman au XVIe Siècle', *Arab Historical Review For Ottoman Studies* 3–4, 51–60.

—— 1993, 'The Ottoman Mappa Mundi of Hajji Ahmed of Tunis', *Arab Historical Review for Ottoman Studies* 7–8, 31–7.

Fallahzadeh, Mehrdad 2005, *Persian writing on music. A study of Persian musical literature from 1000 to 1500 AD*, Uppsala: Uppsala Universitet.

Farmer, H. G. 1934, *Al-Fārābī's Arabic-Latin writings on music*, Glasgow: The Civic Press.

—— 1941, 'Oriental influences on occidental military music', *Islamic Culture* 15, 235–42, repr. in *Studies in Oriental music: Instruments and military music* (The science of music in Islam, vol. 2), Frankfurt am Main: Institute for the History of Arabic-Islamic Science at the Johann Wolfgang Goethe University, 1997, 679–86.

—— 1946, 'Turkish influence in military music', *Journal of the Society for Army Historical Research* 24, 177–82, repr. in *Studies in Oriental music: Instruments and military music* (The science of music in Islam, vol. 2), Frankfurt am Main: Institute for the History of Arabic-Islamic Science at the Johann Wolfgang Goethe University, 1997, 687–92.

—— 1949, 'Crusading martial music', *Music and Letters* 30, 243–9 repr. in *Studies in Oriental music: Instruments and military music* (The science of music in Islam, vol. 2), Frankfurt am Main: Institute for the History of Arabic-Islamic Science at the Johann Wolfgang Goethe University, 1997, 693–9

—— 1957, 'The music of Islam', in Egon Wellesz (ed.),*The new Oxford history of music*, 1. Oxford University Press, London, 421–77.

Faroqhi, Suraiya 1980, 'Textile production in Rumeli and the Arab Provinces: Geographical Distribution and Internal Trade (1560–1650)', *Osmanli Araştirmalari* 1, 61–83.

——— 1982–1983, 'Mohair Manufacture and Mohair Workshops in Seventeenth-Century Ankara', *Ord. Prof. Ömer Lütfi Barkan'a armağan*. İstanbul Universitesi İktisat Fakültesi mecmuası 41, 1–4, 211–36.

——— 1984, *Towns and Townsmen of Ottoman Anatolia, trade, crafts and food production in an urban setting*, Cambridge: Cambridge University Press.

——— 1986, 'The Venetian Presence in the Ottoman Empire', *The Journal of European Economic History*, 15, 345–84.

——— 2000, *Subjects of the Sultan: Culture and Daily Life in the Ottoman Empire*, London: I.B. Tauris, Reprint, 2007.

——— 2002, 'Ottoman Views on Corsairs and Piracy in the Adriatic', in Elizabeth Zachariadou (ed.), *The Kapudan Pasha. His Office and his Domain,* Rethymnon: University of Crete Press, 357–71.

——— 2013, 'Ottoman Textiles in European Markets', in Anna Contadini and Claire Norton (eds), *The Renaissance and the Ottoman World,* Farnham: Ashgate, 231–44.

Fatouros, G. 1998, 'Theodosius Zygomalas', in F. W. Bautz and T. Bautz (eds), *Biographisch-Bibliographisches Kirchenlexikon*, vol. xiv, cols 675–6.

Febure da Novì, Michele 1674, *Specchio, o vero descrizione della Turchia*, 2nd impr., Florence: Francesco Livi.

——— 1675, *L'estat present de la Turquie.*

——— 1683, *Teatro della Turchia, dove si rappresentano I disordini di essa, il genio, la natura, ed i costumi di quattordici nationi che l'habitano*, Venice: Steffano Curti.

Feldman, W. 1996, *Music of the Ottoman court: makam, composition and the early Ottoman instrumental repertoire,* Intercultural Music Studies, 10, Berlin: VWB – Verlag für Wissenschaft und Bildung.

Fenlon, Iain 2006, *The Ceremonial City: History, Memory, and Myth in Renaissance Venice*, New Haven: Yale University Press.

Fichtner, P. S. 2001, *Emperor Maximilian II*, New Haven: Yale University Press.

Fidora, Alexander 2004, 'Ramon Llull – Universaler Heilswille und universale Vernunft', Matthias Lutz-Bachmann and Alexander Fidora (eds), *Juden, Christen und Muslime. Religionsdialoge im Mittelalter*, Darmstadt: Wissenschaftliche Buchgesellschaft, 119–35.

Finkel, Caroline 1988, *The Administration of Warfare: the Ottoman Military Campaigns in Hungary, 1593-1606*, Vienna: VWGÖ.

——— 1992, 'French Mercenaries in the Habsburg-Ottoman War of 1583–1606. The Desertion of the Papa Garrison to the Ottomans in 1600', *Bulletin of the School of Oriental and African Studies* 55/3, 451–71.

——— 2005, '"The Treacherous Cleverness of Hindsight": Myths of Ottoman Decay', in MacLean and Dalrymple 2005, 148–74.

——— 2005b, *Osman's Dream: The Story of the Ottoman Empire 1300-1923*, London: John Murray, also published in 2005 in New York by Basic Books.

—— 2008, 'Ottoman History: Whose History is It?', *International Journal of Turkish Studies* 14, 1–10.

Fleet, Kate 1999, *European and Islamic Trade in the Early Ottoman State: the merchants of Genoa and Turkey*, Cambridge: Cambridge University Press.

Flötner, Peter 1882, *Das Kunstbuch des Peter Flötner*, Berlin (facsimile of the original edition, Zurich 1546).

Folena, Gianfranco 1973, 'Introduzione al veneziano "de là da mar"', in Agostino Pertusi (ed.), *Venezia e il Levante fino al al secolo XV*, 2 parts, Florence: Olschki, vol. I, Part I, 297–339.

Fomichova, Tamara D. 1992, *The Hermitage Catalogue of Western Paintings: Venetian Painting, 14th- 18th Centuries*, Florence: Giunti.

Fontana, Maria Vittoria 1993, 'L'influsso dell'arte islamica in Italia', in Curatola 1993, 455–98.

—— 1993b, 'Corano stampato in caratteri arabi', in Curatola 1993, 480–81, cat. 298.

—— 1999, 'Byzantine Mediation of Epigraphic Characters of Islamic Derivation in the Wall Paintings of Some Churches in Southern Italy', in Burnett and Contadini 1999, 61–75.

Forster, Thornton, and F.H. Blackburne Daniell (eds.) 1881, *The Life and Letters of Ogier Ghiselin de Busbecq, seigneur of Bousbecque, Knight, imperial Ambassador*, 2 vols, London: Kegan Paul.

Forstner, M. 1972, 'Zur Madonna mit der Šahāda', *Zeitschrift der Deutschen morgenländischen Gesellschaft* 122, 102–107.

Forti Grazzini, Nello 1982, *L'Arazzo Ferrarese*, Ferrara: Cassa di Risparmio di Ferrara.

Gaborit-Chopin, Danielle 1986, 'Suger's Liturgical Vessels', in Paula Lieber Gerson (ed.), *Abbot Suger and Saint-Denis: A Symposium*, New York: Metropolitan Museum of Art, 281–93.

Gabrieli, Francesco 1974, 'Islam in the Mediterranean World', in Joseph Schacht and C.E. Bosworth (eds), *The Legacy of Islam* (2nd ed.), Oxford: Clarendon Press, 63–104.

Gabrieli, Francesco and Umberto Scerrato 1979, *Gli Arabi in Italia*, Milan: Garzanti-Schewiller.

Gacek, A. 1990–1991, 'Arabic bookmaking and terminology as portrayed by Bakr al-Ishbīlī in his "Kitāb al-taysīr fī ṣināʿat al-tasfīr"', *Manuscripts of the Middle East*, 5, 106–13.

Gaeta, Franco 1965, 'Sulla «Lettera a Maometto» di Pio II', in *Bullettino dell'Istituto storico italiano per il medioevo e archivio muratoriano* 77, 127–227.

Galilei, Vincenzo 2003, *Dialogue on ancient and modern music*, tr. with intro. and notes, by C.V. Palisca, New Haven & London: Yale University Press.

Gallo, Rodolfo 1943, 'Le mappe geografiche del Palazzo Ducale di Venetia', *Archivio Veneto* 5a serie, XXXII–XXXIII, 47–113.

Galuppo, Martina 2001, 'Corona votiva di Leone VI', in Angela Donati and Giovanni Gentili (eds), *Deomene: L'immagine dell'orante fra Oriente e Occidente*, Milano: Electa, 2001, 221–22, cat. 85.

Geary, Patrick 1986, 'Sacred Commodities: The Circulation of Medieval Relics', in Arjun Appadurai (ed.), *The Social Life of Things: Commodities in Cultural Perspective*, Cambridge: Cambridge University Press, 169-191.

Georgewitz, B. 1544, *De turcarum ritu et caeremoniis*, Antwerp.

Georgius de Hungaria 1993, *Tractatus de moribus, condictionibus et nequicia Turcorum*, ed. R. Klockow, Cologne: Böhlau Verlag.

Gerelyes, Ipolya (ed.) 1995, *Süleyman the Magnificent and his Age*, Budapest: The Hungarian National Museum.

Geuffroy, A. 1543, *Briefve description de la court du grant turc et ung sommaire du regne des Othmans*, Paris.

Giovo, Paolo 1531, *Commentario delle cose de' Turchi*, Venice.

Giraldi, Philip Mark 1976, *The Zen Family: patrician office holding in Renaissance Venice*, PhD thesis, University of London.

Glei, Reinhold F. and Makus Köhler (eds) 2001, *Pius II. Papa. Epistola ad Mahumetem. Introduction, critical edition, translation: Einleitung*, kritische Edition, Übersetzung, Bochumer Altertumswissenschaftliches Colloquium 50, Trier: WVT, Wissenschaftlicher Verlag Trier

Goffman, Daniel 1998, *Britons in the Ottoman Empire 1642-1660*, Seattle and London: University of Washington Press.

––– 2002, *The Ottoman Empire and Early Modern Europe*, Cambridge: Cambridge University Press.

––– 2007, 'Negotiating with the Renaissance state; the Ottoman Empire and the new diplomacy', in Aksan and Goffman 2007, 61-74.

Goitein, S.D. 1967-1993, *A Mediterranean Society: the Jewish communities of the Arab world as portrayed in the documents of the Cairo Geniza*, 6 vols: I, 1967 (Economic Foundations); II, 1971 (The Community); III, 1978 (The Family); IV, 1983 (Daily Life); V, 1988 (The Individual); VI, 1993 (Cumulative Indices), Los Angeles and London (Reprinted in paperback by University of California Press in 1999).

Goldthwaite, R.A. 1993, *Wealth and the Demand for Art in Italy 1300-1600*, Baltimore and London.

Göllner, Carl 1961-8, *Turcica: Bd. I-II: Die europäischen Türkendrucke des XVI. Jahrhunderts*, Bibliotheca bibliographica Aureliana, 23, Bucharest.

Gordon, Dillian 2003, *The Fifteenth Century Italian Paintings. Volume I*, London: National Gallery Company.

Grabar, Andre 1971, 'Corona di Leone VI', in Hahnloser 1971, 81-82, cat. 92 and pls. LXXII-LXXV, CXLVIII.

Grabar, Oleg 1992, *The Mediation of Ornament*, Princeton: Princeton University Press.

Granzotto, O. 1995, 'Alcune Note su Felice Feliciano Legatore', in A. Contò e L. Quaquarelli (eds), L'"Antiquario" Felice Feliciano veronese, tra epigrafia antica, letteratura e arti del libro, Atti del Convegno di Studi, Verona, 3-4 giugno 1993, Padova, 221-229.

Greene, Molly 2000, *A Shared World; Christians and Muslims in the Early Modern Mediterranean*, Princeton: Princeton University Press.

Grelot, Guillaume Joseph 1680, *Relation nouvelle d'un voyage de Constantinople*, Paris.

Grendler, Paul F. 1982, 'What Zuanne read in school: vernacular texts in sixteenth century Venetian schools', *Sixteenth Century Journal* 13/1, 41–54 (republished in Paul Grendler, *Books and Schools in the Italian Renaissance*, Aldershot: Variorum, 1995, essay VII).

Grimme, Ernst Günther 1972, 'Der Aachener Domschatz', *Aachener Kunstblätter* 42.

Groto, Luigi 1572, *Trofeo della Vittoria Sacra*, Venice.

Grubb, James S. 1986, 'Memory and Identity: Why Venetians didn't keep ricordanze', *Renaissance Studies* 8, 357–87.

Grube, Ernst J., Stefano Carboni and Giovanni Curatola (eds) 1989, *Arte veneziana e arte islamica: atti del Primo simposio internazionale sull'arte veneziana e l'arte islamica*, Venice: L'Alta Riva.

—— 1989b, 'Le lacche veneziane e i loro modelli islamici', in Grube, Carboni and Curatola 1989, 217–229.

Gruner, O. Cameron 1930, *A Treatise on the Canon of Medicine of Avicenna: Incorporating a Translation of the First Book*, London: Luzac.

Guidi, Ignazio 1899, 'Di Un Vaso Arabo', in *Actes du Onzième Congrès International des Orientalistes: Paris-1897*, 3rd section, Paris: Imprimerie Nationale, Ernest Leroux, 39–43.

Guilmartin, John 1980, *Gunpowder and Galleys: Changing Technology and Mediterranean Warfare at Sea in the Sixteenth Century*, Cambridge: Cambridge University Press.

Gulácsi, Z. 2005, *Medieval Manichaean Book Art: A Codicological Study of Iranian and Turkic illuminated book fragments from 8th-11th Century East Central Asia*, Leiden: Brill.

Günergun, Feza 2007, 'Ottoman encounters with European science: sixteenth- and seventeenth-century translations into Turkish', in Peter Burke and Porchia Hsia (eds), *Cultural Translation in Early Modern Europe*, Cambridge: Cambridge University Press, 192–211.

Gürsu, N. 1988, *The Art of Turkish Weaving: Designs Through the Ages*, English editor: Edmonds, William A., Istanbul: Redhouse Press.

Gutas, Dimitri 1998, *Greek Thought, Arabic Culture. The Graeco-Arabic Translation Movement in Baghdad and Early 'Abbāsid Society (2nd-4th/8th-10th centuries)*, London: Routledge.

—— 2002, 'The Study of Arabic Philosophy in the 20th Century. An Essay on the Historiography of Arabic Philosophy', *British Journal of Middle Eastern Studies* 29, 5–25.

Hagemann, Ludwig 1976, *Der Ḳur'ān in Verständnis und Kritik bei Nikolaus von Kues. Ein Beitrag zur Erhellung islāmisch-christlicher Geschichte*, Frankfurt: Knecht.

—— 1983, *Nikolaus von Kues im Gespräch mit dem Islam*, Altenberge: Verlag für christlich-islamisches Schrifttum.

Hahnloser, H.R. (ed.) 1971, *Il Tesoro di San Marco: Il tesoro e il museo*, II, Firenze: Sansoni.

Hamilton, A. 1994, *Europe and the Arab World: Five Centuries of Books by European Scholars and Travellers from the Libraries of the Arcadian Group*, Dublin, London and Oxford: The Arcadian Group, in association with Azimuth Editions and Oxford University Press.

––––– 2011, *The Arcadian Library: Western Appreciation of Arab and Islamic Civilization*, London and Oxford: The Arcadian Library with Oxford University Press.

Harley, J.B. 2001, *The New Nature of Maps: Essays in the History of Cartography*, Baltimore: Johns Hopkins University Press.

Harrison, F. 1973, *Time, place and music. An anthology of ethnomusicological observation c. 1550 to c. 1800*, Amsterdam: Frits Kunf.

Harvey, David 2003, *Paris, capital of modernity*, New York: Routledge.

Hasse, Dag Nikolaus 2001, 'Die humanistische Polemik gegen arabische Autoritäten. Grundsätzliches zum Forschungsstand', *Neulateinisches Jahrbuch* 3, 65–79.

––––– 2004, *Arabic Sciences and Philosophy in the Renaissance: Motives and Techniques of Reception*, Habilitationsschrift submitted to the University of Freiburg i.Br.

Haug, Judith I. 2010, *Der Genfer Psalter in den Niederlanden, Deutschland, England und dem Osmanischen Reich (16.-18. Jahrhundert)* (Tübinger Beiträge zur Musikwissenschaft, Band 30), Tutzing: Hans Schneider.

Hayton 1529, *Liber historiarum partium orientis, sive passagium terrae sanctae*, Hagenau.

Heath, M.J. 1979, 'Renaissance Scholars and the Origins of the Turks', *Bibliothèque d'humanisme et renaissance* 41, 453–71.

Helmrath, Johannes 2000, 'Pius II und die Türken', in Bodo Guthmüller and Wilhelm Kühlmann (eds), *Europa und die Türken in der Renaissance*, Tubingen: Niemeyer, 79–138.

Hering, Gunnar 1961, 'Das islamische Recht und die Investitur des Gennadios Scholarios (1454)', *Balkan Studies* 2, 231–256.

Hess, Andrew 1972, 'The Battle of Lepanto and its Place in Mediterranean History', *Past and Present* 57, 53–73.

Heywood, Colin 1993, 'Bosnia Under Ottoman Rule, 1463–1800', in Mark Pinson (ed.), *The Muslims of Bosnia-Herzegovina: Their Historic Development from the Middle Ages to the Dissolution of Yugoslavia*, Cambridge: Harvard University Press, 22–53.

Hieronymus F. in *Griechischer Geist aus Basler Pressen* www.unibas.ub.ch/kadmos/gg ad loc. (retrieved 17.5.2012).

Hitti, Philip K. 1942, 'The First Book Printed in Arabic', *The Princeton University Library Chronicle* 4, no. 1 (November), 5–9.

Hobson, Anthony 1989, 'Islamic influence on Venetian Renaissance bookbinding', in Grube, Carboni and Curatola 1989, 111–123.

―――― 1989b, *Humanists and Bookbinders, The Origin and diffusion of the humanistic bookbinding*, Cambridge: Cambridge University Press.

―――― and P. Culot 1991, *Italian and French 16th century bookbindings*, rev. edn., Brussels: Bibliotheca Wittockiana.

Hobson, G.D. 1939, 'Some early bindings and binder's tools', *The Library* IV, 19, 202–249.

Hodgson, Marshall 1974, *The Venture of Islam: Conscience and History in a World Civilization*, 3 vols. Chicago: University of Chicago Press.

Hodges, Richard and David Whitehouse 1983, *Mohammed, Charlemagne & the Origins of Europe*, London: Duckworth.

Hoffman, Eva R. 2001, 'Pathways of Portability: Islamic and Christian interchange from the tenth to the twelfth century', *Art History* 24, no. 1 (February), 17–50.

―――― 2007, 'Remapping the Art of the Mediterranean', in Eva R. Hoffman (ed.), *Late Antique and Medieval Art of the Mediterranean World*, Malden and Oxford: Blackwell Publishing.

Horden, Peregrine and Nicholas Purcell 2000, *The Corrupting Sea. A Study of Mediterranean History*, Oxford: Blackwell Publishing.

Howard, Deborah 2000, *Venice and the East: The Impact of the Islamic World on Venetian Architecture, 1100-1500*, Yale: Yale University Press.

―――― 2003, 'Death in Damascus: Venetians in Syria in the mid-fifteenth century', *Muqarnas* 20, 143–157.

―――― 2004, *The Architectural History of Venice*, revised edition, New Haven: Yale University Press.

―――― 2005, 'The Status of the Oriental Traveller in Renaissance Venice', in MacLean and Dalrymple 2005, 29–49.

―――― 2005–2006, 'Venice, the Bazaar of Europe', in Campbell and Chong 2005-2006, 12–31.

―――― 2006, 'Venice and the Mamluks', in Stefano Carboni (ed.) *Venise et l'Orient*, exh. cat., Paris and New York: Institut du Monde Arabe, Paris and Metropolitan Museum, New York, 72–89.

―――― 2007, 'Cultural transfer between Venice and the Ottomans in the fifteenth and sixteenth centuries', in Herman Roodenburg (ed.), *Cultural Exchange in Early Modern Europe. Forging European Identities*, vol. 4, Cambridge: Cambridge University Press, 138–77.

Husner, F. 1949, 'Die Editio Princeps des "Corpus Historiae Byzantinae" Johannes Oporin, Hieronymus Wolf und die Fugger', in *Festschrift Karl Schwarber: Beiträge zur schweizerischen Bibliotheks-, Buch- und Gelehrtengeschichte*, Basel: Schwabe, 143–62.

Huth, Hans 1970, '"Sarazenen" in Venedig?', in Peter Block and Gisela Zick (eds), *Festschrift für Heinz Ladendorf*, Cologne-Vienna: Böhlau, 58–68.

Imber, Colin 2002, *The Ottoman Empire, 1300-1650: The Structure of Power*, Houndmills: Palgrave.

―――― 2006, *The Crusade of Varna 1443-5*, Aldershot: Ashgate.

Inalcik, Halil 1973, *The Ottoman Empire, The Classical Age 1300-1600*, trans. Norman Itzkowitz and Colin Imber, London: Weidenfeld and Nicolson.

––––– 1974, 'Lepanto in the Ottoman Documents', in Gino Benzoni (ed.), *Il Mediterraneo nella seconda metà del '500 alla luce di Lepanto*, Firenze: Olschki Editore, 185-92.

––––– 1980-1981, 'Osmanlı İdare, Sosyal ve Ekonomik Tarihiyle İlgili Belgeler: Bursa Kadı Sicillerinden Seçmeler', *Belgeler* X, 14, 1-91.

––––– and Cemal Kafadar (eds) 1993, *Süleyman the Second and His Time*, Istanbul: Isis Press.

––––– 2008, *Türkiye Tekstil Tarihi üzerine Araştırmalar*, Istanbul: Türkiye İş Bankası Kültür Yayınları.

Infelice, Mario 2001, 'The war, the news, and the curious: Military gazettes in Italy', in Brendan Dooley and Sabrina Baron (eds), *The Politics of Information in Early Modern Europe*, London: Routledge, 216-35.

Irwin, Robert 2006, *For Lust of Knowing. The Orientalists and their Enemies*, London: Allen Lane.

Ishay, Micheline R. 2004, *The History of Human Rights: from Ancient Times to the Globalization Era*, Berkeley: University of California Press.

Isom-Verhaaren, Christine 2004, 'Shifting Identities. Foreign State Servants in France and the Ottoman Empire', *Journal of Early Modern History* 8, 109-34.

Israel, Jonathan 1989, *Dutch Primacy in World Trade, 1585-1740*, Oxford: Clarendon Press.

Ivanoff, V. 1994, 'Illustrationen osmanischer Musikausübung in europäischen Publikationen (1500-1800). Versuch einer Typologie', in H. Heckmann, M. Holl and H.J. Marx (eds), *Musikalische Ikonographie*, Hamburger Jahrbuch für Musikwissenschaft, 12, Laaber: Laaberverlag, 171-82.

Jacoby, David, 1986, 'Pélérinage médiéval et sanctuaires de Terre Sainte: La perspective vénitienne', *Ateneo Veneto* 173 (24 n.s.), 27-58

––––– 1989, 'A Venetian manual of commercial practice from Crusader Acre', in *Studies on the Crusader States and on Venetian Expansion*, Northampton: Variorum, 403-28.

––––– 2000, 'Dalla materia prima ai drappi tra Bisanzio, il Levante e Venezia: La prima fase dell'industria serica veneziana', in Luca Molà, Reinhold C. Mueller and Claudio Zanier (eds), *La seta in Italia dal Medioevo al Seicento: Dal baco al drappo*, Venice: Marsilio, 265-304.

––––– 2004, 'The Silk Trade of Late Byzantine Constantinople', in Sümer Atasoy (ed.), *550th Anniversary of the Istanbul University International Byzantine and Ottoman Symposium (XVth century) (30-31 May 2003)*, Istanbul, 129-44.

Janssens, Jules L. 1991, *An Annotated Bibliography on Ibn Sînâ (1970-1989): Including Arabic and Persian Publications and Turkish and Russian References*, Leuven: University Press.

––––– 1999, *An Annotated Bibliography on Ibn Sīnā: First Supplement (1990-1994)*, Louvain-la-Neuve: Fédération Internationale des Instituts d'Études Médiévales.

Jardine, Lisa 1996, *Worldly Goods, A New History of the Renaissance*, London: Macmillan.
—— and Jerry Brotton 2000, *Global Interests: Renaissance Art between East and West*, London: Reaktion Books.
Jones, Robert 1994, 'The Medici Oriental Press (Rome 1584-1614) and the Impact of its Arabic Publications on Northern Europe', in G.A. Russell (ed.), *The 'Arabick' Interest of the Natural Philosophers in Seventeenth-Century England*, Leiden, New York, Köln: Brill, 88-108.
Jorge Ameruzes de Trebisonda 2000, *El Diálogo de la fe con el sultán de los turcos*, ed. and trans. Óscar de la Cruz Palma, Madrid: CSIC.
Jukko, R. 2007, *Trinity in Unity in Christian-Muslim Relations. The Work of the Pontifical Council for Interreligious Dialogue*, Leiden: Brill.
Kadi, I.H. 2012, *Ottoman and Dutch Merchants in the Eighteenth Century*, Leiden: E. J. Brill.
Kaempfer, Engelbert 1712, *Amoenitatum exoticarum politico-physico-medicarum fasciculi V, quibus continentur variae relationes, observationes & descriptiones rerum Persicarum & ulterioris Asiae, multa attentione, in peregrinationibus per universum Orientem, collectae ab auctore Engelberto Kaempfero*, Lemgoviæ : Typis & impensis Henrici Wilhelmi Meyeri, Aulæ Lippiacæ typographi.
Kafadar, Cemal 1986, 'A Death in Venice (1575): Anatolian Muslim merchants trading in the Serenissima', *Journal of Turkish Studies* 10, 191-218.
Kaminsky, Howard 1959, 'Pius Aeneas among the Taborites', *Church History* 28, 281-309.
Karatay, F.E. 1964 and 1966, *Topkapı Sarayi Müzesi Kütüphanesi, Arapça Yazmalar Kataloğu*, Istanbul: Topkapı Sarayi Müzesi.
Karrow, Robert 1993, *Mapmakers of the Sixteenth Century and Their Maps*, Chicago: Newberry Library & Speculum Orbis Press.
Kātib Chelebi 1957, *The Balance of Truth*, trans. G.L. Lewis, London: Allen and Unwin.
—— 1972, *Mizanü'l-hakk fi ihtiyari'l-ahakk*, ed. Orhan Şaık Gökyay, Istanbul: Millî Eğitim Basımevi.
Kircher, Athanasius 1650, *Musurgia universalis sive ars magna consoni et dissoni*, Rome.
Klinger, Linda and Julian Raby 1989, 'Barbarossa and Sinan: A Portrait of Two Ottoman Corsairs from the Collection of Paolo Giovio', in Grube, Carboni and Curatola 1989, 47-59.
Knapp, A. Bernard and Peter Van Dommelen 2010, 'Material Connections. Mobility, Materiality and Mediterranean Identities', in Peter Van Dommelen and A. Bernard Knapp, *Material Connections in the Ancient Mediterranean*, Abingdon and New York: Routledge, 1-18.
Knecht, R.J. 1994, *Renaissance Warrior and Patron: the reign of Francis I*, Cambridge: Cambridge University Press.
Koeman, Cornelis 1967, *Atlantes Neerlandici*, Amsterdam: Theatrum Orbis Terrarum.

Kollarius, A.F. 1762, *Analecta monumentorum omnis aevi Vindobonensia*, 2 vols, Vienna.
Kraemer, Joel L. 1992, *Humanism in the Renaissance of Islam: the Cultural Revival During the Buyid Age*, 2nd rev. ed., Leiden: E. J. Brill.
Kramp, Mario (ed.) 2000, *Krönungen: Könige in Aachen – Geschichte und Mythos*, Mainz: Philipp von Zabern.
Krek, Miroslav 1979, 'The Enigma of the First Arabic Book Printed from Movable Type', *Journal of Near Eastern Studies*, Vol. 38, No. 3 (July), 203–212.
Kreutel, R. 1957, *Im Reiche des goldenen Apfels*, Graz: Verlag Styria.
Krumbacher, K. 1897, *Geschichte der byzantinischen Litteratur*, 2nd ed. Munich.
Kunt, Metin, and Christine Woodhead (eds) 1995, *Süleyman the Magnificent and His Age: The Ottoman Empire in the Early Modern World*, London: Longman.
Kybalova, Jana 1997, 'Das Kunsthandwerk', in Eliška Fučíková et al. (eds), *Rudolf II und Prag, Kaiserlicher Hof und Residenzstadt als kulturelles und geistiges Zentrum Mitteleuropas Ausstellung Prager Burg-Wallenstein Palais 30. Mai–7. September 1997*, Prague, London, Milan: Thames & Hudson, and Skira, 376–86.
La Niece, Susan 2007, 'Master Mahmud and Inlaid Metalwork: A Scientific Perspective', in Carboni 2007, 226–9.
La Stampa 2007, May 30.
Lambranzi, Gregorio 1966, *New and curious school of theatrical dancing*, Nuremberg, 1716, repr. New York: Dance Horizons.
Lamm, Carl Johan 1929–30, *Mittelalterliche Gläser und Steinschnittarbeiten aus dem Nahen Osten*, 2 vols, Berlin: D. Reimer.
Landry, Donna 2011, 'Anglo-Ottoman Enlightenment? Thoroughbreds and the Public Sphere', in Gerald MacLean (ed.), *Britain and the Muslim World: Historical Perspectives*, Cambridge: Cambridge Scholars Publishing, 69–84.
Langmuir, Erika 2004, *The National Gallery: Companion Guide*, London: National Gallery Company.
Lazari, Vincenzo 1859, *Notizie delle opere d'arte e d'antichità della raccolta Correr*, Venice, 214–15.
Le Roy, L. 1568, *Les Politiques d'Aristote*, Paris.
Le Thiec, G. 2004, 'L'Empire ottoman, modèle de monarchie seigneuriale dans l'oeuvre de Jean Bodin', in G.-A. Pérouse, N. Dockès-Lallement, and J.-M. Servet (eds), *L'Oeuvre de Jean Bodin: actes du colloque tenu à Lyon à l'occasion du quatrième centenaire de sa mort (11–13 janvier 1996)*, Paris: Champion, 55–76.
Leech-Wilkinson, Daniel 1981, 'Il libro di appunti di un suonatore di tromba del quindicesimo secolo', *Rivista italiana di musicologia* XVI, 16–39.
Leemhuis, Fred 2000, 'Heiligenscheine fremder Herkunft', *Der Islam* 77/2, 286–306.
Legrand, E. 1885, *Bibliographie Hellénique des XVe et XVIe Siècles*, vol. 1, Paris.
Leo Africanus (Hasan al-Wazzan) 1550, *La descrittione d'Africa*, published in G. B. Ramusio, *Le navigatione et viaggi*, 3 vols, vol. 1, fols 1r–103v, Venice: heredi di Lucantonio Giunti. There is also a French translation by Jean Temporal, 1556 *Historiale Description de l'Afrique*, Lyon, Jean Temporal.

Lepie, Herta and Ann Münchow 2006, *Elfenbeinkunst aus dem Aachener Domschatz*, Petersberg: Michael Imhof.

Levenson, Jay A. (ed.) 1991–1992, *Circa 1992: Art in the Age of Exploration*, exh. cat., Washington, DC: National Gallery of Art.

Levi della Vida, Giorgio 1939, 'Ricerche sulla formazione del più antico fondo dei manoscritti orientali della Biblioteca vaticana', *Studi e Testi* 92, 324–6.

Lewis, Bernard 1993, *Islam and the West*, New York: Oxford University Press.

Lockhart, L. R. and R. Morozzo della Rocca et al. 1973, *I viaggi in Persia degli ambasciatori veneti Barbaro e Contarini*, Rome: Istituto poligrafico dello Stato.

Lovejoy, Arthur O. and George Boas 1935, *Primitivism and Related Ideas in Antiquity*, Baltimore: John Hopkins Press.

Lucchetta, Francesca 1968, 'L' affare Zen in Levante nel primo cinquecento', *Studi Veneziani* 10, 109–219.

Lucchetta, Giuliano 1985, 'Viaggiatori e racconti di viaggi nel Cinquecento', in A. Siliotti (ed.) *Viaggiatori veneti alla scoperta dell'Egitto*, Venice, 43–68.

Lunde, Paul 1981, 'Arabic and the Art of Printing', *Aramco World Magazine* 32, no. 2 (March/April), 20–35.

Lupprian, Karl-Ernst 1981, *Die Beziehungen der Päpste zu islamischen und mongolischen Herrschern im 13. Jahrhundert anhand ihres Briefwechsels*, Città del Vaticano: Biblioteca apostolica vaticana.

Lütteken, Laurenz 1998, 'Renaissance', in Ludwig Finscher (ed.) *Musik in Geschichte und Gegenwart*, Sachteil 8, Kassel: Bärenreiter, and Stuttgart: J.B. Metzler, 143–56.

Luzzatto, Gino 1954, *Studi di storia economica veneziana*, Padua: Cedam.

Mack, Rosamond E. 2002, *Bazaar to Piazza: Islamic Trade and Italian Art, 1300-1600*, Berkeley: University of California Press.

Mackie, Louise 1973–1974, *The Splendor of Turkish Weaving: An Exhibition of Silks and Carpets of the 13th-18th Centuries, November 9, 1973 Through March 24, 1974*, Washington, DC: Textile Museum.

—— 2004, 'Ottoman *kaftans* with a Venetian Identity', in Suraiya Faroqhi and Christoph Neumann (eds), *Ottoman Costumes, From Textile to Identity*, Istanbul: Eren, 219–29.

MacLean, Gerald 2004, *The Rise of Oriental travel. English visitors to the Ottoman Empire, 1580-1720*, Basingstoke: Palgrave Macmillan.

—— and William Dalrymple (eds) 2005, *Re-Orienting the Renaissance: Cultural Exchanges with the East*, Hampshire: Palgrave Macmillan.

—— 2005b, 'Introduction: Re-Orienting the Renaissance', in MacLean and Dalrymple 2005, 1–28.

—— 2007, *Looking East: English Writing and the Ottoman Empire Before 1800*, Hampshire: Palgrave Macmillan.

—— 2011, *Britain and the Muslim World: Historical Perspectives*, Cambridge: Cambridge Scholars Publishing.

—— and Nabil Matar 2011, *Britain and the Islamic World, 1558-1713*, Oxford: Oxford University Press.

Maetzke, Anna Maria (ed.) 2001, *Cimabue ad Arezzo: Il crocifisso restaurato*, Firenze: Edifir Edizioni Firenze.

Magni, Cornelio, *Quanto di piu curioso, e vago ha potuto raccorre C M nel primo biennio da esso consumato in viaggi, e dimore per la Turchia resta distribuito in questa prima parte in varie lettere Aggiontavi la relazione del Serraglio del Gran Signore distesa da A Bobovio, etc*, Parma: G. Rosati, 1679.

Malcolm, Noel 2003, 'The Crescent and the City of the Sun: Islam in the Renaissance Utopia of Tommaso Campanella', *Proceedings of the British Academy* 125, 41–67.

——— 2006, 'Jean Bodin and the Authorship of the *Colloquium heptaplomeres*', *Journal of the Warburg and Courtauld Institutes* 69, 95–150.

Mansi, J. D. (ed.) 1755–59, *Pii II P. M. olim Aeneae Sylvii Piccolominei Senensis Orationes politicae et ecclesiasticae*, 3 vols, Lucca.

Mantran, Robert 1985, 'Venezia e i Turchi (1650–1797)', in Carlo Pirovano (ed.), *Venezia e i Turchi: Scontri e confronti di due civiltà*, Milano: Electa Editrice, 250–67.

Manuel II. Palaiologos 1993, *Dialoge mit einem Muslim*, ed. and trans. Karl Förstel, 3 vols, Würzburg: Echter.

Manutio, Antonio (ed.) 1543, *Viaggi fatti da Vinetia alla Tana, in Persia, in India et in Costantinopoli*, Venice: Manutius.

Al-Maqrīzī, A.I. 'A. 1853, *Al-mawā'iẓ wa'l-i'tibār bi-dhikr al-khiṭaṭ wa'l-āthār*, 2 vols, Cairo.

Marcuse, S. 1975, *A survey of musical instruments*, Newton Abbot: David & Charles.

Marra, Ornella 1993, 'Astrolabio planisferico ispano-moresco in ottone', in Curatola 1993, 178–80, cat. 79.

Matar, Nabil 1998, *Islam in Britain 1558-1685*, Cambridge: Cambridge University Press.

——— 1999, *Turks, Moors and Englishmen in the Age of Discovery*, New York: Columbia University Press.

——— 2005, 'Arabic Views of Europeans, 1578–1727: The Western Mediterranean', in MacLean and Dalrymple 2005, 126–47.

——— 2005b, *Britain and Barbary 1589-1689*, Gainesville: University Press of Florida.

Mathews, Karen Rose 1999, 'Expressing Political Legitimacy and Cultural Identity Through the Use of *Spolia* on the *Ambo of Henry II*', *Medieval Encounters* 5, no. 2, 156–83.

Matoušek, L. 1994, 'Regional signs of medieval musical instruments', in H. Heckmann, M. Holl and H.J. Marx (eds), *Musikalische Ikonographie*, Hamburger Jahrbuch für Musikwissenschaft, 12, Laaber: Laaberverlag, 207–11.

Mattingly, Garrett 1955, *Renaissance Diplomacy*, London: Cape.

Mayes, Stanley 1956, *An organ for the Sultan*, London: Putnam.

McJannet, Linda 2006, *The Sultan Speaks: Dialogue in English Plays and Histories about the Ottoman Turks*, Houndmills: Palgrave.

Melanchthon, Philipp 1834–1860, CR, *Philippi Melanthonis Opera quae supersunt omnia: Corpus Reformatorum*, C. G. Bretschneider (vols 1–14) and H. E. Bindseil (vols 15–28) (eds), Halle: C. A. Schwetschke.

Membré, Michele 1993, *Mission to the Lord Sophy of Persia*, A.H. Morton, trans and ed. London: School of Oriental and African Studies.

Menavino Giovani Antonio 1548, *I cinque libri della legge, religione, et vita de' Turchi: et della corte, & d'alcune guerre del Gran Turco*, Venice.

—— 1560 *Trattato de' costumi et vita de' Turchi*, in F. Sansovino, *Historia universale dell'origine et imperio de' Turchi*, Venice.

Mercati, Angelo 1943, 'Le due lettere di Giorgio da Trebisonda a Maometto II', *Orientalia Christiana Periodica* 9, 65–99.

Mersenne, Marin 1636, *Harmonie universelle: contenant la théorie et la pratique de la musique*, facsimile edition, Paris: Centre national de la recherché scientifique, 1965.

Meserve, Margaret 2000, 'Medieval Sources for the Renaissance Theories on the Origins of the Ottoman Turks', in Bodo Guthmüller and Wilhelm Kühlmann (eds), *Europa und die Türken in der Renaissance*, Tubingen: Niemeyer, 409–36.

—— 2003, 'From Samarkand to Scythia: Reinventions of Asia in Renaissance Geography and Political Thought', in Zweder von Martels and Arjo Vanderjagt (eds), *Pius II, 'el più expeditivo pontifice'*, Selected Studies on Aeneas Silvius Piccolomini (1405–1464), Leiden: Brill, 13–39.

—— 2008, *Empires of Islam in Renaissance Historical Thought*, London: Harvard University Press.

Mesnard, Pierre 1969, *L'Essor de la philosophie politique au XVe siècle*, Paris: Vrin.

Meyer, E.R. 1973–4, 'Turquerie and eighteenth-century music', *Eighteenth-century Studies* 7, 474–88.

Meyer zur Capellen, Jürg 1985, *Gentile Bellini*, Stuttgart: Franz Steiner Verlag Wiesbaden.

Miyamoto, Gabriella R. 2008, 'The Ambo Of Henry II In The Aachen Palatine Chapel: The Use Of Multivalent Imagery To Express Divine And Temporal Legitimization', paper presented at the 43rd International Congress on Medieval Studies, Kalamazoo (forthcoming).

Molà, Luca, *La Comunità dei Lucchesi a Venezia. Immigrazione e Industria della Seta nel Tardo Medioevo*, Venezia: Istituto di Scienza, Lettere e Arti.

—— 2000, *The Silk Industry of Renaissance Venice*, Baltimore, London: Johns Hopkins University Press.

Mollat, Michel and Monique de la Roncière 1984, *Sea charts of the early explorers: 13th to 17th century*, New York: Thames and Hudson.

Monconys, Balthasar de 1973, *Le voyage en Egypte de Balthasar de Monconys 1646-1647*, presentation et notes d'Henry Amer, [Cairo]: L'institut français d'archéologie orientale du Caire.

Monfasani, John 1976, *George of Trebizond. A Biography and a Study of his Rhetoric and Logic*, Leiden: Brill.

―――― (ed.) 1984, *Collectanea Trapezuntiana. Texts, Documents, and Bibliographies of George of Trebizond*, Binghamton: Renaissance Society of America.
Monnas, Lisa 2008, *Merchants, Princes, and Painters: Silk Fabrics in Italian and Northern Paintings, 1300–1550*, New Haven and London: Yale University Press.
Monneret de Villard, U. 1946, 'Le chapiteau arabe de la cathédral de Pise', *Comptes-rendus des séances de l'Académie des Inscriptions et Belles-Lettres*, 90e année, n. 1, 17–23.
Münster, Sebastian 1540, *Geographia universalis, vetus et nova, complectens*. Basel.
Murphey, Rhoads 1983, 'The Ottoman Attitude towards the Adoption of Western Technology: the role of the *Efrenci* technicians in civil and military applications', in P. Dumont and J.L. Bacqué-Grammont (eds), *Contributions à l'Histoire Économique et Sociale de l'Empire Ottoman*, Louvain: Éditions Peeters, 287–298.
Mustafa Ali 1975, *Mustafā 'Alī's Description of Cairo of 1599*, Andreas Tietze, ed. and trans., Österreichische Akademie der Wissenschaften, Philosophisch-Historische Klasse Denkschriften, 120 Band, Wien: Verlag Österreichischen Akademie der Wissenschaften.
Nagel, Alexander 2011, 'Twenty-five notes on pseudoscript in Italian art', in *Res: Anthropology and Aesthetics* 59/60 (Spring/Autumn), 228–48.
National Museum in Cracow 1992, *The Orient in Polish Art, Catalogue of the Exhibition June–October 1992*, Cracow: National Museum in Cracow.
Neander, Michael 1586, *Chronicon sive Synopsis Historiarum*, Leipzig, 162r.
Necipoğlu, Gülrü 1989, 'Süleyman the Magnificent and the Representation of Power in the Context of Ottoman-Hapsburg-Papal Rivalry', *The Art Bulletin* 71 (September 1989), 401–27.
―――― 1990, 'From International Timurid to Ottoman: A Change of Taste in Sixteenth-Century Ceramic Tiles' in Margaret B. Sevcenko (ed.), *Muqarnas*, VII, 136–70.
―――― 1991, *Architecture, Ceremonial and Power: The Topkapı Palace in the Fifteenth and Sixteenth Centuries*, Cambridge, MA: The MIT Press.
―――― 1993, 'Challenging the Past; Sinan and the Competitive Discourse of Early Modern Islamic Architecture', in Margaret B. Sevcenko (ed.), *Muqarnas* X, 169–79.
―――― 1995, *The Topkapi Scroll – Geometry and Ornament in Islamic Architecture: Topkapı Palace Library MS H. 1956*, Santa Monica: Getty Center for the History of Art and the Humanities.
―――― 2005, *The Age of Sinan: Architectural Culture in the Ottoman Empire*, London: Reaktion Books.
―――― 2012, 'Visual Cosmopolitanism and Creative Translation: Artistic Conversations with Renaissance Italy in Mehmed II's Constantinople', *Muqarnas* 29, 1–81.
Newton, Stella Mary 1988, *The Dress of the Venetians*, Aldershot: Ashgate.
Neubauer, E. 2008, 'Īqā'. Musikalische Metrik bei al-Fārābī (gest. 950) und ihr Ebenbild bei Thoinot Arbeau (gest. 1595)', in B. Gruendler (ed., with the

assistance of M. Cooperson), *Classical Arabic humanities in their own terms. Festschrift for Wolfhart Heinrichs on his 65th birthday presented by his students and colleagues*, Leiden, Boston: Brill, 127–47.

Nicol, D.M. 1992, *The Immortal Emperor: The Life and Legend of Constantine Paliologos, last Emperor of the Romans*, Cambridge: Cambridge University Press.

Nicolet, Jean and Michel Tardieu 1980, 'Pletho Arabicus. Identification et Contenue du Manuscrit Arabe d'Istanbul, Topkapi seraî, Ahmet III 1896', *Journal Asiatique* 18, 35–57.

Nordenskjöld, E. 1910, 'Intorno all'influenza dei "Viaggi di Marco Polo" sulla carta dell'Asia di G. Gastaldi', *Rivista geografica italiana* VIII, 496–511.

Norton, Claire 2008, 'Nationalism and the Re-Invention of Early-Modern Identities in the Ottoman-Habsburg Borderlands', *Ethnologia Balkanica* 11, 79–101.

––– 2007, 'Conversion to Islam in the Ottoman Empire', *Wiener zeitschrift zur geschichte der neuzeit* 7/2, 25–39.

Norwich, John J. 1981, *Venice: The Greatness and the Fall*, London: Penguin Books.

Nuovo, Angela 1987, 'Il Corano Arabo Ritrovato (Venezia, P. e A. Paganini, tra l'agosto 1537 e l'agosto 1538)', *La Bibliofilia* LXXXIX/iii, 237–71.

––– 1990, 'A Lost Arabic Koran Rediscovered', *The Library* XII, no. 4 (December), 273–92.

Nuvoloni, L. 2000, 'Commissioni Dogali, Venetian Bindings in the British Library', in David Pearson (ed.), *For the Love of Binding, Studies in Bookbinding History presented to Mirjam Foot*, London: The British Library, 81–111.

Obelkevich, M.R. 1977, 'Turkish affect in the land of the Sun King', *The Musical Quarterly* 63/3, 367–89.

Ohta, Alison 2004, 'Filigree Bindings of the Mamluk Period', in Doris Behrens-Abouseif and Anna Contadini (eds), *Essays in Honor of J.M. Rogers, Muqarnas* 21, 267–76.

––– 2013, 'Binding Relationships: Mamluk, Ottoman and Renaissance bookbindings', in Anna Contadini and Claire Norton (eds), *The Renaissance and the Ottoman World*, Farnham: Ashgate, 221–30.

Orsi Landini, Roberta 2006, 'Tessuti turchi nella guardaroba medicea', in Chiara Lastrucci et al. (eds), *Intrecci Mediterranei, Il tessuto come dizionario di rapporti economici, culturali e sociali*, Prato: Museo del Tessuto, Edizioni, 36–41.

Orsi Landini, Roberta and Bruna Niccoli 2005, *Moda a Firenze 1540 - 1580*, Florence: Edizioni Polistampa.

Owens, J.A. 1990, 'Music historiography and the definition of "Renaissance"', *Notes* 47, 299–330.

Öz, Tahsin 1950, *Turkish Textiles and Velvets*, Ankara: Turkish Press, Broadcasting and Tourist Department.

Pacha, Yacoub Artin 1906, 'Les armes de l'Égypte aux XVe et XVIe siècles', *Bulletin de l'Institut Égyptien* 4th series, 7, 89–90.

Pagani, Zaccaria 1875, *Viaggio di Domenico Trevisan, Ambasciatore Veneto al Gran Sultano del Cairo nell'anno 1512, descritto da Zaccaria Pagani di Belluno*, Venice: Tipografia Antonelli.

Palisca, Claude V. 1985, *Humanism in Italian Renaissance musical thought*, New Haven: Yale University Press.

Papadakis, Aristeides 1972, 'Gennadius II und Mehmet the Conqueror', *Byzantion* 42, 88–106.

Paris, Robert 1957, *Histoire du commerce de Marseille*, vol 5, *Le Levant, de 1660 à 1789*, Paris: Plon.

Parker, Kenneth 1999, *Early Modern Tales of Orient, A Critical Anthology*, London: Routledge.

Pedani [Fabris], Maria Pia 1994, *In nome del Gran Signore. Inviati ottomani a Venezia dalla caduta di Costantinopoli alla Guerra di Candia*, Venice: Deputazione editrice.

――― 1996–1997, 'Simbologia Ottomana nell'Opera di Gentile Bellini', *Atti dell'Istituto Veneto di Scienze, Lettere, ed Arti* 155, 1–29.

――― 2008, 'Ottoman Merchants in Venice', in Suraiya Faroqhi and Gilles Veinstein (eds), *Merchants in the Ottoman Empire*, Paris, Louvain, Dudley, MA: Peeters, 3–21.

Pedersen, Johannes 1984, *The Arabic Book*, trans. Geoffrey Finch, Princeton: Princeton Univesity Press.

Peirce, Leslie 1993, *The Imperial Harem: Women and Sovereignty in the Ottoman Empire*, Oxford: Oxford University Press.

――― 2004, 'Changing Perceptions of the Ottoman Empire: the Early Centuries', *Mediterranean Historical Review* 19/1, 6–28.

Pellegrino, Francesco 1908, *La Fleur de la science de pourtraicture: façon arabicque et ytalique*, Paris: Jacques Niverd, 1530 (facsimile, Paris: Jean Schemit, 1908).

Pelusi, Simonetta 2000, 'Corano, in arabo', in Simonetta Pelusi (ed.), *La civiltà del Libro e la stampa a Venezia: Testi sacri ebraici, cristiani, islamici dal Quattrocento al Settecento*, Civiltà Veneziana Studi 51, Fondazione Giorgio Cini and Biblioteca Marciana, Padua: Il Poligrafo, 162, cat. 100.

Perkuhn, E.R. 1976, *Die Theorien zum arabischen Einfluss auf die europäische Musik des Mittelalters*, Beiträge zur Sprach- und Kulturgeschichte des Orients, 26, Walldorf-Hessen: Verlag für Orientkunde.

Perocco, Daria 1997, *Viaggiare e raccontare: Narrazione di viaggio ed esperienze di racconto tra Cinque e Seicento*, dell'Orso, Alessandria.

Perrault, Charles 1688, *Parallèle des Anciens et des Modernes en ce qui regarde les arts et les sciences...*, Paris.

Pertusi, A. 1970, 'I primi studi in Occidente sull'origine e la potenza dei Turchi', *Studi veneziani* 12, 465–552.

Peruzzi, E. 1997, 'Girolamo Fracastoro', *Dizionario Biografico degli Italiani*, Rome: Enciclopedia Italiana, vol. 49, 543–8.

Pfeiffer, G. 1968, *Studien zur Frühphase des europäischen Philhellenismus (1453-1750)*, Friedrich-Alexander University Erlangen-Nürnberg, PhD Thesis.

Piazza, Simone 2006, 'Vase with Falcons of Sayyid al-Malik al-Mansur', in M. Andaloro (ed.), *Nobiles Officinae: Perle, filigrane e trame di seta dal Palazzo Reale di Palermo*, 2 vols, Catania: Giuseppe Maimone, vol. 1, 615–16, cat. II.9.

Piccolomini, Æneas Silvius 1454, *Oratio ... de Constantinopolitan Clade et bello contra Turcos*, Frankfurt.

——— 1685, *Historia rerum Friderici tertii imperatoris*, Strasbourg: Staedel, Josias Staedel and Johann Friedrich Spoor.

——— 1990, *Epistola ad Mahomatem (Epistle to Mohammed II)*, ed. and trans. Albert R. Baca, New York: Peter Lang.

——— 1994, *Carmina*, A. van Heck (ed.), Vatican: Biblioteca Apostolica Vaticana.

Piemontese, Angelo Michele 1999, 'Le iscrizioni arabe nella *Poliphili Hypnerotomachia*', in Burnett and Contadini 1999, 199–220.

Pirenne, Henri 1939, *Mohammed and Charlemagne*, trans. Bernard Miall, London: George Allen & Unwin.

Pocock, J.G.A. 2005, *Barbarism and Religion. The First Decline and Fall*, volume 3, Cambridge: Cambridge University Press, 2005 (first edition 2003).

Polo, Marco 1496, *De le meravegliose cose del mondo*, Venice: G. B. Sessa (second edn. Venice: M. Sessa, 1508)

Postel, Guillaume 1560, *De la République des Turcs: & là ou l'occasion s'offrera, des moeurs & loy de tous muhamedistes*, Poitiers: Enguilbert de Marnef.

——— 1560b, *La Tierce Partie des orientales histoires, ou est exposée la condition, puissance, & revenu de l'Empire Turquesque*, Poitiers.

Praetorius, Michael 1884, *Syntagma, II. Teil. Von den Instrumenten*, Wolfenbüttel, 1618, Neuer Abdruck, Berlin: Trautwein.

Preto, Paolo 1975, *Venezia e i turchi*, Firenze: G.C. Sansoni.

Ptolemaeus, Claudius 1966, *Geographia*, ed. Sebastian Münster, with an Introduction by R. A. Skelton, Amsterdam: Theatrum Orbis Terrarum Ltd., 1st ed. Basle 1540.

Ptolemy 1475, *Geographia*, Vicenza: Hermannus Levilapide.

——— 1548, *La geografia di Claudio Ptolemeo Alessandrino*, Venice: Giovanni Battista Pedrezano.

Pulido-Rull, Ana 2012, 'A Pronouncement of Alliance: An Anonymous Illuminated Venetian Manuscript for Sultan Süleyman', *Muqarnas* 29, 101–50.

Raby, Julian 1980, 'Cyriacus of Ancona and the Ottoman Sultan Mehmed II', *Journal of the Warburg and Courtauld Institutes* 43, 242–6.

——— 1981, *El Gran Turko. Mehmed the Conqueror as a Patron of the Arts of Christendom*, 3 vols, PhD thesis, University of Oxford.

——— 1982, 'A Sultan of Paradox: Mehmed the Conqueror as a patron of the arts', *Oxford Art Journal* 5/1, 3–8.

——— 1982b, *Venice, Dürer and the Oriental Mode*, London: Islamic Art Publications.

——— 1983, 'Mehmed the Conqueror's Greek Scriptorium', *Dumbarton Oaks Papers* 37, 15–62.

—— 1985, 'Exotica from Islam', in Oliver Impey and Arthur Macgregor (eds), *The Origins of Museums: the Cabinet of Curiosities in Sixteenth- and Seventeenth-Century Europe*, Oxford: Clarendon Press, 251–8.

—— 1987, 'East & West in Mehmed the Conqueror's Library', *Bulletin du Bibliophile* 3, 296–318.

—— 1989, 'The European Vision of the Muslim Orient in the Sixteenth Century', in Grube, Carboni and Curatola 1989, 41–6.

—— 2000, 'From Europe to Istanbul', in Filiz Çagman (ed.), *The Sultan's Portrait: Picturing the House of Osman*, Istanbul: İşbank, 136–63.

Raby, Julian and Z. Tanındı 1993, *Turkish Bookbinding in the 15th Century*, London: Azimuth Editions.

Ramberti, Benedetto 1539, *Libri tre delle cose de Turchi*, Venice: In casa de' figlioli di Aldo.

—— 1542, *The order of the greate Turckes courte, of hys mene of warre, and of all his conquests, with the summe of Mahumetes doctrine*, translated out of the French, [London]: Ricardus Grafton.

Ramusio, Gian Battista (ed.) 1583, 'Viaggio di un mercante che fu nella Persia', in *Navigationi et viaggi*, vol. II, Venice: fols 78a–91a.

—— 1967–1970, *Navigazioni et viaggi, Venice 1563–1606*, introd. R. A. Skelton and George B. Parks, 3 vols, Amsterdam: Theatrum Orbis Terrarum.

Rawson, Jessica 1984, *Chinese Ornament: the Lotus and the Dragon*, London: British Museum.

Reinhard, Kurt and Ursula Reinhard 1984, *Musik der Türkei, 1: Die Kunstmusik*, Wilhelmshaven: Heinrichshofen.

Reinsch, D. 1994, 'Editionen und Rezeption byzantinischer Historiker durch deutsche Humanisten', in H. Eideneier (ed), *Graeca recentiora in Germania: Deutsch-griechische Kulturbeziehungen vom 15. bis 19. Jahrhundert*, Wiesbaden: Harrassowitz, 47–63.

Riant, Paul-Edouard-Didier, Comte 1875, 'Des dépouilles religieuses enlevées à Constantinople au XIIIe siècle et des documents historiques nés de leur transport en Occident', *Mémoires de la Société Nationale des Antiquaires de France* 36 (series 4, 6), 1–214.

—— 1885, 'La part de l'évêque de Bethléem dans le butin de Constantinople en 1204', *Mémoires de la Société Nationale des Antiquaires de France* 46 (series 5, 6), 225–37.

Richards, G.R.B. (ed.) 1932, *Florentine Merchants in the Age of the Medici*, Cambridge, MA.

Ridolfi, Carlo 1914–24, *Le maraviglie dell'arte, ovvero Le vite degli illustri pittori veneti e dello stato*, 2 vols, ed. Detlev von Hadeln, Berlin: G. Grote.

Rizzo, Adriana 2007, 'Venetian "Lacquer": A Scientific Approach', in Carboni 2007, 244–51.

Robertson, Giles 1954, *Vincenzo Catena*, Edinburgh: University of Edinburgh.

Robinson, B.W. 1967, 'Oriental Metalwork in the Gambier-Parry Collection', *The Burlington Magazine* 109, no. 768 (March), 167–71, 173.

Roellenbleck, G. 1964, *Offenbarung, Natur und jüdische Überlieferung bei Jean Bodin: eine Interpretation des Heptaplomeres*, Gütersloh: G. Mohn.

Rogers, J.M. 1986, *The Topkapi Saray Museum: Costumes, Embroideries, and Other Textiles*, London: Thames and Hudson, translated, expanded, and edited by J.M. Rogers from the original Turkish by Hülye Tezcan and Selma Delibaş.

―――― 1990, Review of *Arte veneziana e arte islamica: atti del primo simposio internazionale sull'arte veneziana e l'arte islamica*, The Burlington Magazine August, 576–7.

―――― 1992, 'Ḳara Meḥmed Çelebi (Ḳara Memi) and the Role of the *Ser-naḳḳâşân*', in Gilles Veinstein (ed.), *Soliman le magnifique et son temps*, Paris: École du Louvre, École des Hautes Etudes en Sciences Sociales, 227–38.

―――― 1993, 'The arts under Süleyman the magnificent', in H. İnalcık and C. Kafadar (eds), *Süleyman the Second and his time*, Istanbul: Isis, 257–94.

―――― 1998, Review of *Islam Christianized: Islamic Portable Objects in the Medieval Churches of the Latin West* by Avinoam Shalem, Bulletin of the School of Oriental and African Studies, University of London 61, no. 1, 134–5.

―――― 1999, 'Ornaments, Prints, Patterns and Designs: East and West', in Burnett and Contadini 1999, 133–65.

―――― 2002, 'Europe and the Ottoman Arts: Foreign Demand and Ottoman Consumption', in Michele Bernardini et al. (eds), *Europa e islam tra i secoli XIV e XVI = Europe and Islam Between the 14th and 16th centuries*, 2 vols, Naples, vol. 2, 709–36.

―――― 2005–2006, 'Mehmed the Conqueror: Between East and West', in Campbell and Chong 2005–2006, 80–97.

Rogers, J. M. and Rachel Ward 1988, *Süleyman the Magnificent*, London: British Museum Publications.

Rose, P. L. 1980, *Bodin and the Great God of Nature: The Moral and Religious Universe of a Judaiser*, Geneva: Librairie Droz.

Rothenberg, Gunther Erich 1960, *The Austrian Military Border in Croatia, 1522-1747*, Urbana, IL: University of Illinois Press.

Rouillard, C. D. 1938, *The Turk in French history, thought, and literature (1520–1660)*, Paris: Boivin.

Rowlands, Eliot 1996, *The Collections of the Nelson-Atkins Museum of Art. Italian Paintings 1300–1800*, Kansas City: Nelson-Atkins Museum of Art.

Runciman, Stephen 1963, *The Fall of Constantinople 1453*, Cambridge: Cambridge University Press.

―――― 1968, *The Great Church in Captivity*, Cambridge: Cambridge University Press.

Rycaut, Paul 1682, *The history of the present state of the Ottoman empire*, 5th ed., London.

Ṣafī al-Dīn al-Urmawī 1980, *Kitāb al-adwār*, ed. al-Rajab, Baghdad: manšūrāt wizārat al-ṯaqāfa wa-l-iʻlām, ed. Ḥašaba and al-Ḥifnī, Cairo, 1986; facsimile in Publications of the Institute for the history of Arabic-Islamic science, series

C, 29, Frankfurt 1986; tr. in D'Erlanger, R., *La musique arabe*, 3, Paris: Geuthner, 1938, 185–565.
Said, Edward 1978, *Orientalism*, London: Routledge and Kegan Paul (and New York: Random House).
Sakisian A. 1934, 'La reliure dans la Perse occidentale sous les Mongols au XIVe siècle au début du XVe siècle', *Ars Islamica* I, 180–91.
Sannazzaro, Giovanni Battista 1982, *Leonardo a Milano*, Milano: Rusconi Libri.
Sansovino, Francesco 1573, *Gli Annali Turcheschi overo Vite de' Principi della Casa Othomana*, Venice.
——— 1581, *Venetia città nobilissima et singolare*, ed. Giacomo Sansovino, Venice.
——— 1604, *Venetia città nobilissima et singolare*, ed. Giovanni Stringa, Venice.
——— 1663, *Venetia, città nobilissima, et singolare*, ed. D. Giustiniano Martinioni, Venice.
Sanudo, Marin 1879–1903, *I diarii di Marin Sanuto*, Rinaldo Fulin et al. (eds), 58 vols, Venice.
Sauvaget, Jean 1945–1946, 'Une ancienne representation de Damas au Musée du Louvre', *Bulletin d'Études Orientales* 11, 5–12.
Saxl, Fritz et al. 1987, *Il Libro del Sarto della Fondazione Querini Stampalia di Venezia*, facsimile edition, Modena: Panini.
Schaeder, H. (ed.) 1958, *Wort und Mysterium: Der Briefwechsel über Glaube und Kirche 1573 bis 1581 zwischen den Tübinger Theologen und dem Patriarchen von Konstantinopel*, Witten: Luther-Verlag.
Schéfer, Charles 1895, 'Note sur un tableau du Louvre naguère attribute à Gentile Bellini', *Gazette des Beaux-Arts* 14, 201–204.
Schiaparelli, C. 1871, *Vocabulista in Arabico*, Firenze: Tipografia dei Successori Le Monnier.
Schmidt, Benjamin 2001, *The Dutch Imagination and the New World, 1570–1670*, Cambridge: Cambridge University Press.
Schmidt, Heinrich 1963, 'Morgenländische und abendländische Seidenmuster im Mittelalter', in Oktay Aslanapa (ed.), *Beiträge zur Kunstgeschichte Asiens, In memoriam Ernst Diez*, Istanbul: İstanbul Üniversitesi Edebiyat Fakültesi, 193–207.
Schmidt Arcangeli, Caterina 2007, '"Orientalist" Painting in Venice, 15th – 17th Centuries', in Carboni 2007, 120–39.
Schmidt Arcangeli, Catarina and Gerhard Wolf 2010, *Islamic Artefacts in the Mediterranean World: Trade, Gift Exchange and Artistic Transfer*, Venezio: Marsilio.
Schnitzler, H. 1957, *Rheinische Schatzkammer*, Düsseldorf: L. Schwann.
Schorske, C.E. 1981, *Fin-de-siècle Vienna: Politics and culture*, New York: Vintage.
Schuckelt, Holger and Claudia Schnitzer (eds), 1995, *Im Lichte des Halbmonds, Das Abendland und der türkische Orient*, Dresden and Bonn/Germany: Staatliche Kunstsammlungen Dresden and Kunst- und Ausstellungshalle der Bundesrepublik Deutschland.

Schweigger, Salomon 1964, *Ein newe Reyssbeschreibung auss Teutschland nach Konstantinopel und Jerusalem*, Nürnberg, Lautzenburgen, 1608, facsimile Graz: Akademische Druck- u. Verlagsanstalt.

Sella, Domenico 1968, 'The Rise and Fall of the Venetian Woollen Industry', in Brian Pullan (ed.), *Crisis and Change in the Venetian Economy in the Sixteenth and Seventeenth Centuries*, London: Methuen & Co Ltd., 106–26.

Sellheim, Rudolf 1968, 'Die Madonna mit der Schahāda', in Erwin Gräf (ed.), *Festschrift Werner Caskel: zum siebzigsten Geburtstag 5. März 1966. Gewidmet von Freunden und Schülern*, Leiden: Brill, S. 307 ff.

Seydī 2004, *Seydī's book on music. A 15th century Turkish discourse*, translated, annotated and edited by E. Popescu-Judetz in collaboration with E. Neubauer (The Science of Music in Islam, 6), Frankfurt am Main: Institute for the History of Arabic-Islamic Science at the Johann Wolfgang Goethe University.

Shalem, Avinoam 1996, *Islam Christianized: Islamic Portable Objects in the Medieval Churches of the Latin West*, Frankfurt am Main: Peter Lang.

——— 1996b, 'A Note on the Shield-Shaped Ornamental Bosses on the Façade of Bāb al-Nasr in Cairo', *Ars Orientalis* 26, 55–64.

Sievernich, Gereon and Hendrik Budde (eds) 1989, *Europa und der Orient 800–1900*, Berlin: Berliner Festspiele, Bertelsmann Lexikon Verlag.

Silvius, Enea 1967, *Opera Omnia*, Basel, 1571; Faks. Ausgabe Frankfurt am Main.

Siraisi, Nancy G. 1990, *Medieval & Early Renaissance Medicine: an Introduction to Knowledge and Practice*, Chicago and London: University of Chicago Press.

Soly, H. and J. Van de Wiele (eds) 2000, *Carolus: Charles Quint 1500*–1558, Ghent.

Sokoly, Jochen 1997, 'Towards a model of early Islamic textile institutions in Egypt', *Islamische Textilkunst des Mittelalters: Aktuelle Probleme*, Riggisberg: Die Stiftung, 115–21.

Southern, R. W. 1962, *Western Views of Islam in the Middle Ages*, Cambridge, MA: Harvard.

Soykut, Mustafa 2001, *Image of the "Turk" in Italy: A History of the "Other" in Early Modern Europe: 1453-1683*, Islamkundliche Untersuchungen, Band 236, Berlin: Klaus Schwarz Verlag.

Spallanzani, Marco 1989, 'Fonti archivistiche per lo studio dei rapporti fra l'Italia e l'Islam: le arti minori nei secoli XIV–XVI', in Grube, Carboni and Curatola 1989, 83–100.

——— 1997, *Ceramiche Orientali a Firenze nel Rinascimento*, 2nd ed. Firenze: Libreria Chiari.

——— 2007, *Oriental Rugs in Renaissance Florence*, The Bruschettini Foundation for Islamic and Asian Art, Textile Studies I, Florence: S.P.E.S.

——— 2010, *Metalli islamici a Firenze nel Rinascimento*, Florence: S.P.E.S.

Speer, Andreas, and Lydia Wegener (eds) 2006, *Wissen über Grenzen. Arabisches Wissen und lateinisches Mittelalter*, Berlin: De Gruyter.

Springborg, Patricia 1992, *Western Republicanism and the Oriental Prince*, Austin: University of Texas Press.

Stein, Mark 2007, *Guarding the Frontier: Ottoman Border Forts and Garrisons in Europe*, London: Tauris Academic Studies.
Strohm, R. and B.T. Blackburn (eds) 2001, *Music as concept and practice in the late Middle Ages* (New Oxford history of music, vol. III/i), Oxford: Oxford University Press.
Strohmaier, Gotthard 1998, 'Die Griechen waren keine Europäer', in Eckhard Höfner and Falk Peter Weber (eds), *Politia Litteraria. Festschrift für Horst Heintze zum 75. Geburtstag*, Berlin: Galda + Wilch, 198–206, reprinted in Strohmaier, Gotthard, *Hellas im Islam: interdisziplinäre Studien zur Ikonographie, Wissenschaft und Religionsgeschichte*, Wiesbaden: Harrassowitz, 2003, 1–6.
Stussi, Alfredo (ed.) 1967, *Zibaldone da Canal, Manoscritto mercantile del sec. XIV*, Venice: Fonti per la Storia di Venezia.
Suchland, K.H. 2001, *Das Byzanzbild des Tübinger Philhellenen Martin Crusius (1526-1607)* Julius-Maximilians University, Würzburg, PhD Thesis.
Suger, Abbot of Saint-Denis 1946, *Abbot Suger: On the Abbey Church of St.-Denis and its Art Treasures*, edited, translated and annotated by Erwin Panofsky, Princeton.
——— 1996, *Oeuvres*, translated by Françoise Gasparri, Paris: Les Belles Lettres.
Suriano, Carlo Maria and Stefano Carboni 1999, *La seta islamica/Islamic silk*, Florence: Museo del Bargello/9th International Conference on Carpets.
Szakály, Ferenc 1994, 'The Early Ottoman Period, Including Royal Hungary, 1526–1606', in Peter Sugar et al. (eds), *A History of Hungary*, Bloomington: Indiana University Press, 83–99.
Tait, Hugh 1999, 'Venice: Heir to the Glassmakers of Islam or Byzantium?', in Burnett and Contadini 1999, 77–104.
Tambrun-Krasker, Brigitte (ed.) 1995, *Oracles Chaldaïques: Recension de Georges Gémiste Pléthon*, Athens: Academy of Athens.
Tanaka, Hidemichi 1989, 'Oriental Scripts in the Paintings of Giotto's Period', *Gazette des Beaux-Arts* 113, 214–26.
——— 1994, 'La testimonianza estremorientale nella pittura italiana nell'epoca di Giotto', in Maria Teresa Lucidi (ed.), *La seta e la sua via*, Roma: Edizioni De Luca, 129–32.
Tanındı, Z. 1990, 'Topkapı Sarayi Müzesi Kütüphanesi'nde Ortaçağ Islam Ciltleri', *Topkapı Sarayi Müzesi* 4, 102–49.
——— 2012, 'Two Bibliophile Emirs: Qansuh the Master of the Stables and Yashbak the Secretary', in Doris Behrens-Abouseif (ed.), *The Arts of the Mamluks in Egypt and Syria-Evolution and Impact*, Bonn: University of Bonn, 267–83.
Tarawneh, Taha Thalji 1994, *The Province of Damascus during the Second Mamluk Period (784/1382-922/1516)*, Al Karak: Mu'tah University.
Taruskin, R. 2005, *The Oxford history of Western music*, Oxford: Oxford University.
Taylor, T.D. 2007, *Beyond exoticism. Western music and the world*, Durham and London: Duke University Press.

Teunissen, Harrie and John Steegh 2003, *Balkan In Kaart: Vijf eeuwen strijd om identiteit*. Catalogus bij een tentoonstelling in de Universiteitsbibliotheek Leiden, 4 September – 16 Oktober 2003, Leiden: Universiteitsbibliotheek.

Tezcan, Hülya 2004, 'Furs and Skins Owned by the Sultans', in Suraiya Faroqhi and Christoph Neumann (eds), *Ottoman Costumes, From Textile to Identity*, Istanbul: Eren, 63–79.

Thenaud, Jean 1884, *Le voyage d'outremer de Jean Thenaud, suivi de la relation de l'Ambassade de Domenico Trevisan auprès du Soudan d'Egypte*, ed. Charles Schéfer, Paris.

Thevenot, Jean de 1664, Relation d'un voyage fait au Levant, Paris: Claude Barbin.

Thomas, Joe A. 1994, 'Fabric and Dress in Bronzino's Portrait of Eleanor of Toledo and Son Giovanni', *Zeitschrift für Kunstgeschichte*, 57. Bd., H. 2, 262–267.

Thornton, Dora 1997, *The Scholar in His Study. Ownership and Experience in Renaissance Italy*, New Haven and London: Yale University Press.

Thornton, Peter 1991, *The Italian Renaissance Interior 1400-1600*, London: Weidenfeld and Nicolson.

Tolias, George 1999, *The Greek Portolan Charts. 15th-17th centuries. A contribution to the Mediterranean cartography of the modern period*, Athens: Olkos.

Tomlinson, Gary 1999, 'Vico's songs: detours at the origins of (ethno)musicology', *The Musical Quarterly*, 344–77, repr. in G. Tomlinson, *Music and historical critique*, Aldershot: Ashgate, 2007, 197–230

Tooley, M. J. 1953, 'Bodin and the Medieval Theory of Climate', *Speculum* 28, 64–83.

Tooley, R.V. 1939, 'Maps in Italian Atlases of the Sixteenth Century, Being a Comparative List of the Italian Maps Issued by Lafreri, Forlani, Duchetti, Bertelli, and Others, Found in Atlases', *Imago Mundi*, 3, 12–47.

Torquemada, Juan de 1615, *Los veintiún libros rituales y Monarchia Indiana, con el origen y guerras de los indios occidentales*, Seville.

Tucci, Ugo 1981, *Mercanti, navi, monete nel Cinquecento veneziano*, Bologna.

—— 1980, 'Mercanti, viaggiatori, pellegrini nel Quattrocento', in *Storia della cultura veneta*, III/II, *Del Primo quattrocento al Concilio di Trento*, Vicenza: Neri Pozza, 317–53.

Turan, Ebru 2006, *The Sultan's Favorite: Ibrahim Paşa and the Making of Ottoman Universal Sovereignty in the Reign of Sultan Süleyman*, unpublished PhD dissertation, University of Chicago.

Turbet-Delof, G. 1974, 'Jean Bodin lecteur de "Léon d'Afrique"', *Neohelicon: acta comparationis litterarum universarum*, 2/1–2, 201–16.

Turner, C. J. G. 1969, 'The Career of George-Gennadius Scholarios', *Byzantion* 39, 420–55.

Ullman, Berthold L. and Philip A. Stadter 1972, *The Public Library of Renaissance Florence. Niccolò Niccoli, Cosimo De' Medici and the Library of San Marco*, Padua: Editrice Antenore.

Urbani, Maria da Villa 2008, 'The Virgin's Grotto', in Robin Cormack and Maria Vassilaki (eds), *Byzantium: 330-1453*, London: Royal Academy of Arts, 122–23, 396, cat. 64.
Valensi, Lucette 1993, *The Birth of the Despot: Venice and the Sublime Porte* trans. A. Denner, New York and London: Ithaca.
Valle, Pietro della 1843, *Viaggi di Pietro della Valle e il pellegrinaggio descritti da lui medesimo in lettere familiari all'erudito suo amico Mario Schipano divisi in tre parte cioè: la Turchia, la Persia e l'India*, vol. 1, Brighton: Garcia, 47–50.
Vallet, Eric 1999, *Marchands vénetiens en Syrie à la fin du XVe siècle*, Paris: Association pour le développement de l'histoire économique.
Vecellio, Cesare 1590, *De gli habiti antichi, et moderni di diverse parti del mondo*, Venice.
Venezia, Comune di 1954, *VII Centenario della nascita di Marco Polo: Il commercio veneziano e l'Oriente*, exh. cat. Venice: Archivio di Stato di Venezia.
Vercellin, Giorgio 2000, 'Venezia e le origini della stampa in caratteri arabi', in Simonetta Pelusi (ed.), *La civiltà del Libro e la stampa a Venezia: Testi sacri ebraici, cristiani, islamici dal Quattrocento al Settecento*, Civiltà Veneziana Studi 51, Fondazione Giorgio Cini and Biblioteca Marciana, Padua: Il Poligrafo, 53–64.
Vicentino, Nicola 1555, *L'antica musica ridotta alla moderna prattica*, Rome: Antonio Barre.
Victoria & Albert Museum (V&A) 1923, *Brief Guide to the Turkish Woven Fabrics*, London.
——— 1931, *Brief Guide to the Turkish Woven Fabrics*, 2nd edition, London.
——— 1950, *Brief Guide to the Turkish Woven Fabrics*, revised edition, London.
——— 2004, *Palace and Mosque*, London.
Vitkus, Daniel 2003, *Turning Turk: English Theater and the Multicultural Mediterranean, 1570-1630*, Houndmills: Palgrave.
van der Krogt, Peter 2003, *Koeman's Atlantes Neerlandici*, v. 3, *Ortelius's Theatrum Orbis Terrarum, De Jode's Speculum Orbis Terrarum...*, Utrecht: Universiteit Utrecht.
von Martels, Zweder 2003, 'The *Studia humanitatis* and the *Studia divina*: the Role of Ethics and the Authority of Antiquity', in Z. von Martels and V. M. Schmidt (eds), *Antiquity Renewed. Late-Classical and Early-Modern themes*, Leuven: Peeters, 185–210.
——— 2005, 'Pope Pius II and the Idea of the Appropriate. Thematisation of the Self', in Martin Gosman, Alasdair MacDonald and Arjo Vanderjagt (eds), *Princes and Princely Culture 1450-1650*, vol. II, Leiden: Brill, 1–21.
——— 2013, 'Old and New Demarcation Lines between Christian Europe and the Islamic Ottoman Empire: from Pope Pius II (1458–1464) to Pope Benedict XVI (2005–)', in Anna Contadini and Claire Norton (eds), *The Renaissance and the Ottoman World*, Farnham: Ashgate, 169–80.
von Wilckens, Leonie 1991, *Die textilen Künste von der Spätantike bis um 1500*, München: C.H. Beck.

Wace, A.J.B. and Muriel Clayton 1938, 'A tapestry at Powis Castle', *The Burlington Magazine* 73, 64–9.
Wansbrough, John 1965, 'Venice and Florence in Mamluk commercial privileges', *Bulletin of the School of Oriental and African Studies* 28, 483–523.
Ward, R. 1993, *Islamic Metalwork*, London: British Museum.
Ward, R., S. La Niece, D.R. Hook and R. White 1995, 'Veneto-Saracenic Metalwork: an Analysis of the Bowls and Incense Burners in the British Museum', in D.R. Hook and D.R.M. Gaimster (eds), *Trade and Discovery: The Scientific Study of Artefacts from Post-Medieval Europe and Beyond*, BM Occasional Paper 109, London: British Museum Press.
Wardwell, A.E. 1989, 'Panni Tartarici: Eastern Islamic Silks woven with gold and silver', *Islamic Art* III, 95–173.
Wearden, Jennifer 1985, 'Siegmund von Herberstein: An Italian Velvet in the Ottoman Court', *Costume – The Journal of the Costume Society* 19, 22–9.
Weinmann, Karl (ed.) 1917, *Johannes Tinctoris (1445-1511) und sein unbekannter Traktat "De inventione et usu musicae"*, Regensburg: F. Pustet.
Weitzmann, Kurt and Herbert Kessler 1986, *The Cotton Genesis: British Library Codex Cotton Otho BVI*, Princeton.
Wellesz, Egon (ed.) 1957, *New Oxford history of music*, vol.1, Ancient and Oriental Music, London: Oxford University Press.
Wendebourg, D. 1986, *Reformation und Orthodoxie: Der ökumenische Briefwechsel zwischen der Leitung der Württembergischen Kirche und Patriarch Jeremias II. von Konstantinopel in den Jahren 1573-1581*, Göttingen, Vandenhoeck & Ruprecht.
Wentzel, Hans 1971, 'Das byzantinische Erbe der ottonischen Kaiser Hypothesen über den Brautschatz der Theophano', *Aachener Kunstblätter* 40, 15–39.
—— 1972, 'Das byzantinische Erbe der ottonischen Kaiser Hypothesen über den Brautschatz der Theophano', *Aachener Kunstblätter* 43, 11–96.
—— 1973, 'Byzantinische Kleinkunstwerke aus dem Umkreis der Kaiserin Theophano', *Aachener Kunstblätter* 44, 43–86.
Wessely, Kurt 1973-1974, 'The Development of the Hungarian Military Frontier until the Middle of the Eighteenth Century', *The Austrian History Yearbook* 9-10, 55–110.
Westermann-Angerhausen, H. 1995, 'Did Theophano Leave Her Mark on the Ottonian Sumptuary Arts?', in Adelbert Davids (ed.), *The Empress Theophano: Byzantium and the West at the Turn of the First Millennium*, Cambridge: Cambridge University Press, 244–64.
Wilson, Bronwen 2005, *The World in Venice: Print, the City, and Early Modern Identity*, Toronto: University of Toronto Press.
Wisnovsky, Robert 2004, 'The Nature and Scope of Arabic Philosophical Commentary in Post-Classical (ca. 1100–1900). Islamic Intellectual History: Some Preliminary Observations', in Peter Adamson, Han Baltussen and M.W.F. Stone (eds), *Philosophy, Science and Exegesis in Greek, Arabic and Latin Commentaries*, 2 vols, London: Institute for Classical Studies, ii, 149–91.

Wolkan, Rudolf (ed.) 1909-1918, *Der Briefwechsel des Eneas Silvius Piccolomini*, Fontes rerum Austriacarum: Österreichische Geschichtsquellen. 2. Abt., Diplomataria et Acta, 61-62, 67-8.

Woodfield, I. 1990, 'The keyboard recital in oriental diplomacy, 1520-1620', *Journal of the Royal Musical Association* 115/1, 33-62.

Woodward, David 1980, 'The Study of the Italian map trade in the sixteenth century: needs and opportunities', in Cornelis Koeman (ed.), *Land- und Seekarten im Mittelalter und in der frühen Neuzeit*, München: Kraus International, 137-46.

——— review of Günter Schilder's *Monumenta Cartographica Neerlandica*, Volume 2: located at http://www.swaen.com/monumenta.html (retrieved on 6 September 2012).

Wright, Owen 1992, 'Music in Muslim Spain', in Salma Khadra Jayyusi (ed.), *The legacy of Muslim Spain* (Handbuch der Orientalistik, Abteilung 1: Der nahe und mittlere Osten, Band 12), Leiden: Brill, 555-79.

——— 2011, 'How French is *frenkçin?*', *Journal of the Royal Asiatic Society* Series 3, 21/3, 261-81.

——— 2013, 'Turning a Deaf Ear', in Anna Contadini and Claire Norton (eds), *The Renaissance and the Ottoman World*, Farnham: Ashgate, 143-65.

Ydema, O. 1991, *Carpets and Their Datings in Netherlandish Paintings 1540-1700*, Leiden: Antique Collectors' Club.

Yekta Bey, Rauf 1922, 'La musique turque', in *Encyclopédie de la musique* (Lavignac), vol. 1, Paris: C. Delagrave, 2945-3064.

Yérasimos, Stefanos 1997, 'De la Collection des voyages à l'histoire universelle: la *Historia universale de' Turchi* de Francesco Sansovino', in Yérasimos, Stefanos, *Hommes et idées dans l'espace ottoman*, Istanbul: Isis, 49-68.

Yildirim, Onur 2007, 'The Battle of Lepanto and Its Impact on Ottoman History and Historiography', in Rossella Cancila (ed.), *Mediterraneo in armi (secc. XV-XVIII)*, Palermo: Associazione Mediterranea, 533-56.

Zäh, H. 1997, 'Wolfgang Musculus und der Verkauf griechischer Handschriften für die Augsburger Stadtbibliothek 1543/44', in R. Dellsperger, R. Freudenberger and W. Weber (eds), *Wolfgang Musculus (1497-1563) und die oberdeutsche Reformation*, Augsburg: Akademie Verlag, 226-45.

Zarcone, Thierry (ed.) 1988, *Individu et société*, Istanbul: Éditions ISIS.

Zarlino, Gioseffo 1558, *Le institutioni harmoniche*, pt. 1, Venice.

Zeitler, B. 1997, '"Sinful sons, falsifiers of the Christian faith": the depiction of Muslims in a "crusader" manuscript', *Mediterranean Historical Review* 12/2, 25-50.

Zimolo, Giulio C. 1964, *Le Vite di Pio II / di Giovanni Antonio Campano e Bartolomeo Platina*, Raccolta degli storici italiani dal Cinquecento al Millecinquecento, Bologna : Zanichelli.

Zorzi, Marino (ed.) 1988, *Biblioteca Marciana Venezia*, Firenze: Nardini.

——— (ed.) 2003, *La vita nei libri: edizioni illustrate a stampa del Quattro e Cinquecento dalla Fondazione Giorgio Cini*, Venice: Edizioni della Laguna, Biblioteca Nazionale Marciana.

Manuscript Sources

OWEN WRIGHT

Cantigas de Santa Maria for Alfonso X, Spain, thirteenth century. Madrid, Biblioteca Real, San Lorenzo del Escorial, MS T.I.1.

Anon., *Histoire universelle*, late thirteenth century, Acre. London, British Library MS Add. 15268.

Anon., *Tractatus de septem vitiis*, probably late fourteenth century, Genoa. London, British Library, Ms Add. 27695.

Ali Ufki, no title, datable to the mid-seventeenth century. Paris, Bibliothèque Nationale de France, Ms. Turc 292.

Ali Ufki, *Mecmua-ı saz ü söz*, ca. 1650. London, British Library Ms. Sloane 3114.

Plato charms the animals, Nizami, *Khamsa*, Lahore (?), 1004 AH/1595 AD. London, British Library Ms. Or. 12208, fol. 298r.

ALISON OHTA

L. Bruni, *Commentarius rerum in Italia suo tempore gestarum*, Bologna?, 1464–1465. Venice, Biblioteca Marciana, Lat.X, 117 (=3844), 19.7 × 11.9 cm.

W. Burley, *De vita et moribus philosophorum*, 1453. Venice, Biblioteca Marciana, Lat. VI 270 (=3671), 14 × 20 cm.

Cicero, *Epistolae ad familares*, Venice, 1475. Paris, Bibliothèque National de France, Vélins 1149.

Commission, Venice, 1500. Venice, Biblioteca Marciana Ms.It.VII, 597 (=7820), 26 × 17.7 cm.

Commission, Venice, 1571. Venice, Biblioteca Marciana, Ms.It.VII, 1366 (=8092), 23.4 × 15.4 cm.

Commission, Venice, 1571. London, British Library, Egerton Ms.757 cm, 23.4 × 15.4 cm.

Dimyati, *Mashāri' al-ashwāq ilā maṣāri' al-'ushshāq*, Cairo, 1490. Istanbul, Topkapı Palace Library, Ms.A.649/1, 36.5 × 26 cm.

Divan of Sultan Ahmed Jalayir, 1406. Istanbul, Museum for Turkish and Islamic Art, Ms. 2046, 27.1 × 18.3 cm.

Fra Giocondo, *Sylloge*, Venice, ca.1520–1530. Chatsworth Library, Chatsworth House, Derbyshire, 25.1 × 15.9 cm.

Hamza b. Hasan al-Isfahani, *Tārīkh-i Iṣfahān*, 1431. London, British Library, Or.2773, 23 × 14 cm.

G. Marcanova, *Collectio Antiquitatum*, Bologna, ca.1464–1465. Modena, Biblioteca Estense, Cod. Alfa, L.5.15.
Petrarch, *Canzoniere and Trionfi*, Florence, 1460–1470. Oxford, Bodleian, Ms.Canon. Ital.78, 21.8 × 13.8 cm.
Sūrat al-anʿām, Istanbul, ca. 1480. Istanbul, Topkapı Palace Library, Ms. B.29, 21 × 14 cm.
Jacopo Tiraboschi, *Carmina*, Padua, ca. 1471, Codex Lippomano. Private Collection, 17.3 × 11.8 cm.
Qadi Ayyad, *Al-Shifā' fī ta'rīf ḥuqūq al-Muṣṭafā*, Cairo, 1391. Istanbul, Topkapı Palace Library, Ms. A. 317, 27 × 17.5 cm.
Qur'an, Cairo, ca. 1481–1496. Istanbul, Museum of Turkish and Islamic Art, TIEM 508, 62 × 38 cm.
Qur'an, Ottoman, 1536. Venice, Biblioteca Marciana, Orientali 68.
Yusuf bin Abd al-Hadi (Ibn al-Mabrid), *Al-Durrat al-muḍiyya wa'l-ʿarūs al-marḍiyya*, 1484. Istanbul, Topkapı Palace Library, Ms.A.2829, 32 × 21.5 cm.

SURAIYA FAROQHI

Başbakanlık Arşivi-Osmanlı Arşivi (BOA), *Düvel-i ecnebiye Defterleri* 13/1, p. 93, No. 460 (Cemaziyelevvel 1021/ July 1612).
BOA, *Düvel-i ecnebiye Defterleri* 13/1, p. 97, No. 481 (Ramazan 1021).
BOA, *Düvel-i ecnebiye Defterleri* 13/1, p. 88, No. 436 (Safer 1021).
BOA, *Düvel-i ecnebiye Defterleri* 13/1, p. 86, No. 420 (Zilhicce 1020).

Maps

PALMIRA BRUMMETT

Camocio, Giovanni Francesco, 1574, *Isole famose, porti, fortezze, e terre maritime, sotto poste alla Sigma Sig.ria di Venetia, ad altri Principi Christiani, et al Sig.or Turco, novamente poste in luce*, In Venetia, alla libraria des segno di S. Marco. Folger Shakespeare Library, G1015 C3., maps 38 and 39.
Giacomo Gastaldi, [Anatolia], Venice, 1566. Newberry Library, Novacco 4F 377.
Antonio Lafreri (d. 1577), 'Ordine con il quale l'esercito Turchesco suole presentarsi in Campagna contro de Christiani, o Persiani...', Rome, 1566. Newberry Library, Novacco 2F 48.
Antonio Lafreri, "Il vero ritratto de Zighet...', Rome, 1566. Newberry Library, Novacco 4F 101.
'Brazo de Maina', [1560]. Newberry Library, Novacco, 2F 32.
Nicolo Nelli, published by Claudio Duchetti, 'Tripoli Citta di Barbaria', Rome, [1570]. Newberry Library, Novacco 4F 404.

Cornelius de Iudaeis, [Cornelis de Jode] (1568–1600), 'Croatiae & circumiacentiu[m] Regionu[m] versus Turcam nova delineatio', undated map, in Cornelis de Jode, *Speculum Orbis Terrae*, Antwerp, 1593. British Library, Maps. C.7.c.13.

Cornelius de Iudaeis, [Cornelis de Jode] (1568–1600), 'Croatiae & circumiacentiu[m] Regionu[m] versus Turcam nova delineatio', undated map. Leiden University Library, COLLBN Port 123 N 138 and Port 168 N 65.

J.S., 'Abris Der Vöstung Hadtwan, Von Den Christen Belegert Und Eröbert, Den. 3. Septemb: A: 1596.' British Library, Maps, C.7.e.2(.31).

Giovanni Francesco Camocio, 'Soppoto fortezza nella provincia della Cimera luoghi del Turcho presa dal Clarissimo M.r. Sebastian Venier ... 10 Giugno 1570', Venice, [1570], map 28, in *Isole famose*. Folger Shakespeare Library, G1015 C3, 1574.

Antonio Lafreri, 'Disegno de l'Isola di Cypro con li Confini della Caramania, Soria, Giudea et Egitta', Rome, 1570. British Library, Maps C.7.e.2.(17.).

Ioani Bussemechers [Johan Bussemacher], 'Thracia Et Bulgaria Cum Viciniis', [Köln], 1596. British Library, Maps, C.39.c.1(.67).

Jocodus Hondius, 'Turcici Imperii Imago', [Amsterdam, ca. 1606]. Library of Congress, Maps, uncataloged.

Giovanni Francesco Camocio, 'Il vero ordine delle due potente armate...', Venice, 1571, map 40, in *Isole famose*. Folger Shakespeare Library, G1015 C3, 1574.

SONJA BRENTJES

Giacomo Gastaldi, *A map of the provinces of Natolia, Caramania, parts of Syria, the Archipelago, Romania*, Venice, 1566. London, British Library, The Map Collection, CXIV/63.

Bolognio Zalteri, *Il vero disegno della Natolia, & Caramania, con gli confini della Soria, Romania, & dell'Arcipelago, di Giacomo Gastaldo cosmografo*, Venice, 1570. London, British Library, The Map Collection, CXIV/64.

Abu l-Fida, *Taqwīm al-buldān*. Città del Vaticano, Biblioteca Apostolica Vaticana, Ar. 266.

Marino Sanudo, *Liber secretorum fidelium crucis*, 1322–1329. Ms Città del Vaticano, Biblioteca Apostolica Vaticana, Reg. Lat. 548.

Benincasa, Grazioso, *Carta nautica*, Ancona, 1482. Biblioteca Universitaria di Bologna, Rot. 3.

Index

Adoration of the Magi, The (Bellini, 1475–80) 120, Plate 30
Adoration of the Magi, The (da Fabriano, 1423) 42, *44*
Ahmed I (sultan, 1603–1617) 67, 159
al-Maraghi 155–56
Alexander the Great 17, 173, 253
Ali Pasha (grand vizier) 177–78
Ali Ufki *see* Bobowski, Wojciech
ambo 28–30, Plate 4, Plate 5
Amirutzes, Georgios 7, 15, 16, 18, 252–54, 255, 256
Anatolia (map, Gastaldi, 1564) *125*, 126–28, 141
    name sources 128–32, *132–33*, 134–35, 136–38, *137*, *138–39*, 140
Anatolia (map, Gastaldi, 1566) 74, *76*, 77
Ankara 232, 237–40, 241, 242, 243–44
Arabic dictionary 25, Plate 2
architecture 4, 11–13, 18, 21
artefacts 9–11, 23–28, 36–37, 232–34
    see also leatherwork; textiles
    ambo 28–30, Plate 4, Plate 5
    astrolabe 25, Plate 1
    ewers 32, 33, 34, 54, *54*, 56, Plate 8
    Grotta della Vergine 31, Plate 7
    halo inscriptions 42–43, Plate 10
    marble capitals *34*, 34–36
    metalwork 42, 53–56, *54*, Plate 11, Plate 18
    Pisa Griffin 34, *35*, 36
    reliquaries 30–32, 34, 60
    rock crystals 9, 23, 24, *33*, 60, Plate 6
astrolabe 25, Plate 1
Athens 186–88, 189, 193, 194
atlas (Lepanto, Camocio) 63–64, *65*, *66*, 84–85, *85*, 89–91
Augsburg, Germany 183

Bellini, Gentile 9, 11, 16–17, 67, 92–93, 97, 100, 119–20, 122
Benedict XVI (Pope, 2005–2013) 179–80, 249
Bertone, Tarcisio (Cardinal, 2004) 170, 179
Bisaha, Nancy 70, 248
Bobowski, Wojciech (Ali Ufki) 162–63, *163*
Bodin, Jean 200–201, 203, 205, 210–13, 214, 217
    Colloquium 204–5, 209, 213–14, 215–17
    Islam 213–14, 215–17
    Methodus 200, 206n47, 207, 209, 210, 212, 213, 214
    monarchy 205–7, 208–10, 212
    religious toleration 202–3, 214, 217
    République 201–3, 204, 207–8, 209, 210, 211, 214, 216, 217
book-bindings 56, 59, 103, 221–30, *229*, Plate 19, Plate 43
books 26, *27*, 102–7, Plate 3
    merchant handbooks 99–100, 102, 103
    pilgrim guides 100–101, 148
    portolans 100, 124, 130
    travel 97–98, 100–103, 104–7, Plate 26
Borgia V (world map) 131, 132, *132–33*, 140
Brotton, Jeremy 232–33
Brummett, Palmira 16, 20
Bursa, Anatolia 45, 47–48, 50, 232, 235, 236
Busbecq, Ogier Ghislain de 189, 198, 199, 200, 238, 239, 243
Busbequius, Augerius Gislenius 170, 172, 177–79
Bussemacher, Johan (map, 1596) 87, Plate 25
Byzantine Empire 5–6, 7, 11–12, 17–18, 19, 24, 181–82
    artefacts 30, 31, 159, Plate 7

Camocio, Giovanni Francesco (Lepanto atlas) 63–64, *65*, *66*, 84–85, *85*, 89–91
carpets 9, *38*, 38–40, *39*, 46, 59–60, 231, 236, 237
cartography *see* maps
Catena, Vincenzo 120–21
Caus, Salomon de 156
Chalcondyles, Laonicus 185, 187–88, 189
Christian Europe 4, 5–6, 71–72, 169, 170
Chytraeus, David 188–89
Colloquium heptaplomeres (Bodin, 1590–1592) 204–5, 209, 213–14, 215–17
commercial networks *see* trade routes
Constantinople 5, 11, 12, 37, 38 *see also* Istanbul
 fall of 67, 171, 174, 185–86, 187, 193, 194
Cotton Genesis 101
Critoboulos 252–53, 254, 255, 256
Croatia (map, de Jode) 80–83, Plate 23, Plate 24
Crucifix (Cimabue, 1265-80) *41*, 41–42, *43*
crusades 145–46, 169, 171, 172, 176–77, 183, 248
Crusius, Martin 181, 182, 183, 191, 192–93
Cyprus 72, 85–86, *87*

da Montalboddo, Fracanzio 104–5
da Santacroce, Girolamo 122
de Jode, Cornelis (Croatia map) 80–83, Plate 23, Plate 24
de Ruzzino, Nicolò 97–98
Dernschwam, Hans 190–91, 192, 233n11, 238, 239
diplomatic gifts 10, 13, 15, 17, 97, 159
Düvel-i ecnebiye Defterleri (Registers of foreign states) 241

Eparchos, Antonios 183–84
epigraphic bands 40, 42, *43*
European Union 169, 170, 180
ewers 32, 33, 34, *54*, 54, 56, Plate 8

faith, Christian 169, 173, 174–75, 176, 179
Faroqhi, Suraiya 6, 9n22, 20
filigree bindings 221, 222, 226–28, 230
Fleet, Kate 5
fortresses 80, *81*, 83–85, *84*, 85

Gastaldi, Giacomo 91, 106–7, 123, 140–41
 Anatolia 1564 map *125*, 126–28, 141
 name sources 128–32, *132–33*, 134–35, 136–38, *137*, *138–39*, 140
 Anatolia 1566 map 74, *76*, 77
 Natolia, Nova Tabula 123, 124, 126, 127, Plate 34
 Tabula Asiae Prima 124, 126, Plate 33
Genoese merchants 6, 7, 37
Geography (Ptolemy) 15, 103, 106, 123, 124, Plate 33, Plate 34
George of Hungary 197, 198, 199
George of Trebizond 15, 16, 254–55, 256
Georgewitz, Bartholomeus 197, 198, 199
Gerlach, Stefan 190, 191–92
Gerung, Matthias (woodcut, 1548) 73–74, *75*, 77, 88
Graeco-Roman civilisation 14, 15, 19, 232, 233
Greek Orthodox Church 182–83, 184–85, 188–89, 190–92, 193
Greeks 14, 182, 183, 184–85, 189–93, 194–95
 Athens 186–88, 189, 193, 194
 Constantinople 67, 171, 173, 185–86, 187, 193, 194
griffin, bronze *see* Pisa Griffin
Gritti, Alvise 7
Grotta della Vergine (The Virgin's Grotto) 31, Plate 7

Hagia Sophia (Byzantine Church) 11, 12, 13
halo inscriptions 42–43, Plate 10
Hasse, Dag Nikolaus 245–46
Hess, Andrew 68–69, 92
Hilten, Johann 186
Hobson, Anthony 221, 223, 226, 227
Holy Roman Empire 18–19, 186, 201, 212
Hondius, Jocodus (map, 1606) 88, *89*

instruments, musical 99, 144–47, *146*, 148–51, *150*, 159–61
Islam 5, 8, 180, 197, 198, 217, 245, 251–52
 Bodin 213–14, 215–17
 Pius II 173, 174–75, 248–49, 250
Istanbul 12–13, 171

just leadership 173, 174, 175, 176

kettledrums 145, 161

Lafreri, Antonio
   Cyprus map 85–86, *87*
   Sighetvar map 77, 78, *78*, *79*
Le Roy, Louis 205–6
leatherwork 10, 56, 57–58, Plate 20
   book-bindings 56, 221, 222, 226–27, Plate 19
   shields 10, 56–58, Plate 21
Lepanto, Venice 63–67, 68–69, 70, 73, 86n51, 92
   atlas 63–64, *65*, *66*, 84–85, *85*, 89–91
Llul, Ramon 251
Ludovisi, Daniello de' 138, *138–39*
lutes 99, 144, *146*, 146–47
Lutheran theologians 182–83, 191–92, 193

Magno, Alessandro 101–2, Plate 26
Malipiero, Nicolò 115–16, *117*
Mamluk, Egypt 5, 9, 10–11, 42–43
   book-bindings 221–27, 228, 230
   Reception of the Venetian Ambassadors in Damascus 109, 110, 112, 118
Mansueti, Giovanni 112, 118–19, *120*, Plate 29
Manutio, Antonio 105
maps 15–16, 73–74, *76*, 85–91, 100
   fortresses 83–85, *84*, *85*
   news maps 73, 77, 78–84, *79*, *81*, *82*, *84*, Plate 23, Plate 24
   socially empty map 74, *76*, 85
   world maps 15–16, 130, 131, 132, *132–33*, 140
marble capitals *34*, 34–36
Marco Polo 101, 103, 104, 129
Martyrdom of Saint Lawrence (da Santacroce, 1505) 122, Plate 32
Matar, Nabil 3n1, 7n12, 69, 91n61
medals 17, 18–19, 21
Medici family 32, 46–47, 235–36, Plate 16
Mediterranean world 4, 5–8, 9–10, 15, 16–18, 19–21, 23–24, 85–87
Mehmed II (sultan, 1432–1481) 9, 10, 11–12, 15, 16, 17, 18, 46, 247–48

Amirutzes 7, 15, 16, 18, 252–54, 255, 256
   Athens 186–87, 188, 189
   George of Trebizond 15, 16, 254–55, 256
   Pius II letter 15, 18, 169, 170, 172, 173–75, 176, 248–49, 250, 252
Mehmed III (sultan, 1595–1603) 67, 87, 89, 159, 181, Plate 25
Melanchthon, Philipp 182, 183, 184–85
   Athens 186–87, 188, 189, 193
   Constantinople 185–86
Membré, Michele 91–92, 137, *137*, 140
Menavino, Giovanni Antonio 197, 198, 199, 200
merchant handbooks 99–100, 102, 103
merchants 6, 23–24, 37–40, 102, 111 *see also* trade routes
metalwork 42, 53–56, *54*, Plate 11, Plate 18
Methodus ad facilem historiarum cognitionem (Bodin, 1566) 200, 206n47, 207, 209, 210, 212, 213, 214
mohair cloth (*sof*) 232, 237–40, 241, 242, 243–44
monarchy 205–7, 208–10, 212
motifs, ornamental 9–10, 24, 45, 50, 52–55, 58–61, *59*, 221–22
Muhammad (prophet) 175, 180, 202n26, 207, 215, 216, 249
Murad III (sultan, 1574–1595) 67, 82, 83, Plate 24
Musculus, Wolfgang 183
music 99, 143–51, 153, 155–58, 159–63, 165
   instruments 99, 144–47, *146*, 148–51, *150*, 159–61
   notation 144, 149–50, 152, *153*, *154*, 162, *163*
   Turkish 147–51, *150*, 152, 153, 155–56, 162–63, 164, 165

name sources (Anatolia map, Gastaldi, 1564) 128–32, *132–33*, 134–35, 136–38, *137*, *138–39*, 140
Natolia, Nova Tabula (map, Gastaldi, 1548) 123, 124, 126, 127, Plate 34
Neander, Michael 194
Necipoğlu, Gülrü 12, 15, 19

Nelli, Nicolo (map, 1570) 80, *82*
news maps 73, 77, 78–84, *79*, *81*, *82*, *84*, Plate 23, Plate 24
Nicholas of Cusa 251–52
Nicholas V (Pope) 175–76
notation, musical 144, 149–50, 152, *153*, *154*, 162, *163*

Octavius (*Colloquium*, Bodin) 204, 209, 213–14, 215–16, 217
Ottoman Empire 3–8, 9–13, 14–19, 20–21, 68–73, 74, 172, 197, 246

Parker, Kenneth and MacLean, Gerald 70
Pellegrino, Francesco 58, *59*
Perrault, Charles 157, 158
Piccolomini, Aeneas Silvius (Pius II after 1458) 169n2, 171, 172, 174, 175–76, 248
pilgrim guides 100–101, 148
Pisa Griffin 34, *35*, 36
Pius II (Pope, 1458–1464) 169, 170, 172, 176–77, 178–79, 180, 249–50, 251, 255–56
  Aeneas Silvius Piccolomini (before 1458) 169n2, 171, 172, 174, 175–76, 248
  Islam 173, 174–75, 248–49, 250
  Mehmed II letter 15, 18, 169, 170, 172, 173–75, 176, 248–49, 250, 252
portolans 100, 124, 130
Postel, Guillaume 129, 148, 149, 198–99
pressure-moulded bindings 221, 222, 226, 228–30, *229*
printing 26, *27*, 102–7, Plate 3

Querini, Marco (map, 1560) 80, *81*

Raby, Julian 10, 14, 112, 247–48
Ramberti, Benedetto 137–38, *138–39*
Ramusio, Gian Battista 105–7, 128, 129, 140
Reception of the Venetian Ambassadors in Damascus (after 1511) 109–12, *113*, 115–18, 119–22, Plate 28
Registers of foreign states (*Düvel-i ecnebiye Defterleri*) 241

religious toleration 199–200, 202–3, 204, 214, 217
reliquaries 30–32, 34, 60
Renaissance 3–4, 11–12, 13–19, 20–21, 23–28, 60, 70–71, 245–46
République (Bodin, 1576) 201–3, 204, 207–8, 209, 210, 211, 214, 216, 217
rock crystals 9, 23, 24, *33*, 60, Plate 6
  ambo 28–30, Plate 4, Plate 5
  ewers 32, *33*, 34, 56, Plate 8
  Grotta della Vergine 31, Plate 7
  marble capitals *34*, 34–36
  Pisa Griffin 34, *35*, 36
  reliquaries 30–32, 34, 60
royal monarchy 205, 206, 207, 209–10, 212
rugs 37–38, 40, 231, Plate 9
Rumelia 74, 87

Salomon (*Colloquium*, Bodin) 215, 216, 217
scholarship 24–25, 26–27, 28, 31
Schweigger, Salomon 149–50, 162n71, 190, 191–92
seigneurial monarchy 205–6, 208–9
shields 10, 56–58, Plate 21
Sideri, Giorgio *132-33*
Sighetvar 77–79, *79*, 80
silks 10, 37, 40, 43, 45–46, 47, 48–49, *51*, 58, 231–32, 235–37, Plate 12
Sinan Bey 11
slavery 197, 207, 209
socially empty map 74, *76*, 85
sof (mohair cloth) 232, 237–40, 241, 242, 243–44
St Peters, Rome 12, 13
Süleyman (sultan, 1520-1566) 8, 19, 67, 77–78, 134, 159, 171, 238
sultans 7, 9, 205–6, 207, 208, 209
  maps 16, 83, 86–89, *89*, Plate 25
Symbolic Representation of the Crucifixion (Mansueti, 1492) 118–19, Plate 29

Tabula Asiae Prima (map, Gastaldi, 1548) 123, 124, Plate 33
textiles 9–10, 37, 40–42, 43, 45–46, 231–32, Plate 22
  carpets 9, *38*, 38–40, *39*, 46, 59–60, 231, 236, 237

rugs 37–38, 40, 231, Plate 9
silks 10, 37, 40, 43, 45–46, 47, 48–49, *51*, 58, 231–32, 235–37, Plate 12
sof 232, 237–40, 241, 242, 243–44
velvets 40, 45, 46–48, 50, *52*, 52–53, 231–32, 235, 237, Plate 13, Plate 16, Plate 17
'the Turk' 64, 67, 70–72, 77, 87, 88–91, 197
trade routes 5–8, 23–24, 27–28, 36, 92, 222–23, 234, 240–44
sof 239–40, 241, 242, 243–44
textiles 37–42, 45–48, 231–32, 235–37
translations 25–26, 71–72, 88n57, 185, 245–46
travel books 97–98, 100–103, 104–7, Plate 26
Trombetta, Zorzi 100, 161–62
Turco-Graecia (Crusius, 1584) 193
Turkey 74, 169, 170, 179–80, 188

Turkish music 147–51, *150*, 152, 153, 155–56, 162–63, 164, 165
tyranny 205, 206, 208

velvets 40, 45, 46–48, 50, *52*, 52–53, 231–32, 235, 237, Plate 13, Plate 16, Plate 17
Venice 5–6, 9, 17–18, 37, 38–40, 107, 109, 231–32
von Raitenau, Wolf Dietrich 32, 56

Wilson, Bronwen 72, 73, 86n53
world maps 15–16, 130, 131
Borgia V 131, 132, *132–33*, 140

zambelotti see sof
zamlot see sof
Zen, Pietro 109, 112, 114–15, 116, *117*, 117–18
Zygomalas, Theodosios 192